A CULTURAL HISTORY OF WESTERN EMPIRES IN THE MIDDLE AGES

A Cultural History of Western Empires
General Editor: Antoinette Burton

Volume 1
A Cultural History of Western Empires in Antiquity
Edited by Carlos Noreña

Volume 2
A Cultural History of Western Empires in the Middle Ages
Edited by Matthew Gabriele

Volume 3
A Cultural History of Western Empires in the Renaissance
Edited by Ania Loomba

Volume 4
A Cultural History of Western Empires in the Age of Enlightenment
Edited by Ian Coller

Volume 5
A Cultural History of Western Empires in the Age of Empire
Edited by Kirsten McKenzie

Volume 6
A Cultural History of Western Empires in the Modern Age
Edited by Patricia Lorcin

A CULTURAL HISTORY OF WESTERN EMPIRES IN THE MIDDLE AGES

Edited by Matthew Gabriele

BLOOMSBURY ACADEMIC
LONDON • NEW YORK • OXFORD • NEW DELHI • SYDNEY

BLOOMSBURY ACADEMIC
Bloomsbury Publishing Plc
50 Bedford Square, London, WC1B 3DP, UK
1385 Broadway, New York, NY 10018, USA
29 Earlsfort Terrace, Dublin 2, Ireland

BLOOMSBURY, BLOOMSBURY ACADEMIC and the Diana logo are trademarks of
Bloomsbury Publishing Plc

First published in Great Britain 2018
Paperback edition published 2023

Copyright © Matthew Gabriele and Contributors, 2018

Matthew Gabriele and Contributors have asserted their right under the Copyright,
Designs and Patents Act, 1988, to be identified as Author of this work.

Cover design: Raven Design
Cover image: St Henry the Great © De Agostini/ Getty Images

All rights reserved. No part of this publication may be reproduced or transmitted
in any form or by any means, electronic or mechanical, including photocopying,
recording, or any information storage or retrieval system, without prior
permission in writing from the publishers.

Bloomsbury Publishing Plc does not have any control over, or responsibility for,
any third-party websites referred to or in this book. All internet addresses given
in this book were correct at the time of going to press. The author and publisher
regret any inconvenience caused if addresses have changed or sites have ceased to
exist, but can accept no responsibility for any such changes.

A catalogue record for this book is available from the British Library.

A catalog record for this book is available from the Library of Congress

ISBN: HB: 978-1-4742-4259-2
       PB: 978-1-3503-5821-8
       ePDF: 978-1-3502-9037-2
       eBook: 978-1-3502-9036-5

Series: The Cultural Histories Series

Typeset by RefineCatch Limited, Bungay, Suffolk
Printed and bound in Great Britain

To find out more about our authors and books visit www.bloomsbury.com
and sign up for our newsletters.

CONTENTS

ILLUSTRATIONS		vii
GENERAL EDITOR'S PREFACE		xii
	Introduction *Matthew Gabriele*	1
1	War *Marcus Bull*	21
2	Trade *Anne E. Lester*	45
3	Natural Worlds *Vicki Szabo*	71
4	Labor *Martha G. Newman*	93
5	Mobility *Shayne Aaron Legassie*	115
6	Sexuality *Patricia E. Skinner*	139
7	Resistance *Brett E. Whalen*	161

8 Race *Cord J. Whitaker*	183
NOTES	211
FURTHER READING	215
NOTES ON CONTRIBUTORS	245
INDEX	247

ILLUSTRATIONS

INTRODUCTION

0.1 Antichrist as king, colored copper engraving by C.M. Engelhardt, 1818, after "Hortus delicarum" of Herrad of Landsberg (1125/1130–95), Bavarian National Museum, Munich.   2

0.2 Silver denarius depicting Charlemagne, ninth century, Paris, Musée du Cabinet des Medailles de la Bibliothèque National de France. Credit: De Agostini Picture Library/Getty Images.   6

0.3 The Coronation of Charlemagne, 1516–17, Fresco by Raphael, Room of the Fire in the Borgo, Vatican Museum. Credit: Godong/UIG via Getty Images.   8

0.4 The territories ruled by Henry II of England and his successors, Richard I and John. An illustration from *A Short History of the English People*, by John Richard Green, illustrated edition, Volume I, Macmillan & Co., London, New York, 1892. Credit: The Print Collector/Getty Images.   14

0.5 St. Maurice, Magdeburg Cathedral Germany, c. 1250 CE. Credit: INTERFOTO/Alamy Stock Photo.   17

CHAPTER 1

1.1 Thirteenth-century Spanish *peones* and *cabellero*, Beatus de Liébana, Explanatio in Apocalypsim, Morgan MS 429 fol. 149v, thirteenth century. Credit: J Pierpont Morgan Library, New York.   27

1.2 Burning of a House, Bayeux Embroidery, late eleventh century. Credit: Photo12/UIG via Getty Images. 31

1.3 David and Goliath in the Morgan Leaf from the Winchester Bible, Morgan MS M 619 verso, twelfth century. Credit: J Pierpont Morgan Library, New York. 35

1.4 Matthew Paris illustration of two Templars on horseback, British Library Royal MS 14 C VII fol. 42v, thirteenth century. Credit: The British Library. 38

1.5 Hereward the Wake, eleventh-century Anglo-Saxon leader, attacking Peterborough Abbey in 1070 in protest at William I's imposition of a Norman abbot, early twentieth century. Credit: Universal History Archive/Getty Images. 40

1.6 Arthur above the kingdoms he has conquered, Peter of Langtoft, Chronicle of England, British Library Royal MS 20 A II fol. 4r, fourteenth century. Credit: The British Library. 42

CHAPTER 2

2.1 Miniature. Gilles de Rome. "Livre du Regime des Princes": Merchants doing business and Plowing scene. Paris, Bibliotheque Nationale. Credit: Christophel Fine Art/UIG via Getty Images. 51

2.2 Gold *ecu* of Saint Louis (r. 1226–70), first minted, 1266. Paris, Bibliotheque Nationale. Credit: Christophel Fine Art/UIG via Getty Images. 55

2.3 Pearl of the Guelph Treasure, treasure relics of Brunswick Cathedral, historical woodcut, *c.* 1870 CE. Credit: Bildagentur-online/UIG via Getty Images. 59

2.4 Gold and precious stones reliquary. Mosan Art, thirteenth century. Colmar, Musée d'Unterlinden. Credit: DeAgostini/Getty Images. 60

2.5 Boucicaut Master, Book of the Marvels of the World (1409–12): the Polo brothers arriving in Bukhara. Paris, Bibliotheque Nationale. Credit: Christophel Fine Art/UIG via Getty Images. 67

2.6 Miniature, Maqama by Al-Hariri, Al-Harith at the Slaves Market, 1237. Paris, Bibliotheque Nationale Manuscript Arabe 5847. Credit: Christophel Fine Art/UIG via Getty Images. 68

CHAPTER 3

3.1 Borg á Myrum, 1,100 years after Skalla-Grimr's landnám. Credit: Vickie Szabo. — 72

3.2 Frederick II miniature from *De Arte Venandi cum Avibus*, Codex Palatina 1071, thirteenth century. Rome, Biblioteca Apostolica Vaticana. Credit: Archiv Gerstenberg/ullstein bild via Getty Images. — 82

3.3 King John hunting, Statutes of England, fourteenth century, f.116 – BL Cotton MS Claudius D II, fol. 116r. Credit: Fine Art Images/Heritage Images/Getty Images. — 87

3.4 Fountain of life, miniature from the Godescalc Gospels, eighth century, Germany. Credit: DeAgostini/Getty Images. — 89

3.5 She-Wolf, Hellenistic bronze, brought to Aachen Münster in the ninth century. Credit: Florian Monheim/Bildarchiv-Monheim/ArcaidImages. — 90

CHAPTER 4

4.1 Eve nursing while Adam tills the soil. Hand-colored woodcut from Hartmann Schedel's *Liber Chronicarum* (Nuremberg, 1493). Credit: AF Fotografie/Alamy Stock Photo. — 97

4.2 Henry I's dream, from John of Worcester's *Chronicon ex chronicis*, *c.* 1140. Credit: Corpus Christi College, Oxford, MS 157 p. 382./Bridgeman Images. — 104

4.3 Adam and Eve tilling the soil. West façade, Modena Cathedral, Italy, *c.* 1106. Credit: Realy Easy Star/Toni Spagone/Alamy Stock Photo. 105

4.4 Cistercian monks at work, in Alexander of Bremen's *Expositio in Apocalypsim*, ca. 1250. Cambridge University Library MS Mm. 5.31 fol. 113. Credit: ART Collection/Alamy Stock Photo. — 110

4.5 Adam tilling and Eve spinning. Fifteenth-century church wall painting. Broughton, UK. Credit: Holmes Garden Photos/Alamy Stock Photo. — 112

CHAPTER 5

5.1 Hoard of silver and Arab coins from a Viking grave, Sweden, tenth century. Credit: CM Dixon/Print Collector/Getty Images. 116

5.2 Adoration of the Magi, by Giotto, detail from the cycle of frescoes Life and Passion of Christ, 1303–5, after the restoration in 2002. Padua, Italy, Scrovegni Chapel. Credit: DeAgostini/Getty Images. 131

5.3 Matthew Paris, illumination from his "Historia Major" depicting the elephant sent by St. Louis to Henry III in 1255, c. 1200–59. Cambridge, Corpus Christi MS 16. Credit: Culture Club/Getty Images. 132

5.4 A goldsmith's shop. Miniature from "The Lapidary" by John Mandeville, fifteenth century. BnF, Ms. fr.9136, f.344r, Paris, France. Credit: Leemage/Corbis via Getty Images. 135

5.5 A goldsmith in his shop, possibly Saint Eligius, by Petrus Christus, Germany, fifteenth century. New York, The Metropolitan Museum of Art. Credit: De Agostini Picture Library/Getty Images. 136

CHAPTER 6

6.1 Miniature taken from the Roman de Godefroi de Bouillon, fifteenth century. Credit: De Agostini Picture Library/Getty Images. 150

6.2 Slave traders. Arabic miniature, twelfth century. Credit: De Agostini Picture Library/Getty Images. 151

6.3 Limestone group depicting Hugh I of Vaudemont greeted by his wife Anna of Lorraine, upon returning from the Crusades to the Holy Land, twelfth century. From the Priory of Belval (Vosges), Church of Cordeliers, Nancy, Meurthe et Moselle, Lorraine, France. Credit: De Agostini Picture Library/Getty Images. 153

6.4 Moorish baths of Ronda, c. thirteenth century. Malaga province, Andalusia, Spain. Credit: Education Images/UIG via Getty Images. 156

CHAPTER 7

7.1 Donation of Constantine, Basilica of Santi Quattro Coronati, Rome. Credit: Fine Art Images/Heritage Images/Getty Images. 163

ILLUSTRATIONS xi

7.2 Lateran Church mosaic: Saint Peter, Leo III, and Charlemagne, ninth century, lithograph 1880.   165

7.3 Gregory VII, Henry IV, and Mathilda of Tuscany, after a miniature from the parchment manuscript "Life of Matilda" (1114 completed) by the monk Donizo of Canossa in the Vatican Library in Rome, published in 1880.   169

7.4 Pope Innocent IV deposes Emperor Frederick II, France, fifteenth century. Credit: De Agostini Picture Library/Getty Images.   177

7.5 Joachim of Fiore, Apocalyptic Seven-Headed Dragon, Liber Figurarum, 1132–1202, by Joachim of Fiore, St. Peter's basilica, Perugia, Umbria, Italy. Credit: De Agostini/Archivio J. Lange.   178

CHAPTER 8

8.1 Medieval knight figurine.   186

8.2 Edmund Spenser is portrayed in this engraving produced in 1834.   192

8.3 Portrait of Genghis Khan. Ink and watercolor on silk. Bridgeman Art Library. Credit: ullstein bild via Getty Images.   197

8.4 A forty-meter-tall statue of Genghis Khan stands atop the Genghis Khan Statue Complex and Museum at Tsonjin Boldog, Tov Province, Mongolia. Credit: Nick Ledger.   198

8.5 The Coronation of Emperor Charlemagne by Pope Leo III. Credit: French School/Getty Images.   200

8.6 The Emperor Frederick I Barbarossa with his sons Henry VI and Frederick, Duke of Swabia, from the Welfenchronik chronicle produced at the Abbey of Weingarten, Germany, in the twelfth century. Credit: De Agostini Picture Library/Getty Images.   201

8.7 Adoration of the Magi by Gerard David. Fifteenth-century work demonstrating the conventional depiction of the three wise men representing Asia, Africa, and Europe. The depiction of the African magus is particularly noticeable. Credit: Superstock.   202

Every effort has been made to trace copyright holders and to obtain their permission for the use of copyright material. The publisher apologizes for any errors or omissions and would be grateful if notified of any corrections that should be incorporated in future reprints or editions of this book.

GENERAL EDITOR'S PREFACE

Histories of empire have been transformed in the last three decades by a combination of new methods, new archives, and a new generation of scholars who have come of age in a postcolonial world. The impact of these historical forces on how imperialism is understood has been remarkable. For decades the province of geopolitics, diplomacy, and the "official mind," imperial history is now just as likely to be told from the bottom up as from the top down. The rise of cultural history has played a significant role in how we think about and narrate imperialism from the ancient world to the twentieth century. With an emphasis on evidence drawn from literature, the arts, life-writing, and a host of fragmentary sources, cultural historians think through patterns of representation and experience that shape the conditions in which histories of all kinds—economic, political, social—happen. They investigate often overlooked subjects and offer new angles of vision on familiar topics through a cultural lens. The ambition of *A Cultural History of Western Empires* is to advance conversations about the work of culture in shaping how empire took root, took shape, was maintained, and faced challenges whether its regimes were of long or short durée. Indeed, no thoroughgoing histories of the subject can afford to ignore the influence that culture has had on the shape of empires in local, regional, and global contexts.

The geographical remit of *A Cultural History of Western Empires* is indicated in its title. As compelling a topic as the wide variety of imperial formations is, and as interconnected as west and non-west have been along the axis of empire from Greece to Beijing and back again, the authors in this volume explore empire's cultural histories in a broadly western European setting. And while the differences between French and German and English imperial experiences are often notable, what is equally striking are the features that cultures of labor, trade, sexuality, race, war, mobility, natural worlds, and resistance share across imperial locales. Even allowing for specificities of time and place, there is a value to taking a very long view of the concept and practice of *imperium*—not simply to note commonalities or differences but to be able to discern through lines across such widely distinctive terrains as the Frankish kingdoms and the world of the post-Versailles settlement. In no small respect, attention to cultural forces, identities, rhetorics, tropes, relationships, and imaginaries make this kind of discernment possible. Reading for culture—which is to say, developing the capacity to plumb a variety of sources and archives for evidence of how meanings and forms were constantly made and struggled over across a range of domains—reveals the work of historical forces that have undergirded and, at times, have redirected or undone imperial power. Empire simply cannot be understood in all its limits and possibilities without an analysis of its cultural histories.

This is a work of scholarly synthesis rooted in the original scholarship and intellectual vision of the volume editors and their contributors. Its audience is students seeking a comparative, interdisciplinary, and evidence-based account of how empires worked at multiple scales. Readers will get a sense, then, of the cultural impact of large-scale territorial expansion and hegemony *and* of the meaning and experience of conquest and colonization in more intimate environments. Contributors have written their essays to make available a broad overview of their theme or topic. Each one draws on a range of materials and case studies to make a larger argument about the history of cultural formations and influences that pertain to their subject. The series is structured around six time periods: Antiquity, The Medieval Age, The Renaissance, The Enlightenment, The Age of Empire, and the Modern Age. These are conceptual and pedagogical, signaling a periodization that modern Western imperialism itself has played an important role in shaping and sustaining. Casting Rome as an imperial touchtone and colonized territories as "ancient" or "medieval" in temporal terms remains an important cultural resource for contemporary empire-building, and it draws on a long cultural legacy that contributors both address and challenge. Each volume takes up the chronological parameters assigned in critical conversation with the historical evidence, allowing readers to see the pros and cons of thinking about empire itself as a maker—and breaker—of time periods. Of equal significance, each volume is organized with the same chapter titles so that readers can either follow a theme across time frames—mobility in the Enlightenment as compared to the twentieth century, for example—or read through a single period by exploring the range of thematic lenses on offer. This combination of diachronic and synchronic affords us a unique opportunity to cultivate comparisons that are as deep as they are broad, and to appreciate the indispensability of cultural history to practically all aspects of imperial regime making and unmaking across this particular swath of the global past.

Such a purposeful focus on culture at this juncture in the history of the historiography of empire is worth remarking on. As an object of historical inquiry, culture is arguably the carrier of a number of historical forces that attention to politics or economics alone cannot capture. Though embedded in and constitutive of every aspect of imperial geopolitics, race, gender, and sexuality were long invisible to the historians' eye because they were considered trivial, or at best inconsequential, to the workings of real power. Cultural history practices, which bring new forms of seeing and reading as well as new subjects to our sightline, open up the imperial archive to aspects of the past, which, in turn, shed new light on old paradigms. Thinking with and through culture also reorients our gaze, pulling us toward sources—diaries, images, discursive motifs—in a diverse array of formations and spaces that illuminate dimensions of hegemony and power otherwise invisible: dismissable, even, as immaterial because they are ostensibly "only cultural." What the collective example of this series accomplishes is to suggest how, why, and under what conditions culture has been a maker of imperial history—indeed, that empires have been done and undone by the cultural forces they sought to control but which were not always completely in their grasp. As twenty-first-century forms of imperial power emerge, claiming historical newness and relying on past models of conquest and occupation all at once, we need narratives that insist on the power of histories attuned to the ideological and material work of culture more than ever.

Culture is at the dynamic heart of all imperial histories. It operates in spaces of high command and conjugal intimacy; in ceremony and in ordinary life; in military documents and botanists' texts; at court and on the plantation; through trade routes and refugee settlements; in the pronouncements of empresses and the movements of the lowly beetle; in the signing of treaties and the violence of the battlefield and the inner workings of the household. Thinking through cultures of empire, in turn, throws us back on the protocols and presumptions of the discipline by encouraging us to be ever vigilant about where—in what spaces and through what repertoires—history happens. Empire is not, perhaps, unique in this regard. The irony is that while imperial ambition and self-regard have often been steeped in convictions about the power of culture to conquer and colonize, imperial narratives on a grand scale are often the most impervious to the argument that culture matters. What follows is a wide-ranging and lively set of arguments about how and why that has been incontrovertibly so from antiquity to modern times.

Introduction

MATTHEW GABRIELE

Allow me to begin with an anecdote that, I hope, will clarify some of the challenges in studying *A Cultural History of Western Empires* in the Middle Ages.[1] Just a few years after 950 CE, the West Frankish queen Gerberga (wife of King Louis IV, r. 936–54) asked the learned men of her realm for a brief tract on the Christians' greatest enemy, the one who was foretold to come at the end of time—antichrist (Figure 0.1). In response, the monk Adso from the monastery of Montier-en-Der produced a brief work entitled *On the Antichrist*. In producing the text, Adso mined the works of authorities from his own day back to the Church Fathers in order to discuss the contours of the evil one's time on earth, beginning with the circumstances of antichrist's birth, continuing through his personal development, rise to power, conquest of Jerusalem, and final defeat just before the Last Judgment. Buried within that tale of woe, one foretelling persecution and suffering for the few righteous Christians willing to resist the wiles of the enemy, is another tale intended to comfort Gerberga. The time of antichrist is not yet upon us, he assured his queen, because Roman *imperium* (usually translated as "empire," but see later) had not faded from the earth. The dignity of that *imperium* persisted in her husband, the king of the Franks. The extent of his power might not be as vast as that of his predecessors but it nonetheless remained. Indeed, Adso assured the queen, the world had not reached that appointed time of tribulation, there was another step in sacred history that had yet to arrive. Just before the time of antichrist, a ruler from among the kings of the Franks would fully restore Rome's *imperium*, defeat all God's enemies, conquer Jerusalem, and then relinquish his crown to God, allowing antichrist to begin his reign (Adso 1979: 89–96).

FIGURE 0.1: Antichrist as king, colored copper engraving by C.M. Engelhardt, 1818, after "Hortus delicarum" of Herrad of Landsberg (1125/1130–95), Bavarian National Museum, Munich.

On its surface, this might seem to be a perfect anecdote with which to begin a cultural history of western empires in the Middle Ages. Here we have an evocation of past empire in Rome, a sense of continuation of empire in the kings of the Franks, a prophetic projection toward a future empire with one version of the so-called "Last Emperor" legend. But it's actually a bit more complicated than that. The "empire" that Adso described in the middle of the tenth century was actually one without an "emperor," or an "empire." All of his Frankish rulers, including the last and greatest one, are called *rex* ("king") throughout. The "kings" of the Franks endure. One from the "kings" of the Franks will arise anew and will be the greatest and last of all "kings." In Adso's telling, Rome itself never has a ruler. Roman only exists as an adjective, modifying *imperium*—*Romanum imperium* (appearing four times). This phrase has, as I noted earlier, traditionally been translated as "Roman empire" but translation is an imperfect art and the act can sometimes inadvertently infuse words with modern sensibilities. Here, to put it bluntly, the word *imperium*, so often translated into English as "empire" by nineteenth- and early twentieth-century scholars, didn't actually mean that. More accurately, it meant "power," "authority," or "jurisdiction" of a supreme sort. Look at what Adso specifically said. He wrote:

> For we know that after the Greek kingdom (*regnum*), or even after the Persian kingdom (*regnum*), each of which in its time had great glory and flourished with the highest power (*potentia*), at last after all the other kingdoms (*regna*) the Roman kingdom (*regnum*), which was the strongest kingdom (*regnum*) of all, took hold and had all the kingdoms (*regna*) of the earth under its control . . . This time [of antichrist] has not yet come, because even though we may see Roman power (*imperium*) for the most part ruined, still, as long as the kings of the Franks, who now hold Roman authority (*imperium*), endure, the dignity of the Roman kingdoms (*regni*) will not pass away because it will remain in its kings. Some of our learned men say that one from the kings of the Franks will hold Roman authority (*imperium*) anew . . . After he has successfully governed his kingdom (*regnum*), at the end he will come to Jerusalem and will lay aside his scepter and crown on the Mount of Olives. This will be the end and consummation of Roman and Christian authority (*imperium*) (Adso 1979: 93).[2]

In Adso's *On the Antichrist*, the "thing" the Romans hold is always a *regnum* but the "idea" they hold is always *imperium*. It is indeed Roman—note that the Greeks and Persians have *potentia*, not *imperium*—but it is not "empire." The last sentence of the long quotation above shows this distinction best. Although this is the end of *imperium*, the many "kingdoms" held together by Roman "power" endure. Roman and Christian *power* has been transferred to God, who will be the one to ultimately defeat the forces of evil (Gabriele 2011: 100–11).

So, in short, we have a tenth-century text about a "Last Emperor" that has neither empire nor an emperor. Yet, it talks about an idealized Rome, universal political and religious authority across multiple polities, and a great ruler who will unite them all to fight a cosmic war between the forces of good and evil. In addition, the text sees fundamental continuity across past, present, and future—no "Fall," no decline, no "medieval" after a separate "antiquity." The tradition of *imperium* stretches backward and forward through time according to Adso, from the beginning to the final End. In other words, our familiar categories seem here to break down, dissipate into air upon closer inspection. But then, underneath, solid ground for analysis. *A Cultural History of Western Empires* in the Middle Ages will therefore tell a story that our subjects don't seem to want to tell us, because they're speaking their own language, not ours. This is a story of ideas enacted, of a lived experience in all its messiness. So, we must start with foundational questions: was there such a thing as an "empire" in what we call the "Middle Ages" generally? Then, related to this query, is there a sense of something "medieval" here that exists as distinct from what came before, or what would come after? Something distinct, a culture discernible from what we call "Antiquity" or "Modernity?"

For now, the answer to both questions must be another question: "maybe?"

* * * * *

Let us start with the "medieval." The chronological scope of this book spans 650 years, from 800 to 1450 CE, from the Carolingians to the Habsburgs, or from the death of Charlemagne's adviser Alcuin to the birth of the famous Renaissance thinker Leonardo da Vinci, or from the birth of the Carolingian noblewoman and author Dhuoda to the death of the writer Christine de Pizan, or from the subjugation of the Saxons to the conquest of the Canary Islands and beginning of Iberian expansion into the Atlantic. The list could go on. We are closer in time today to the end of this period than the end of it was from the beginning. Those dates thus provide structure, even as they suggest fluidity. Throughout this book, we ought to think of those dates as guideposts rather than firm boundaries. Indeed, the boundaries of the Middle Ages have always been so.

In 1948, Wallace Ferguson published *The Renaissance in Historical Thought: Five Centuries of Interpretation*. This masterful work revealed how the so-called (Italian) Renaissance was constructed after-the-fact, primarily by positioning the events and activities in the fourteenth- to sixteenth-century Italian peninsula as a radical break with what had come before. Although he by no means invented this myth, consider what Jacob Burckhardt famously wrote in his 1860 *The Civilization of the Renaissance in Italy*:

> In the Middle Ages both sides of human consciousness . . . lay dreaming or half awake beneath a common veil. The veil was woven of faith, illusion, and childish prepossession, through which the world and history were seen clad in strange hues . . . In Italy this veil first melted into air; an *objective* treatment and consideration of the state and of all the things of this world became possible (Burckhardt 1904: 129).

The Middle Ages were supposedly a time of cultural and intellectual immaturity, characterized by a vision of the world cloaked in superstition and untethered from reality. But it had not always been like that, Burckhardt continued. Greeks/Romans/Arabians had not held such ideas. Italians during the fourteenth and fifteenth centuries cast them off. What was left was an in-between, a *medium aevum*—a "middle age." The Renaissance emerged from the "dark ages" as light followed darkness.

In reality, of course, those who lived during that period thought no such thing. Historical periodization has always been an artificial construct. Humans of all time think, at times, that things have radically changed from what came before, but invocations of novelty, a new age, modernity, stretch back centuries and were particularly acute, for instance, during the late ninth century (Dutton 1994: 195–224). The real construction of the "Middle Ages," the subject of our study here, began during the Enlightenment with a rejection of the "superstition" that the *philosophes* believed to have characterized the period (and by "superstition," they meant religion). Then, that characterization of the time between Rome and the "Renaissance" was cemented into its current form by nineteenth-century Protestant historians who agreed that Europe reemerged from darkness, first with art and culture, but only to reach maturity with the Reformation of the sixteenth century (Ferguson 1948; Bull 2005: 42–61; Arnold 2008: 1–22).

The history of "empire" still, to a large part, fits within this paradigm. The Middle Ages remain largely one cloaked under a veil of superstition/religion. For example, a recent textbook on political theory highlights only two medieval thinkers—Augustine of Hippo (d. 430 CE) and Thomas Aquinas (d. 1274) (though it does also mention John of Salisbury, d. 1180). Indeed, the only reason Augustine seems to have been placed in the "Medieval: 500–1500 CE" section is because of his Christianity (Heywood 2015, especially table on p. 5). Other modern overviews of theories of empire almost entirely skip the Middle Ages. Anthony Pagden's introductory survey tellingly ends its section on Rome with a note about Constantine's conversion, then spends three pages on Byzantium and Charlemagne before leaping about 1200 years forward to Charles V (r. 1516–58) (Pagden 2003). Other surveys similarly—but oftentimes more directly—jump that same distance in time from Rome to the Ottomans and Spanish of the fifteenth and sixteenth centuries, presumably when reason "returned" to western thought (Doyle 1986; Colás 2007). This is not so subtly reinforced elsewhere, when some studies of empire in "modern" political thought begin with Machiavelli (Muthu 2012).

There are necessarily exceptions to these examples but the general point remains that the Middle Ages are, by and large, excluded from these overviews and analyses. That period, the thinking seemingly goes, was a culture without complex political forms. My intention is not to suggest that all modern scholars still subscribe to this periodization but rather to show how pervasive and subtle this Enlightenment myth remains. We scholars, I would argue, remain stuck in a historiographical trap, allowing an aspect of the past (in this case, "empire") to be defined anachronistically. Here, nineteenth-century scholars, writing in the age of imperialism compared their own political formations to what they saw in the past. They found what they were looking for in ancient Rome but not in the Middle Ages. As François Guizot wrote in his tremendously influential 1828 *General History of Civilization in Europe*, "empire" formed because Rome needed to control its disparate provinces. It only fell because those provinces weren't loyal to the capital. It never reemerged in the Middle Ages, despite the attempt by Charlemagne (Guizot 1838: lecture II). Guizot was arguing that there could be no empire in the Middle Ages because what did exist didn't resemble later European colonial and imperial projects in Africa, Asia, and Latin America. This is a trap we must escape. To do so, we must be true to our sources, conscious of anachronism, honest and thoughtful about how the people of the time thought about what they were doing.

Let us begin with Charlemagne (r. 768–814 CE) (Figure 0.2). The details of his life need not be rehearsed here. Suffice it to say that he conquered a continent, with his power extending from Catalonia to Saxony, from Rome to southern Denmark. In the middle of his reign, on Christmas Day 800 CE, Charlemagne was crowned in St. Peter's basilica in Rome by Pope Leo III (795–816). According to the early ninth-century *Royal Frankish Annals*, as King Charles was rising for mass, Pope Leo III placed a crown on his head and the

FIGURE 0.2: Silver denarius depicting Charlemagne, ninth century, Paris, Musée du Cabinet des Medailles de la Bibliothèque National de France. Credit: De Agostini Picture Library/Getty Images.

assembled crowd cried: "To the august Charles, crowned by God, the great and peaceful emperor of the Romans [*imperatori Romanorum*], life and victory!" (Scholz and Rogers 1970: 81) This act did not—I cannot emphasize enough—create the "Holy Roman Empire." That would come some 450-plus years later (see later). Instead, it intended to resurrect what had come before, reviving the office ruling the western part of Rome, one that had fallen into disuse toward the end of the fifth century (Davis 2015: 347–50, 359–62). But the meaning of "Roman" had changed in the interim. No longer necessarily a universal title sought across the continent, "Rome" now meant "the city". Charlemagne never was, nor did he seek to become, emperor of the Franks or the Lombards or the Saxons. For them, he was a king. Even after the coronation in 800, his diplomas (royal decrees) revealed that his power derived from the multiplicity of titles he held. He was an emperor of the Romans, a king of the Franks, a king of the Lombards. All of those titles, in their own ways, allowed him to rule the various peoples he did (Garipzanov 2008: 101–56).

So what actually changed on Christmas Day 800 CE? It seems clear that Charlemagne and his circle had been planning something related to the coronation since at least 798 CE. One of the signs he had begun this cultural process was the accelerated pace with which he exchanged emissaries with perceived equals, namely the "Persians" (actually the Abbasid Caliph Harun al-Rashid [r. 786–809]) and the ruler of the Byzantines, Irene (r. 797–802) (Fried 2016: 398–408). But the more immediate spark was likely something closer to home. In April 798, a Roman mob attacked Pope Leo III as he led a public procession through the streets of the city. Mutilating him in some way—accounts vary—the mob declared Leo deposed and had him thrown into a monastery prison, there to live out his days. Yet he escaped. Spirited quickly away from Rome by sympathetic churchmen and Frankish envoys who had been sent south by Charlemagne when he learned the news, Leo III made his way to meet Charlemagne at Paderborn in Saxony. What they discussed there is unknown but it more than likely was at least in part about the coming coronation, for the pope soon returned to Rome accompanied by a sizeable Frankish army. Once there, he reestablished himself by celebrating mass once again in St. Peter's and helping the accompanying Franks conduct an investigation into the events that led to his deposition and flight.

Charlemagne himself arrived in Rome in late November 800 CE. After being received warmly outside of the city by the newly restored pope, Charles convened a great council of churchmen in St. Peter's to determine the "truth" of what happened those two years earlier. At the end of this gathering, on December 23, 800, Leo III "voluntarily" confessed his sins and swore a solemn oath that he was innocent of the charges levied against him. The matter resolved, Charlemagne remained in Rome to celebrate Christmas. The coronation occurred on Christmas Day (Figure 0.3). All accounts of the event seem generally to agree on what

FIGURE 0.3: The Coronation of Charlemagne, 1516–17, Fresco by Raphael, Room of the Fire in the Borgo, Vatican Museum. Credit: Godong/UIG via Getty Images.

happened. Where they disagree, and where it becomes interesting for our purposes, is on what it all meant. Who could make an *imperator Romanorum* ("emperor of the Romans")? From where did *imperium* derive?

A contemporary pro-papal source said that the coronation was thought up by the Romans themselves, who intended to thank Charlemagne for his patronage and protection of their city and their bishop. In that version of the story, the assembled Romans hailed Charles as the pope carried out their plan. The pope was an important, constitutive part of the plan. Another source composed close to Charlemagne's court, however, said that this idea all originated across the Alps, with the Franks, intended to provide Charlemagne with a fitting title to match the actual extent of his power. So, on Christmas Day 800, a commingled crowd of Franks, Romans, Saxons, and others acclaimed him with the pope simply being an agent of their will. The pope, in this version, just happened to be there. So, in the former text the title is much more local in scope, granting Charlemagne a power that applied primarily to Rome (and likely the central part of the Italian peninsula). In the latter account, the title is expansive, a cultural signifier in its own right, one that supplements and reinforces the titles he already held but ultimately is a recognition of power that he already possessed (Fried 2016: 412–30). What are we to make of this? Was the coronation, in the pro-papal Roman view, an act centered primarily around Rome and one dependent upon papal designation? Or was it, in the Frankish view, a recognition of actual power, a necessary step conveyed at the end of a process of conquest of many kingdoms? These are the questions that would bedevil relations between pope and emperor for centuries to come.

But in 800 CE, it seems best to lean toward the pro-Frankish accounts and see the coronation as an acknowledgment of an already existing reality. First, given that he owed his position (and life) to Charlemagne, the pope was not really in a position to argue or attempt to assert his primacy. Second, and perhaps more importantly, there is the issue of *imperium*, the "power" that lies behind the acclamation as "emperor." Consider Charlemagne's actions following his coronation. He never attempted to govern from Rome, leaving the city shortly after his coronation in favor of his palace at Aachen. He restarted diplomatic conversations both with the Byzantines and "Persians" (actually, again, the Abbasid Caliph), and increased his aid to the churches and Christian communities in the Holy Land, particularly those around Jerusalem. Moreover, he issued capitularies and amended law codes, waged war, and promoted reform. All of the above seems to have been in the service of demonstrating his status as *the* protector of Christendom and caring for the "good order" of the places under his control (Fried 2016: 440–57). It seems he was taking his job as emperor seriously. But that's a problematic understanding. He had done all of these things before the coronation as well. Here, we should keep in mind Jennifer R. Davis' conclusion that Charlemagne's "practice of empire" was generally consistent and extended throughout his entire reign. Thus, it could (and perhaps should) be argued that the coronation on Christmas Day 800 CE was not so much a turning point, as a stage along the way of the Franks' expanding power (Davis 2015: 429–33). When Charlemagne gained the title of *imperator* in Rome in 800, he did not suddenly acquire *imperium*, he added to what he already had. In other words, he did not gain "empire" but added to his "authority." *Imperium* in the Middle Ages was about the peoples it collected under its umbrella (Ellenblum 2002: 105–19). Franks, Lombards, Saxons, and Romans—all the peoples of his kingdoms (*regni*)—together acclaimed Charlemagne as emperor.

The coronation of 800, however, did not settle the question of who could make an emperor, what could constitute an empire, for the remainder of the Middle Ages. On the contrary. These remained highly contested cultural questions, erupting—oftentimes into actual physical violence—for centuries thereafter. If Charlemagne's rulership "established the boundaries of what was politically possible for the rest of the Middle Ages," effectively delimiting the field of action within which rulers could operate until the nineteenth century (Davis 2015: 433–4), he also haunted the collective imagination of the continent during that same time and inspired bitter conflicts over aspects of his legacy.

For instance, he was the basis for the legitimacy of nearly everyone who ruled the eastern part of Francia (roughly modern Germany) even beyond the late Middle Ages, with this association perhaps coming to its greatest prominence during the reign of Frederick I Barbarossa (r. 1152–90). Following Charles' precedent, Frederick was crowned "emperor of the Romans" by the pope in Rome in 1155 CE. But he found himself almost immediately embroiled in conflict with the bishop of Rome over the question of primacy, the same one that haunted texts produced in the immediate aftermath of Christmas Day 800. Indeed, the meaning of the coronation—the question of whence the title "emperor" derived—could be said to have been the animating antagonism between the pope and Frederick I during the late 1150s and 1160s. And both sides relied upon cultural memory, reached back to Charlemagne for support, with the papacy arguing that they had made Charlemagne what he was, while Frederick's party argued that the event was merely a recognition of actually held power. The framing of this debate in the twelfth century was different from what it was in the ninth though, as one of the primary ways that Frederick tried to wrest control of the debate from his papal opponents was to reframe the meaning of *imperium*. For example, after 1157 CE, Frederick's chancellery began to attach the phrase "*sacrum imperium*" (often, again, translated as "holy empire," but perhaps better "sacred authority") in his official documents. Doing so seemed to suggest that the *imperium* Frederick held derived directly from God, without the necessity of papal intervention. The emperor reported directly to God, not the papacy. Frederick thought he was at the top of Christendom's org chart. The challenge to the papacy became even more direct after *c.* 1180, when the phrase *sacrum imperium* began to be amended for the first time ever in order to include "*Romanum*," thus the inception of the (misnamed) "Holy Roman Empire" we know of today. This was a more direct, explicit challenge to the papacy. Now, it seemed Frederick didn't need the pope or the Romans to justify his power over Rome (Whalen 2014: 125–8; Freed 2016: 197–217, 269–76).

In the midst of this, Frederick presided over the canonization of Charlemagne in 1165 CE. Intended to show that Frederick was the true successor to the great Frankish ruler, that Aachen (under Frederick's control) was the true home to the multi-ethnic polity Charles had established, and that the power to make and unmake popes resided with Frederick as it had with his predecessor, everything about the event, from the performed actions to the sung liturgy to the gifts bestowed on Aachen by Frederick afterwards, went toward reinforcing this link to the past and, more importantly, emphasizing that the power (*imperium*) held by Charlemagne (and now his successor, Frederick) derived from God, not the pope (Latowsky 2013: 139–214; Freed 2016: 330–4). In fact, it would seem that canonization had much in common with coronation. The making of a saint (canonization) was to be read, in Frederick's mind, in the same way as the making of an emperor—it was not so much an act of creation as a recognition after-the-fact. A holy person's life and posthumous miracles would be formally recognized and his/her veneration ritualized. Nothing a pope did made the saint holy. That had already happened (Vauchez 1997: 11–58). So, when we consider all these elements together, Frederick and his circle were fighting the same battle over the meaning of his position as his predecessor some 350 years before. As the Frankish version of Christmas Day 800 said, coronation and acclamation were acts of recognition, not creation. An emperor received *imperium* (even over the Romans) directly from God; *imperium* created the title, not the other way around.

To the west of Aachen, the Capetian successors to the West Frankish kingdom sometimes struggled with Charlemagne's legacy, hesitant at times to explicitly exploit any connection to a dynasty they had supplanted in the late tenth century. Since at least the time of King Hugh Capet (r. 987–96), the Capetians had staked their legitimacy as kings (*reges*) of the Franks on their claim to *imperium*, not from the Romans but from the Franks. Position depended upon *imperium*, and *imperium* depended on the cultural memory of Charlemagne. Even during the eleventh century, when royal power has been characterized as particularly "weak" in what is now modern France, rulers were deeply concerned with the legacy of *imperium*. During the reign of King Philip I of Francia (r. 1060–1108), for instance, the king and his entourage embarked on a subtle, sustained campaign to capture the specter of Carolingian legitimacy for himself. Though Philip's program fizzled for practical, political reasons in the mid-1090s (he ran off with another man's wife—another story entirely), Philip laid the groundwork for the ambitious process that would eventually lead to a modern "nation," a process fully launched during the reign of his son and led by and centered at the abbey of Saint-Denis (Gabriele 2011: 13–40, 97–128; Gabriele 2016: 9–32).

That new polity—what could, perhaps by the end of the twelfth century, be called "France"—continued to look back to the Franks, to Charlemagne for legitimacy. Beginning *c*. 1200 CE and continuing thereafter, French royal chroniclers argued that with the birth of Philip II (r. 1180–1223) "Augustus" the royal line *reditus ad stirpem Karoli* ("was returning to the lineage of Charles [the Great]"). Although this was a claim made on and off since at least the time of Philip I, it had never been made so explicitly until the middle of the twelfth century. Indeed, it enjoyed a particular resonance at that time because of the way this particular connection looked not backward but *forward* toward an ambitious political program that aimed to expand Capetian influence across the continent and even, perhaps, link Philip II to the king prophesized to come in works such as Adso of Montier-en-Der's tract on antichrist. Effectively, the twelfth-century ideology animating *reditus regni* "redefined the intellectual framework by which events could be understood and evaluated, legitimized, and accepted." Or, to put it another way, this was an attempt by the Capetians to cement their claim that the legitimacy of the Frankish king rested upon a link back to Charlemagne, back to Frankish *imperium*. In Philip II's case, much like Frederick I Barbarossa, his rough contemporary across the Rhine, this meant arguing that the possession of *imperium* transformed a ruler, pushed him beyond being a "mere king" to be recognized as something more, what Gabrielle Spiegel has termed a *Rex-Imperator* ("king-emperor") (Spiegel 1997: 111–37).

Much like the *reditus ad stirpem*, the "king-emperor" ideal was a much older one that had found new life in differently fertile soil. Likely in the early 1080s, emerging from a monastery connected in some way to the Capetians, an anonymous monk composed a brief text that has come to be known as the *Descriptio qualiter Karolus Magnus*. At its core, this is a narrative about the translation of some saints' relics from east to west. But within that overarching plot, the *Descriptio qualiter* also tells of Charlemagne's (fictional) trip to Jerusalem and Constantinople to acquire those relics and transfer them to Aachen, Compiègne, and Saint-Denis (Gabriele 2008). At about the same time, an anonymous Anglo-Norman scribe wrote out another legendary tale of Charlemagne's exploits, namely the defeat he suffered in the Pyrenees at the hands of the "Saracens" and Charles' subsequent vengeance upon them. This is the *c*. 1100 CE Oxford version of the *Song of Roland*. Let us compare their respective opening lines.

The first line of the *Descriptio qualiter* reads: "In the time when the king [*rex*] and great emperor [*imperator*] Charles ruled the kingdom of Gaul . . ." The Oxford *Song of Roland* opens thus: "Charles the king [*reis*], our great emperor [*emperere*] . . ." In both sources, king and emperor, both together. An uncanny echo. I have argued elsewhere that these opening lines are not cases of scribal confusion about titles but rather reveal a subtle, historically located distinction. Indeed, the *Descritptio qualiter* explains the difference between the two titles later in the first paragraph of its text. The anonymous author explains that Charlemagne was a king (chronologically) first because he was in charge of Gaul. Then, after he had won many victories, having demonstrated his claim to *imperium* to the Romans, they allowed him to choose the pope. It is only then that God's providence (*dei providentia*) was made manifest and Charles was made emperor (*imperator*). By now, this should be a familiar story to us, mimicking as it does the version of events that the ninth-century Franks themselves crafted after the coronation in Rome in 800 CE. The same is true in the Oxford *Roland*. Though there is no mention of Charlemagne's coronation, it is quite clear throughout the poem that Charlemagne's status as king derives from his rule over the Franks, while the title of emperor belongs to him because of his many conquests—a recognition of the power he wields over many peoples, over all of Europe including Italy, Iceland, Constantinople, and the British Isles (Gabriele 2011: 32–3, 99–100). In both cases, the title of emperor derives from the possession of *imperium*, a rule over multiple peoples, a path of conquest, but most importantly a recognition of an established fact.

It is significant—and too often overlooked by commentators—that the Oxford *Roland* survives in Anglo-Norman, not Frankish, not Latin. That version of the poem likely originated in England. After the conquest in 1066 CE, the Norman kings of England had pretensions about their power that rivaled any ruler across Europe—and with good reason! In the second half of the twelfth century, King Henry II controlled England, Ireland, Scotland, and more of what is now modern France than the king of the Franks himself (Figure 0.4). And holding dominion over numerous peoples, it should not surprise us that Henry II also adopted the same language as his cross-channel rivals, seeing in his numerous conquests the realization of *imperium*. As Wendy Hoofnagle has recently demonstrated, Henry II did this in a number of ways that could be analogized to modern colonialism, namely through a rhetoric of civilizing barbarian peoples. This could take the form of religious conversion, construction across the disparate parts of the realm, and the taming of the wilderness/forest. But those were just the means; the justification for such a claim lay elsewhere, in a more familiar setting. If in antiquity, it could be said that all roads led to Rome, perhaps in the Middle Ages, we should say that all roads led to Charlemagne. This is even more of an apt analogy when we see the way the construction of roads during the reign of Henry II was viewed as a sort of literalization of the Carolingian idea of the *via regia* ("royal road")—the "road" the king was to walk as a good ruler, imposed on the landscape for all his peoples to walk themselves (Hoofnagle 2016).

* * * * *

But that is not all there is to say. The narrative provided does not include the so-called Investiture Contest, the long-running conflict that began in earnest during the eleventh century and raged in Europe between secular rulers and papacy over who had the authority to create bishops (Miller 2005). Much, much ink has been spilled on that topic. Another glaring omission is Byzantium. Ruling from Constantinople, the *basileus* ("king" in Greek) continued to rule in the same tradition as Constantine I (r. 306–37) when he moved his residence eastwards. In them, Rome survived and in their legacy remained very much a part of the European consciousness. There was no moment in our period 800–1450 CE in which envoys, merchants, and pilgrims were not moving to and from Byzantium. There was no moment in our period in which the ruler in Constantinople was not a potential ally or enemy of some other western power. Byzantium was very much a part of the medieval west, a part with similar yet distinct understandings of political and cultural power (Harris 2015).

In addition, the narrative also does not include things too often omitted in considerations of "medieval empire." The chapter here omits issues of dissent, of resistance to *imperium*. Although Charlemagne and his son, for instance, strove for unity and comity within, there were those who felt that a

FIGURE 0.4: The territories ruled by Henry II of England and his successors, Richard I and John. An illustration from *A Short History of the English People*, by John Richard Green, illustrated edition, Volume I, Macmillan & Co., London, New York, 1892. Credit: The Print Collector/Getty Images.

heavy yoke and fought back (Gillis 2017). Moreover, narratives of "medieval empire" have too often focused on the "core" of Europe, leaving out what has traditionally been called its "fringes." Geographically, this means we have not discussed Iberia, Anatolia (other than the note about Byzantium), the Middle East, and North Africa. Culturally, this means women, Jews, and Muslims have also been left out. This is no longer acceptable, and shouldn't be.

Scholars have now shown how those areas and those people, so long considered (or at least treated as) peripheral, were absolutely central to the cultural world of medieval Europe. As already discussed, Charlemagne's decision to pursue his coronation was shaped by his relations with the Byzantine ruler Irene, as well as the Abbasid Caliph Harun al-Rashid. Charlemagne's expeditions into Iberia, his conquests across the Pyrenees (expanded beyond Barcelona by his son, Louis the Pious) became the stuff of legend in the *Song of Roland* and its subsequent imitators. Constantinople, Cordoba, and Baghdad were very much a part of his ninth-century world, even ruling as he did from Aachen in northern Europe. In addition, the women of the Carolingian world were always central to its intellectual, social, and political life. The noblewoman Dhuoda's letter to her son stands as one of the most important witnesses to aristocratic and imperial life of the ninth century (Garver 2009). Moreover, it is fundamentally impossible to understand any Frankish ruler's reign—let alone Charlemagne's!—without consideration of his relations with the Islamic Abbasid Caliphs in Baghdad or the Islamic rulers in Iberia. With the former, Charlemagne plotted against the Byzantines in southern Italy and burnished his own reputation (as mentioned earlier). With the latter, he played petty rulers off against one another to help them secure their power, as well as expand his own into and beyond Catalonia (Sénac 2002; Ottewill-Soulsby 2017).

All of this, as with just about everything else Charlemagne and his court did during his reign, echoed forward for the remainder of the Middle Ages. Iberia, both Christian and Islamic, was absolutely integral to the mind of the medieval west. The Pyrenees were not nearly the barrier we often can think them to have been. Culture crossed mountains (Sahlins 1991; Purkis 2008; Lecaque 2018). The same was true of the rest of the Mediterranean world, from North Africa to the Middle East—and this is all to say nothing about the later Middle Ages. By 1450 CE, the end of our period, the Portuguese had reached Senegal in West Africa and merchants and missionaries had been going back-and-forth to China for more than a hundred years. Culture crossed oceans (Phillips 1988). People who were born in Europe did not—ever—just stay in Europe but moved constantly, as pilgrims to holy sites, as merchants, as diplomats, as warriors, as marriage entourages, as rulers—yet another reason why we must avoid thinking of *imperium*, of rule, as extending over places but rather as encompassing people (Verdon 2003; Legassie 2017). Much of this outward expansion, similar to how it was during the life of Charlemagne, was led by those seeking/holding *imperium*.

This was true on both sides of the Rhine. Emperor Frederick I's successors understood his invocation of *sacrum imperium* expansively, likely as Frederick himself would have liked. As such, those rulers constantly looked east. The two Fredericks, Barbarossa and his great-grandson Frederick II (r. 1211–50), participated in military expeditions to Jerusalem, the latter even regaining the city for the Christians (albeit only for a brief time) through diplomacy. Many of Frederick's other successors sanctioned expansion through Poland and into the Baltics, conquering non-Christians throughout. Oftentimes working in concert, the French kings and papacy sanctioned repeated expeditions—usually led by Franciscans—to Asia, hoping for converts, alliances, and the fabled realm of Prester John. For example, William of Rubruck was sent in the early 1250s by King (Saint) Louis IX of France (r. 1226–70) to the Mongol Khan. In William's account of his journey, we never learn the contents of Louis IX's letter in detail but we do get hints that its primary goal was to secure an alliance with the Mongols against the Muslims, as well as attempt to secure the Mongols' conversion to Christianity. Although nothing came of it and King Louis reportedly regretted sending emissaries, that he did still speaks to his ambition, his embrace of the title "most Christian king," and his assumed role as protector of all Christendom because of his heritage, because of his *imperium* (Jordan 1979; Husain 2011: 245–58; Khanmohamadi 2014: 57–87). The most powerful rulers in western Europe paid little heed to boundaries, to borders. Their *imperium* extended over peoples—different peoples—not places.

This better contextualization of medieval *imperium*, of "empire," is particularly important because it allows us to better understand that other "fringe" of medieval society, that variety of peoples that populated the west between 800 and 1450 CE. Europe was not—was never—simply white, nor was it simply Christian. Jewish communities were present and active in Europe since at least Republican Rome, though primarily in Italy at first. By the ninth century, however, there were substantial and expanding communities in Italy, Iberia, as well as in some parts of modern France and western Germany. Indeed, there's some anecdotal references to Jews in and around the entourages of Frankish kings (Toch 2005). Muslims, too, were no strangers to Europeans. Most of Iberia, parts of southern Italy, and parts of what is now southern France were, after all, under Islamic control for portions of our period and a large portion of the population of those areas were converts to Islam, not "foreign" invaders. Beyond that, however, and although there is evidence of Muslims living in northern Europe (mostly though not all, initially at least, as hostages or slaves), the vast majority lived together with Christians in Hungary, Italy, the so-called Crusader States, and Iberia. In those areas, they were simply part of the landscape, part of the population, part of the same *imperium* as anyone else: "in the thousands of charters and royal orders that survive in the Iberian Peninsula alone, the Latin rulers addressed them and their communities [simply] as 'all Our faithful Muslim subjects'" (Catlos 2014: 12; Metcalfe 2009).

Finally, we must note that there is increasingly strong textual and archeological evidence that there were Africans on the British Isles (and elsewhere in Europe) from the time of Rome onwards and certainly in the early Middle Ages (Green 2016). Geraldine Heng documents, for example, the striking case of the portrayal of Saint Maurice at Magdeburg Cathedral from the first half of the thirteenth century (Figure 0.5). Almost certainly tied in some way to the Emperor Frederick II, this statue serves to remind the viewer that this saint—patron of the *sacrum Romanum imperium* itself—represents the horizons of Frederick's power, the former power that Christian rulers held in the Middle East and beyond and a spur to recreate that power in the present. In this way,

FIGURE 0.5: St. Maurice, Magdeburg Cathedral Germany, *c.* 1250 CE. Credit: INTERFOTO/Alamy Stock Photo.

Maurice's blackness is crucially important for its inclusivity, a signal that those like the saint also fell under Frederick II's *sacrum imperium* (Heng 2014).

Now, the above must come with some caveats. That there were places and moments of interaction and engagement across all vectors of difference in the Middle Ages does not mean that there weren't also places and moments of horrific violence as well. We must not focus on either the former or the latter without regard for the other. Jews may have lived among Christians but were also massacred by them and expelled from their communities. Muslims were considered paragons of chivalry but also quasi-demonic killers. Black skin could be representative of evil but also of saintliness. So, given that variability, we must acknowledge that all populations of medieval Europe—Christian, Muslim, Jewish, white, black, men, women, etc.—thought deeply at times about the variety of human experience. How they responded to that difference was oftentimes situational, formed by their particular historical context (Whitaker 2015 and other essays in that issue; also Heng 2011a, 2011b; Ramey 2014).[3] But for our purposes here, the one constant was that *imperium* didn't much care about any of that difference, at least not in the ways that we today might. In some ways, a ruler's *imperium*—his claim to medieval "empire"—derived its strength from that difference. It relied upon multiplicity and the ruler's ability to bring them all together under his authority. It spanned cultures and created its own. This is not to say that rulers didn't act differently toward different groups of people; of course they did. What it means is that the power rulers claimed allowed them to act on bodies regardless of any of those differences, allowed them (depending on the historical circumstances) to extend control beyond geographical limits.

* * * * *

Despite the chronological constraints of this volume, the story that began in 800 CE does not really end until *c.* 1800 CE, some one thousand years later. The only "real" western medieval empire, the *sacrum Romanum imperium*—more commonly known as the "Holy Roman Empire" begun during the reign of Frederick I Barbarossa—was dissolved by Napoleon I Bonaparte (r. 1804–14, 1815) after he defeated the forces of Emperor Francis II (r. 1792–1806) at Austerlitz in 1806. But just as one empire ended, another began. By 1806, Napoleon himself had become "Emperor of France," a title wholly invented at the time of his coronation in 1804. And even then, the debate about the meaning of that title continued along much the same lines as before. Right up until the time of the French Revolution at the end of the eighteenth century, the French continued to argue about the nature of political authority (*imperium*), with royal and bourgeois historians seeking to prove—via recourse to Charlemagne(!)—from whence the king's power really derived. This time, however, the argument left the pope out of it. The question debated in the eighteenth century became: did *imperium* derive from God directly, or from the acclamation (and consent) of the people? The French Revolution and deposition of the monarch seemed to settle that question in the favor of the people but Napoleon reversed course when he became "Emperor of the French" in 1804. Although Pope Pius VIII was present at the ceremony in Notre Dame in Paris, along with an assembled crowd, there was no acclamation, and no real role for the pope. All the pope did was hand Napoleon the crown, which he himself placed on his own head (Baker 1990: 31–56; Morrissey 2003).

So, by 1800, are we so far from the Middle Ages? Perhaps not. "Empire" in 1800, in 1400, in 800, was about *imperium*, was about authority/power that extended over a multiplicity of peoples. That *imperium* recognized no fixed borders but could move with the political winds, expanding or contracting as necessary, useful as a metric for measuring populations but not geography. There was also a consistent recognition that *imperium* could be held by multiple rulers, oftentimes with different titles, at the same time. This wasn't *Star Wars* and there was no one "empire" to which all needed subscribe. Where medievals disagreed was whence that power derived. They agreed, for example, that it had been given to Charlemagne but disagreed who had bestowed it upon him— perhaps by God, perhaps the Franks through conquest, perhaps the pope, or perhaps the Romans by safeguarding the Eternal City. That question was never answered to everyone's satisfaction then, nor perhaps will it ever be now. We still, after all, write and speak volumes about whence power derives in modern democratic societies. This, too, is a debate about empire in that it is a debate about *imperium*.

If this is the case, if the story told in this essay is one that might well extend far beyond the chronological limits of the volume, we have to return, here at the end, to the questions with which we began. That discussion of Adso of Montier-en-Der's *De antichristo* led us to ask: was there such a thing as "medieval empire," was there something distinct about those two words in combination? Now, I think, we must answer that question only slightly differently than we tentatively did at the start. There was—and wasn't—such a thing as "medieval empire." Once we dig back through the opaque layers piled upon the Middle Ages by colonialist/imperialist scholars of the nineteenth and early twentieth centuries, we do realize that there was *imperium* and there were *imperatores* and *augusti*. These were terms that medievals themselves used in different contexts, at different points between 800 and 1450 CE. Charlemagne was an *augustus* and *imperator*, as was Frederick I, as was Frederick II, as was Napoleon. Rulers in the areas of modern France, Germany, England, and Spain all claimed *imperium*. Yet, as we have also seen, those terms as we understand them in English—"empire" and "emperor"—did not mean the same things then as they do in modernity. "Empire" did not mean territory, nor did it mean hegemonic power over a unified polity, even if it did carry hints of those ideas in the Middle Ages. An "emperor" did not always sit at the top of a strict hierarchy of titles of which it sat at the top, even if at some moments some in the Middle Ages claimed he did. In other words, *A Cultural History of Western Empires* in the Middle Ages is a story that is both familiar and foreign, recognizable and alienating, and a story that once investigated tells us something about how people of the period thought about politics, culture, religion, society, gender, sex, economics, and how porous—almost at times non-existent—the lines between those categories often are.

CHAPTER ONE

War

MARCUS BULL

The embodiment *par excellence* of the medieval vision of empire, and someone who loomed large in the European imagination for many centuries after his death, was Charlemagne, king of the Franks between 768 and 814. As is well known, the signature event of Charlemagne's reign was his coronation as emperor in St. Peter's basilica in Rome on Christmas Day, 800; this made him the first person to bear the title in western Europe for more than three hundred years (McKitterick 2008). Much about Charlemagne's new status was unclear or ambiguous; he and his advisers, and then his son and successor Louis the Pious (r. 814–40), would spend many years trying to work through the implications of possession of the imperial title. What qualitative difference, they needed to establish, did it bring to simply being a king? Whatever the uncertain future of the revived emperorship, however, those present at Charlemagne's coronation would have been in no doubt that the principal reason why he had reached this pinnacle of achievement was his remarkable record as a war leader. Like his grandfather Charles Martel (d. 741) and his father Pippin the Short (d. 768) before him, Charlemagne presided over a war machine that was launched against a wide range of opponents in a relentless series of annual campaigns (Reuter 1985). When an annalist close to the royal court recorded for 792 that there had been no campaign that year, it was as if this was an odd break from the norm (Scholz and Rogers 1970: 70). True, Charlemagne's military system had limitations, and some of his opponents proved hard nuts to crack: the emperor's biographer Einhard, for instance, speaks of thirty-three years of relentless, hard, and savage fighting between the Franks and their Saxon neighbors to the east (Ganz 2008: 22–3). But a key moment in Charlemagne's eventual rise to the emperorship had been a much shorter, sharper campaign against the Lombard kingdom in northern Italy in 773–4. In taking the Lombard capital, Pavia, and deposing and exiling the king, Desiderius, Charlemagne made a significant new move. In the past, when one ruler had overcome another in the early medieval west, the vanquished were typically expected to accept the victor's overlordship and to pay tribute; at most, one finds the replacement of the defeated ruler by a more pliant client (Halsall 2003). In 774, however, Charlemagne assumed the title of king of the Lombards for himself, thereby establishing the plurality of kingships over diverse peoples that was to be one of the rationales for the elevation to emperor some years later. In short, naked aggression and the mobilization of overwhelming military force had underpinned Charlemagne's rise to imperial greatness.

And the formula worked again, for when the German king Otto I assumed the imperial title, which had fallen into abeyance, in 962—in so doing inaugurating the primary association of the western idea of empire with the German-speaking lands that was to last until 1918—he too had built up his status and authority principally as a war leader (Reuter 1991: 148–74). The military resources at Otto's disposal were fewer than those of the Carolingians at the height of their success but his East Frankish ("German") kingdom was that part of the former Carolingian world in which vigorous leadership in war could be parlayed most effectively into political dominance (Arnold 1997: 133–7). Otto's principal external adversaries were the Magyars, a steppe people who had begun raiding deep into central and western Europe shortly before 900. Otto's father Henry I (r. 919–36) had exploited a nine-year respite between Magyar invasions to effect fundamental reforms of his military organization (Leyser 1968), and Otto carefully built on this foundation. The apotheosis of Otto's exploitation of his military resources was his crushing defeat of the Magyars at the Lechfeld, near Augsburg in what is now southern Germany, in 955 CE (Leyser 1965). The revival of the imperial title seven years later was in large part a direct consequence of that victory and his political dominance in Germany, and by extension northern Italy. Once again, empire was the child of war.

Although warfare was intimately connected to medieval ideas of "empire" in its formal, institutional sense, as the careers of Charlemagne and Otto I make clear, it is important to remember that the Latin word *imperium*, the root of the modern English word, had a wide range of meanings. It was an easy matter to extend it to the authority and power of kings, who were obviously the closest in status to emperors (Niermeyer 1997: 514). But medieval writers were also aware that in the classical Latin that they tried to imitate, *imperium* referred to powers of command and forms of authority of various sorts. At its most basic, the word simply meant the capacity to hold sway over one or more others. The notion of "empire" is, therefore, a useful route into thinking about the ways in which medieval people were caught up in myriad and overlapping networks of power that affected their lives on multiple cultural levels.

It is difficult to think of any such networks in which violence was not a fact of life: if not always the application of actual active physical force, then the threat of or potential for violence that hung over people's social interactions and constrained their behaviors (Brown 2011). One thinks, for example, of the remarkable physical violence visited on the twelfth-century English holy woman Christina of Markyate by her parents because she refused their demands that she marry (Talbot 2008: 24–5)—a rare window on what one suspects was a whole world of routine domestic abuse. At the level of the extended family group, notions of face and shame fueled vendettas: in many medieval cultures, the institution of the feud mounted a strong resistance against central authorities' attempts to gain a monopoly over the legitimate use of violence (Fletcher 2003). Until the Church withdrew its endorsement of such procedures in the thirteenth century, legal cases were often decided by ordeals that either inflicted considerable violence on the body of the accused or pitted him or her against their accuser in a trial by combat (Bartlett 1986). Convicted criminals were executed or mutilated for a wide range of offences.

Medieval warfare was, in effect, simply the scaling up of the endemic violence in society as a whole. Medieval armies were generally small compared to those in the ancient and early modern periods, usually comprising no more than a few hundred combatants and seldom more than one or two thousand, so such a process of scaling up would have seemed natural and straightforward. Different levels of violence easily bled into one another. The early eleventh-century German chronicler Thietmar of Merseburg tells the story of a judicial duel arranged in August 1017 CE to resolve a long-running dispute between Duke Godfrey II of Lower Lotharingia and Count Gerard I of Alsace (Warner 2001: 351–2). Thietmar does not specify the nature of their dispute: it is as if the premise that two men such as these should be at loggerheads was wholly unremarkable in itself and did not require further comment. When the two parties met in a meadow to hold the duel, it quickly descended into a mass fight: three hundred died on Gerard's side, whereas Godfrey lost *only* thirty of his best men, Thietmar dryly notes. There are many other indications of spillage to and from large-scale violence in our sources. Charlemagne's successors tried to require soldiers who served in their armies to put their weapons aside promptly when they returned home: the violent cultural ambience of the public war in which they had been immersed could potentially spill over into feuds or acts of lawlessness when they were thrust back into their local communities. Similarly, Einhard wrote to the abbot of Fulda concerning one of the abbot's men who was worried that his enemies would exploit an upcoming military expedition as cover to pursue a vendetta against him (Dutton 2009: 137–8).

One way in which to imagine the many "empires" or networks of power that governed people's lives, and the significant cultural role that violence played in their world, is to picture a late medieval castle, a complex of defensive structures, dwellings, stables, workshops, and storage spaces that was home to several hundred people. The walls, perhaps surrounding a stone keep that had been the first structure to be built on the site, proclaimed the castle as a place of military power; this was its main *raison d'être* (Coulson 2003). But the castle would have been more than a military stronghold. It would have been the site of its lord's hall, where his literate, school-trained administrators busied themselves with the exploitation of his estates, where lawsuits were heard, and where the lord could project much of his "soft" power through the staging of courtly assemblies and the giving of feasts. If the castle were in royal hands, it might be the site of a mint. One or more churches within or just beyond the castle walls added the force of religious sanction to the lord's authority. The castle would probably be the economic hub of its locality, the location of regular markets; and clinging to its walls would be clusters of homes and workshops, embryonic suburbs that had grown up as people gravitated to the castle to earn their livings in various service industries. The castle would not simply occupy a site that was defensible in its immediate environment; it would be plugged into larger networks of authority by being situated on a navigable river or important road. In other words, the status that the lord was able to project by means of the castle viewed as a military asset was interwoven with other forms of power—economic, religious, social, and cultural (Creighton 2012: 109–51).

A phrase that one often finds used of medieval Europe is that it was a society, or a number of societies, "organized for war." That is to say, war was not simply something that medieval people participated in from time to time, or found themselves swept up by, alongside the many other kinds of activity that filled their lives. Instead, warfare profoundly shaped the social structures and cultural horizons of their worlds: it governed the hierarchies of lordship and dependence that told people who they should obey and why obedience was due to them; it determined who got to benefit from the hard-earned surpluses that peasants wrung from the soil; and it was one of the main ways in which distant authority figures, kings and other rulers, projected their power onto the scattered communities, many of them remote and isolated, that lay within their dominions (Halsall 2003: 1–39). As is the case with all large generalizations, the claim that medieval society was organized in this way must be treated with some caution, for the political, economic, and geographical conditions in which social groups lived varied considerably from place to place and from one period to another; and with that variety came corresponding differences in the ways in which war impinged upon people's lives (Contamine 1984). That said, it is not difficult to find medieval communities in which the needs of war significantly influenced the social structures that governed people's day-to-day cultural experience and suffused the ideologies and paradigms upon which they drew in order to make sense of their world. Two examples help to show how deeply the demands of war could drill into the operations of medieval societies big and small.

The first example comes from the Iberian peninsula, specifically the struggle for political power, economic resources, and military ascendancy between Christian rulers to the north and their Muslim adversaries to the south (Lomax 1978). Between the later eleventh and later thirteenth centuries—broadly speaking a period of Christian territorial gain, though this was neither consistently sustained nor inevitable—an important way for Christian kings to prosecute effective wars of conquest and to hold on to the territories they conquered, as well as to project an image of themselves as active and vigilant warrior-rulers whose writ ran to the very edges of their realms, was to mobilize the human and material resources of frontier towns. The towns were granted formal charters—in Castilian, *fueros*; there were equivalent terms in the other Romance languages spoken in the peninsula—that set out the rights and obligations of the citizens as participants in war (Powers 1988). The origins of the towns varied: some were existing centers of Christian population, others were towns recently captured from the Muslims or clusters of exposed villages relocated to within newly built city walls. The red thread that runs through all the *fueros*, however, is the primary need for the towns to maintain effective militias and to so organize their affairs that the needs of those militias always took precedence. In theory, the militias were to be adaptable, able to operate in a number of roles as independent raiding forces, as a first line of defense against Muslim raids and as units serving in royal armies. In practice, several of the towns organized in this way were not situated on or near the religious frontier, but rather in the borderlands between one Christian kingdom and another; the kings clearly meant for these assets to be available to them in their many conflicts with their coreligionists as well as in their wars against the Moors. But wherever the towns happened to be situated, the ethos that the *fueros* sought to instill was one of edgy, constant vigilance and a sense of cultural distance from one's enemies that seemed consonant with life on the very fringes of Latin Christian civilization.

This ethos underpins all the practical arrangements that the *fueros* set out, for example concerning the structure of the municipal governments and the division of the towns into residential zones, or *collaciones*, which doubled up as subunits of the urban militias (Powers 1988: 93–205). Officials were appointed to supervise the distribution of booty after a successful raid. In some cases, in particular when a Muslim town was captured and its population was wholly or substantially displaced, there is evidence that priority was given to those members of the Christian force who intended to settle when it came to organizing the *repartimiento*, the division of dwellings, parcels of land, and other captured resources. Only later would a second wave of settlers be invited in to fill any remaining gaps. A town repopulated in this manner effectively sought to perpetuate the sense of collective purpose and militant identity that had been forged among the participants during the conquest itself; in such circumstances, the town became a continuation of an act of war by other means. Numerous provisions in the *fueros* speak to the demands that came with being on a constant war-footing (Powers 1971). Regulations governed, for example, the length of time that the militiamen could be required to serve, and the distances from home that it was expected they might range. Members of a town's militia, typically the large majority of the fit adult males living there, were expected to keep their arms, armor, and military gear in good condition; inspections were regularly held and punishments were meted out to those whose slacking was tantamount to letting the side down.

Two illustrations of the way in which *fuero* towns were at the sharp end of a "society organized for war" are particularly revealing because they show how the exigencies of militia organization could revise social norms that equated to deep-rooted habits of mind in the Christian interior. In the first place, frontier conditions encouraged an unusual degree of social mobility. In most of Europe at this time, the ability to equip oneself as a knight and to call oneself by that title was increasingly becoming the birthright of a more or less closed social caste. But in the Spanish towns, ownership of a horse and related equipment as well as a sufficient income could rank a citizen among the militia's mounted troops, the *caballeros*, as opposed to the footsoldiers, or *peones* (Figure 1.1). Indeed, in some *fueros*, reaching a certain property qualification *required* the owner to serve on horseback. This strictly functional approach to the provision of mounted troops accounts for the emergence of "commoner knights" (*caballeros villanos*), a conjunction that seemed natural and necessary on the Spanish frontier but which would have amounted to a cultural contradiction in terms elsewhere (MacKay 1977: 47–50). Second, many *fueros* granted women tax exemptions, control of their own property, and rights of inheritance that were seldom matched in other parts of Latin Christendom: such women were forces for stability and continuity if, for example, their fathers died without male heirs, or their husbands died before their son or sons had reached manhood; while the property rights that they enjoyed would attract would-be husbands willing to submit themselves to the life of a frontier militiaman (Dillard 1984). As the balance of power between Christian and Muslim Iberia began to shift in favor of the former, and as the frontier consequently nudged southwards in fits and starts, towns that had once been on the front line found themselves deep within the relatively safe interior. This raised delicate questions about the extent to which the municipal authorities needed to sustain the fiction of living in a danger zone. In time, one finds former frontier towns moving closer to the sorts of economic and social paradigms that shaped urban life elsewhere in Europe, for example as markets and trading centers, places of manufacture, or royal residences. But through the early modern period, one also sees in the towns' municipal governance and in their relationship with central authority persistent traces of their frontier pasts.

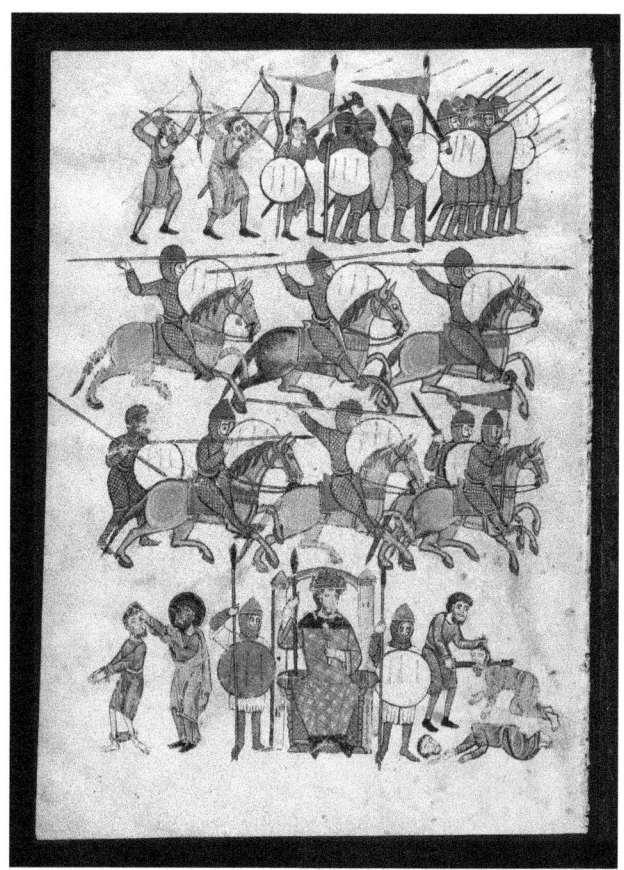

FIGURE 1.1: Thirteenth-century Spanish *peones* and *cabelleros*, Beatus de Liébana, Explanatio in Apocalypsim, Morgan MS 429 fol. 149v, thirteenth century. Credit: J Pierpont Morgan Library, New York.

The second illustration was born of acute, short-term crisis, but it too reveals the ways in which war could have profound impacts on people's lives. The Viking, predominantly Danish, invasions of central and southern Britain in the ninth century wrought great destruction and lasting political change: the kingdoms of Northumbria and East Anglia were swept away, and that of Mercia severely truncated. Wessex, in the south-west, likewise came under severe pressure, and for a time in the 870s and 880s its very survival was up in the air (Keynes 1997: 48–63). One of the principal means by which the king of Wessex, Alfred (r. 871–99), was able to revive his kingdom's fortunes was the construction of a network of about thirty fortified centers, or *burhs* (Abels 1998: 198–207). The *burhs* used and improved what remained of old Roman fortifications where these were available, such as in London, while others were located on the sites of long-abandoned Iron Age hill-forts. Those built from scratch consisted of ditch and rampart defenses, surmounted by wooden palisades, that could be put in place more quickly than stone walls but would still have required the mobilization of tens of thousands of man-hours of labor. Alfred's contemporary biographer Asser reveals that there was some resistance to the king's building program, probably on the part of local landowners unhappy at being made to meet much of the cost as well as farmers taken away from their fields to work on the fortifications (Keynes and Lapidge 1983: 101–2). But the ambition and scope of Alfred's vision are nonetheless remarkable (Lavelle 2010: 209–17). Each *burh* was situated no more than a day's march from at least one other in order to aid defense in depth (Hill 1981: 85–6). And they were sited on major rivers and estuaries—a favored route for Viking raiders—as well as on Roman roads and the pathways traditionally taken by Anglo-Saxon armies. In this way, the *burhs* were more than individually well-positioned and defensible strongpoints; they represented a carefully planned, joined-up system designed to frustrate the free movement of the Viking armies.

The true nature of Alfred's achievement emerges from a remarkable document known as the Burghal Hidage, in which the *burhs* are listed and each allocated a number of hides, which were units of agricultural exploitation used for the assessment of taxes and other dues (Hill 1969). In its surviving form the Burghal Hidage must date from the reign of Alfred's son Edward the Elder (r. 899–924), but in its substance it almost certainly preserves administrative arrangements overseen by Alfred himself (Keynes and Lapidge 1983: 193–4). The document applies a formula for matching a given number of hides to a given length of *burh* wall or rampart, which allows us to calculate what the king's administrators believed to be the length of the defense works at each site. Where archaeological survivals and surviving street patterns—for example, the traces of the Roman walls at Winchester—permit a comparison of conditions on the ground with the Burghal Hidage's totals, the correspondences are sometimes extraordinary (Hill 1981: 85–6). At Winchester, the allocation of 2,400 hides translates to a figure of 3,017 meters of wall, whereas the archaeological remains suggest that this calculation was out by only 16 meters, a margin of error of about half a percent. Although some of the other matches are not as close, the Burghal Hidage is nonetheless impressive evidence for the administrative capacities of Alfred's regime, as well as its ambition: if one assumes that each hide was expected to provide one man for garrison duty in his assigned *burh*, Alfred's system would have mobilized 27,000 people—this on top of those serving in the royal field army, or *fyrd*, another target of Alfred's military reforms. This figure would have been even larger if, as seems likely, men were asked to serve in rotation with colleagues from their localities. It has been estimated that the burghal garrisons made a proportionately greater demand on the available manpower in Wessex than did Prussia, a notably militaristic polity, during the Napoleonic era (Abels 1998: 207).

The mobilization of such large numbers was doubtless unsustainable over more than the short term: Alfred's first priority was to prevent Wessex from going the way of the other Anglo-Saxon kingdoms at a time when the West Saxons had their backs to the wall. But the burghal model proved adaptable, and was extended by Alfred's son and grandsons into the areas north of Wessex that they wrested from the Danes in the early decades of the tenth century. Significantly, it seems that Alfred and his successors fully appreciated the long-term potential of the *burhs* beyond their utility as military bases; there is evidence for the early siting of royal mints and the holding of law courts in these places, as well as the encouragement of markets. In other words, the kings were actively planning for life after the immediate demands of warfare had passed. The *burhs* were also a model that could be adapted to other conditions. The Saxon chronicler Widukind of Corvey describes how King Henry I of Germany (r. 919–36) organized the garrisoning of fortifications with every ninth man from among his forces, the other eight pooling what they grew in order to supply the ninth (Widukind of Corvey 2014: 49). The fortifications were to be the sites of law courts and assemblies as well as training camps. Although there is some scholarly debate on this matter, it is likely that Henry was adapting the West Saxon *burh* system to his own military needs (Schoenfeld 1995). In support of this view is the fact that we know of close cultural ties between the West Saxon and continental Saxon courts in the early tenth century. The main problem is the absence of the sort of archaeological evidence that is so compelling in the West Saxon case. Perhaps Henry and his advisers independently arrived at similar solutions to deal with foes, the Magyars, as mobile and dangerous as were the Vikings. But even if the West Saxons were not paid the flattery of direct imitation in this particular instance, the fact that the burghal system did its job, helping to take Wessex from the brink of extinction to the successful containment of the Viking threat in less than a generation, speaks to the ability of medieval societies to be profoundly reconfigured when the needs of warfare so required.

Not all medieval societies were on the sort of high military alert that characterized life in one of the *fuero* towns or Alfred's *burhs*. So were these places unusual, or are their lessons of wider application? As we noted earlier, it is important not to over-generalize. Although medieval approaches to warfare tended to be quite conservative, there were significant changes over the course of our period: for example, the transformation of the human landscape brought about by the emergence of stone castles in the eleventh and twelfth centuries; the growth of towns, some of whose surplus populations found employment as highly organized mercenary bands that became synonymous with their places of origin—"Flemings," "Brabançons," "Basques," and others; and the introduction of gunpowder into western Europe in the fourteenth and fifteenth centuries

(Keen 1999). Although a single picture of medieval conditions is therefore impossible, there were, nonetheless, two constants that transcended changes in the technologies, organization, and conduct of warfare and allow us to speak of a medieval culture of war in the round. One was the way in which a military identity was almost invariably hard-wired into the self-image and self-worth of secular male elites (we shall turn to this later). The other was the fact that the human and material costs of warfare were disproportionately borne by the poor—the majority of the population. Whether this involved so-called "customs" devised by an exploitative lord in a corner of eleventh-century France in order to generate the cash he needed to build and garrison a new-fangled stone *donjon*, or the burdensome taxation paid by late medieval English peasants to fund a distant king's wars in Wales, Scotland, or France, or some other money-making device, the basic mechanism was much the same. Peasants were forced to divert substantial portions of the frequently exiguous and always vulnerable agricultural surpluses that they generated for the needs of belligerents. The fact that they were able to do so, at least much of the time, given what we know of the very modest returns from the land that were possible in a world before modern intensive farming, is nothing short of remarkable. Medieval warfare in all its forms was ultimately a function of the powers of command and coercion—the *imperium*—that landowners had over the people who grew their crops and tended their livestock.

But it was not only as the ultimate cash cows of war that the poor suffered. They were frequently its direct victims. To be in the path of a medieval army in motion would have been a devastating experience. In the absence of mechanized transport and the effective preservation of food, it was very difficult indeed to supply a large group of belligerents adequately. The expectation was, therefore, that armies should live off the land, a euphemism for systematic pillaging usually accompanied by the widespread burning of villages, barns, and other agricultural infrastructure. Medieval armies did not march down the road in neat soldierly fashion line abreast; they fanned out over the countryside, often over several miles. An eyewitness account of the First Crusade (1095–9) reports that one of the crusade's leaders, Bohemond, made a point of ordering his men to refrain from plundering the land as they marched through the central Balkans, and to take only the food that they strictly needed. This is meant to show Bohemond in a positive light, as a leader who maintained firm discipline. But a few sentences later the author goes on to comment, without a trace of irony or criticism, that as soon as the crusaders encountered a lack of cooperation from the local people—understandably, for Bohemond's south Italian Normans had invaded that same region some years earlier—they eagerly set about seizing livestock and anything else they could lay their hands on (Hill 1962: 8).

Systematic pillaging was not simply a matter of satisfying one's immediate needs and moving on. Fire was one of the major weapons of medieval warfare, and was remarkably effective in a world of predominantly modest wooden buildings. To cut a swathe of destruction through a territory was to intimidate and demoralize one's enemy, to destroy his resources, or to goad him into precipitate action. One of the most revealing "cut-away" scenes in the Bayeux Tapestry that stands apart from the main story of the Norman Conquest of England involves a distressed mother and child emerging, hand in hand, from a burning building that is flanked by two larger, looming figures with lit torches in their hands (Wilson 1985: 50–1) (Figure 1.2). But why include this scene if, as its positioning implies, the figures with the torches are members of Duke William of Normandy's forces and the victims are a local English family swept up in events? Would this not put William and his cause in a bad light? Not necessarily, for the scene takes place in the interval between the Normans' landing in Sussex and the Battle of Hastings. Many of the family lands of William's rival, Harold II, were concentrated in that part of southern England where the Normans were ravaging (Barlow 2002). Perhaps Harold was being goaded. If so, it worked, for, as is well known, Harold drove his forces hard from northern England in order to offer battle at the earliest opportunity, rather than pursue a more cautious strategy of attrition. His defeat at Hastings was the result.

Worse was to follow a few years later. Over the winter of 1069–70, William's forces, now masters of England but still not entirely secure in their new conquest, engaged in one of the most brutal exercises in scorched-earth tactics

FIGURE 1.2: Burning of a house, Bayeux Tapestry, late eleventh century. Credit: Photo12/UIG via Getty Images.

on record. The target was northern England, particularly Yorkshire, as a punishment for having given aid to a recent Danish invasion. Not only were villages burned and food destroyed, every effort was made to ensure that agricultural production would be disrupted for years to come (Bates 2016: 313–21). This was, in effect, an attempt to contrive a long-term famine. Many thousands of peasants were killed outright. Numerous others were forced to become refugees, meeting lingering deaths on the sides of roads. There are even reports of people resorting to cannibalism. One modern historian has not baulked from describing this "Harrying of the North," as it is known, as an act of "genocide" (Kapelle 1979: 3). And though scholars continue to debate the true extent of the Normans' destruction of the region, there is no disguising the anguish of the usually well-informed Anglo-Norman chronicler Orderic Vitalis when he evokes an image of "helpless children, young men in the prime of life, and hoary gray-beards perishing alike of hunger" (Orderic Vitalis 1968: 230–3). In 1086, when William's commissioners assembled the vast survey of England's resources that we know as Domesday Book, much of Yorkshire was still classified as "waste," that is to say as land not in active use. Agricultural land and rural communities could often bounce back quite quickly after setbacks, but the Domesday waste suggests that there had been a systematic and intensive campaign of depopulation and destruction sixteen years earlier.

It was not just people living in dispersed rural communities who were vulnerable to the formidable destructive power of medieval armies. One of the most striking set-pieces in Jean Froissart's *Chronicles*, one of our main narrative sources for the Hundred Years War (1337–1453), concerns the storming of the French city of Limoges by the forces of Edward, the Black Prince, in 1370. Froissart is known as the chronicler of chivalry, a writer who wasted no opportunity to sing the praises of men such as the Black Prince, the eldest son of King Edward III of England (r. 1327–77), as paragons of noble virtue (Ainsworth 1990). In a sense, Froissart's Hundred Years War is a kind of cultural stage upon which high-status men are able to disport themselves and parade their chivalric masculinity. So it is all the more remarkable when we encounter Froissart's narrative penetrating beneath the aristocratic veneer and capturing something of the lived experience of those who were on the receiving end of the war. According to Froissart, when the English breached the walls of Limoges and poured into the city, they had orders to kill indiscriminately, presumably because the inhabitants had resisted their rightful lord:

> There were pitiful scenes. Men, women, and children flung themselves on their knees before the Prince, crying: "Have mercy on us, gentle sir!" But he was so inflamed with anger that he would not listen. Neither man nor woman was heeded, but all who could be found were put to the sword, including many who were in no way to blame. I do not understand how they could

have failed to take pity on people who were too unimportant to have committed treason. Yet they paid for it, and paid more dearly than the leaders who had committed it. There is no man so hard-hearted that, if he had been in Limoges that day, and had remembered God, he would not have wept bitterly at the fearful slaughter which took place. More than three thousand persons, men, women, and children, were dragged out to have their throats cut (Froissart 1978: 178).

The Harrying of the North and the storming of Limoges struck contemporary observers as especially heinous, but not because violence of this sort was unusual in and of itself. On the contrary, it took acts of exceptional brutality to provoke comment because the base level of violence to which people were more or less inured, what the celebrated medieval historian Marc Bloch with only a little exaggeration termed "the distinguishing mark of an epoch" (Bloch 1962: 410–11), was already so high.

Froissart's vignettes also draw our attention to the large role that sexual violence played in the abuse that medieval armies visited on those in their path. One of the very first acts in the Hundred Years War was a French naval raid on Southampton in October 1338. Froissart tells us that the Norman and Genoese sailors sacked the town thoroughly. Then they killed large numbers of people, raped women and girls, which was "a deplorable thing," Froissart thinly observes, and loaded their ships with the plunder they had seized, before catching the tide and sailing back to France (Froissart 1978: 61). The fact that the act of mass rape is sandwiched between other actions that the raiding party undertook, as if part of a natural and expected pattern of behavior in such circumstances, and the implication, too, that the rapes were every bit as pre-planned and organized as the raiders' other predations, not something that they somehow fell into in the moment, offer up a chilling view of the role of sexual violence as an instrument of power and subjugation in medieval warfare.

Another striking piece of evidence takes the form of the penitential ordinance that was imposed in 1070 by the pope's representative, Bishop Ermenfrid of Sion, on those who had taken part in the Norman Conquest of England (Douglas and Greenaway 1981: 649–50). Although the Conquest was vigorously sold by the victors as a legitimate war fought in vindication of a just cause, and it had been endorsed by important voices in the Church, those who had taken part were still expected to atone for the various sins that they had committed during the campaign (Cowdrey 1969). Most of Ermenfrid's ordinance concerns thefts, woundings, and killings—how archers might do penance for those they had killed at Hastings when it was impossible to know how many deaths they had caused, for example. But toward the end of the document Ermenfrid turns to those who had committed adultery, rape, or acts of fornication. These men must do penance "as if these sins had been committed in their own country." In other words, the Normans' relocation to a new land, full of vulnerable, culturally alien victims who spoke an unfamiliar language, would seem to have encouraged a relaxation of the self-restraint—such as it was—that was expected of such men back in their homeland. The larger question underpinning Ermenfrid's reference to rape, then, was how much longer the Normans would continue to regard themselves as an army of occupation in a foreign land, and thus tolerate and indeed encourage the widespread sexual violence that their situation, in their eyes, validated.

As noted earlier, the second constant of the medieval culture of war was the way in which society's male elites drew upon images and habits of mind associated with warfare in order to fashion their images of themselves (Crouch 1992). There was little in the way of formal schooling in military manhood in the Middle Ages, nor were there institutions that did a similar job to the training camps that had been run by the Roman state. To rise to the estate of an elite warrior in medieval Europe was largely a matter of acculturation from a young age as boys were taught to ride and to use weapons (Karras 2003: 20–66). Emphasis was placed on physical toughness and on teamwork, which is one reason why elite males spent much of their free time hunting, an excellent training ground for real war. Although by the late Middle Ages there were how-to manuals of chivalry, such as that by Geoffroi de Charny, which gave the ethical education of the sons of the aristocracy a slightly more bookish feel (Kaeuper and Kennedy 1996), the essential mechanism remained the same: constant practical training and the studied imitation of the men and older boys around you. It is important to remember that medieval elite culture had not retained the Roman *cursus honorum*, or "course of offices," in which the career trajectories of high-status males oscillated back and forth between civilian and military responsibilities. In medieval Europe, unless one had been earmarked by one's family for a career in the Church, there was effectively only one life path available to the male children of the aristocracy. It is true that as youths or adults some were able to "opt out" for reasons of religious scruple and became hermits or monks; and there were times when this was in vogue, such as in the twelfth century when the Cistercians and other new religious orders grew thanks to many acts of conversion on the part of members of the aristocracy (Newman 1996: 23–37). But religious conversion was never a route open to anything more than a minority. For most male aristocrats, their lives were simply the inexorable working through of a set of cultural expectations, attributes, and attitudes that had been programmed into them since childhood (Orme 1984). Given the depth of this acculturation, it is not surprising that aristocratic culture prized physical prowess, loyalty, reliability and other martial virtues so highly (Keen 1984) (Figure 1.3).

Elite males valued honor and had a concomitant abhorrence of shame as well as a lively horror of the loss of face. Sometimes men cracked or failed in some way to live up to what was expected of them, and they suffered accordingly.

FIGURE 1.3: David and Goliath in the Morgan Leaf from the Winchester Bible, Morgan MS M 619 verso, twelfth century. Credit: J Pierpont Morgan Library, New York.

For example, Henry of Essex, who served as constable and standard-bearer for King Henry II of England (r. 1154–89), a position that placed him right on the king's shoulder in moments of acute danger, became notorious for mistakenly dropping the royal standard—which was the signal that the king was dead—during an expedition into Wales in 1157. Only the prompt action of others prevented Henry's actions from triggering a rout (Strickland 1996: 122–3). Six years later Henry was accused of treason and required to fight his accuser in a judicial duel on an island in the River Thames. As described with relish by one chronicler, Henry was knocked senseless and, his defeat serving as proof of his guilt, he was carried to the nearby abbey at Reading, where he became a monk once he had recovered (Jocelin of Brakelond 1989: 61–3). In effect, Henry was pushed into early retirement and turned into a non-person for his infraction of the powerful aristocratic norms that applied in times of war.

A different but equally revealing case is that of King Stephen of England (r. 1135–54), whose forlorn heroics in the thick of battle helped to salvage an otherwise unfavorable reputation. Stephen's father, Stephen of Blois, had gained notoriety by deserting the First Crusade, only to be sent back east by his mortified wife (Brundage 1960). This legacy doubtless contributed to the difficulties faced by the younger Stephen when he seized the throne after the death of his uncle Henry I (King 2010: 41–81). After a brief honeymoon period during which Stephen spent down Henry's treasure, the hard-nosed Anglo-Norman magnates came to see their king as injudicious, profligate, unreliable, and weak. An inconclusive and poorly led campaign in Normandy in 1137 added strategic incompetence to the growing list of shortcomings. So when Henry I's daughter, the empress Matilda, decided to press her claims to the English throne, Stephen lacked both the resources and the reserves of respect and loyalty to prevent the country from slipping into civil war. Nonetheless, a single act of personal fortitude in battle was able to silence the chorus of disapproval, at least in the short term. For when Stephen found himself hemmed in on all sides at the end of the battle of Lincoln in February 1141, the worst defeat of his career, he redeemed himself by manfully holding off his assailants as they came at him in wave after wave. Brandishing a battle-ax, and after this broke a sword, he managed to keep his attackers at bay with just a handful of followers until he was finally overcome. According to one of the best informed chroniclers of Stephen's reign, when his enemies saw the king in such straits, "they were all so much softened by tender emotions of pity and compassion that they broke forth into tears and lamentation [and] repentance was very deeply imprinted on their hearts and faces" (Potter 1976: 114). A highly visible and physical, and tenaciously sustained, performance of the basic virtues of elite military masculinity could even rehabilitate someone like Stephen.

The ways in which the aristocracy internalized the skills and deportment of a warrior and made them the central element of their identity emerge particularly clearly from attempts to discipline and channel aristocrats' martial instincts. A case in point is the experience of the Military Orders. Emerging in the twelfth and thirteenth centuries, these were organizations that combined a military way of life, mostly on the frontiers of Christendom, with the disciplines and devotional routines of an order of monks or canons (Forey 1992). Unlike some religious orders that took in entrants as children and so had an extended period in which to instruct the next generation in their way of life, the Military Orders relied on adult recruits, in particular members of the knightly class—in other words, men who had already received at least an adequate military training (Forey 1986). But with these grown-up recruits came habits of mind and ingrained behaviors that might undermine the orders' collective ethos and strong emphasis on obedience and discipline. The rules and statutes that regulated the lives of the Military Orders thus include fascinating attempts to strain out what was useful in a member's military upbringing from those elements of aristocratic martial culture that were considered undesirable. For example, the Primitive Rule of the Templars, the foundational set of regulations for the first Military Order to be founded, strictly forbade the wearing of fine robes or any show of pride (Upton-Ward 1992: 24). Pride was a sin traditionally condemned in the monastic regulations that heavily influenced the Templar Rule, but it was also a vice traditionally associated with the haughtiness of aristocrats confident in their military superiority (Little 1971). One sees further attempts to destabilize and suppress the competitive, boastful culture of the male elite in the Primitive Rule's insistence that strong and weak members of the order were to be considered as strictly equal; that in order to ensure that "no brother should fight or rest according to his own will," members should routinely move around in self-policing pairs; and that there should be no chatting about the brave deeds that a member claimed to have performed in his days before joining the order (Upton-Ward 1992: 29–31).

Some of the regulations' prohibitions seem trivial on the surface, such as those concerning pointed shoes, shoelaces, and long hair (Upton-Ward 1992: 25). But the legislators knew full well that such attention to appearance was part of a larger cultural habit, or "schema," that characterized the secular warrior and had to be tamed. It is for this reason that one finds the Templars and other Military Orders frequently passing regulations against individual members taking gifts from outsiders—for the giving and receiving of gifts was one of the principal ways in which medieval elite cultures created and sustained social ties. There were frequent strictures against the ornamentation of saddles and other equipment; the fact that the second international Military Order to emerge after the Templars, the Hospitallers, came back to this issue again and again in its thirteenth-century legislation suggests that its members were constantly pushing the limits of what they could get away with under the impulse of aristocratic military display. In a similar vein, the German order of the Teutonic Knights had to forbid its members from participating in tournaments. And all the orders routinely legislated against hunting. Membership of a Military Order was only for a select few. Indeed, their small numbers allowed the Military Orders to play up the idea that they were a pristine "new knighthood," a radical departure from the norms of the warrior class (Barber 1994: 38–63). It is significant that the Templars' favored visual marker, their "logo" on their seals and in other representations, was a picture of two helmeted knights humbly mounted together on a single horse, a powerful statement that the order retained, in fact accentuated, the military identity of its members while rejecting many of the cultural norms that were associated with such an identity (Barber 1994: 181) (Figure 1.4).

Further revealing demonstrations of the ways in which the male aristocracy defined itself through war emerge from what might be called "fantasy history," stories about the past that purported to be accurate historical narrative—indeed, even insisted on this point—but were in fact largely exercises in fantasy, myth-making, and wishful thinking. It is striking how often, when authors decoupled themselves from even a modest adherence to historical reality as they understood it, and let their own and their readers' imaginations run loose, tales of the deeds of ruler-figures and other aristocratic alpha-males exaggerated the scale and effectiveness of the fighting in which their protagonists engaged.

FIGURE 1.4: Matthew Paris illustration of two Templars on horseback, British Library Royal MS 14 C VII fol. 42v, thirteenth century. Credit: The British Library.

A good example concerns Hereward, a minor lord from the Fenlands who is known to have made some difficulties for the Normans a few years after the Conquest (Hayward 1988). In Charles Kingsley's overblown 1866 novel *Hereward the Wake*, Hereward is a noble freedom fighter, the last man to hold out against the cruel Norman yoke (Kingsley 1889). But this is far from the truth. Hereward was not the leader of an Anglo-Saxon *maquis*, but a freebooter who had been exiled from England before 1066 and served various lords in Flanders, probably as a mercenary, before returning to his homeland and getting caught up in a rebellion against the new regime. It is probable that Hereward was reconciled with King William when the rebellion collapsed, and he may even have died serving in William's army in France. But in the hands of the author of a text known as *The Deeds of Hereward*, probably a monk of Ely called Richard who was writing between 1109 and 1131, Hereward was transformed into a paragon of military virtue (Ohlgren 2005: 28–99).

Although it can be shown that there are traces of historical fact in the *Deeds'* account of Hereward's career, for example in its descriptions of his time in Flanders (van Houts 1999b) and its identifications of his companions and enemies (Dalton 2009), there can be no doubt that we are in the presence of a substantially enhanced, "reimagined" hero. It is significant, then, that the principal means at the author's disposal to rewrite Hereward involved exaggerating his qualities as a warrior. Hereward is presented as physically tough, brave, and magnanimous toward his enemies. He is supremely resourceful, plans intelligently, and can improvise solutions to tactical crises. His manhood extends to the slaying of wild beasts, and his exploits are celebrated in song and dance by the common people. Even when he is in disguise, his skill in battle betrays his true identity; and the more fair-minded of his foes come to acknowledge his prowess and nobility. Perhaps most importantly of all, he excels as a leader: young men, many of them of high status, flock to join his warband in the confident expectation that they will receive first-rate training as knights under his tutelage. What the Hereward of the *Deeds* principally delivers to his gang of followers is, therefore, what the author calls the "comradeship of battle" (Ohlgren 2005: 52). And this makes him nothing short of a model for anyone wishing to pursue the military life (Ohlgren 2005: 40) (Figure 1.5).

Kingsley's novel made Hereward a minor public hero in Victorian England, but his fame and cultural significance are hugely eclipsed by another celebrity of the fantasy history genre, King Arthur. The writer who did more than any other to launch Arthur's career was Geoffrey of Monmouth, whose *History of the Kings of Britain* was written in the mid 1130s (Geoffrey of Monmouth 2007). As is well known, almost all of the content of Geoffrey's *History* is at best confabulation and huge exaggeration, at worst pure fiction (Echard 1998: 31–67). Scholarly debate has long raged over what Geoffrey intended his text to be and to achieve (Jankulak 2010), but three things are clear: most of Geoffrey's readers accepted the *History* as a more or less straight exercise in historical writing, despite the efforts of a handful of defiant naysayers to point out the text's absurdities; the *History* was extremely popular, surviving in a large number of manuscript copies; and the history of Britain that Geoffrey gave his many—accepting—readers was above all a history of relentless warfare. More than any other political act or social process, war, invasion, and rebellion fill the narrative across its broad sweep from the first inhabitants of Britain to the end of Roman rule and the arrival of the Saxons. The reign of Arthur was clearly a time that Geoffrey wished to foreground, for it occupies a large portion of the text (Geoffrey of Monmouth 2007: 192–253); and it is no surprise that it is mostly as a warrior that Arthur's career plays out. Much like Hereward, though on a far larger scale, Arthur treats warfare as essentially a political and cultural resource: it gives expression to a shared aristocratic ethos, it builds consensus among the elites of his kingdom, and it supplies the lands and titles

HEREWARD AND HIS MEN ATTACK THE NORMANS

FIGURE 1.5: Hereward the Wake, eleventh-century Anglo-Saxon leader, attacking Peterborough Abbey in 1070 in protest at William I's imposition of a Norman abbot, early twentieth century. Credit: Universal History Archive/Getty Images.

with which he rewards his followers. The logic of cause and motivation is little explored. True, the Britons' titanic struggle against the Romans, which represents the climax of Arthur's wars of conquest, is prompted by an insulting Roman demand for tribute and then animated by the desire to avenge Roman mistreatment of the Britons in times past. But almost all of Arthur's other acts of aggression simply happen: warfare in this world just *is*.

Arthur begins his reign threatened by the Saxons, so his first actions involve campaigns of self-defense, and the aura of holy war that attends this fighting and the crusade-inspired spiritual rewards that are offered to Arthur's troops reinforce a sense of legitimate violence (Geoffrey of Monmouth 2007: 196–9). But then defense shades into attack, and attack into spectacular aggression, without comment or explanation on Geoffrey's part. Victorious against the Saxons, Arthur turns his forces against the Picts and Scots, then the Irish, then Iceland, Norway, and Denmark, and so on in a cascade of unstinting violence.

In a moment of strangely vacuous reasoning, we are told that Arthur conceived the idea of conquering the whole of Europe simply because he discovered that the leaders there were all terrified of him (Geoffrey of Monmouth 2007: 204–5). Thus war simply becomes a sort of self-fulfilling prophecy or an end unto itself. Gaul is reduced in a nine-year campaign; the Romans are defeated in a climactic battle; and Arthur is only prevented from capping his achievements by a descent on Rome itself by the news that his nephew Mordred has rebelled against him, which forces him to return to Britain. Geoffrey does not palliate the calculated and grimly effective brutality of Arthur's war machine. We are told, for example, that as many as 6,000 Saxons are killed in one day, drowned or put to the sword (Geoffrey of Monmouth 2007: 145–6); Arthur sets out to exterminate the Picts and the Scots, contriving starvation and famine much like William the Conqueror in the Harrying of the North, and wiping them out "with utter ruthlessness" (Geoffrey of Monmouth 2007: 200–1); and in Norway and Denmark his troops scatter the local peasants "with unabated fury" (Geoffrey of Monmouth 2007: 206–7). A snowball momentum informs Arthur's relentless pursuit of *imperium*, as defeated peoples swell the ranks of his armies, and the brutalized become the brutalizers. We know that historical empire-builders such as Charlemagne did much the same: there is evidence, for example, that Saxons were serving in Charlemagne's armies within a few years of the infamous massacre at Verden, in 782, in which the king, angered by a recent defeat, ordered the mass execution of several thousand of their fellow countrymen. But this in itself does not adequately account for Arthur's constant resort to war. Perhaps the nearest Geoffrey comes to offering up an explanation is when he has one of Arthur's followers, Duke Cador of Cornwall, chafe at the debilitating effects of peace, which he argues turns the Britons into emasculated, slothful cowards and undermines their bellicose reputations (Geoffrey of Monmouth 2007: 216–17). In Arthur's world of implacable warfare for warfare's sake, then, one must relentlessly press ever forward simply to stand still (Figure 1.6).

A further example of the fantasy history genre is the *Historia Turpini*, or "Turpin's History" (Poole 2014). Written very close in time to Geoffrey of Monmouth's *History*, and like it widely read and copied—in both its Latin original and various translations into vernaculars—the *Historia Turpini* purports to be a partly eyewitness account of Charlemagne's campaigns in Spain written by one of his close companions, Archbishop Turpin of Reims. The narrative's historical basis is extremely slight, but this frees the author to cast Charlemagne in a similar light to Geoffrey's Arthur. One finds the same relentless drive for *imperium*; the same easy mobilization of vast human and material resources; the same near-effortless traversing of large distances when on campaign. As in Geoffrey's narrative, battles can be hard fought and close run, and defeats are possible, but in other respects this is warfare made to seem effortless and

FIGURE 1.6: Arthur above the kingdoms he has conquered, Peter of Langtoft, Chronicle of England, British Library Royal MS 20 A II fol. 4r, fourteenth century. Credit: The British Library.

natural. There are no inconvenient logistical problems. Soldiers willingly join and mobilize without fuss, and their own motivations and reactions to what they are asked to do are virtually unexplored; they are simply tools. Like Geoffrey, the author of the *Historia Turpini* offers up a fantasy of epic warfare and epic achievement. In his treatment, warfare becomes not simply the main expression of political power, but also much of its very substance and its central justification.

In a sense, the *Historia Turpini* brings us full circle, for we began with the Carolingian war machine as a tool for the relentless pursuit of empire; and we conclude with a caricature of that same dynamic. To the extent that the *Historia*

Turpini and the *History of the Kings of Britain* wish the difficulties and inconveniences of war away, they gesture toward an aristocratic fantasy of easy, untrammeled, and brutally effective power, that is to say "empire," as a direct outgrowth of the elite's social conditioning as warriors and their expertise, or claimed expertise at any rate, in the arts of war. This cultural ennobling of violence nonetheless implicitly invokes the harsh experience of war that it tries to sanitize. These far-fetched narratives thus capture something of the reality of warfare in medieval culture—a reality that those who paid for war with their hard-won surpluses, and those who were simply unlucky enough to get in the way, knew all too well.

CHAPTER TWO

Trade

ANNE E. LESTER

At the turn of the eleventh century, along the border between northern China and eastern Mongolia, a Laio princess and her consort were buried in true imperial style. Following the practices that formed the backbone of local religion, their tombs were adorned with all that they would need to pass into an afterlife. The princess' body was laid to rest bedecked in silks and jewels. Among the gold and jade one might expect to ornament a Chinese princess, a double-stringed amber necklace fell around her neck. Made of small round well-tooled beads of a dark orange and brown hue, interspersed along the necklace were much larger carefully carved rounded beads depicting dragons with bent necks, bearded warriors contorted in battle, and water birds curved to fit their oval-carved spaces. Unlike indigenous Chinese or Asian varieties, the princess' amber was iridescent with reds, oranges, and yellows known only in amber from the Baltic. The shapes worked into the larger beads also betray the objects' provenance: over thousands of kilometers to the west, from the shores of northern Europe (Flecker 2001; Shen, 2006; Xiaodong 2009).

Two centuries earlier, along the banks of the River Yonne in central Francia, the canons of the Cathedral of Sens received a prodigious gift of relics, carefully wrapped in hundreds of pieces of fine, brightly colored silks. Some of these silks were of Byzantine origin, but others, bearing medallions depicting facing birds, or foxes, woven in greens, yellows, and reds, were produced on looms in Central Asia (Muthesius 1997: 198–9; McCormick 2001; Smith 2012). Preserved, traded, bought, or sold, these fabrics made their way across the great stretches of land that charted the early medieval Silk Road. The distant provenance, fine quality, and vibrant colors made them worthy to wrap the bones of Saint Paula, Saint Colombe, and Saint Loup, and still other unnamed saints. Like the Baltic amber found in the Laio tomb, we no longer know the precise routes these objects traveled or the hands that manufactured and later carried them. Their presence, however, so far from the site of their making, says much about the workings of empire, and the role objects and trade played in defining and displaying power and determining the contours of an empire's imagined bounds.

Imperial power and presence, whether in amber or silk, in western China or northern Francia, displayed itself through things: in objects moved from afar to command a sense of near-limitless authority, or the extent of reputation and the ambitions of consumption. To follow objects, their makers, and those who transported them is to trace a cultural history of empire(s) and an imperial ideology put into practice through the rhythms and regulations of trade. The extent and meaning of "empire" in the west can be charted along the contours of trade routes, their contraction and expansion, and in the very goods that moved within borders and beyond. These objects tell two different, but interconnected, stories. One is a story of the growth and accumulation of capital; capital needed to acquire goods from a distance and whose flourishing was often the result of long-term peace established under successful rulers. Thus, following a discussion of scale and scope in recent historiography, this essay begins with rural surpluses and their conversion into movable wealth, a process that spoke to the consolidation of political authority that could harbor ambitions for imperial rule. The second story analyzes the structures and mechanisms that fostered the movements of things across the empires of the west. The regulation of trade through lordly guarantees of safe passage, open markets, fair pricing, and similar practices, all surface in the records that preserve the collection of taxes and tolls and that, in turn, communicate claims to power that lie at the core of empire's everyday impress on the lives of men and women. But these same records, coupled with surviving luxury objects, also speak to the habits of consumption and desires for things that shaped the cultural history of trade. Over the course of the medieval period, cultural and religious interactions that spanned the Mediterranean came to shape ideological claims to empire in Europe. Finally, looking closely at the individuals behind the movement of things—those involved in the trade itself: merchants, laborers, creditors, and the like—reveals much about the medieval culture of trade and its imperial designs.

SCALE AND SCOPE: MEASURES OF "IMPERIAL" TRADE AND THE MEDIEVAL IMAGINARY

In economic terms, scale has always been the primary marker of imperial trade, trade that could sustain the population of cities like Rome, Constantinople, London, and Seville. In the transition between the end of the Roman world and the early medieval period, the contraction of economies of scale transformed, circumscribed, and provincialized the economic life of early Europe (Wickham 2005; Burton 2015). The collapse of systematic taxation signaled the slow disappearance of the Roman imperial administration in Gaul, Italy, Spain, and especially North Africa and Egypt. Coupled with the loss of grain imports, felt acutely from North Africa, internal exchange networks collapsed and stable agricultural surpluses contracted. The loss of an imperial economy of scale left the early medieval European countryside to fend for itself in a world without long-distance trade. European elites were left to reconstitute local, small-scale networks of trade in foodstuffs and basic commodities (Wickham 2005: 56–150). Indeed, by this measure, the scale of trade throughout the medieval period was far smaller and much more localized than in the Roman period, but we would be wrong to imagine that it was any less far-reaching. The silks we began with moved across these local worlds.

The scale and scope of trade during the Roman period suggests that medieval historians also need to understand "space as a technology of imperial power" (Ballantyne and Burton 2009: 2). The ways that empires used space to move people and goods was one aspect of the delineation of imperial cultural authority. In the Roman and early medieval world, the Mediterranean Sea was the connective space through which imperial authority could be felt, regulated, and delineated (Braudel 1966, 1972; Horden and Purcell 2000). Bound by the natural limits of geographic space the Roman empire based its claims to sovereignty on spatial markers: the River Danube, the Atlantic Ocean, the Sahara, and the Euphrates. While this did not end during the medieval period—the Mediterranean continued to dominate aspects of trade and encounter as well as ambitions for imperial control in particular—the role of space did shift to become both more localized and ideologically more charged. Intellectual, religious, and ideological conceptions of space came to define the ambitions of imperial power and its practice more clearly. The space and claims for the extent of Christendom, built on the Roman tradition and its rituals, defined imperial power. Thus, the imperial impressed itself on medieval people both through ideological constructions and practiced networks (Effros 2017).

If, as many historians have shown, by 800, or even 1100, the spaces of trade became more localized, they remained forcefully interconnected. Capillary exchanges, that is, intensive, small-scale trade networks fostered along and through river-ways and central corridors largely determined local trading patterns: the Po River carried objects from east to west across the Italian peninsula; the River Rhine conveyed goods from Flanders into the heart of the German lands; the Seine and Aube tributaries created a networked plane across northern France (Bloch 1962; McCormick 2001; Wickham 2005). Likewise, the Adriatic, Baltic, English Channel, the Indian Ocean, and the western (between Aragon and Sicily) and eastern (between Cyprus to Syria and Cairo)

Mediterranean all fostered local networks of trade and consumption. And, as we shall see, these capillary routes were linked by longer-distance trading ambitions that cut across and through the lordly dominions of the medieval world. The cultural history of trade during the Middle Ages is thus a history of boundary crossing, of multilingual interactions, of documents created for long-distance needs and negotiations, and of the spreading out of regional practices and habits.

Moving our analysis of trade beyond scale means examining anew sources that offer a window onto cultural practices as well as economic successes. For decades, histories of trade have focused on specific types of records: diplomas, accounts, tax records, inventories, and the like, all of which sought to delineate zones of trade and profit. More recently, however, historians have followed the movement of objects as they appear in a much more expansive set of sources: literary texts, letters, hagiographies, chronicles, and romances, but also the archaeological record (McCormick 2001; Wickham 2005; Jones 2007; Effros 2017). Thus, if the medieval world does not meet the standards of scale, it did maintain its scope, its reach and at points exceeded it (Unger 2015). Culturally, as Antoinette Burton and Manu Goswami have identified, it was the "accumulate[ed] interconnections" that ultimately informed imperial ideas, ambitions, and consumptive habits and desires (Goswami 2004: 107; Ballantyne and Burton 2009: 3). This may be especially true in the medieval period, when small, local interactions often seem to defy broader normative pronouncements or declarations of empire. Rather it was in the local, everyday production, movement, marketing, and trade that the cultures of empire made themselves manifest, slowly and carefully, translated across vast distances. In this way, empire can be untethered from a specific space and scope, and from a classical definition of imperial sovereignty, and opened to include the ways that medieval individuals thought, used, collected, and assembled things.

And in this discussion, if measured by the movement of things, the years on either side of 800 were a defining cultural moment for empire in the west. According to the Royal Frankish Annals, in 799 an emissary from the patriarch of Jerusalem arrived at Charlemagne's court with relics and blessings, a sign of the Frankish ruler's recognition in the east. The following year, the same Charles received—reluctantly we are told—the imperial crown from the pope in Rome. At that same time, Charlemagne had a great list drawn up enumerating all the religious houses and Latin clerics residing in the Holy Land and making provisions for the regular distribution of alms to support the Latin clergy, especially those who served the Holy Sepulchre. Two years later the same Annals records another delegation's arrival in Aachen, this one bearing an illustrious diplomatic gift: a white elephant named Abul Abaz. Harun al-Rashid, the Abbasid caliph ruling from Baghdad, had learned of Charlemagne's renown and sent a gift worthy of a true king of kings (Krauze 1895: 799, 802; Scholz and Rogers 1970: 80–3; Brubaker 2004; Gabriele 2011: 34–47). Over the centuries that followed, the stories of these early ninth-century imperial gifts would grow in their retelling, fostering a memory of empire that held great cultural force in the European imaginary. That there were regular shipping routes in place that could facilitate the movement of such things is itself revealing. The exchange of luxury and diplomatic gifts suggests that connections between the east and west remained well enough trafficked to make such gifts possible, plausible even. The channels needed for an elephant's transport also suggest that everyday trade, its management and upkeep, relied upon more localized interactions and labor: the social and economic networks with which empires were made.

PRODUCTION AND SURPLUS

The history of trade is often presented as a history of luxury networks. It is thrilling to read of the silks and furs that lined aristocratic capes, the exotic foods, well-spiced, that outfitted a king's table, or the pounds of iron or timber arriving into English ports only to be forged into the means of aristocratic warfare. But to focus on such objects is to miss the broad and more pervasive history that fueled trade: the history of rural labor, of the exploitation of the land, of growing personal franchises, of peasant success, and the quiet transfer of technologies (Brubaker 2004; Cutler 2004). All trade in the medieval world was fueled by agricultural surplus and its consequences. Peasant households and peasant production were the engines behind economic growth in the premodern world. Charlemagne's alms to the Holy Land came from the great success of his estates (McCormick 2011).

Trade beyond the old boundaries of Europe and certainly outside the "Carolingian core" depended on the reorganization of manors, estates, and single-plots, all of which generated the surplus of agricultural goods that were marketed, taxed, converted to coin, and used to propel long-distance trade and increase demand for exotic goods. As McCormick has argued, "[d]emographic growth, the expansion and stability of political structures, innovative methods of marshalling and compelling labor on the land and extracting its fruits—the story of water mills and the great estate—shifting cultural values and ambitions (including, probably for the first time since late antiquity, a small but positive trend toward literacy, and an application of literacy to land management), a currency which was solid and unified were essential elements" in the opening up of Europe (McCormick 2001: 791–2). From the end of the Roman period through the early Middle Ages, economic scholars have traced the increasing autonomy of the peasantry in the face, initially, of weak aristocratic authority (Wickham 2005). This led to increased production and greater purchasing power, which fostered the development of local and regional markets as the backbone and framework for a steady expansion of trade and the circulation of goods and people. From the ninth century onwards, records from the great Carolingian and post-Carolingian estates show a new interest on the part of administrators in tracking, organizing, and encouraging surplus production (Devroey 1993; Davis 2015: 303–22). And indeed, it may be that in record-keeping and estate management the practice of empire, as a cultural technique, was maintained even in the face of political fragmentation.

During the eleventh and twelfth centuries, in the absence of a centralizing political authority, the large estates that formed the center of community organization and peasant labor dependence were increasingly consolidated under the management of great monastic houses, episcopal domains, and local lordships (Bartlett 1993; Contamine *et al.* 2003). Robert Berkhofer has shown how the management of both land and people relied on increased record-keeping and more intensive administrative regimes (Berkhofer 2004). Such techniques facilitated the growth and proliferation of well-managed estates; of the cooperative work of assarting—that is, the backbreaking labor that converted forest lands or wastes into arable; of the foundation of *villesneuves*, or new towns; and contributed to the growth of large urban centers, the great nodes of trading networks (Figure 2.1). Increased production led to significant changes at the local level. Between 900 and 1200, for example, the number of water mills constructed and in use expanded exponentially, bringing to a crescendo a trend that had begun centuries before. Mills, used for grinding grain, were also the site of fishponds, which could be stocked with indigenous fish, fen eels (a stable of the European diet), and imported fish; all of which contributed to growing the population and expanding the possibilities for marketing goods (flour, ground in the same mills, and fish, in this case), for charging fees (banal rights to use the mills), and for further specialization of labor (millers, fishermen, toll collectors, etc.) (Bartlett 1993: 106–66). Thus, the local micro-economics were the foundation on which longer-distance networks emerged. And local production was the cornerstone on which ambitious elites, like Norman and Ottonian noble families, carved out wealth and influence that nurtured aspiration of imperial culture and imitation, as we shall see.

Even as political boundaries shifted in different regions, increased production and demographic growth was a European-wide phenomenon during our period. Part of what united Christendom and presented similar challenges in different locales, was the rapidity of change and the increased social and physical mobility of a wealthy peasant population. Indeed, agricultural surplus, which could be converted into capital used to acquire goods from near and far, propelled the return of trade both locally and over great and growing distances. The yields from the fields of northern Europe generated the possibility of the consumption of silk woven in Kashgar. The tenth- and eleventh-century story

FIGURE 2.1: Miniature. Gilles de Rome. "Livre du Regime des Princes": Merchants doing business and Plowing scene. Paris, Bibliotheque Nationale. Credit: Christophel Fine Art/UIG via Getty Images.

of political fragmentation and the rise of so-called feudal society persists alongside a very different narrative of economic growth, trade networks, and cultural connectivity. Trade and exchange kept the European core—from the Danube to the Baltic, from the Channel to the Mediterranean—part of a culturally cohesive world, with a common written language (Latin), exchangeable currencies, and a shared ideological and historical past that would shape how individuals imagined and sought to recreate a culture of empire. Indeed, the "imperial fusion" of territory first brought into being during the Carolingian period—a territory that now roughly defines the modern European Union—framed an area that was both a cultural idea and economic unity that would thrive in the centuries that followed (Devroey 2017).

Although local studies focused on medieval trade proliferate for the High Middle Ages (c. 1000–1400), less work has been done to synthesize these results into an overview, much less a cultural history of trade (Lopez 1987; Postan 1987; Reyerson 1999). Moreover, an artificial and anachronistic sense of national identity and nation-states has confined some research to consider trade only in France, Castile, England, or local zones within the German lands and the Italian peninsula. Often the survival of documentation determines why certain regions and activities are highlighted. The amazing cache of documents preserved in the Cairo Geniza, for example, has enabled two generations of scholars to give life—in abundant detail—to the trade networks, business contacts, and rhythms of daily life for Jewish merchant families operating out of Cairo and trading across the Mediterranean (Goitein 1967–93; Goldberg 2012; Rustow 2017).[1] We know a great deal about trade and traders in Muslim

Spain thanks to the survival of records in the Geniza as well as in Iberian archives (Constable 1994). Sources for Venice and Genoa, London and Bristol, Bremen, Bruges, and Naples, to name only a few trading hubs of the period, offer a robust picture of trade and merchant life in specific metropolises of the medieval world. Stitching together these examples remains to be done.[2]

STRUCTURE AND REGULATION

Trade flourished during periods of peace and stability. The history of successful states, moreover, is closely tied to the development and regulation of markets and long-distance trade (Haldon 1993; Wickham 2005; Bang 2007; Bisson 2010). For most of the premodern period, much of what was traded was locally produced: grain, wine, beans, wax, honey, and cloth in great qualities and varieties. Beginning in the late eleventh century, the cultivation of new markets spurred the simultaneous growth of trade and local power. The creation and the regulation of regional markets was a key feature of lordship. Convened under the auspices of local lords and monastic communities, markets began to proliferate and to meet regularly in specific nodal towns, that is, centers that functioned as hubs of connection to promote the marketing and trade in goods produced from farther afield. The great Lendit Fair of Saint-Denis outside of Paris drew merchants and local patrons from the growing city and surrounding regions (Berkhofer 2004: 68; Baldwin 2010). By the middle of the twelfth century, under the patronage of Count Henry I, "the Liberal," the fairs of Champagne, which rotated between Lagny, Troyes, Bar-sur-Aube, and Provins, functioned as a continuous market, meeting throughout the year, connecting merchants from Germany, England, Flanders, Provence, and Italy to northeastern France, only a day's journey from Paris (Bautier 1991; Evergates 2016). Regular markets convened at Arras, Ypres, Bruges, and Lille, like those along the Rhine in Worms, Speyer, Mainz, and Cologne, united the region of Flanders and the Rhineland respectively and fostered commercial, monetary, credit, and familial networks that enabled further prosperity into the later Middle Ages (Nicholas 1997; Murray 2005). As the demand for goods increased and local markets became stable venues for regular commerce, regional trade zones to the north, which connected the Baltic region and Scandinavian world, came in contact with those of the south, particularly the Po River trade, which channeled Mediterranean goods across the Alps and up the Rhine or Rhône corridors to markets along the Atlantic coast, in Flanders, and in Champagne. Europe's rivers, far more than its roads, fostered the making of Europe.

Cloth was the most significant commodity of the twelfth century to be traded over long distances. The differences in cloth produced in Lagny, Bruges, London, Cypress, Damascus, and Barcelona were parsed in their weave, thickness, color, material, quality of wool, linen, hemp, and the like. And each was desired in its own way for its own use. In turn, each type of cloth had its own cultural meanings. Cloth and clothing, perhaps more than anything else, was a mark of distinction, used to differentiate lay from religious, rich from poor (or deliberately humbled), Jew from Christian and Muslim (after 1215) (Lipton 2014; Farmer 2017). While trade in cloth was the backbone of most medieval markets, other goods of high value came to influence networks of exchange: metal tools and implements like shears, knives, needles; dishware and pottery that varied greatly by region; candlesticks and ornaments for houses and chapels; shoes, saddles, belts, and leather goods, all formed an expanding repertoire of things in circulation—things whose production, marketing, and consumption can be traced to delineate the webs of trade at work in the medieval world. A culture of empire no doubt influenced habits of production and consumption, changing to reflect current desires, trends, and tastes.

The cultural work of empire can be traced also in forms of regulation that influenced behaviors, habits, and perception. Trade depended on the protections and regulations of kings, counts, dukes, bishops, and local governments, and the enforcement of those regulations served as a further proof of their power (Contamine *et al.* 2003). Rules governing when markets were convened and how long they lasted gave order to regional networks that reflected the rhythms of religious celebrations, harvests, and traditions of commemoration. A lord's authority guaranteed safe passage along the comital roads, provided for the upkeep of bridges, maintained the safety of towns and market squares, oversaw the value of currency and the regulations for changing money (Watson 2010; Evergates 2016). The tolls, taxes, and fees rulers charged was a small price for the safety and openness they fostered. Unlike in the Roman period, when such regulation was relatively consistent across vast distances, during the Middle Ages each principality had its own customs, privileges, and provisions, but they worked to a common purpose and fostered a common culture of interaction. Guarantees that coinage would be "good"—that is, worth its stated value—were fundamental for exchange across political borders. Thus, for example, as King Henry I moved to establish peace across England during the early years of his rule, he decreed that

> the false and bad money should be amended, so that he who was caught passing bad denarii should not escape by redeeming himself, but should lose his eyes and members. And since denarii were often picked out, bent, broken, and refused, he decreed that no denarii or obol, which he said were to be round, or even a *quadrans*, if it were whole, should be refused. By reason of this, he did much good throughout the whole kingdom, because he did these things to relieve the land of its troubles forever (Stubbs 1913: 113).

Good lordship, moreover, could ensure that merchants, pilgrims, and travelers enjoyed the lord's safe passage along roadways and within borders, protected from bandits and thieves. Tolls and taxes, collected at bridges, crossroads, and major natural boundaries, supported such protections (Evergates 2016). Toll lists from the tenth and eleventh centuries show that merchants, travelers, and pilgrims paid, for example, to traverse the Alpine passes that connected northern Europe to Italy, in the hopes of enjoying safe passage. Such lists also offer detailed inventories of individuals and things on the move. The toll list Bishop Giso of Aosta issued in 960, recording the charges for a host of goods that crossed the Alpine passes *en route* between Rome and the Ottonian cities of the north, inventories military equipment, including swords, spears, shields, and armor as well as horses, spurs, and reins all made in Italy for use in the German lands. Spices such as pepper, ginger, cloves, cinnamon, and myrrh traveled across the Alps to monasteries in northern France and even exotic animals, like an African ape, made its way north at a cost three times greater than that of a horse. We know of these movements and their values because there was money to be made along the way (Bruce 2015: 12–15). Moreover, should disagreements arise that needed to be peacefully adjudicated, the protections of a lord's court could offer peaceful resolutions if needed. Growing credit mechanisms also fostered long-distance connections and facilitated the movement of wealth between France and Italy, England and the Levant. By the early thirteenth century, many merchants came to reside, at least part-time, in the towns that they traded in most frequently. Tax lists and deeds of sale show German, English, and Italian merchants and creditors who rented properties in London, Paris, Troyes, and Cologne, marrying into local families and rising to positions of prominence in local governance. Even as lordships remained small and separate during the medieval period, trade networks, abetted by familial connections, provided the connective tissue that bound Europeans in a common cultural frame (Kowaleski 2006).

Over the course of the twelfth century, other mechanisms developed to foster longer-distance trade. Coinage and credit offer two good examples. For centuries, the right to mint coins was carefully guarded by local bishops, abbots, and lay lords. Each lord who had a right to mint coins within his domains exercised that right and a diverse assortment of denarii, solidi, pounds, or marks circulated that required exchange. As a consequence, coins were extremely diverse in weight, size, iconography, and value from region to region. As farther-reaching trade networks developed, many of the great lordships of Europe adopted a standardized coinage to create consistent exchange ratios. The German and English mark became the dominant currency through the Rhine valley and North Sea; the Paris pound *tournois* emerged as the coin against which all others were measured in France and the currency measure used to pay taxes to the crown. Agreements were created among local towns to recognize a common weight and value for the most common coins in circulation. By the early thirteenth century, the currency of Provins became the money of account in the Champagne fairs. Italian merchants, who frequented the fairs with regularity, used the pound *provinois* as the measure for exchange when calculating exchanges with Italian currencies. By the later thirteenth century, the papacy set its currency value by the coins of Provins (Spufford 1987; Spufford 1988). By no means imperial in its ambition, the common value of coinage facilitated the growth of international markets across medieval Europe. But the silver-based currency of Europe was always overshadowed internationally by the gold-based standard that ran in the Islamic world. Although no European government could hope to possess enough gold to mint anything more than symbolic currency, the iconographic and material power of such coins was never lost on rulers. Frederick II set his neo-classical imperial image on the gold coin he first minted in 1230 (Lopez 1956; Abulafia 1988). And Louis IX of France, in part in emulation of Frederick's imperial and antique claims, minted the gold French *ecu d'or* with the fleur-de-lys and the cross for the first time in 1266 (Figure 2.2). It bore the legend *Christus Vincit, Christus Regnat, Christus Imperat* (Christ conquers, Christ reigns, Christ commands). With this, the crusader king expressed to all who held it the religious and political ambitions of French imperium (Jordan 1979: 210).

Instruments of credit, perhaps one of the most brilliant and imaginative innovations of the central Middle Ages, opened trade networks and facilitated economic interactions in ways previously unimagined. Credit agreements and bills of exchange allowed a merchant in Genoa to draw up a contract or deed for payment to be rendered in cash on the other side of the Mediterranean. Such agreements, which required a grant of trust, meant that coinage did not

FIGURE 2.2: Gold *ecu* of Saint Louis (r. 1226–70), first royal money, 1266. Paris, Bibliotheque Nationale. Credit: Christophel Fine Art/UIG via Getty Images.

have to travel across the sea in large quantities, but could be credited and arranged for in advance. Such arrangements required networks with depth, built on reputations for trustworthiness. They also formed the backbone for the success of international orders like the Templars and Hospitallers, which offered credit to many involved in the crusades and in the long-distance networks that formed in their wake. Indeed, the crusades and the continuous need for cash and credit that occasioned that religious movement, as we shall see, greatly spurred on the mechanisms of trade (Spufford 1988).

Other things, too, were traded, shared, and thus spread out across Europe as towns and major trade routes grew. Stories—hagiographical, historical, and romance—passed from mouth to mouth and found their way onto parchment pages. Passages of the gospel read aloud, so the story goes, inspired Francis of Assisi to strip his worldly clothes from his body and take up a humble brown robe as a sign of his new life, unfettered by mercantile connection or the taint of coinage in the hand. The first ateliers to produce copies of books, whether the romances of Chrétien de Troyes, copied in his native Champagne, or copies of the Bible, its commentaries and exegesis, or play scripts, were located in towns like Arras, Troyes, and Provins, close to the houses of canons and monks. And so too, business techniques were traded up the Rhône and through the Rhine and Seine vallies. Historians have noted repeatedly the proliferation of new forms of charters, dating clauses, guarantee clauses, and the eclipse of the witness list with the notary's double copy or official's seal. Trade and interaction were the engines of change (Clanchy 2013).

IMPERIAL DREAMS: RELICS, PILGRIMAGE, AND MOVEMENT

Although technical advances and structural developments facilitated the mechanisms of trade, by the close of the eleventh century, changes in the religious landscape of Europe also expanded the horizons of the west. The Gregorian reform movement, with its emphasis on clerical purity and freedom of the church from lay control, spurred much of this new religiosity. The movement had galvanized many in Christendom, from the papacy down to local parish communities, to engage in practices of prayer, penance, and pilgrimage in new ways. Such a religious realignment gave new prominence to the role of saints and the practice of pilgrimage as a way to expedite the forgiveness of sins and the efficacy of one's prayers. To go on a pilgrimage and to pray before the earthly remains of saints and apostles who had walked in Europe or, better yet, in the Holy Land, promised a more direct communion with God. The reform movement also galvanized the interests and commitments of laymen and women in new religious movements, including the religious renewal behind the explosion of religious orders and the crusades to the east.

The cultural and religious work of small bits of bone and wood, scraps of cloth, stones, sand, water, and oil can be traced throughout the medieval world and in the connections they generated between Europe and the Holy Land (Smith 2012). As things, these relics, understood to be the remains of the saints, were valued as the material presence of the divine that continued to adhere in the world. Relics offered tangible proof of God's physical form and formed the foundation for a broader imperial imaginary that propelled trade in ways hardly conceivable at the end of the Carolingian period. Relics had been an important part of the Late Antique religious experience and served to connect people and places in powerful ways (Hahn and Klein 2015). When Saint Helena, mother of the Roman Emperor Constantine, commissioned the recovery of the True Cross and sponsored the excavation of Golgotha in Jerusalem in 326, she reaffirmed Christian imperial authority through the possession of one of Christianity's most holy relics—the wood of the cross on which Christ died. Because God consented to let relics of his son come to Helena and her son, it was believed that the Lord had also given divine assent to their rule. The ideological relationship—initiated by Constantine and Helena—between holy objects and imperial claims would have a profound impact on the movement of things and the cultural contours of trade during the Middle Ages. It also served as a model for future claims to imperium that could be shored up and affirmed through the possession of the holy.

A cascade of other objects followed and complemented the movement and acquisition of relics. Sacred objects required a great deal of care. By the eleventh century, if not earlier, most relics were set into reliquaries made of precious materials—gold, silver, crystal, gems and wrapped in silks—used to adorn and enshrine them. These opulent containers, as Cynthia Hahn has shown, made the sacred quality of the otherwise mundane material evident to those who venerated them. From the Carolingian period onwards, relics, especially those collected from Rome and the Holy Land, traveled from east to west with increasing regularity. Deposited into royal, episcopal, and monastic treasuries or kept in personal collections, their possession was a mark of aristocratic identity and its cultivation of devotion.

Although Charlemagne never personally traveled to the Holy Land, monastic and episcopal collections in Aachen, Corbie, Conques, and Paris, for example, traced their beginnings to gifts from the great ruler and imagined his journey to the east. The creation of such legends linked objects, narratives, and imperial claims about authority and authenticity (Remensnyder 1995; McCormick 2011; Latowsky 2013). The formidable collection of relics, reliquaries, and other objects amassed in the treasury at the abbey of Conques offers a glimpse into the wealth mobilized to display devotion and affirm the imperial history of the abbey. As the monks described, they had been given relics of the True Cross, Christ's foreskin, and Christ's umbilical cord (two of the bodily remains it was believed Jesus left behind before his ascension) (Remensnyder 1996). These were enshrined in elaborate reliquaries, each of silver-gilt and encrusted with a panoply of gemstones and Roman cameos. These reliquaries, like myriad others found in aristocratic and ecclesiastical treasury collections, visualized the reach of imperial trade networks: none of these materials were locally produced. Gold hailed from Africa, silver from the mines far to the east of the Frankish border, rubies, pearls, amethysts from the far east, and cameos from the distant Roman past. Whereas the construction of the great abbey could be seen as the work of local labor, local trade and donations of stone and timber, the creation of elaborate reliquary shrines announced cultural claims that stretched to what was imaginatively associated with the Holy Land, Egypt, and beyond. An ornate reliquary shrine embodied and projected the consumption and decoration of the divine described in John the Evangelist's *Apocalypse*. Reliquaries gave material form on earth to the literal "stuff" of heaven and, in doing so, allowed those who commissioned and possessed them to imagine their place and part in Christian imperium.

Objects offer their own narratives of trade and interaction. Ecclesiastical inventories tell of the steady assemblage of aristocratic or diplomatic gifts to adorn altars, chapels, and parish churches: chalices, patens, linens to cover the altar, processional crosses, altar pieces, candlesticks, books and book covers, among a host of other items. Stunning Ottonian reliquaries and Gospel books, for example, often reused Byzantine or Late Antique carved ivory plaques and cameo stones, embedding them in a new western imperial context that announced the ambition of uniting eastern and western Christian devotional culture and displayed their power to do so by means of possession and re-appropriation. The Guelph Treasure (*Welfenschatz*), assembled in the late eleventh century by the German princely house of Guelph and later housed in Brunswick Cathedral, makes powerful visual and material arguments for the authority of the dynasty, an authority anchored to Byzantine objects and imitation (Figure 2.3). In Flanders, famed Mosan work of silver-gilt and elaborate cloisonné enamel flourished during the twelfth and early thirteenth centuries and artisans of the region must have relied upon a network of contacts to provide them with precious metals and stones, including aristocratic patrons whose gifts of household tableware or jewelry could be metaled down and recycled to adorn the table of the Lord (Figure 2.4). Now housed in the Morgan Library in New York, the so-called Stavelot Tryptich is a spectacular example of such artistic production as it flourished in northern Europe, suggesting a local knowledge that had become adept at working with materials that traveled great distances. The Stavelot Triptych embeds at its center two small Byzantine tryptich reliquaries of the True Cross, each opening out to the viewer, enshrined within the larger gothic assemblage. In this case, not only does the reliquary announce its sacred contents through its material, but it also amplified the

FIGURE 2.3: Pearl of the Guelph Treasure, treasure relics of Brunswick Cathedral, historical woodcut, c. 1870 CE. Credit: Bildagentur-online/UIG via Getty Images.

west's possession of the east and Byzantine forms of devotion and imperium (Hahn 2012). The contents of relic collections and the construction of opulent reliquaries to contain them detail the movements of unnamed merchants, artisans, and pilgrims who carried forth objects of veneration, gathered and gave materials for their construction, and who carved out well-traveled routes to venerate the holy. These sacred things displayed and defined a culture of Christian imperium that connected the medieval world—its ideas, things, and people—in ever tighter and vivid regimes of circulation (Markovits *et al.* 2003).

THE CRUSADE MOVEMENT AND CULTURAL DIASPORA

While religious and aristocratic patronage spurred long-distance trade ambitions, three other phenomena contributed to the rise of what we might call

FIGURE 2.4: Gold and precious stones reliquary. Mosan Art, thirteenth century. Colmar, Musée d'Unterlinden. Credit: DeAgostini/Getty Images.

"international" trade during the High Middle Ages: the so-called aristocratic diaspora or outward movement of the European elite; the cultural and literary cultivation of images of eastern luxury; and the crusade movement. All three phenomena opened the frontiers of Europe and connected the old "Carolingian core" to the wider worlds of the Baltic, the Atlantic, the Mediterranean, the Levant coast, and the growing reach of the Silk Road to the far east. As many scholars have shown, Europe's growth and prosperity coincided with what Robert Bartlett has termed an "aristocratic diaspora," that is, the movement and relocation eastward and across the Mediterranean of generations of men and women over the course the eleventh, twelfth, and thirteenth centuries. For Bartlett, this is the story of the "making of Europe" (Bartlett 1993). The spur behind such outward movement is still hotly debated. Whether the product of a contracting aristocratic and martial culture, competition for landed resources, or a proto-chivalric ideal that propelled lords, knights, and lesser families beyond their natal borders, the allure of making a name for oneself and one's family through heroic deeds and in turn carving out new lordships and landed wealth clearly propelled men of status to embark for Sicily, Pomerania, and the Levant.

As men and women began to settle along the "fringes" of Europe, the cultural imaginary became more diverse and inclusive, playing with images of interactions, intermarriage, miscegenation, and cultural appropriation. Whereas the heroic landscape of *chansons des geste*, like the *Song of Roland*, presented a world of binaries, the Romances that emerged by the second half of the twelfth century traced the movements of men and women on merchant ships, in landscapes foreign and diverse where they can pretend at new identities, swath themselves in textiles made of linen and gold, ride Arabian horses, and find golden trinkets revealing of a hidden Byzantine royal lineage. The bodies of German and Byzantine princes and princesses—the protagonists of, for example, Chrétien de Troyes' *Cligés*—are used to showcase red and purple silks from the east, gold embroidered edgework stitched by women's nimble fingers, and the possibilities of intermarriage as a harbinger of noble imperial peace. Romance fantasies of boatloads of eastern imperial wealth shaped how Europeans imagined the real wealth of empire and spurred many generations to test their fate at sea and in the face of inhospitable conditions to seek a new life with new access to the flow of such wealth (Kinoshita 2006, 2008). And many Norman noble families attempted to live this ideal, carving out lordships that stretched from Sicily to Syria to the British Isles (Bartlett 1993; Cutler 2001; Davis-Secord 2017).

Yet far less tangible than a desire for wealth, materialism, or social mobility is the importance of the religious dimension to the burgeoning of trade with the east (Abulafia 1995). By the mid-eleventh century, the realignment of the Muslim world, occasioned by the dominance of Fatimid Egypt and the new prominence of the Seljuk Turks, gave a new urgency in the Latin west to intervene in the Holy Land (Cobb 2014). Although Jerusalem had long been a pilgrimage destination for the exceptionally devout, beginning in the eleventh century the numbers of men and women who traveled to follow in the literal footsteps of Jesus—seeking to walk and to die where the Lord had—expanded exponentially. In 1063, the so-called the Great German Pilgrimage saw an alleged 7,000 people plod their way to the Holy Land (Riley-Smith 1987; Bull 1993). By 1095, however, reports of the mistreatment of pilgrims at the hands of the Muslims who had come to rule in the Levant, including the city of Jerusalem, prompted what chronicles described as an official response from the pope: a call to arms for men to take up a new kind of pilgrimage and to travel to the east as armed warriors for Christ to lead the charge in taking back the patrimony of the Lord. The popes had sanctioned—even blessed—previous armed campaigns against the Muslims in the Mediterranean, especially along the Sicilian coast, but the response in 1095–6 was unprecedented. Many men and women sewed cloth crosses onto their garments, or took up wooden crosses, and progressed as *crucesignati* (those signed with the cross) in two waves to the east. Most historians estimate that between 80,000 and 100,000 individuals made their way across the roadways and fields of Europe, following the Rhine through Germany or the Rhône to southern France then across Italy, through the lands of the Hungarian rulers and into Byzantium. From Constantinople, the armies moved southward along the Levant coast, slowly and persistently taking cities into their control: Antioch (1098), Bethlehem (1099), and finally Jerusalem (July 15, 1099). Although they had come initially to aid the Byzantine ruler in taking back territory once under Greek control and in liberating the city of Jerusalem, once there a small handful of nobles carved out eastern principalities of their own. The events of 1095–1110, which later came to be called the First Crusade, opened to Europe access to the eastern Mediterranean and the Levant coast in ways unknown since the fourth century. With this, especially as settlement in the east became a priority, the port cities of the Levant served to reorient and open trade to the east in ways that historians now appreciate to have been transformative economically and culturally (Riley-Smith 1987, 1997; Tyerman 2006).

Although rule in the east fell mostly to the northern French lords who had led the campaigns, Genoese, Pisan, and Venetian merchants were largely responsible for the profound flourishing of trade that followed after 1099. The participation of merchants from the Italian cities was certainly spurred by religious devotion, but their role also complemented trading networks and connections already in place in the Mediterranean. The opening of the ports of Acre, Tyre, Sidon, and later Ascalon (briefly) to western ships served to expand networks already in place that connected Italian cities, especially Genoa, to North Africa and Egypt and afforded the opportunity to expand the eleventh-century volume of trade exponentially. Indeed, over the course of the twelfth century, rulers in the Levant granted Italian merchants extensive rights, franchises, and privileges within Acre and in other crusader port towns often in recognition of their critical role in transporting and provisioning western crusaders (Abulafia 1995; Pryor 2006). In this way, the ports of the Levant, and later in Cyprus and Crete, augmented trade connections that had been in place between Amalfi and Tunisia and Alexandria, locales that had long been the end of the gold caravan routes. Crusader trade complemented patterns of circulation such that,

> by 1150 Italian ships arrived each autumn in the Levant, and put in first at Acre. There they sold their own goods or used western silver to obtain gold, which was in short supply in the west. They carried the gold out of the Latin kingdom, primarily to Alexandria, where they bought spices, drugs and other luxury articles. They then returned to the west, perhaps directly without calling again at Acre (Abulafia 1995: 14).

As had long been the case, merchants along the coasts rarely ventured into the interior, but the Genoese and Venetians came to trade with indigenous

Christian and Muslim merchants who came down to the ports of the Latin states from Damascus and Aleppo primarily, and from other Muslim inland cities as well, bearing goods intended for sale in western markets or in Alexandria. From the Levant ports, merchants transported such items to Byzantium, Sicily, and Alexandria and then on to Europe. Alexandria remained crucial to trade for it was at the head of routes that linked across the Red Sea carrying spices and cotton from India, gold out of Africa, and silk, pepper, and cinnamon from China and Ceylon. To the north, Damascus funneled mostly finished goods, including tempered steel and finely worked cloth like silk and damask (which took its name from the city) (Freedman 2008; Jackson 2017). These items were exchanged for European silver, timber, and later for whole ships, and Flemish wool. Occasionally, the sources shed light on the activities of merchants operating at the expense of crusader endeavors. In 1169, and again in 1174, and 1213, the rulers of Jerusalem put sanctions on Pisan merchants for supplying arms—shields and timber—to the Muslims in Egypt (Abulafia 1995: 17). Over time, particularly as losses in the east became chronic and as the French and Angevin commitment to the crusade cause grew, other merchant groups were offered privileges in eastern ports in return for material support, including the Amalfitans, Marseillais, Montpelliérains, Catalans, and merchants from Occitania and Provence.

The long project of crusading in the eastern Mediterranean slowly and steadily reshaped the contours of trade economically and culturally. Far more difficult to grasp than the constant flow of ships and goods transported and recorded with increasing detail in notarial registers is the cultural, religious, and social assimilation and integration that must have occurred throughout this landscape. We catch snatches of such living together from the pens of the great intellects living in twelfth-century Syria. William of Tyre and Usama Ibn-Munqidh both describe their circumstances and perceptions of the Christian-Muslim "other" with similar degrees of curious, circumspect disapproval. But both author also share anecdotes of a world peopled with captives, refugees, adoptions, intermarriages, conversions, and all that comes with inhabiting a shared religious and cultural world (Edbury and Rowe 1988; Cobb 2008).

By the turn of the thirteenth century, it was loss rather than triumph that spurred a renewed pursuit of empire through the movement of things. A turning point for the crusade project and the aristocratic diaspora came in 1187 when Muslim forces under the leadership of Saladin won a series of decisive victories that returned the city of Jerusalem to Muslim control. These Christian losses precipitated numerous calls to crusade in the hope of recovering the Holy City, but interests in the Levant had grown complex and increasing energy was devoted to strategic planning which drew crusaders and their resources to Greece, Cyprus, and Egypt. In 1204, Venetian, French, and Flemish crusaders embarked on what would come to be known as the Fourth Crusade, but debts and the allure of Byzantine wealth drew the expedition to the city of Constantinople, which they eventually captured, establishing the short-lived Latin Empire of Constantinople (1204–61). While this appeared to be a diversion from the crusade mission, French and Flemish contingents yoked their victory to the trove of relics and other holy objects they found in the city, which they proceeded to send to churches, chapels, and cathedrals in the west.

The outpouring of holy objects, in an unprecedented number, counteracted the loss of the cross and the holy city and began to transform cities in the west—Amiens, Paris, Troyes, Halberstadt—into "new Jerusalems," new centers of devotion that could trace the biographies of their holy objects to Constantine's treasury and before that directly, and authentically it was believed, to the Holy Land (Laiou 2005; Lester 2017). This phenomenon reached its apogee in 1237, when Louis IX purchased the Crown of Thorns and other Passion Relics from Venetian merchants to redeem a loan made to the Latin emperor. The king's decision to acquire the relics and enshrine them in the newly built Sainte-Chapelle displayed the Capetian monarchy's ambition for cultivating a new Christian empire in France, with the French as the new Chosen People (Strayer 1969a; Cohen 2015). The translation of Byzantine claims to empire through the medium of religious culture shows how deeply entwined objects, imperium, and circulation had become by the middle of the thirteenth century. Numerous rulers anchored in the Mediterranean, including the Hohenstaufen, Angevin, and Aragonese, would take up the ambition for imperium and its many titles (Kelly 2003; Jones 2007). The inability to recover Jerusalem after its loss to the Muslims in 1187, however, meant that crusaders and leaders in the west had to reconceptualize a Christian culture of empire as something not rooted in a place, but in its practice, display, and divine right.

PEOPLE AND THINGS: MERCHANTS, LABOR, AND "CULTURE BROKERS"

The pace and production of trade accelerated profoundly in the decades after the Fourth Crusade. As many scholars have observed, this was in part the product of greater connectivity among separate commercial spheres, which linked traditional Mediterranean networks with those of the Atlantic coast, the Silk Road, the Baltic sphere, and the Indian Ocean (Miller 2013; Margariti 2014; Unger 2015). Although no one imperial agent or merchant vessel sailed the totality of this span, the incremental labors of trade fostered through piecemeal but interconnected regimes of circulation grew ever more significant and culturally transformative. Consumption patterns and economic practices shaped cultural perceptions and informed the imaginary of imperial culture. But this dynamic also allowed for the labor behind trade—the work that went into fashioning damask from Syria or harvesting pepper from Ceylon—to be elided, removed from view, collapsing the spaces and differences between the flow of goods and how such movements were conceptualized.

The close analysis of material culture and materiality, however, has drawn renewed attention to the role of labor and the shared technologies that lie behind the production and movement of things. Building on the detailed work of S.D. Goitein, Robert Lopez, and Olivia Remie Constable, for example, scholars have come to see the role of merchants and merchant networks in new ways. Business relationships, family interests, even tracing the long arc and patterns of merchant movements, have yielded new ways of seeing the flows of culture (Goldberg 2012; Rothman 2012). As Richard Unger has recently reminded us, trade and empire were predicated on technologies of communication and commerce: the use of parchment giving way to paper, the adoption of documents of credit and exchange; the formation of institutions in colonial cities that functioned as hubs of a metropole or corporation (Unger 2015). Technologies of communication and record, like bills of credit and notarial registers, had behind them the force of local authority and specialized skills learned in university and professional training. The use, adoption, and dissemination of such techniques spread across an ever-wider class of participants and geographies. In short, we can find the cultural role of empire—of power and regulation—in an ever-widening set of written texts, skills, practices, and interactions.

Technologies of production were traded as frequently and easily as their finished goods. The aristocratic diaspora brought with it the trade and dissemination of cultures of production: how to make saddles, weave silk, paint on fresco, among myriad other skills traveled with men and women as they moved and resettled. *Techne*, or know-how, could be redeployed and replicated through captivity and slavery as well as through economic inducements and invitations. The cultural and economic dimensions of the exchange of *techne*, as scholars like Judith Bennett, Martha Howell, Sharon Farmer, and Kathryn Reyerson have shown, depended intimately on the domestic economies of the household and thus on the roles of women within those networks (Bennett 1999; Howell 2009; Reyerson 2016; Farmer 2017). The labors of women, as wives, mothers, widows, and sisters, were an integral part of the consumption/production puzzle (Mummey and Reyerson 2011). As Sharon Farmer has shown, the advent of a luxury silk industry in Paris at the end of the thirteenth century depended on the physical relocation of female labor and eastern ateliers in the heart of the French capital. Teaching how to work with silk from afar did not work; one needed the physical laborers to be present for such a complex technological transfer (Farmer 2017). Relatedly, the ways that women used and passed on things—relics, tokens, letters, patronage—to foster ideas of family, tradition, and aristocratic culture further underpin their role in galvanizing and shaping the exchange of ideas and habits of consumption (Van Houts 1999a; Paul 2012; Lester 2014). Likewise, the role of women as "makers" of art and luxury goods as well as everyday items shows that women were an integral part of trade networks in ways that can no longer be overlooked (Martin 2012, 2016).

The protections, regulations, and innovations that fostered the growth of towns and trading centers also spurred the emergence of a new class of burghers, artisans, and merchants and thus a new cultural sensibility. Burghers, as a vibrant urban or bourgeoisie class, were defined in part by their access to capital, but much more so through the networks they created that facilitated exchange. Yet as Martha Howell has argued, it was not capital that animated this world, but rather *moveables* and moveable wealth. Burghers, moreover, were part of a world of moveable people—merchants, creditors, bankers, pilgrims, slaves, refugees—all of whom came to play a new and more prominent role in the creation of culture: in the regulation of time, the mediation of distance, and the language of commerce and governance (Howell 2009, 2010). It was these individuals, too, who took part in shaping fashions, cultivating tastes, and forming aesthetic ideas. Although very few records reflect how this process of cultural transmission and diffusion worked, the increased use of the vernacular for recording bills of sale, credit, and exchange; the emergence of a local vernacular chronicle tradition in northern Italy, for example; the circulation of play-scripts in French; and a new recognition of voluntary poverty and the *vita apostolica*, all reflected the interests of a burgher and merchant class. The exchange of styles, moreover, like the dissemination of Gothic design forms, glazing, and book production, and the rise of a French "court-style" within Europe and beyond its borders, fostered an aesthetic ideal that suggests the cultural unity of the period.

As the horizons of exchange widened, it became incumbent upon the men and women who traveled its limits not simply to exchange goods, but to serve as culture brokers (Rothman 2012: 3–7). Conversant in new languages, customs, and foods, men like Friar William Rubruck and Marco Polo understood their roles not only as connectors within trade networks, but as ambassadors of European ideas, practices, and—crucially—religious beliefs leading to Christian salvation. As these men traveled the Silk Road and encountered marvels worthy of recounting, they also served to broker the cultural differences that separated them as representatives of the Christian world from the forms of prestige, display, and authority they recognized in Mongol wealth, hierarchies, customs, and rituals (William of Rubruck 1990; Kinoshita 2006) (Figure 2.5). The tantalizing prospect of bridging such divides through conversion also suggested the possibility of a cultural empire of near limitless potential, an ideal that Jesuit missionaries would attempt to put into practice (Ditchfield *et al.* 2017; Jackson 2017). The familiarity with cultural practices from afar made merchants into crucial translators capable of "brokering empires." Merchants from Genoa, Venice, Pisa, and later Cyprus and Constantinople would continue to play this role far into the seventeenth century (Rothman 2012). But in this moment of

FIGURE 2.5: Boucicaut Master, Book of the Marvels of the World (1409–12): the Polo brothers arriving in Bukhara. Paris, Bibliotheque Nationale. Credit: Christophel Fine Art/UIG via Getty Images.

transition, at the end of the Middle Ages, we can also see the work of empire in its ability to create both subjects and objects of its power. Subjects were individuals included in the privileges of power, networks, and the accumulation of capital; objects—slaves, outsiders, foreigners—felt the power to control movement, to restrict access, and to deny personhood. Empire's power to subjugate, regulate, and control became increasingly linked to ethnic, religious, and racial markers of difference and the role of trade in catalyzing and propelling the use of power cannot be overlooked (Heng 2011a, 2011b). It should be no surprise that trade in slaves continued throughout the later Middle Ages and became a means of expressing an imagined and idealized form of imperial power that was performed and displayed in Ottoman, Habsburg, and Valois courts by the fifteenth century (Epstein 2001a; Blumenthal 2009; Rothman 2012) (Figure 2.6). The movement of people as objects was yet another—long-lasting—expression of the culture of empire.

CONCLUSION

With this framework in mind, empires of things become visible and readable. Set behind glass in an early seventeenth-century reliquary, one finds in the sacristy of the Lower Church of San Francesco in Assisi a cloth relic of extremely

FIGURE 2.6: Miniature, Maqama by Al-Hariri, Al-Harith at the Slaves Market, 1237. Paris, Bibliotheque Nationale. Credit: Christophel Fine Art/UIG via Getty Images.

delicate, near transparent, fabric made of the finest silk thread. Known as the "veil of the Mother of God," it was a gift from the merchant, Tommaso Orsini, who brought it from Damascus following a trip to the east. It was given to the Sacro Convento in 1320 in fulfillment of a vow and has been ritually displayed to the faithful at Easter and Pentecost ever since. It is badly damaged now, and as a result of frequent touching the warp threads have been pushed together forming stripes in some places. The material and its manufacture tells us that it hailed, not from the Levant and the towns near Bethlehem or Nazareth, but from a Tiraz workshop still active in Iberia, from the labor of Muslim women (Flury-Lemberg 1988: 318–19). This object, like so many others described and alluded to earlier, moved along long-established networks connecting the Muslim Mediterranean from the shores of Spain to North Africa to Syria, and then passed, quite easily, into a Christian chapel, into a growing Christian cultural ambit of imperial design and ideology that connected, and in the imaginary of Italian merchants, reconnected the Mediterranean. But this object, like so many other things in the medieval world, also speaks to mobility and the power of narrative in the world of cultural commerce during our period. This cloth, too, was called on to perform many things: to stand in for the authentic power of the holy coming from the east; to suggest the far reaches of Christian imperial fantasies; and to bind through an object one merchant's devotions to his home, the place at the end of his trade and travels. In this object, like so many things traded in the medieval world, are parts seen and unseen, made and remade, moved and removed with greater agility than scholars often credit or relate. The intertwined relationships of things and people in motion, of cultures in motion, is one of the cultural narratives of "empire" at work in the world (Rogers *et al.* 2014).

It is perhaps a great irony that the transformative event of the later Middle Ages was precipitated by trade, borne along—unknowingly at first—the familiar and well-worn networks described earlier. In 1346, a Genoese ship sailed out of port at Kaffa, a Genoese trade entrepôt on the Black Sea, and carried among other goods the pathogen later identified as *Yersinia pestis*, more commonly known as the plague. The *bacilli* moved with the speed of rumor, passing unseen from person to person and by 1353 it spanned the width and breath of the European and Mediterranean west (Green 2014). The extent of the plague's spread reflects almost perfectly the networks of trade and interaction that animated and connected the medieval world. Trade in this disease had devastating consequences. Roughly one-third of the European population died during the successive outbreaks of the plague, with urban centers—the hubs of all networks of exchange—especially devastated. The chronicle reports, manorial records, and notarial registers all describe the collapse and stagnation that followed. Learned technologies were lost, labor forces disappeared, the circulation of raw and worked goods receded (Pamuk 2007). One consequence of this was a slow but profound transformation of the culture of empire reflected in the advent of new economic structures and the opening up of the scale and scope of trade with the Atlantic world.

CHAPTER THREE

Natural Worlds

VICKI SZABO

Grímur Kveldúlfsson, better known as Skalla-Grímr, "bald-Grim," was not the founder of an empire. Neither was his son Egil, who would become one of medieval Iceland's more colorful outlaws, a warrior-poet famous for the notorious exploits recorded in his eponymous saga. While Egil is perhaps the more historically noteworthy figure, his father also boasts an impressive résumé. Son of Kveldulf, a shape-shifter and powerful warrior, Skalla-Grímr fled along with his father from Norway after an attack against King Harald Fairhair in the late ninth century. King Harald's reign was a tumultuous time in Norway. According to *Egil's Saga*, Harald seized properties from sea to mountain, farming land, estates, lakes, and all resources: "Every farmer and every forester had to become his tenant, every salt-maker and every hunter on land or sea had to pay taxes to him. Many a man went on the run from this tyranny and many a wilderness became inhabited ... And that's when Iceland was discovered" (Pálsson and Edwards 1976: ch. 4). As Harald seized properties and resources for his growing kingdom, Kveldulf and men of his ilk were brought into conflict, left with few choices other than war or emigration.

Iceland-bound, Skalla-Grímr's landing spot was selected by his father, although in an unorthodox manner. Kveldulf died during the journey from Norway, physically spent after one last berserker fit, so it was Kveldulf's coffin that washed ashore at Skalla-Grímr's new homestead in western Iceland's township of Borgarnes. Skalla-Grímr's new home, Borg á Myrum ("rock in the marshes"), has been described as an ecological ideal, a deeply resourced landscape and an archetype of *landnám* (land-taking) (Figure 3.1). The renowned poet and politician Snorri Sturluson, who lived for a time at Borgarnes, recorded the tale of Egil and his family in the early thirteenth

FIGURE 3.1: Borg á Myrum, 1,100 years after Skalla-Grimr's landnám. Credit: Vicki Szabo.

century. Skalla-Grímr's land-taking underscores medieval appreciation for and recognition of the necessity of diverse ecosystems and natural resources in settlement patterns and success:

> "Skallagrim put in near a big headland jutting out into the sea and only linked to the mainland by a narrow neck of land . . . [He] set out to explore and could see that there were great marshes and woods there, with plenty of land between the mountains and the sea, as well as ample seal-hunting and fishing. Exploring the land southwards to the sea they found a vast fjord . . . Skallagrim took possession of everything between the mountains and the sea, . . . all the land bounded by the rivers right down to the sea . . . There he built his farm and called it Borg . . . Not far from there where a small creek cuts into the coast, they saw a good many ducks, so they called the place Andakil (Duck Channel) . . . Skallagrim explored the whole district . . . They soon realized that every one of the rivers was teeming with fish . . . What livestock they had were left to fend for themselves over winter in the woods . . . There was plenty of driftwood to be had west of Myrar, so he built and ran another farm at Alftaness and from there his men went out fishing and seal-hunting, and collecting the eggs of wild fowl, for there was plenty of everything. They also fetched in his driftwood. Whales often got stranded, and you could shoot anything you wanted, for none of the wildlife was used to man and just stood about quietly . . . There are some islands lying offshore where a whale had been washed up, so they called them the Hvals Isles. Skallagrim also had his men go up the rivers

looking for salmon . . . As Skallagrim's livestock grew in number the animals started making for the mountains in the summer. He found a big difference in the livestock, which was better and fatter when grazing up on the moorland, and above all in the sheep that wintered in the mountain valleys" (Pálsson and Edwards 1976: chs. 28–9).

This Icelandic excursus offers several useful points of departure for this survey of the natural worlds of medieval empires. First, it captures the interplay of lands, waters, and the panoply of resources needed by nearly all successful medieval societies. The excerpt reveals the diversity of landscapes and natural resources that Skalla-Grímr and his men exploited in order to succeed in Iceland. This strategy of a diverse resource base was reproduced by thriving societies large and small across medieval Europe. Second, Skalla-Grímr and his father had evaded the overreaching control of Norway's expansionist and resource-hungry king, at least for a while. *Egil's Saga* underscores the fact that power and the natural world were synonymous in the Middle Ages. The empires of medieval Europe were dependent upon the same environmental control that Skalla-Grímr recognized as essential in his own small-scale land-taking. As would be faced by Skalla-Grímr and other heroes of the Icelandic sagas, no resource was safe from competition, destruction, or exhaustion. The capacity to adapt and control natural resources sustainably was of greatest importance to successful medieval empires. While Skalla-Grímr and his fellow Icelanders were pioneers of sustainability, other Europeans were perhaps not so nuanced, culturally or economically, in their appreciation for the long-term use of the natural worlds which they controlled. Third, Kveldulf and son may have escaped Norway during a climate optimum, an ideal environmental window of opportunity. The era when Skalla-Grímr founded Borg, when other medieval kingdoms and empires across western Europe were established and began to thrive is known, imprecisely and perhaps erroneously, as the Medieval Warm Period (MWP) or the Medieval Climatic Anomaly (MCA) (Lamb 1965; Stine 1994; Bradley *et al.* 2016). Climate did not dictate, but could certainly impact, a settlement, kingdom, or empire's success or failure. Fourth and finally, unlike the medieval kingdoms and empires of continental Europe, Skalla-Grímr moved into a virgin space which he shaped and exploited, not competing with or adapting to the resource customs of earlier inhabitants. Expansionist empires of western Europe faced altogether different conditions, adapting to new terrains and challenges, testing the limits of resource extraction or introduction, with the benefit or detriment of extant local populations. Imagining Skalla-Grímr's *landnám*, for example, in the eleventh century landscape of Domesday England or in the competitive and parched lands of contemporary Outremer, accentuates both the unique condition of early Iceland and the challenges faced by medieval kingdoms and empires of western Europe. This successful farm, founded by an outlaw son of an outlaw, offers the first of this chapter's explorations of medieval engagements with the natural world.

Environmental history, the means by which we reconstruct encounters and exploitation of the natural worlds, frequently benefits from a transdisciplinary and broad perspective, being so diverse that it can be vexing to define or contain, given the many forms of evidence, subjects, approaches, periods, and regions which it can encompass (Brady 2015). While resources, field systems, forests, weather, waters, and animals are still disciplinary essentials, scholars of medieval environmental history have elevated the field beyond simple questions of tangible environmental resources, engaging with deeper questions of memory, perception, culture, and complex social ecologies in the medieval world. Given the breadth of material subject to environmental scrutiny, it is a broad task to survey or encapsulate medieval interactions with and cultural perceptions of the natural world, especially in the ecologically dynamic ninth through fifteenth centuries.

First and foremost, the natural world, including both local environments and broader climate forces, was critical to medieval European development, success, and failure. No environmental historian today would argue that the environment singularly determined or dictated the fate of kingdoms, empires, or communities, but the impact of environmental forces on these premodern societies could be felt more acutely than we may appreciate today: "even small changes in the overall scope of Holocene climate variability can, under certain conditions, have notable effects on civilizations" (McCormick *et al.* 2012). Second, to distinguish how natural worlds were experienced in an empire, as opposed to some other constructed unit of medieval experience—a kingdom, monastery, village, city, town, *emporion* or other foundation—requires a selective approach. Medieval empires forged expansive strategies to acquire and manage resources, to subsist through disaster, and to produce on levels that met or exceeded needs, but so did successful monasteries, kingdoms, or even cities. The encompassing nature of an empire perhaps allowed, on a practical level, a higher fortitude in times of stress and recovery, in that the resource base of empires may have been more extensive than those found in kingdoms or smaller political or social units.

Medieval monarchs and emperors alike were bound to the natural world with its shifts and (in)stability. The capacity of an emperor to control nature, or appear to do so, or to simply exist in equilibrium was important and effective cultural propaganda, particularly in a period when so many societies lived on the ecological edge. While control of nature was, and is, a lofty goal, and one typically transitory and won at the expense of another competitor, strategies that maximized impressions of control or dominion over the natural world could be ideologically, culturally, and economically beneficial to an emperor. Whether during a period that was climatically calm or turbulent, the control over some aspect of the natural world that an emperor could demonstrate advertised his prowess and prominence. This chapter, rather than attempting a broad environmental history of empires, focuses on examples of emperors and their unique engagements, perhaps even "dominion," with some aspect of the natural world. By framing emperors within culturally bounded natural contexts, we remind ourselves of the importance of environments which emperors aimed to exploit or control.

MEDIEVAL CONCEPTIONS OF NATURE

The natural worlds of medieval Europe, high and mountainous, dense and wooded, deep and cold, filled with fearsome and at times useful denizens, were seen by contemporaries as imbued with the power and providence of God but also the threat of the devil. Nature could be mundane and plentiful, challenging or supernatural. Encyclopedists, natural philosophers, scholastics, and students of God's creation observed and explained, cataloged and illuminated the natural worlds around them. Popular bestiaries recounted the creatures with which God had populated the earth, skies, and waters, some vexing and some helpful to humankind. While largely derivative from classical and late Roman scholarship, such as Pliny the Elder's first-century *Naturalis Historia* and Isidore's seventh-century *Etymologiae*, among others, medieval natural historians like Vincent of Beauvais (*c.* 1190–1264) or Albertus Magnus (*c.* 1200–80) knew that understanding of the natural world was essential for both civilization and salvation. Knowledge of nature was knowledge of God and God's plans, so scrutiny, observation, and experience of natural worlds revealed much. As historians, we may fail to appreciate the utter omnipresence of natural worlds in medieval minds, the constant intrusion of nature upon thought and action. As Hanawalt and Kiser mused in a recent volume on premodernity and nature, "the most daunting problem is that in both the visual and written records of the time, nature appears to be both everywhere and nowhere . . . for many writing in these early periods, 'nature' was arguably not even a discursive category; it simply went without saying" (Hanawalt and Kiser 2008: 1–2).

The natural world was ubiquitous, challenging, spiritually enlightening, terrifying, and—above all else—sustaining. Abbot Ælfric of Eynesham's late tenth-century *Colloquy* provides a useful reminder into the simple and pragmatic value of nature to medieval people. The quaint *Colloquy*, a didactic text for Ælfric's Latin students, recounts the engagement of late tenth-century English tradesmen and laborers with the natural world, including discourse among ploughmen, shepherds, oxherds, hunters, fishermen, and fowlers. From bitter winters to scorching summers, through encounters with wolves, boars, and whales, hard work yielded profits, despite the risks of attack, storm, and travel (Ælfric 1993: 169–77). Ælfric was no original observer of the natural world, but his *Colloquy* underscored at its most basic the daily proximity and partnership between medieval society and diverse environments. A monarch or emperor who could bring stability or a modicum of control to that world, through proximity to God or by other means, would be favored and remembered.

Through intrepid exploration and hard labor, medieval monks, merchants, farmers, craftsmen, peasants, nobles, kings, and even emperors made great impacts, positive and negative, on the natural worlds that sustained them. While not, perhaps, at an imperial Roman pace in their proclivities or capacities to consume natural resources without heed, medieval communities and empires across western Europe had complex relationships with the natural world, ranging from humility in the face of nature's great force to a desire for dominance. Ascription of a simplistic worldview of dominion over nature to people of the Middle Ages, as scholars of the past were wont to do, masks the complexity of medieval thought. Dominion over nature may have been a goal for many, particularly emperors, but it was far from a universally held perspective (Arnold 2013; Hoffmann 2014: 85–91). The medieval desire to dominate nature was held as a historical truth for decades, based in large part on Lynn White's 1967 "The Historical Roots of our Ecologic Crisis" (White 1967: 1203–7). The White thesis asserted that medieval Christians sought control over nature based on biblical sanction: "And God blessed them and said to them, 'Be fruitful and multiply and fill the earth and subdue it and have dominion over the fish of the sea and over the birds of the heavens and over every living thing that moves on the earth'" (Genesis 1:28). This perceived dominion, argued White, began with the plow, which "profoundly changed . . . man's relation to the soil," and led to a divorce of mankind from nature (White 1967: 1205). Although famous within environmental historiography, countless historians have subverted White's thesis through thoughtful analysis of medieval sources, especially monastic literature and natural histories. Richard Hoffmann notes that White's article is not without value, in that it captured the medieval notion that God could work through nature, both in creation and action, and that "Nature thus necessarily reflected the mind and purpose of God" (Hoffmann 2014: 88).

At times benevolent and, seemingly, more often hostile, medieval Christians knew that God rewarded and tested them through his creation of nature. Medieval encyclopedists and natural historians could attribute changes in the natural world to physical forces, celestial or earthly, and to disruptions in the Great Chain of Being. Or, like the broader medieval populations, they could look to God Himself, to God's own agents, or, at worst, malevolent forces. Ultimately, nature was synonymous with God. Environmental historians recognize that concepts like "nature" or "the natural" are complex cultural constructions without singular definition (Bartlett 2008; Epstein 2012). To call something natural—behavior, qualities, or an environment—assumes an original state or status of purity. The landscape of medieval Europe was by no means a "natural" one when the Middle Ages began. Centuries of modification, exploitation, and degradation had changed European fields, forests, farmland, meadows, wastelands, coastlines, rivers, and more, long before Charlemagne or any later emperor came to his throne. Human impacts on land, water, species, even air quality, all shifted with time and space, creating territories at times hospitable or hostile across continental Europe. When the western Roman empire withered in the fifth century, much of Europe was left profoundly changed. Deforestation, pollution, industrial wastes, diminished animal populations, altered and sedimented rivers, lakes, and harbors were part of Rome's environmental legacy (Thommen 2012: 3). By the sixth century, as the dust of Rome settled, the natural worlds of the West had been reprieved and recovery began.

MODERN APPROACHES TO MEDIEVAL CLIMATE

In addition to human impacts on medieval environments, greater forces of change were constantly at play as Europe rose and thrived or declined. Climate scientists rely on a wide array of indicators and sources that replace or augment scientific means of reconstructing past environments. Texts like Matthew Paris' thirteenth-century *Chronica Majora* (1872–83) have long provided insight into medieval environments, but climatologists also rely on chemical or physical analysis of important proxy datasets, including human, animal or insect remains, pollen, corals, ice cores, tree rings, and sediments. From such proxy data, we know that western Europe was subject to broad-ranging climate shifts throughout the Middle Ages, particularly from the ninth through the sixteenth centuries.

In this period, the climate alone did not shape or determine the rise or fall of medieval powers, but it provides a useful framework to consider emperors and their environmental interactions. From the rise of Charlemagne (r. 768–814) through the birth of the Early Modern era and well beyond, Europe and the Mediterranean worlds saw numerous, perhaps innumerable, shifts and fluctuations, major and minor, in climate patterns. Weather tends to attract a great deal of attention in medieval chronicles and accounts, but weather is simply a short-term and changeable state. Climate is the matrix within which weather performs and dissipates. McCormick, Dutton, and Mayewski compellingly connect ideas of climate and weather with Bernard Bailyn's ideas of latent and manifest history, noting that "latent" events are deep developments whose effects contemporaries felt but of which they were unconscious, while "[m]anifest events . . . are those that contemporaries perceived" (McCormick *et al.* 2007: 865–95). Climate change, whether modern or historical, is controversial. Nothing underscores this more effectively in academia than reference to the Little Ice Age (LIA) or the Medieval Warm Period (MWP) (Fagan 2000, 2008).[1] The LIA and MWP have become popularly accepted paradigms and determinist explanations of successes and failures, changes or developments in medieval European history. Climate scientists have expressed skepticism for such broad application of debated climate models, providing more pointed analyses of regional variations, including the duration and extent of the impacts of changing climate phases. Notwithstanding controversy, a contextualization of medieval empires through the lens of climate offers important preliminary perspectives on successes, failures, and choices made.

In brief, as the Roman empire ended in the west, Europe is thought to have experienced several centuries of climatic variation or disturbance (McCormick *et al.* 2012). As noted earlier, Romans had affected rather than impacted Europe's landscape in profound ways during the high and late empire, but coincident with Rome's western decline, Europe entered "an extended period of wet and cold climate" (Cheyette 2008: 127). The impact of twin volcanic disturbances in the mid sixth century produced a "mystery cloud" that contemporary authors linked with crop failures, plague, famine, and cooling that persisted for a decade or more (Toohey *et al.* 2016: 402, 406). Using proxy evidence including tree rings, glacial cores, landscape surveys, texts, and pollen, scientists have suggested that climate played a key role in western Europe's transition from an ancient to a medieval landscape through the agricultural, economic, and political disruptions of the so-called "Late Antique Little Ice Age" (Büntgen *et al.* 2016: 231–6). The formative kingdoms of sixth-century western Europe, struggling with political and social upheavals, and none of the benefits of Rome's infrastructure, were less equipped to adapt and rebound from inhospitable climate episodes. Shortly thereafter, Carolingian Europe suffered from its own "messy history of crisis and climate" (Newfield and Labuhn 2016). The story we tell of the Carolingians, however, is more often one of agricultural success, territorial expansion, and the imperial reassertion of control over rewilded Europe, but not consistently so. While Charlemagne's reign occurred during a particularly hospitable period, useful propaganda to underscore God's favor for the emperor, his successors were not so fortunate. Decades of harsh winters, flooding rains, famines, and pestilence plagued the Carolingians (McCormick *et al.* 2007: 117–72). Coinciding with Viking raids on the continent and into the British Isles, it is no wonder that so many authors looked to Divine punishment, or at least the removal of Divine favor, as the cause.

With time came solace, prosperity, and growth. As the first millennium passed, a new climate phase began. Western Europe entered the supposed Medieval Warm Period (MWP) (Mann *et al.* 2009: 1258). Controversy abounds with this "climate phase," but in short, as the popular narrative goes, a more favorable climate allowed settlements to spread, agriculture to resume with new effective tools and technologies, and land to be cleared and claimed with alacrity, for dykes to be pushed from shallows to the deep, and for population, better fed, bigger and longer-lived, to abound. Proxy data indicate a lengthy and productive period of climate stability for much of western Europe:

> The onset of wetter and warmer summers is contemporaneous with the societal consolidation of new kingdoms that developed in the former WRE [Western Roman Empire]. Reduced climate variability from ~700 to 1000 CE, relative to its surroundings, matches the new and sustained demographic growth in the northwest European countryside and even the establishment of Norse colonies in the cold environments of Iceland and Greenland. Humid and mild summers paralleled the rapid cultural and political growth of medieval Europe under the Merovingian and Carolingian dynasties and their successors (Büntgen *et al.* 2011: 580).

One article recently referred to the period from *c.* 725 to 1025 as a "Medieval Quiet Period" [MQP]: "a prolonged period with both minimal explosive volcanic activity, and no significant perturbations in solar forcing, either positive or negative. The world was thus in a period of relative stability, . . . an 'unperturbed' state" (Bradley *et al.* 2016: 990). The MQP may be preferable to many scholars, who have noted that the so-called "warm" period was neither uniformly nor ubiquitously warm across western Europe. A recent study of glacial moraines has showed growth rather than retreat of alpine glaciers in Norse Greenland during the MWP, indicating, alongside other forms of proxy data, that the warm period was not a universal phenomenon in the North Atlantic and Northern Europe (Young *et al.* 2015: 1–8).

The reversal of growth began with the Little Ice Age, which seems to have begun around the early fourteenth century.

> Wetter summers during the 13th and 14th centuries and a first cold spell at ~1300 CE agree with the globally observed onset of the Little Ice Age, likely contributing to widespread famine across central Europe. Unfavorable climate may have even played a role in debilitating the underlying health conditions that contributed to the devastating economic crisis that arose from the second plague pandemic, the Black Death . . . The period is also associated with a temperature decline in the North Atlantic and the abrupt desertion of former Greenland settlements (Büntgen *et al.* 2011: 582).

Just as some scholars reject the universality of medieval warmth from 950 to 1250, so too the "Little Ice Age" has recently been recast as more regional and varied in its impact (Kelly and Gráda 2014: 57–68). Scientists and medievalists alike would benefit from consideration of climate within more nuanced contexts, namely geographical and temporal constraints, to better understand impacts upon medieval societies (Xoplaki *et al.* 2016: 229–52). This brief foray into climate science underscores the potential centrality and impact of environmental change on the rule of medieval emperors or monarchs.

GOD, EMPERORS, AND DOMINION OVER NATURE

Given the challenging matrix of medieval climate stability or change, medieval emperors varied in their capacity or desire to effect control over the natural world. Hoffmann has reminded us that "the European Middle Ages lacked self-conscious or even coherent tacit discourse on relations of humans to nature or on nature as an entity, to say nothing of such concepts as environment or ecology" (Hoffmann 2014: 86). It is unlikely, then, that any monarch or emperor overtly acknowledged a goal of environmental control, dominion over nature, as a governing strategy. But reference to the natural world and the emperor's role within it infuses imperial rule, from cultural symbols of power to economic enterprises. The many chapters and approaches to empire in this volume underscore the complex worlds that emperors governed, with military, political, economic, social, and cultural concerns that varied over time and space. But control, or appearance of control, over nature must have been symbolically valuable for medieval emperors too, given the proximity of God to nature. While discounted as a universal thread of medieval thought, the idea of dominion over nature may have found traction in royal and imperial actions. This chapter now turns to vignettes of emperors and their dominion—intellectual, cultural, economic, social, and ideological—over natural worlds under their control. While only God truly possessed dominion over the medieval world, emperors recognized the value of expressing control even if only in microcosms. The intellectual dominion of Frederick II over the avian world and the sylvan and bucolic control of Carolingians and Angevins offered important means of propaganda for emperors to varying degrees of effectiveness.

Emperor Frederick II (1194–1250), known to contemporaries as "the wonder of the world" (*stupor mundi*), is enveloped by stories, both attractive and repulsive, that distinguish him from other medieval rulers, particularly in his intellectual endeavors and his penchant for experimentation. Frederick's interest in science and nature, beyond the sportsman's pursuits, elevated him above his noble contemporaries. Frederick's study of animals extended well beyond the typical noble fare of horses, hounds, and hawks, to his personal menagerie, which included giraffes, elephants, and other exotics. Ownership of expansive menageries, from the Roman world to Charlemagne to the Hohenstaufens, conveyed and "reinforce[d] the symbolic—and actual—distance between [wealthy, largely royal, medieval families] and those of lower social stations" (Kiser 2007: 106). Possession of a menagerie was impressive, but more so was Frederick's ability to take his animals on tour: "Frederick . . . traveled with his elephants, camels, lions, panthers, and leopards, occasionally displaying them publically in parades" (Kiser 2007: 105). Mary Refling's detailed study of the sources relating to Frederick's menagerie observes that this traveling display marked Frederick's zoo above that of others and demonstrated his imperial power: "the difficulty and expense of feeding, transporting, and caring for such an odd assortment of animals . . . [and] the decision to bring the animals along on such a difficult trip over the Alps was a deliberate attempt to exploit their symbolic power—to cultivate Frederick's image as the stupor mundi . . . What an uncanny knack for image control" (Refling 2005: 5). While the menagerie may have served as useful propaganda, Frederick's true passion in nature was more narrow in scope.

The massive *De Arte Venandi cum Avibus*, written in the 1240s, is indicative of his broader cultural and intellectual curiosity for the natural world. The work spans six illustrated books, including analysis of structure, care, and behavior of the falcons and prey birds, and emphasizes the intellectual and experiential distance between Frederick and other authors or commentators on the noble sport (Frederick II 1943; Haskins 1921). While Frederick acknowledged his debt to Aristotle's *De animalibus*, he also articulated his intellectual and practical transcendence of The Philosopher: "we do not follow the prince of the philosophers on all points, as he seldom or never was engaged in falconry" (Beullens 2007: 145–6). Many historians have commented that Frederick, through the course of his research on falconry, was known to correct translations of Arabic treatises on falconry, "using his own knowledge of Arabic" (Haskins 1924: 247; Refling 2005: 5; Bressler 2010: 124). As such, moving well beyond being a mere sportsman, Frederick establishes himself as an ornithologist and scientist. Book 1 of *De Arte Venandi*, "The Structure and Habit of Birds," includes fifty-seven chapters on anatomy, behaviors, flight, diet, refuge, and more, underscoring not only years of observations but detailed analysis of a range of species. As a whole, Frederick's tome has been declared, even with errors abounding, "the first zoological treatise written in the critical spirit of modern science" (Egerton 2012: 27).

In the prologue to the work, Frederick notes the great expense, time, and effort required to produce the comprehensive tome, which was necessary given the "misleading and often insufficient statements to be found in the works of certain hackneyed authors" (Frederick II 1943: 3). He also reminds his audience that the codification of knowledge that he has provided had come at great personal expense and effort: "As the ruler of a large kingdom and an extensive empire we were very often hampered by arduous and intricate governmental duties, but despite these handicaps we did not lay aside our self-imposed task and were successful in committing to writing at the proper time the elements of this art" (Frederick II 1943: 3). In his introduction to the translation of Frederick's treatise, Wood noted that perhaps the Emperor was perhaps too absorbed in his hobby, to the detriment of empire: "he failed disastrously in one important engagement because he made the mistake of indulging in a day of sport with his birds instead of pressing the siege of a fortress" (Frederick II 1943: xxxv) (Figure 3.2).

Through *De Arte Venandi*, Frederick is linked to a rising interest in the natural world that embraced new scrutiny and observation with revelation of God's will and plan: "Because the natural world and natural values had been created by God, there can be no inherent conflict between what humans experience in the natural world and what God wishes for them to understand" (Hoffmann 2014: 106). Alongside other contemporary observers of animals and the natural world, including the philosophers Albertus Magnus (d. 1280),

FIGURE 3.2: Frederick II miniature from *De Arte Venandi cum Avibus*, Codex Palatina 1071, thirteenth century. Rome, Biblioteca Apostolica Vaticana. Credit: Archiv Gerstenberg/ullstein bild via Getty Images.

Roger Bacon (d. 1292), and Thomas of Cantimpré (d. 1272), Frederick "saw observations of falcons as informing about nature in general ... Frederick apprehended nature also as a source or site of recreation and in that sense his book reflects another newly visible way of thinking about it relative to civilized humans" (Hoffmann 2014: 107). While not all subjects could appreciate Frederick's work, he implored both nobles and the poor to consider its "manifold and far-reaching uses, ... both classes will find in bird life attractive manifestations of the processes of nature" (Frederick II 1943: 4). The emperor himself, though, found elevation and singularity in his capacity to observe and record God's work through his favored avian agents. Frederick signs off in his prologue as "The author of this treatise, the august Frederick II, Emperor of the Romans, King of Jerusalem and Sicily, is a lover of wisdom with a philosophic and speculative mind" (Frederick II 1943: 4).

Frederick offers us here an instance of intellectual dominion of nature, unchallenged and unparalleled in his age and even after. He impresses this dominion upon all nobles who might fancy themselves as sportsmen, but who would likely need assistance in understanding falconry. Acknowledging his work's value, he implores noblemen to "order it read and explained ... by some master of the science," underscoring that not everyone will be able to comprehend this most specialized work (Frederick II 1943: 4). Intellectual dominion, while impressive, may have held little sway across the expanse of Frederick's empire. Centuries before Frederick, another emperor set the pace for imperial dominion across a broad range of natural worlds, from cultivated fields to dark forests. Charlemagne's dominion was both palpable and conceptual, and set the stage for all who would follow him.

Charlemagne's dominion over nature could be found on royal estates and in the deep forests of Germany rather than Frederick's sunny Sicily. Notker the Stammerer (d. 912) painted a dramatic scene when the Emperor's dominion was challenged in his account of bold and tireless Charlemagne's fateful hunt of the auroch. Standing up to six feet at the shoulder, European aurochs were among the most formidable quarry of the north. Perhaps seeking to impress the visiting Persian envoys at his court, who had kindly brought the emperor a range of eastern exotics, including "some monkeys ... [and] an elephant," Charlemagne took his guests out to a memorable hunt:

> Charlemagne, who could never endure idleness and sloth, prepared to go off into the forest grove to hunt bison and wild oxen. He took the Persian envoys with him; but when they set eyes on these immense animals, they were filled with mighty dread, and they turned and ran. Our hero Charlemagne, on the contrary, knew no fear: sitting astride his spirited horse, he rode up to one of the beasts, drew his sword and tried to cut off its head (Einhard and Notker the Stammerer 1969: 143–5).

What follows is perhaps a bit less glorious, as the animal survived the blow and landed his own on Charlemagne: "The huge beast ripped the Emperor's Gallic boot and leg-wrap and pinked his skin with the point of its horn" (Einhard and Notker the Stammerer 1969: 143–5). Chased down by a courtier who had earlier fallen from the Emperor's favor, the auroch's "still palpitating" heart was brought to Charlemagne, a thoughtful gift that mended those old wounds. In recounting the episode at Aachen, "the enormous horns were brought in, as proof of his story" (ibid.). What would have been more impressive to Charlemagne's imperial subjects: his violent encounter with a forest beast or his brand new Asian elephant, known to history as Abul Abbas, presented to him by the very envoys who had just witnessed the hunt?

Charlemagne's Europe was a wild place, or perhaps it was a rewilded place. Following Rome's decline in the west, Europe's new monarchs continued to rule in ways inspired by Rome, but far from reproducing Rome's control. From Athawulf's declaration to restore the Roman state with Gothic vigor to Clovis' Constantinian battlefield conversion, Europe's barbarian kings imitated Romans, but never attained a semblance of empire until Charlemagne. From Charlemagne's succession to the end of his wars, his vastly expanded territory encompassed many peoples, languages, cultures, religions, and environments. Einhard notes that "the Frankish kingdom which he inherited . . . was already far-flung and powerful," but came to include lands from the Atlantic to "a considerable part of Germany," from the Rhine, Loire, Danube, and Ebro, to the Pyrenees to the whole of Italy (Einhard and Notker the Stammerer 1969: 68–9). While much of Charlemagne's reign was spent on improving his kingdom, in sponsoring churches, building his great palace complex, and investing in economic infrastructure in *emporia* and related constructions, his engagement with his empire's natural spaces, as witnessed in Notker's story, was politically, economically, and culturally profound. And Charlemagne himself, if his biographers Einhard and Notker are to be believed, as a Frank by culture and a Roman by necessity, was most comfortable in these very wilds, or at least the managed wilds, on horseback, hunting, exercising, and even swimming.

The Carolingian empire "has special importance for environmental history," says Richard Hoffmann, in the "path-breaking new syntheses for organizing human use of European nature," but also in the contemporary documentation of these activities (Hoffmann 2014: 79). Carolingian sources from Einhard's biography to Carolingian capitularies to the works of Alcuin and his scholarly successors at the court school at Aachen reveal both pragmatic details and intellectual scrutiny of the natural world. The organizational capacities of Carolingians are witnessed in the defense and management of royal forests and in restoration of agrarian control as seen in Charlemagne's capitularies, especially the early ninth-century *Espistola Generalis* or *Capitulare de Villis*.

Here it says, "our wood and forests shall be well protected; if there is an area to be cleared, the stewards are to have it cleared, and shall now allow fields to become overgrown with woodland ... they shall keep our fields and arable land in good order" (Capitulare de Villis 2008: chs. 36–7). Charlemagne's royal forests and management of royal estates both demonstrate effective reign over both the wilds and domesticated natural worlds.

Control of forests, first contrived by the Carolingians and emulated for centuries thereafter by monarchs, emperors, and nobles, may be the most enduring symbol of medieval power over nature. Royal or imperial forests were artificial constructions, encompassing fields, pastureland, and of course woods, both managed and natural, set aside for noble pursuits of the chase. The quarry of the hunt, stags, deer, boars, and other animals, wild or managed, were protected both for sport and for food. More importantly, the forests were locales for elite enculturation and identity reproduction: "Since the reign of Charlemagne, when the great royal forest had become a symbol of imperial authority, activities within it (i.e. hunting) became a performance of the king's supremacy" (Hoofnagle 2013: 169).

Charlemagne sought to create paradise on his personal villas and in his royal forests, but his capacity to control his forests, aurochs notwithstanding, was not easily replicated by emperors or monarchs elsewhere. Beginning with William's conquest in 1066, Norman and Angevin emperors sought to create in England wooded refuges, the forests, where pastimes and prey could be pursued and elite status reinforced. In this way, William the Conqueror's control over England was, by most measures, complete. The Domesday Book (1086) must stand as the most impressive and enviably comprehensive account of newly acquired imperial possessions from the Middle Ages. Among his many claims upon his newly conquered land, William set aside forest land as hunting preserves, well within the traditions and rights of his continental forbearers, in an "extraordinary application of central authority" (Aberth 2013: 97). However, unlike Charlemagne's age, when dissent remained undocumented, many sources record the disdain of local populations for William's seizure of culturally traditional and economically essential forests and fields, used for scavenging, hunting, wood, and foraging land, or pannage, for pigs. "The Anglo-Saxon Chronicle and later historians such as John of Worcester and Orderic Vitalis decry the king's arrogant presumption and abuse of royal privilege, especially his disenfranchisement of the English people in order to enjoy the pleasures of the hunt" (Hoofnagle 2013: 165). Upon arrival in England, William "sought to express and legitimate [his] newly acquired power ... through the integration of symbols of Carolingian authority" (Hoofnagle 2013: 166). The forest served not only as a physical manifestation of the king's legal power, but his symbolic "authority over man and beast alike" (Hoofnagle 2013: 166). The awe which control of forests may have carried on the continent seems to have translated in England with some measure of derision. The Anglo-Saxon Chronicle says of William: "He was sunk in greed, And utterly given up to avarice. He set apart a vast deer preserve and imposed laws concerning it. Whoever slew a hard or a hind, Was to be blinded. He forbade the killing of boars, Even as the killing of harts. For he loved the stags as dearly, As though he had been their father. Hares, also, he decreed should go unmolested. The rich complained and the poor lamented, But he was too relentless to care though all might hate him" (Garmonsway 1990: 221). While Anglo-Saxons simmered and occasionally rose up in resentment, the Norman and Angevin forests served the sociopolitical and cultural needs of the Anglo-Norman empire in England, symbolizing "the transformation of the woods from wilderness to tamed arena," allowing William, or his later Angevin heirs, to "impose his will on the forest landscape and tame it to serve his needs" (Hoofnagle 2013: 167). The woods were theirs alone.

Royal forests of England were held and expanded for centuries with a range of officials charged to maintain and preserve the lands and creatures, and to ensure poaching and trespass were met with firm fines. Perhaps, in more practical terms, this was the real point of forests, symbolic value aside. "When William the Conqueror first introduced the Forest Law to England, . . . he was not so much initiating a tyrannical system for the exploitation of natural resources at the expense of the needs of indigenous peoples, . . . as he was instead establishing the forest as one vital expression of his royal authority the revenues from which would support the crown" (Hoofnagle 2013: 169). Landscape historians and ecologists have questioned the fertility and productive value of the lands upon which forests were established, noting that many royal preserves and forests were located upon lands at best marginal for agriculture (Aberth 2013: 97–8). Rhetorically, however, contemporary complaints note that the loss of traditional forest, riverine, and coastal resources was unbearable for the poor. In England, traditions of forest resistance spawned vigorous new cultural dissent in the form of popular outlaw tales, culminating in very real and popular resentment against ruling powers in the age of King John (r. 1199–1216) and thereafter (Figure 3.3).

As John lost his continental holdings, diminishing the Angevin empire of his predecessors, so too he began to lose the symbolic prestige of his royal forests. Articles 47 and 48 of the 1215 Magna Carta demanded restoration of recently afforested land as well as correction of the "evil customs connected with forests and warrens, foresters and warreners, sheriffs and their officials, riverbanks and their wardens." In addition to the forests, William and his successors had seized coastal rights to wreck, including fish, whales, and other drift goods, as well as possessions of waterways and riverbanks. While symbolic control of natural lands may have been tolerated for a time, with the failures of John and the loss of empire, the king's dominion, including that over the

FIGURE 3.3: King John hunting, Statutes of England, fourteenth century, f.116 – BL Cotton MS Claudius D II, fol. 116r. Credit: Fine Art Images/Heritage Images/Getty Images.

natural world, fell to question. No such questions plagued Charlemagne or even, for a time, his heirs. Control of the forest was expanded by Louis the Pious, offering both symbolic power and economic revenue (Rothwell 1975; Hoofnagle 2013: 169, n. 13).

While Charlemagne's creation of the forest inspired nobles, monarchs, and emperors of Europe, his control of the forest may have been bested by the agrarian order seen on his numerous royal estates, as documented in the late eighth-century *De Villis*.[2] Largely focused on the administration and maintenance of royal agricultural estates, *De Villis* offers insight into the economics and natural resources of Charlemagne's kingdom as it sat on the eve of empire.[3] While the capitulary "never once mentions how to plant or harvest the crop, how to breed cattle, or when to collect eggs or milk," and falls short on many practical matters of estate management, readers glean a sense of high functioning and productive farms, fish ponds, barns, and fields (Campbell 2010: 244). Charlemagne's *De Villis* made clear the distinction between royal estates and public lands. The people would have no harm but also no benefit from royal lands. In the absence of the chronicles, uprisings or legal actions seen in England or later empires, the negative impacts of Charlemagne's regulation of natural spaces upon local peasant communities become secondary to the message of Charlemagne's capacity to control.

Charlemagne's role upon his royal estates, like that of most medieval elites, was removed and symbolic, as his *iudices*, royal estate managers, were charged with property maintenance. Their numerous duties included the care, keeping, and defense of the royal animals. Domesticates are peppered through the capitulary, both in the feeding and service of the court. Some of the animals—oxen, goats, pigs, bees, fish, chickens, and geese—appear as essential stock with little elaboration, but others, notably horses, dogs, hawks, and falcons, are subject to more extensive discussion due to their utility both in war and courtly leisure (Capitulare de Villis 2008: chs. 13–15, 36, 47, 50, 58). Dutton highlights as most notable the ornamental birds, "swans, peacocks, pheasants, ducks, pigeons, partridges and turtle doves," kept *pro dignitatis causa* (Dutton 2004b: 51; Capitulare de Villis 2008: ch. 40). Dutton emphasizes the phrase "for the sake of dignity" as an indicator of the king and later emperor's exceptional estates, but more so his social distance from subjects.

The presence of the peacock and varieties of decorative and exotic birds in particular, he writes, also represents the paradisiacal qualities of the royal estates: "Charlemagne was, in miniature imitation, stocking his estates with God's creatures like some Noah and naming them as had Adam" (Dutton 2004b: 56). Thomas Allsen cites Einhard's description of Charlemagne's "verdant pleasure park, 'encircled by many walls,' ... [within which] were meadows, streams, woods, and 'shady glades' alive with fowl, deer, and 'all kinds of wild beasts'" (Allsen 2006: 20; Smets and van den Abeele 2007: 59–79). Underscoring the paradisiacal quality of Aachen and its surroundings, this park described by Einhard represented Charlemagne's recreation of paradise in the midst of German forests. Abul Abbas would have rounded out this Germanic paradise nicely, but Charlemagne's menagerie may not have ended there, at least perhaps not in the minds of contemporaries (Dutton 2004b: 59). The eleventh-century *Song of Roland* would recall a gift offered from King Marsile to Charlemagne of "Bears and lions and chained hounds, Seven hundred camels and a thousand moulted hawks" (Burgess 1990: 128–9).

In his history of royal hunting traditions, Allsen emphasizes the symbolic "political prestige" of the gifts of exotic animals, like Abul Abbas:

The sender demonstrated generosity and command over Nature, and the recipient's status was elevated by a convincing display of distant connections ... [N]othing better demonstrated on home ground a ruler's great reach, knowledge of distant places, and his far-flung fame than a zoological garden full of strange, foreign animals. Moreover, since such beasts were ... imbued with mystery, they revealed a ruler's spiritual resources as well as his earthly powers (Allsen 2006: 234–45).

The peacocks, though, as seen in the Godescalc Evangelistary (Figure 3.4), had particularly enduring and potent cultural and religious meaning. Dutton notes that the peacock was "a standard symbol in Christian art for immortality and a token of paradise on earth ... In the golden age of his animal park, all creatures ... would return to God through Charlemagne as part of his grand

FIGURE 3.4: Fountain of life, miniature from the Godescalc Gospels, eighth century, Germany. Credit: DeAgostini/Getty Images.

scheme of world order" (Dutton 2004b: 54, 68). More impressive even, perhaps, than subduing an auroch, was the recreation of this exotic paradise.

With all of those peacocks and perhaps even more exotics strutting about and embellishing the royal estates, wardens must have been attentive to the very real threats upon these novel creatures, particularly intrusions from wild animals. Few wild beasts haunted Europe more than wolves (Pluskowski 2006; Marvin 2012). Chapter 69 of *De Villis* states that the *iudex* must inform the king of how many wolves are annually caught, with the delivery of skins to serve as verification. Eradication of wolf pups would be conducted in May, using "poison and hooks as well as . . . pits and dogs" to ferret out pests before they could grow to maturity (Capitulare de Villis 2008: ch. 69). Wolves and wild animals presented challenges to Carolingian pastoral peace, with great culls periodically in the late eighth century: "Charlemagne waged a never-ending war on wolves" (Dutton 2004b: 63; Pluskowski 2006: 103; Pastoureau 2007: 90) (Figure 3.5).

While prominent, both for strength and menace, in Germanic art and culture, wolves could challenge the stability of the pacified Christian landscape which Charlemagne had constructed. Dutton expounds upon the proliferation of animal imagery and related scholarship found at Aachen, including playful animal nicknames that brought Germanic wildness into the civilized court. Rhetorical play was one thing, but the reality of wild threats would not be tolerated: "The wild was increasingly being separated off from the civilized, the forest from the farm" (Dutton 2004b: 49). In addition to the responsible *iudices* terminating

FIGURE 3.5: She-Wolf, Hellenistic bronze, brought to Aachen Münster in the ninth century. Credit: Florian Monheim/Bildarchiv-Monheim/ArcaidImages.

wild threats, Charlemagne and his court symbolically asserted control over the wilds in recreation and hunts: "Where woods are supposed to exist they should not allow them to be excessively cut and damaged. Inside the forests they are to take good care of our game" (Capitulare de Villis 2008: ch. 36). Themes of domestication and wildness pervade Charlemagne's court, from actual to metaphorical animals. "For his courtiers," Dutton writes, "one of Charlemagne's special gifts was his power to transform the natural world" (2004b: 67).

Between his effective control of the wilds and his very own pet elephant, Charlemagne would seem to rival Roman emperors as a master of the natural world. But, returning here at the end of the chapter to where we began, larger forces could confound Charlemagne's empire and that of his successors. Even with wild threats like wolves held at bay, beyond Charlemagne's control, and more spiritually foreboding, were the larger effects of climate and weather. From 750 to 950 CE, proxy data indicate decadal or century-length episodes of warming and cooling in the northern hemisphere that produced "nine truly major winter anomalies" (McCormick *et al.* 2007: 871, 877). Beginning in the winter of 763 and ending in 940, none of the major events occurred during the reign of Charlemagne. The 763–4 episode concluded in March, while Pepin still reigned, and the next episode began in 820 under the rule of Louis the Pious. Charlemagne's era must have seen crises of some magnitude and certainly suffered from food pressures, epizootics, and, later on, ravages from metaphorical wolves from the north (perhaps including some of Skallagrim's ancestors). However, his reign did not experience widespread crop failures, severe cold, flooding, or storms of his predecessor or successor (Newfield 2013: 172). Contemporaries must have attributed some of their fortune to their dynamic and godlike king and emperor. The much later *Song of Roland* remembered his reign as a Golden Age, attributing Charlemagne with the capacity to beseech God to alter the course of nature to suit his needs:

> The emperor . . . Lies down on the ground and prays to God
> That for him he should stop the sun in its tracks,
> Postpone nightfall and maintain daylight.
> See, an angel now comes again and speaks to him;
> Immediately he commanded the king:
> "Charles, ride on, daylight will not fail you . . ."
> God performed a great miracle for Charlemagne,
> For the sun remained where it was (Burgess 1990: lines 2443, 2449–52, 2458–9).

One could argue that Charlemagne was more profoundly engaged than most emperors with the natural world because his empire had emerged from a rewilded world, following the ecological and industrial degradation brought upon Europe by Rome. In part, this is true. Charlemagne's Europe was renewed, more wild, wooded, and ready for taming than the natural worlds of his successors. Still, while not tamed, as seen in his violent encounter with an auroch or in the storms that could abrade his coasts and lands, Charlemagne's Europe was on the path to domestication. Charlemagne inherited a reforested Europe, so by degree, his engagement with nature may have been more palpable in fact. The agricultural and pastoral landscapes of Emperor Charlemagne's Europe, while occasionally assailed by real wolves and storms, was more pacified than the world which King Charlemagne had inherited. His gardens and imperial estates underscore the bucolic dominion—gardens in the wilds— that a strong emperor could create and control.

For most medieval people, we must imagine that the natural world beyond their known surroundings was a fearful place. Monstrous creatures, diabolical agents, wild animals, diseases, and disasters feature prominently in literature, art, homilies, sermons, saints' lives, and histories. In the twin disasters of the Great Famine and Black Death of the fourteenth century, along with later medieval epizootics, outbreaks of plague, changeable weather and crop-vexing storms, the age of Charlemagne must have been a rewarding era to consider, and one to which later medieval societies returned with wistful memory. Few emperors, kings, or elites of later eras, though, could reproduce the comparative splendor of Charlemagne's age, when that emperor brought order to a wild Europe, resplendent with at least one elephant and a handful of peacocks.

CHAPTER FOUR

Labor

MARTHA G. NEWMAN

"When Adam delved and Eve span, who was then the gentleman?" This famous couplet appears in Thomas Walsingham's account of the English Peasants' Revolt of 1381 (*Historia Anglicana* 2.33). According to Walsingham, the priest John Ball used the phrase in a sermon criticizing political hierarchies. Such hierarchies, Ball believed, originated in "the unjust and evil oppression of men, against the will of God, who, if it had pleased Him to create serfs, surely in the beginning of the world would have appointed who should be a serf and who a lord." Walsingham claimed that Ball advocated "first killing the great lords of the realm, then slaying the lawyers, justices and jurors, and finally rooting out everyone whom they knew to be harmful to the community in future." If they did this, the peasants could procure their "original liberty." Walsingham himself had a different opinion about peasants, viewing them as "most vile rustics," and describing them as vermin and animals gone wild. Yet it seems that most of the peasants in 1381, as well as the village officials, artisans, and Londoners who joined them, did not wish to throw off all political subjugation. Rather, they hoped to remove their immediate lords or reform their arbitrary practices, leaving in place a political system with the king at its apex (Strohm 1992; Justice 1994; Freedman 1999). Ball's sermon and Walsingham's reactions illuminate the variations within medieval discourses about labor. Walsingham reproduced demeaning language about those who worked, seeing in their rebellion animal-like qualities that further justified peasant servitude. John Ball's couplet, however, suggests that he and those who joined him had heard religious and political ideas that offered hope for the amelioration of their condition. Yet the rebels' willingness to maintain a monarchy, along with John Ball's expression of a Christian ideology of work, indicates that even these efforts to resist exploitation ultimately reproduced rather than overturned imperial discourses of hierarchy and difference.

This essay defines empire broadly. Scholars of comparative empires, including Burbank and Cooper (2010) and Tim Parsons (2010), note the prevalence of imperial organizations before the modern formation of the nation-state. Studies of premodern empires posit minimal differences between the ruling strategies of kings and emperors. According to one definition (Morris and Scheidel 2009: 18), an empire is "a territory ... ruled from a distinct organizational center ... with clear ideological and political sway over varied elites who in turn exercise power over a population in which a majority have neither access to nor influence over positions of imperial power." Other definitions emphasize cultural differences among elites and between the elites and the general population. They suggest that empires "maintain distinction and hierarchy as they incorporate new peoples," that they assume different populations within their territory will be governed differently, and that a key marker of an imperial state is that those who are without access to political power are defined as "foreign" to elites and thus subject to exploitation (Doyle 1986: 45; Burbank and Cooper: 2010: 8). Imperial ideologies also present sovereigns as responsible for linking divine and earthly order, thus creating a sacral and divinely sanctioned rule (Strathern 2016). Medieval rulers, whether Carolingian emperors, Anglo-Saxon, Angevin, or Capetian kings, or reformed popes, possessed such imperial characteristics. Even without explicitly claiming an imperial title, they asserted sovereignty over regionally powerful elites with distinct linguistic and cultural differences, and they developed discourses of universality, hierarchy, mutuality, and difference that legitimized the extraction and redistribution of the products of labor from the workers who produced them.

With the exception of archeological materials and artifacts, most of the evidence about medieval labor and those who worked was produced by educated elites. Even works of art that appear to offer realistic depictions of peasant life have ideological messages that often overshadow accurate social descriptions. As a result, a cultural history of medieval labor is more a history of attitudes toward those who worked than it is an examination of the culture of workers themselves. These discourses maintain the perspectives of their authors. They thus tend to notice the work of men more than that of women and to emphasize forms of labor that produce commodities rather than subsistence work. Still, there was no single medieval discourse on labor, and there were multiple ideologies that both supported and critiqued forms of political power and exploitation. As Thomas Walsingham's account of the Peasants' Revolt suggests, workers' own understandings of labor and politics could draw on these discourses.

An examination of labor in the context of a cultural history of medieval European empires upends the usual approaches to the study of medieval work. Most investigations of medieval labor are expressed in a Weberian key. They examine the relationship between religious conceptions of work and the nascent development of capitalist practices and ask whether there were medieval articulations of productive labor before the advent of Protestantism. Lynn White (1962) and Jacques Le Goff (1980) were two of the first scholars to discuss medieval work and social change, and many recent investigations, such as those by Ovitt (1987), Van den Hoven (1996), and Ranft (2006), continue to consider the relation of penitential and productive labor. A focus on the discourses of empire shifts the question. Instead of exploring the formation of capitalism, this essay investigates the interactions between economic developments, representations of labor, and expressions of political power. Religious ideas still play an important role, for churchmen created many of these representations, but these bishops, monks, preachers, and scholars combined interpretations of biblical ideas with the political and socioeconomic conditions they understood and supported. In creating a varied repertoire of ideas about work and workers, these churchmen reinforced the imperial positions of both secular and ecclesiastical rulers. Some of their ideas emphasized the mutual dependence of social groups arrayed under a single sovereign while others created sharp social differences that justified exploitation and servitude. Some presented a radical Christian equality, others the transformational quality of work as a penitential act that led toward salvation. In recognizing the value of work and the contributions of labor, these authors articulated ideas that workers themselves could and at times did adopt. Their root assumptions, however, supported a sociopolitical hierarchy and an elite extraction of production that remained unquestioned.

LABOR AND WORK

In modern English, "labor" is usually an abstract concept. As Raymond Williams (1983: 176–8) argues, the word designates either an economic abstraction of productive activity, as in the accumulation of labor statistics, or the social abstraction of a working class. At times, it still connotes work that involves effort and pain, but more frequently, it refers to the human activity of producing commodities by mixing material with capital. Medieval authors, however, emphasized the pain and toil. In this essay, I will use "labor" as a subset of the broader category of work and will explore not just the production of commodities but also the non-commodified work of peasants, slaves, women, and clergy that could be reproductive, penitential, or intellectual as well as productive of agricultural goods and artisanal objects.

The book of Genesis provided medieval Christian authors with two conceptions of work. On the one hand, the God in Genesis is a creator who worked for six days to form the cosmos and intended Adam and Eve to care for the garden he had created. The Latin Vulgate employs forms of *operari* to denote both God's act of creation and Adam's care for Eden. Other passages and figures from Hebrew scriptures also valorize creative work. These include Tubal-Cain in Genesis 4:22 who instructed people in metal-working, and the praise accorded to the craftspeople in Exodus 36:2 "whom the Lord had given skill" to decorate the Tabernacle. On the other hand, God's curse of Adam and Eve for their disobedience condemned them to a life of toil, pain, and sweat. In Latin, these words formed a triad of words—*labor, dolor, sudor*—that medieval authors often employed together. God's condemnation made the difficulties of labor, whether productive or reproductive, into a punishment, and God's second curse in Genesis 4:12, condemning Cain to work ground that would no longer yield to him "its strength," further amplified the point.

Passages from the New Testament also provided medieval authors with multiple messages about work and labor. In the Gospels, Jesus praised Mary's contemplation over Martha's work (Matthew 6:25–9), and he compared the apostles to the birds of the air and the lilies of the field who neither worked nor spun (Luke 12:27); he also offered rest to those who labored (Matthew 11:28). Paul's first epistle to the Thessalonians (2:9) presents the apostles' missionary work as a form of labor, for Paul included the apostles among those who, with "toil and labor," work day and night. 2 Thessalonians 3:10 also asserts that those who do not work should not eat. Yet in Galatians 3:28, Paul also advocated a radical egalitarianism, probably connected to his expectation of immanent end times, which taught that in Christ there is "neither Jew nor Gentile, neither slave nor free, nor is there male or female." As Christianity became more established within the Roman empire, the challenge faced by Christian authors was how to interpret biblical passages in ways that explained and supported rather than overturned the existing social order.

SERVITUDE AND SERFDOM

The economy of the Roman empire depended on slavery. Roman imperial ideologies seldom mentioned those who worked, but imperial monuments such as the Arch of Titus celebrated the enslavement of conquered peoples. Christopher Wickham (1994) argues that the Roman dependence on slave production began to decline as early as the second century, although archeological evidence of slave chains and shackles suggests that slavery persisted inside the Rhine-Danube borders until at least the fifth century (Henning 2008). Even if slavery was in decline, gradually replaced by the subsistence agriculture of independent peasants, late antique theologians still considered slavery a social reality in need of explanation. In seeking to justify the continuation of subjugation in a Christian empire where all Christians were equal before God, these theologians provided the underpinnings for a medieval imperial ideology in which both slaves and serfs, neither of whom had access to political power, were defined as foreign and considered subject to exploitation.

Augustine of Hippo presented political domination and the continued existence of both work and slavery as a consequence of human sinfulness. His understanding of dominion started with the household, for God's curse of Adam and Eve for their disobedience placed Eve under a new form of male control. Whereas in Eden, Eve had been subject to Adam out of affection for him, now she was subject to him because of her status as a woman. Augustine also distinguished female and male labor. Even in Eden, Eve's work was reproductive while Adam's was productive, and after the Fall, Eve was cursed to endure pain in childbirth while Adam toiled to bring forth crops from a land of thorns and thistles. Early medieval images of Adam and Eve, such as those in the Moutier-Grandval Bible (*c.* 840), depict this gendered distinction between productive and reproductive labor (Camille 1995) and such images persisted throughout the middle ages (Figure 4.1). Augustine extended this correlation

FIGURE 4.1: Eve nursing while Adam tills the soil. Hand-colored woodcut from Hartmann Schedel's *Liber Chronicarum* (Nuremberg, 1493). Credit: AF Fotografie/Alamy Stock Photo.

between sinfulness and servitude to include not only a husband's dominion over his wife but also a master's dominion over his slaves. He recognized that some people might be slaves because of the misfortunes caused by the human condition, but others were slaves because of their inferior character and their need for control and direction. He found biblical justification for these human differences. If Adam's curse had affected all of humanity, Noah's curse of Ham and his descendants explained why some people were condemned to servitude (Freedman 1999: 75–6).

Gregory the Great and Isidore of Seville echoed Augustine's argument that labor and servitude resulted from human sinfulness. Yet, as Paul Freedman (1999: 98) astutely points out, the differences between these theologians had important implications. Gregory placed more emphasis than did Augustine on the essential equality of Christians despite social distinctions. While he did not advocate the abolition of slavery, he did insist that Christ had removed the bondage of sin and made possible the restoration of human nature to its original state. Nor did Gregory link servitude to Noah's curse of Ham. Neither did Isidore of Seville, but Isidore instead hardened Augustine's position, insisting that servitude results from human sinfulness and that the dominion of some humans over others accords with the will of God since it punished people for an iniquity that has its roots in the Fall.

Medieval economies, like the Roman empire, depended on unfree labor. At times in medieval Europe, the labor and sale of slaves provided crucial resources for the elites, but more frequently, such resources were supplied by the work of serfs who owed their lords their labor but who could not be sold independently from their land. The transition from slavery to serfdom has long been considered a marker designating the advent of the medieval economy, but the dating and extent of this shift is now disputed. Slaving never fully disappeared in medieval Europe. Michael McCormick (2002) argues that the sale of enslaved people, probably captured along the eastern border of the Carolingian empire, gave the Carolingian elites the resources needed to participate in long-distance trade and to obtain the silks, spices, drugs, and gold that they desired. Adriaan Verlhust (2002: 43) notes that many Carolingian estates were still worked by slaves. Ruth Mazo Karras (1988: 10–12) and David Wyatt (2009) both associate slavery with the humiliation of conquered peoples, and they demonstrate the presence of domestic slaves, most often women, in both Anglo-Saxon and Scandinavian households. While a slave trade centered on the Baltic and North Sea seems to have diminished by the thirteenth century, the possession and sale of slaves increased in many Mediterranean lands in the later Middle Ages (Stuard 1986; Epstein 2001a; W.D. Phillips 2013). Some slaves competed against free labor in workshops, others worked large plantations in Crete and Cyprus, some rowed on galleys, but many, both male and female, worked as domestic labor. Steven Epstein suggests that slavery in Italy died out in the late

Middle Ages because the supply of white slaves for household labor disappeared, pointing toward the beginning of racial distinctions based on color that became so important for slaving in the empires of the Atlantic world. In the fifteenth and sixteenth centuries, African slaves became prominent in the Iberian peninsula and on sugar plantations of the eastern Atlantic islands, but while slavery in Europe may have provided a model for New World slavery, the number of slaves diminished in Europe as it rose in the Americas (Epstein 2001a: 191; W.D. Phillips 2013: 151–2).

Whereas the fortunes of war and conquest supplied the majority of medieval slaves, serfdom entailed the long-term subjection of a population within a ruler's territory. Adriaan Verhulst argues that it was the Carolingians who developed the bipartite estate, divided between the lord's demesne and the holdings of unfree peasants who owed their lords labor and services. Other scholars, however, associate the formation of serfdom with the "seigneurial revolution" around the year 1000 that subjected peasants to increased control and exploitation by newly powerful knights. Paul Freedman (2012) points out that there are many regional variations. Some areas of Europe, such as western France, had little serfdom; in other areas, serfdom died out by the thirteenth century; and in still others, serfdom was not imposed until the late Middle Ages. The growth of a money economy, the commutation of labor services to rents, and the expansion into newly colonized territories in the east could mitigate the conditions of an unfree peasantry.

As did patristic theologians, medieval authors sought to explain the continuation of servitude and inequality within Christian realms. Churchmen in the Carolingian imperial court repeated Augustine's position that slavery stemmed from a combination of human sinfulness and misfortune, and both Alcuin and Hrabanus Maurus again emphasized the consequences of Noah's curse for the descendants of Ham (Freedman 1999: 98). At times, Carolingian churchmen expressed a concern for the enslavement of Christians: the council of Koblenz in 922, for instance, considered the sale of Christians as slaves to be a crime similar to homicide. More often, however, legislation prohibited Jews and Muslims from holding Christian slaves rather than forbidding Christians from enslaving one another (Freedman 1999: 81; McCormick 2002: 47–9). This remained the case in the later Middle Ages as well. In the early fourteenth century, Frederick III's legislation for Sicily sought to ameliorate conditions for Christian slaves, perhaps as incentive for non-Christian slaves to convert; similarly, the fifteenth-century laws passed by the Great Council in Dubrovnik, while invoking the idea that all humans were created in the divine image, regulated rather than prohibited the traffic in slaves (Freedman 1999: 81–2; Epstein 2001a: 95). For the most part, authors who wrote about slavery associated it more with the consequences of conquest and defeat and the power of the state than with forms of labor, and they seldom noted its economic contributions.

The subjection of serfs and the exploitation of peasants created a more formidable problem, for peasants were not conquered people subject to the degradation of slavery. Nonetheless, they came to be defined as alien to the elites physically, religiously, and intellectually so as to justify the exploitation of their labor. Already in the sixth century, Caesarius of Arles emphasized the ignorance and superstition of peasants, whom he considered predestined to specific sins and vices, especially lechery, drunkenness, and the disease of leprosy (Le Goff 1980: 93). By the later Middle Ages, peasants appear in literary works as hairy, dark, and bestial. In *Aucassin and Nicolette*, Chrétien de Troyes described a cowherd as possessing a black snout, red lips, and yellow teeth, while in other romances, peasants resemble boars, wolves, oxen, or asses. Often, they appear filthy and black, a darkness that contrasts with the whiteness of the nobility. Peasants in literary depictions live amid manure, they are stupid and ignorant of Christianity, and they are either asexual or oversexed, traits that made them seem like animals (Freedman 1999: 137–73).

Explanations for these traits made them hereditary. Like slaves, peasants were considered the descendants of Ham and thus subject to Noah's curse. In the ninth century, proverbs and riddles used Ham's sin to explain the origin of *servi*, but it is unclear if these *servi* were serfs or slaves. Around 1100, Honorius Augustodunensis also associated *servi* with Ham. By the later Middle Ages, Ham became a literary character who is servile as well as ignorant and foolish. German authors made extensive use of the figure of Ham, at times associating peasants with Jews, witches, and heathens as cursed peoples. In other areas, especially those with stronger monarchies, secular narratives replaced biblical explanations for serfdom. In France, stories of Charlemagne's campaigns in Spain, drawn from the twelfth-century *Pseudo-Turpin Chronicle* but elaborated in later vernacular translations, depict Charlemagne as debasing all those who refuse to accompany him to Pamplona and condemning them to serfdom. Some versions of this story make the original crime cowardice, others desertion, but most assume the punishment became hereditary, inflicted not only on those who initially refused to fight but on their descendants as well. Such a tale also allowed later French monarchs to act with mercy in commuting this ancient punishment; royal letters of 1315 and 1318 that freed serfs in royal territory recognized the "misdeed" of their ancestors but also observed that as "Franks" they should be free (Freedman 1999: 100–13).

In Catalonia and Hungary, a late medieval imposition of serfdom made these myths politically powerful. In Catalonia, the story of Charlemagne merged with the Catalans' own heroes to create a narrative in which a Christian population enslaved by the Muslims is too timid to help the Christian princes restore the territory to the Franks. As a result, the Christian princes, who could have killed this captive population with impunity, instead in an act of mercy agree to perpetuate its servitude. The Hungarian version explained that

Hungarian serfs are descended from those who refused to muster and fight against the Magyars (Freedman 1999: 107–26). Interestingly, in England, where conquest might have been used to explain villeinage, it was not; instead, the Normans were viewed as subjecting "the English" more generally, a story which instead supported a conception of "Englishness" and suspicion of "foreigners" who controlled their government.

In his study of images of the medieval peasant, Paul Freedman (1999: 300–2) warns against a simplistic picture of peasants as alien. He argues that the broad idea of an "Other" can obscure differences between marginalized groups. Peasants differed from Jews, heretics, and Muslims in part because they comprised a majority of the European population, in part because of their proximity to the elites who tried to emphasize their differences, and in part because of their status as Christians. Sometimes, as in the case of the fourteenth-century French king, the idea that all royal subjects were Franks and thus free took precedent over ideologies of difference that explained servitude and exploitation. But the possibility of such commonality made the need to explain economic exploitation all the more pressing. In fact, many of the ideas that justified slavery were applied to peasants as well. Both slaves and peasants had been humiliated, either by defeat or cowardice, and both had inherited the curse of Ham. And even more than medieval slaves, medieval peasants seemed bestial, dark, and only partially human, characteristics that seemed all the more real in the moments when they tried to throw off their subjugation and rebel against their lords.

MUTUALITY AND CONCORD

Political and cultural discourses of concord and mutual cooperation offered an alternative way to understand the relationship of labor to political power. Medieval Europeans inherited from classical Rome the idea of an emperor as a divinely instituted ruler who not only accepted tribute from client-states but also issued laws that regulated the order of the realm and united its diverse social groups. Roman imperial ideology acknowledged a tripartite social classification of senators, equestrians, and plebians and a bipartite division between *honestiores* and *humiliores*, but these schemata did not connect the activities and products of those who worked with the power of those who ruled. Medieval sovereigns adopted Roman conceptions of peace and concord but they modified imperial ideas to stress the ways that different groups contributed to the order and wellbeing of their realms. In so doing, they recognized the importance of labor and the resources provided by those who worked. Yet these discourses of imperial concord and reciprocal relations did not fully negate discourses of difference and subjection, for their language of political cooperation ultimately excluded both peasants and women.

Carolingian emperors and the churchmen in their court drew on Roman imperial ideas but modified them. Like the Romans, the Carolingians thought emperors were responsible for regulating a universal social order, but their social categories were not those of the Romans. In his instructions to his *missi* in 802, Charlemagne commanded everyone to live in peace and love according to God's order, and he noted the different responsibilities of clerics, religious women, and laymen. Carolingian authors also divided the social orders into clergy and warriors or into clergy, monks, and "the people" (Constable 1995: 275–6). At times, agricultural laborers appear in these lists. Haimo of Auxerre, for instance, described a Carolingian social order consisting of priests, soldiers, and *agricultores* as he thought these groups corresponded to the Roman tripartite categories. The ninth-century *Capitulare de Villis*, which describes the management of imperial estates and asserts an imperial ordering of agriculture, animal husbandry, and crafts, also suggests the Carolingians recognized the importance of workers for the maintenance of their empire (Nelson 2002: 38–9). At times, emperors even regulated the exactions lords could expect from their peasants. Responding to a complaint from peasants, for instance, Charlemagne in 800 limited the labor services lords could demand (Verhulst 2002: 48). Later emperors also at times issued legislation that demonstrated an interest in regulating the social order. In 1152, for instance, Frederick Barbarossa's *Landfriede* invoked the idea of a *pax Romana*, through which he not only sought to enforce human and divine laws, but he also distinguished between peasants and knights and established fair prices and practices in economic activities (Freedman 1999: 85–7).

Such imperial expressions of interest in labor did not always reflect actual working conditions. Charlemagne's court produced the first artistic renderings of the agricultural labors associated with each month, but, as Carl Hammer (1997: 27) argues, these images derived from classical mosaics rather than an interest in the tools and tasks of contemporary peasants. As parts of two computational and astronomical manuscripts from the early ninth century, these pictures demonstrate Charlemagne's imperial task of "ordering human affairs in the context of nature and the cosmos," a task that included his renaming the months and winds as well (Hammer 1997: 51). Similarly, in the twelfth century, when Frederick Barbarossa's imperial laws attempted to separate peasants from military men, Frederick paid little attention to the reality of the *ministeriales* who, as unfree knights, actually participated in both categories. Even the Luttrell Psalter, a fourteenth-century English manuscript that has often been used as a mirror of medieval life and labor, is an ideological construct that depicts a divinely established social hierarchy in which peasants peacefully produce bounty from the earth to support a lord who rules his household as God rules the heavens. It portrays an imagined world, not an actual one (Emmerson and Goldberg 2000: 62).

The idea that sovereigns controlled a harmonious society that included workers became an important way to express royal power. In ninth-century England, as Alfred the Great restructured the kingdom of Wessex to resist Viking invasions and as his successors gained control over other English kingdoms, churchmen described the "prayer-men, army-men, and work-men" as the tools needed for these kings to reign. As with the laborers on Charlemagne's calendar, this classification probably did not depict social reality since many of the Anglo-Saxons who labored also fought, but it was an assertion of monarchical power and ideology at a time when the monarchy was in peril (Duby 1978: 100–1). The classification emerged again in the late tenth and early eleventh centuries when the kings of the English again faced invasions and the churchmen Aelfric and Wulfstan described the *laboratores* as one of the three pillars supporting the throne. In continental Europe, two eleventh-century bishops, Adalbero of Laon and Gerard of Cambrai, also articulated this trifunctional view of society. Their classifications too supported a threatened sovereign, this time a Carolingian king endangered by the seigneurial revolution of the early eleventh century (Duby 1978: 13–60; Constable 1995: 279).

Scholars disagree as to whether this trifunctional social theory recognized the importance of labor and whether it ameliorated conditions of work. Georges Duby argues that the theory supported seigneurial exploitation and that any expression of concern for those who worked was a pious fabrication. Paul Freedman disagrees, pointing out that figures such as Adalbero of Laon not only noted the productive nature of agricultural work but also recognized the labor by which peasants furnished their masters with riches (Freedman 1999: 23–4). Just as Charlemagne had sought to regulate what lords could extract from their peasants, so at times authors depicted the kings' obligations toward the social groups in their realms. In the twelfth century, for instance, the English chronicler John of Worcester described a dream of King Henry I; the illustration of this dream shows a sleeping Henry threatened by the three social groups over whom he ruled. Peasants, knights, and churchmen each hold their characteristic tools and implements, and the images imply that the king has not kept his obligations to any of these groups, including the peasants (Figure 4.2). Other twelfth-century authors also recognized that it was due to the work of the *aratores* that those who fought and those who prayed could avoid living in poverty (Constable 1995: 315).

Not every scheme to classify the orders in a harmonious political society was tripartite. In his mid-twelfth-century *Policraticus*, John of Salisbury provided a picture of the body politic, claiming he based his image on a letter of instruction to the Roman emperor Trajan. John's commonwealth has the clergy at its soul and the king at its head, but its limbs and organs were those whom John thought supported royal power. Most of the body consists of royal officials—the kings' counselors, his judges, his financial officers, tax collectors, and soldiers—but

FIGURE 4.2: Henry I's dream, from John of Worcester's *Chronicon ex chronicis*, c. 1140. Credit: Corpus Christi College, Oxford, MS 157 p. 382./Bridgeman Images.

the feet are artisans and peasants since they "erect, sustain and move forward the mass of the whole body" (5.1–2). Similarly, a fourteenth-century *Book on the Game of Chess* also divides political society into king and queen, royal officials, and the "humbler occupations," represented by the pawns (Constable 1995: 339). In these political discourses, female labor remained invisible. Not only responsible for the reproductive labor of childrearing, peasant women joined their husbands in agricultural labor (Figure 4.3), they received wages for their work—although at a lesser rate than the men—and, by the later Middle Ages, they participated in local commerce, especially in the part-time activities of brewing and baking that could supplement household income (Bennett, 1986; Hanawalt 1986). Yet women's work was not recognized in discussions of the labor that supported the political order.

FIGURE 4.3: Adam and Eve tilling the soil. West façade, Modena Cathedral, Italy, c. 1106. Credit: Realy Easy Star/Toni Spagone/Alamy Stock Photo.

Already by the twelfth century, John of Salisbury's image of the body politic recognized artisans and differentiated them from peasants. By the early thirteenth century, as urban-based commerce and trade became an increasingly important source of revenue for sovereigns, this distinction became more common, separating townspeople, sometimes now called *cives* in an echo of Roman republican ideas, from the rural peasantry. In many cases, agricultural labor became less visible. The *Philippiad*, a Vergilian epic celebrating King Philip Augustus's victory at Bouvines in 1214, presents Philip as a French sovereign supported by the clergy, the knights, the townspeople, and the *rustici*. In his analysis of this poem, however, Georges Duby shows that these *rustici* are depicted as outsiders to the political order, unable to sing praises to the victor and stupefied by their participation in a celebration for which they did not have an accustomed place (Duby 1978, 346–53). By the fourteenth century, when Jean Gerson wrote to the teacher of the French Dauphin, he described the three orders in the French kingdom as the "fighters, the clerics, and the townsmen" (Constable 1995: 399). Later royal entries, which echoed imperial processions of Roman emperors, also excluded rural labor, celebrating instead the three estates where the third estate comprised the bankers and the guild masters who controlled the labor in their shops rather than those who actually worked (Bryant 1986; Ruiz 2012). Such ideologies presented the actors within a political body and started to distinguish the civic participation of a new urban class from the toil of peasants, a distinction that continued through the meeting of the Estates General leading up to the French Revolution (Duby 1978: 355–6).

The inclusion of urban citizens in these political discourses did not mean the full political participation of urban artisans and wage laborers. As Steven Epstein (1991) and Antony Black (1984) have argued, urban guilds in medieval cities were only one of many possible corporate entities, and except for a few cities in which a select number of guilds became politically powerful, most medieval cities were controlled by merchants, by magnates with rural interests, or, as in the case of Paris, directly by a king. The formation of guilds in the twelfth and thirteenth centuries recognized the importance of artisanal production and trade, but for the most part they expressed the regulatory and communal interests of the masters who owned the shops rather than the interests of the wage laborers and apprentices (Epstein 1991: 190–204). The guilds' lack of political participation in urban government allowed women to work and control workshops and to act within a market economy, for as long as these shops were considered part of a domestic economy, women could be employed by their spouses and, as widows, could act as head of the household. However, as Martha Howell (1986) has shown, once these economic organizations entered the political realm, women were pushed out of such high-status work in part by the actions of guilds and city councils and in part by the animosity of journeymen who competed with women for wage positions.

In thirteenth-century Paris, royal efforts to regulate and tax urban artisans illuminate many of the occupations in the city and the precision with which the kings' officials categorized them. The *Livre des métiers*, assembled by the provost of Paris in the mid-thirteenth century, contains the regulations of some 101 different communities of workers, while tax roles from the decades around 1300 list well over 1,000 occupations (Archer 1995: 156). Both men and women were among those with enough revenue to be taxed; women made up nearly fourteen percent of the names on the tax roles, and they worked in some 253 different *métiers*. Many of these women worked in sales, peddling, cloth-making, and needlework professions. Some guilds had so many women that their regulations used female pronouns. These included the silk spinners, the ribbon makers, and those embroidering in gold; the guilds of small purse makers, bath house keepers, and poulterers also had large numbers of women (Archer 1995: 108–10). Still, only a quarter of the households in Paris were subject to this taxation. Nobles, the clergy, and students were excluded, but so were the wage earners without business inventories or with insufficient income to tax. These people probably comprised the great majority of the population within the city. Missing as well from such royal surveillance were the large numbers of domestic servants as well as the non-working poor who relied on begging and charity and whose inability to work was viewed with suspicion (Farmer 2002: 60–70).

Political discourses of concord and mutual cooperation recognized the importance of labor but only to the extent that workers seemed to contribute to the wellbeing of the realm. Such work was productive, for it supplied political elites with food, goods, and taxes and, as with any system in which people lived off the labor of others, exploitation and brutality were tempered by the need to have a living and reproducing workforce. Discourses of mutuality thus allowed sovereigns to express their magnanimity and offer their protection to the poor and powerless who, at times, reminded their kings of their obligations. Nonetheless, the language of mutual cooperation maintained a hierarchy in which the peasants and wage laborers comprised the feet of the body politic, if they were present at all. Mutuality and subjection formed two sides of the same coin, for both served to justify the extraction of surplus production from those who created it.

WORK, PENANCE, AND THE PRODUCTION OF THE SELF

Medieval sovereigns were not alone in making imperial claims. The institution of the Church did as well, asserting a universal rule that could create a divine order on earth and institute peace. Many churchmen who had articulated discourses on labor in support of a political economy and royal sovereignty also considered labor within an economy of salvation, developing a variety of biblical interpretations that understood labor not only as productive of goods but also as productive of the self. Work reshaped natural resources into useful commodities but concurrently served as a form of penance that reshaped the virtues of those who undertook it. This created a discourse of work that extended its possibilities to all Christians. At the same time, however, churchmen also limited the universality of this language, creating social and intellectual hierarchies and distinctions that disparaged manual labor and allowed religious elites to live off the production of others.

Augustine of Hippo viewed servitude as the result of sin and misfortune but he also understood work as part of the process of redemption. Certainly, the toil and pain of labor—whether productive or reproductive—stemmed from Adam and Eve's disobedience, but like other early monastic writers, he also viewed work as part of God's initial plan for his creation, for Adam had been formed in order to work and care for Eden (MacCormack 2002: 231–3). In his treatise *De opere monachorum*, written to rebuke monks in Carthage who wished to be like the lilies of the field and devote themselves to a labor-free life of prayer, Augustine used both Genesis 2:15 and the Pauline injunction that those who do not work should not eat to insist that monks had a duty to work, especially at agricultural labor and crafts. Such labor was not intended for the production of goods so much as to prevent the dangers associated with idleness and sloth. Furthermore, not all were fit to work. Augustine noted that monks from the upper classes who could not endure the strain of manual work could be exempt, as could those who were occupied in pastoral cares such as preaching and administering the sacraments (van den Hoven, 1996: 144–5; MacCormack 2002: 227–30).

The Benedictine Rule also advocated manual labor for monks. In offering a rule for beginners, it placed less emphasis on the possibility that monks might become a community resembling the apostles and more on the importance of controlling human willfulness. Monks should work, Benedict thought, to avoid temptation, and his chapter on manual labor emphasized the importance of reading as well as agricultural work, for both could prevent idleness and gossip. Benedict repeatedly insisted that manual labor should not burden the monks or drive them away. Those who were "truly monastics" he wrote, "live by the labor of their hands as did our Fathers and the Apostles," but at the same time, "let all things be done in moderation, for the sake of the faint-hearted" (48.8–9). A similar concern for preventing idleness appears in women's rules. Caesarius of Arles' late antique rule for women, for instance, prescribed the manufacture of cloth as part of the process of learning devotion and humility (Ovitt 1987: 185).

Carolingian interpreters of the Benedictine Rule continued to advocate the importance of manual labor for religious communities, in part to encourage institutional independence but also to combat luxury and *acedia* and encourage a growth in the virtues (Williams 2012: 19–42). The Benedictine Rule may have offered a picture of a self-sufficient community with workshops and gardens staffed by the monks, but it also presented the mix of manual labor, prayer, and reading in such a way as to allow later monks to consider intellectual and spiritual activities as satisfying their obligations to avoid idleness. Cluniac monastic ideals downplayed the manual labor of monks, emphasizing instead the importance of prayer and the enactment of an angelic life on earth. Cluny's estates, in fact, provide a prime example of a new seigneurial exploitation around the millennium, as the monastery's revenues depended on the labor services and payments of its subject peasantry.

Similarly, just as Carolingian churchmen understood *agricultores* as one of the components of a social order supporting the emperor, so churchmen viewed those who worked as supporting those who provided for society's salvation. In articulating a tripartite vision of society, Haymo and Heiric of Auxerre assumed it was the role of those who labored, whether as peasants or as military men, to support those who prayed and performed masses (Nelson 2002: 40). Haymo went further, distinguishing those with wisdom from those with practical knowledge of organizing human affairs. While all who carried out their work faithfully would receive a reward, Haymo nonetheless argued that the common folk who "toil for the benefit of others, by planting, building, working the land," would receive a lesser reward due to their less perfect state (Nelson 2002: 39–40). Yet some churchmen also worried that they exacted too much. In 858, the bishop Hincmar of Reims addressed a letter to other bishops, asking them to ensure that estate agents not oppress their peasants or ask more of them than they had in the past (Verhulst 2002: 48). As local lords increased their control over their peasants in the tenth and eleventh centuries, other churchmen expressed similar concerns. Still, they were more likely to articulate a general concern for "the poor" than for particular categories of laborers, and they still assumed that the other orders of society, whether agricultural workers or those wielding a sword, existed to support the clergy's salvific work of prayer (Duby 1978: 134–9). In the early thirteenth century, the English archbishop, Stephen Langton, composed a set of commentaries on the biblical prophets that warned prelates against oppressing others and accused them of being tyrants who drank the blood of the poor (Freedman 1999: 47–9).

In the eleventh and twelfth centuries, the communities of monks and nuns who experimented with new ways of enacting a penitential life articulated a variety of attitudes toward work and labor. Some, such as the early Cistercians and other communities of hermits, insisted on manual labor for all their members. Bernard of Tiron, who lived with a group of followers in the woods in Brittany, limited the number of daily psalms so that his community could live off its own labor; similarly, a group of hermits at Affligem in Belgium asserted that "we could not discover a more rightful or devout path of salvation than that we should gain nourishment and clothing by the labors of our hands and remain content with these" (Leyser 1984: 56). Among the Cistercians, aristocratic men voluntarily took on the work of peasants. Bernard of Clairvaux argued that the only form of labor with spiritual value was work done voluntarily in conformity with the labor, sweat, and pain of Christ; labor done out of necessity or because of the desire for the goods produced had no merit (Newman 2012: 112) (Figure 4.4). The Cistercians' stories about their lay brothers—men who, over the course of the twelfth century, took on the majority of the monasteries' agricultural tasks—suggest that the lay brothers' tasks would bring them into contact with God and conform them to the model of Jesus. Cistercian women who, among other tasks, cared for the poor and sick in hospices, viewed their work in much the same way (Lester 2011). Interestingly, when the lay brothers started to rebel in the late twelfth century, it was not their labor that they objected to but their unequal treatment (Newman 1996: 101–6).

Other new monasteries placed less stress on the pain and sweat of manual labor and more on the concord of communities whose members each contributed using the skills they possessed. The Carthusians, for instance, divided their monasteries between monks and lay brothers and made room in their daily schedule for manual labor, but they distinguished the manual labor of their lay

FIGURE 4.4: Cistercian monks at work, in Alexander of Bremen's *Expositio in Apocalypsim*, ca. 1250. Cambridge University Library MS Mm. 5.31 fol. 113. Credit: ART Collection/Alamy Stock Photo.

brothers from the monks' work copying manuscripts. Manuscript copying, the monks argued, was a form of preaching: "we preach the word of God with our hands since we cannot do so with our lips," one Carthusian prior argued. Similarly, once the followers of the hermit Stephen of Muret established a community with defined customs, the rule for Grandmont too divided tasks between the monks and the lay brothers, giving the lay brothers the authority to run the community but noting that "the better part which the Lord praised so highly in Mary, we impose upon the clerics alone . . . they will be the servers of spiritual realities both to themselves as well as to the other brethren who confess their sins to them." Like the Carolingian churchmen who described the mutual contribution of different orders of society, these monks emphasized the cooperation of the different groups with their monasteries and the utility of different forms of work as they assisted one another. As one Carthusian wrote, "all are called to a life in which manual labor and prayer are indissolubly united, albeit in different ways" (all quotes from Ranft 2006: 142).

Other monastic authors, however, found this new emphasis on labor to be demeaning. Rupert of Deutz, for instance, criticized the Cistercians' manual labor, finding it shocking that they neglected the priestly office of the mass to spend time cutting down trees and gathering the harvest (van Engen 1983:

319). Many priests, whether regular canons, monks, or secular clergy, understood their own work preaching, baptizing, and administering the sacraments to be the work of Christ (Ranft 2006: 94). This view of work was associated with the growing self-consciousness of a priestly caste that emphasized its control of the sacraments and its care for the salvation of the laity. It was an attitude tied more to the growing authority and evangelical impulses of a newly imperial Church than to either the economic impact of the laboring classes or the penitential efforts of religious figures who desired to reform themselves.

By the early thirteenth century, moral theologians and preachers became interested in classifying groups within Christian society so that they could help people avoid the sins and foster the virtues considered characteristic to specific occupations. The preacher Jacques de Vitry used a corporeal metaphor similar to John of Salisbury's body politic to describe a Church that united in one body under the head of Christ people "of differing conditions" and with "different types of talents entrusted to them by the Lord." Both he and the Dominican Humbert of Romans divided Christian society into categories: at times they separated society by monastic order and clerical status, at times by occupation, and at times by marital status. Both Jacques and Humbert celebrated the manual labor of peasants. Jacques thought agricultural labor a particularly praiseworthy form of work since "without agriculture and manual labor, society would not be able to survive." When arguing that "those who labor with the intention that they fulfill the penance ordered by God" were more praiseworthy than churchmen or praying monks, however, Jacques at the same time implied that peasants should be satisfied with their difficult life on earth (Freedman 1999: 33; Farmer 2002: 49). Humbert too suggested that peasant life could best please God since work is not only penitential but also necessary for food, for providing alms to the poor, and for preventing idleness (van den Hoven 1996: 235–6). Thomas Aquinas provided nearly identical explanations for work in his *Summa theologica* (2.2.187.3), for he argued that work provides food, prevents idleness, curbs desire, and offers the wherewithal for alms, and he offered five biblical passages (Genesis 3:19; Psalm 128:2; Sirach 33:28–9; 2 Corinthians 6:5–6; Ephesians 4:28) in support of his argument.

Both Jacques and Humbert recognized women's work. Jacques celebrated the manual labor of his friend, the beguine Mary of Oignies, seeing the voluntary work of religious women as a form of penance. Nonetheless, when Jacques and Humbert addressed sermons to secular women, they classified women's work according to reproductive labor and focused on issues of sexuality. Jacques's sermon to maidservants warns about sexual dangers and reproduces language that degraded those who worked by describing female servants as "lusting cows" and over-sexed cats; Humbert worried that peasant women were particularly susceptible to sorcery and to sexual promiscuity and that their simplicity and intellectual failings would lead them astray (Farmer 2002:

FIGURE 4.5: Adam tilling and Eve spinning. Fifteenth-century church wall painting. Broughton, UK. Credit: Holmes Garden Photos/Alamy Stock Photo.

109–16). It is also possible to see a new recognition of female work in the iconography of urban cathedrals. In the windows in the cathedrals at Chartres and Lincoln, as well as in late medieval wall paintings, Adam digs and Eve spins. Both sexes had become responsible for productive labor, but this labor was distinguished by gender (Figure 4.5).

Intertwined with these moralists' recognition of labor and work was an insistence that intellectual work be superior to manual labor. In defending mendicant ideals against those who criticized the friars for living off the alms of the faithful, some medieval scholars repeated earlier arguments that preaching and other pastoral tasks are a "labor of wisdom" that can replace other forms of work. They drew on Aristotelian ideas about natural fitness, accepting as natural the rule of elites over inferiors and arguing that some people were especially suited for servile labor because of their physical strength and lack of reason (Freedman 1999: 82–3). Even Humbert of Romans, who articulated a sympathy for those who labored, compared those who lacked intellect to beasts; Jacques de Vitry, who considered the penitential labor of husbandmen more praiseworthy than the prayers of monks, worried that the poor would detest and blaspheme God for their difficulties (Farmer 2002: 46–9). Churchmen may have articulated the universality of a labor that could reform the self but they did not upend ingrained social and political hierarchies.

CONCLUSION

Medieval sovereigns did not always call themselves emperors. Yet medieval polities, whether secular or ecclesiastical, royal or imperial, possessed imperial characteristics in that their sovereigns ruled over culturally diverse elites who themselves controlled people who had little if any access to political power. The imperial ideologies that supported these sovereigns may have sought to unite disparate elites, but they also separated those who labored from the rest of society so as to make workers alien to those who profited from their work. Agricultural workers supported the rest of society, but this support placed them at the bottom of the social hierarchy; wage laborers remained invisible in urban political systems that recognized those who owned the shops but not those who worked in them; and women were still generally associated with their reproductive rather than productive labor. Even the idea of labor as penance, which could be applied to all Christians due to the consequences of the Fall, maintained sociopolitical distinctions for such work had greater penitential value when voluntary.

Yet these imperial discourses also contained elements that ameliorated the conditions of those who worked. Ideologies of mutual cooperation implied that sovereigns should care for all in their realm, and when rulers issued laws, they at times enacted this magnanimity. The images of Henry II's dream suggest that sovereigns could be haunted if they forgot such obligations. Churchmen also worried about the mistreatment of the poor, and figures such as Stephen Langton invoked the language of the biblical prophets to warn elites about their behaviors. By the late Middle Ages, agricultural and urban laborers drew on some of these ideas to speak and protest for themselves (Freedman 1999: 60–3). Still, their rebellions were neither long-lived nor successful, and in many cases, the protests themselves further solidified discourses of difference and exploitation.

Historians studying work have often asked when medieval conceptions of labor shifted from penitential to productive. The assumption behind this question associates productive labor with the development of capitalism. Although the question considers the nature of work, it is less interested in the worker. In fact, as Christopher Wickham (2008) reminds us, factors that create "economic development" might not benefit those whose production spurs such development. An exploration of labor and empire in medieval Europe does not help us hear directly the voices of those who worked, for at best these voices are mediated through the language of the literate elites who described them. Yet, as Sharon Farmer's work on the poor in Paris has shown, understanding discourses of power can help us reconstruct these mediated voices. The medieval churchmen who articulated imperial ideologies associated labor with both a political economy and an economy of salvation, and they viewed labor as simultaneously productive and penitential, capable of producing goods, children, and a reformed self. Perhaps workers too celebrated their production and their position supporting the rest of society, and perhaps they patiently accepted that the penitential value of their work would bring them rest in a world to come. But perhaps, as the preachers and moralists feared, they cursed and resented their lot in life and desired rest on earth. John Ball's couplet suggests that they may have heard the implications of the discourses of mutuality and demanded that they be enacted. Such requests did not overthrow the political and gendered hierarchies of medieval Europe but they did ask for their reformation.

CHAPTER FIVE

Mobility

SHAYNE AARON LEGASSIE

If you close your eyes and try to picture everyday life during the Middle Ages, chances are that you will conjure up a relatively predictable tableau. Perhaps it will be peasants toiling away in a field, or a solitary monk poring over ancient tomes in a gloomy, vaulted cell. You might picture a crenellated tower besieged by catapults or a tapestried hall made merry by feasts and dancing. There is always the market town with its winding alleyways, snaking inward into itself behind its stout, gated walls. The romantically inclined might imagine a gargoyle-encrusted cathedral vaulting toward the sky, or—if so disposed—a tenebrous dungeon filled to capacity with luckless captives. Simply put: the settings most routinely associated with the Middle Ages are some combination of craggy and imposing, isolated and self-enclosed, traditional and agrarian; they paint, in other words, the picture of an epoch that seems utterly antithetical to the idea of "mobility."

There is no doubt that hoary myth of the Dark Ages has conditioned the way that scholars and non-specialists alike think about mobility in the period that spans 800–1450. In discussions of the earlier side of the Middle Ages, for instance, underwhelmed comparisons to classical Rome and late antiquity are not uncommon. Let us stipulate, as seems reasonable, that the collapse of the western Roman empire in 476 inaugurated a prolonged period of "decreased" mobility in much of Europe. Such an observation may be generally true, but it is not very useful, precisely because it subsumes many significant, interesting qualitative differences under the umbrella of a single quantitative one. For example, the construction of roads in early medieval Europe was less centralized than it had been under the Roman empire, but it also linked places that imperial roads had not, since medieval road construction met the needs of more local nodes of administration and commerce, as opposed to being dictated by a single military strategy hatched by the denizens of a capital city. As a result, certain small settlements were connected to more trade routes than they had been before the period of "decreased" mobility (Verdon 2003: 15–28) known as the early Middle Ages.

In general, dark-ages rhetoric obscures the regional and temporal variation in long-distance travel and trade. The flourishing trade in elephant ivory objects in Carolingian Cologne is one of many tangible indications that Peregrine Horden and Nicholas Purcell are correct to suggest that some previous scholars have exaggerated the isolation of Frankish Europe from the medieval Mediterranean during the early Middle Ages (2000: 153–73). The Vikings voyaged over a vast geographical expanse, which included the North Atlantic, central Eurasia, and the Mediterranean. In fact, archaeologists continue to unearth Viking hoards in Scandinavia and northern Britain that contain coins minted in Samarkand, Cordoba, and Baghdad (Figure 5.1). Of course, between the ninth and eleventh centuries, the Vikings also colonized Iceland, Greenland, and Newfoundland, by certain measures outstripping even the Roman empire in the process (Jones 1968: 145–311; Seaver 1996).

FIGURE 5.1: Hoard of silver and Arabic-inscribed coins from a Viking grave, Sweden, tenth century. Credit: CM Dixon/Print Collector/Getty Images.

As is true of the early Middle Ages, the material realities of later-medieval mobility shifted in response to ongoing commercial and territorial disputes. The evolution of routes taken by crusading armies offers one dramatic example. During the First Crusade (1095–9), Latin Christian forces voyaged from modern-day France and Germany to Jerusalem almost entirely by land, via the Baltics, Constantinople, central Anatolia, and Syria. This route would not have been viable were it not for the crusaders' temporary military victories over Seljuk forces in Anatolia—gains that were decisively and permanently reversed by 1103 (Mackay 1997: 86–7). Future military leaders could not, therefore, count on following in the footsteps of the first crusaders, nor did they have to. The crusading campaigns of Holy Roman Emperor Frederick II (1228–9) and King Louis IX of France (1248–50) took advantage of the expansion of Latin Christian power in the eastern Mediterranean, transporting troops to the Holy Land almost entirely by sea, in stark contrast to the overwhelmingly terrestrial routes that characterized the First Crusade (Mackay 1997: 88–90). Frederick departed from Brindisi, passed along the increasingly Venetian-dominated coastline of the Peloponnese, and onward to Crete (which had been conquered by Venice in 1212) before arriving to the crusader stronghold of Acre. Louis reached Acre having embarked from Aigues-Mortes and having first stopped over in Cyprus, which had been under Francophone control since 1192, when it was purchased from the Knights Templar by Guy of Lusignan. Almost all of the above-mentioned Latin Christian gains came at the expense of the Byzantine empire, which notoriously came under the attack of crusading armies in the Third and—especially—the Fourth Crusades (1189–92 and 1202–4, respectively).

On the other side of 1450 looms another factor that distorts modern perceptions of medieval mobility: "The Renaissance," with all of its attendant hyperbole regarding the new and unprecedented. In reality, the ideologies and circuits of mobility that define the early modern world are, in many cases, built upon the footprint of the high-to-late Middle Ages. For this reason, this essay will focus primarily on the period spanning 1100–1500. During these centuries, Eurasia enjoyed a degree of cross-cultural integration that seldom ceases to surprise even those who have devoted their scholarly lives to studying late-medieval trade and travel. In the wake of the First Crusade, the victorious Latin Christians suddenly found that they had political, economic, and spiritual interests in parts of the world that, up until that point, had seemed far removed from their daily concerns. Along with the Crusades, the Norman conquests of England and southern Italy heralded the expansion of a French-speaking "aristocratic diaspora," which spread from the British Isles to central Europe, from Sicily to the Holy Land (Bartlett 1993: 18–21, 101–5). Scholars continue to shed new light on the slightly later, but no less remarkable, expansion of Aragonese influence in the Mediterranean (Fernández-Armesto 1987; Abulafia 1994). The same is true of the contemporaneous Castilian and Portuguese explorations of the Atlantic, which "discovered" Madeira, the Azores, and the Canary Islands, while paving the way for the circumnavigation of Africa and Columbus' journeys to the Americas (Fernández-Armesto 1987; Russell 2000). Late-medieval Venice and Genoa established rival commercial empires in the Mediterranean and Black Seas, often triumphing over powerful military adversaries such as the Byzantine empire and the Crowns of France and Aragon (Abu-Lughod 1989: 102–34; Epstein 2001b; Georgopoulou 2001).

From these eastern Mediterranean bases, Italian merchants and missionary friars followed land and maritime routes into Persia, India, China, and other regions of east Asia, thanks to the Mongol empire's efficient administration of trans-Eurasian traffic. Together, these developments laid the foundations for the journeys of unprecedented numbers of missionaries, pilgrims, traders, crusaders, diplomats, and scholars. Even after the Black Death (1346–53) and the fragmentation of the Mongol empire rendered overland travel through central Asia less feasible than before, maritime trade routes continued to connect India to the eastern Mediterranean and—by extension—to western Europe. Collectively, these realities challenge many of the assumptions that depict the early modern period as one that broke radically with a medieval past that was insular and complacent in its attitude toward the larger world.

NEW HORIZONS

On an otherwise dull Italian evening in 1332, the Dominican friar Menentillus of Spoleto unexpectedly intercepted a letter sent from Khanbaliq (modern-day Beijing). Its author was the late Franciscan missionary John of Montecorvino (1247–1328), who oversaw the construction of the first two Latin Christian churches in China (in 1299 and 1305). Menentillus copied the epistle—which included astronomical measurements taken by John in various regions of Asia—and dispatched it with all possible haste to fellow Dominican Bartolomeo of Santo Concordio, with the affectionate salutation: "Dear Brother, I know the great curiosity (*chura*) you have about all branches of learning ... especially those things that are unknown to you" (Yule 1914–16: I.209–10).

This exchange typifies the late medieval enthusiasm for cutting-edge geographical knowledge, and—for this same reason—it flies in the face of much received wisdom. Stereotype depicts the Middle Ages as a period that cleaved dogmatically to ancient *auctores* such as Aristotle, Cicero, and Augustine, while greeting new geographical ideas with a mixture of indifference and twitching paranoia. Anthony Grafton (1992: 13) serves up a typical version of this alleged attitude when he writes: "In 1500, European thinkers saw their world as a narrow, orderly place ... in which few surprises could await the explorer of the past or the present." In reality, not only did medieval people eagerly seek out new geographical knowledge, they also engaged in searching debates about the reliability of the ancient texts, even though they certainly respected and placed considerable faith in them.

Anticipating the wonderstruck pronouncements that accompanied the "discovery" of the Americas, numerous medieval voices lauded their age as one of unprecedented advance in the field of geographical exploration. Marco Polo boasted that he had traveled more widely than any man "since Adam" (Polo 1928: 305–6). This apparently included Alexander the Great, one of the only figures from antiquity mentioned by Polo and his writing partner Rustichello da Pisa. Alexander's quasi-historical conquests of Persia and south Asia were the subject of a fantastical body of literature that, for centuries, served as a principal source of European information about Asia (Cary 1956; Boyle 1977). Indeed, the Greek hero became a benchmark against which medieval travelers like Polo measured themselves. In the 1350s, John Marignolli, a Franciscan missionary from Florence, proclaimed that he had seen—*and* had ventured *beyond*—the monument that marked the easternmost extent of Alexander's Asian itinerary. Not to be outdone, John erected his own marble memorial, to the east of Alexander's. Bearing his family crest and inscriptions in Latin and "Indian," the monument was "intended to last until the world's end" (Yule 1914–16: III.218). Nearly a century later, Poggio Bracciolini (1857: 4) asserted that the Venetian merchant Nicolò di Conti had voyaged "farther than any other traveler" including Alexander the Great—and, one assumes, Marco Polo.

Although humanism is often imagined as an epochal break with the Middle Ages, its early practitioners, like Poggio, spoke of the history of mobility and geographical discovery in ways that seem perfectly "medieval" in their competitiveness. In addition to recording Nicolò's recollections of India, Sri Lanka, and Sumatra, Poggio also quizzed an Ethiopian dignitary visiting Rome about the source of the Nile, motivated by "a great desire to learn things unknown to ancient writers, *and especially to Ptolemy*, who was the first to write upon this subject" (Bracciolini 1857: 34, emphasis added). Even Petrarch grudgingly conceded that his contemporaries had surpassed the cultural achievements of antiquity in at least one area: navigation. In a 1363 letter written from Venice, Petrarch describes the departure of a towering cargo ship, and imagines its itinerary as it "crosses the Ganges and the Caucasus . . . [and] arrives in India, farthest China, and the Eastern Ocean." He also notes that, if Tiphys—the helmsman of the Argonauts—were still alive, he would "blush" at the fame he had won for the paltry pond-hop that yielded the Golden Fleece (Petrarch 2005: I.62).

As the earlier comments collectively suggest, medieval intellectuals were acutely aware that they could not rely on classical texts for a full and accurate picture of the world. Indeed, travelers were struck by the inaccuracies of not only pagan philosophers but also Christian *auctores*. John of Montecorvino was met with blank stares when he asked residents of India and China about the location of the Garden of Eden, which theological speculation often placed in east Asia (Yule 1914–16: III.213).[1] Franciscan William of Rubruck measured the circumference of the Caspian Sea, and, in so doing, discovered that Isidore of Seville had been wrong when he wrote that it emptied into the ocean (Wyngaert 1929: I.211; Dawson 1966: 213). William's investigations also led him to refute the claim—made by both Isidore and Solinus—that monsters inhabited the eastern extremities of the world map (Wyngaert 1929: I.269; Dawson 1966: 170). In a similar vein, John Marignolli—perhaps thinking of the legends surrounding Alexander—criticized "histories and romances" for perpetuating belief in dragons, dog-headed humans, and the like (Yule 1914–16: III.254–5).

Somewhat more surprisingly, John cited his experience as a traveler in order to argue that the official Bible of the Roman Church should be revised to correct what he believed was a glaring error. According to John, the Vulgate Bible erred in stating that Adam and Eve wore animal skins after they were ejected from Eden. He proposed that a careless scribe had somehow converted the word *filiceas*—vegetable fiber—into *pelliceas*—fur hood. John first hatched this theory in India, after acquiring a comfortable waterproof tunic fashioned from a plant-based fabric. The much-cherished garment accompanied John back to Florence, and his fellow Franciscans deposited it in the sacristy of the Church of Santa Croce, perhaps because they were convinced of the object's relevance to scripture (Yule 1914–16: III.22, III.240–1). The case of John illustrates that not even *the* most authoritative of texts—the Vulgate Bible—was immune from the repercussions of geographic discovery in this era of ever-expanding horizons.

MOBILITY AND IDENTITY

The reintegration of Latin Christian societies into broader circuits of travel and commerce gave rise to new models of individual and group identity. Among the most enduringly influential of these conceptions was the phenomenon known as courtly love, which emerged in the early twelfth century. The love song (*canso*) of the Occitan troubadours popularized many of the conventions that would come to define elite identity as it related to erotic passion. As is well known, a fundamental feature of courtly love was the impossibility of its fulfillment. The most common obstacles to amorous satisfaction included: the disinterest or disdain of the beloved, the fact that one—or both—parties was married, and the communal suspicion of romantic love in general (often based on the assumption that erotic desire compromised the lover's spiritual salvation or commitment to his or her social responsibilities). Traditionally portrayed as a *sui generis* invention of "western," "European," and—even more curiously—"French" civilization, the troubadour corpus has been convincingly reassessed as the product—at least in part—of cultural exchanges between the Latin Christian societies of Occitania and northern Iberia on the one hand, and Muslim-ruled Al-Andalus on the other (Menocal 1987). (The contemporaneous, and far better documented, movement of scholars and books across the very same geographical boundaries reintroduced Aristotle to Latin Christian intellectuals, a development that revolutionized education and the methods of academic argumentation.)

There is another sense in which courtly love can be viewed as the outcome of circuits of mobility and modes of geographical consciousness particular to the twelfth century. In the troubadour *canso*, the psychological and social impediments that thwart the lover are frequently coded in spatial terms as *geographical distance*. This poetic convention gave rise to the concept of *amor de lonh*—"love from afar"—a phrase that predates, and has become synonymous with, "courtly love." The term was coined by twelfth-century troubadour Jaufré Rudel, in the opening stanza of his "Lanquan li jorn son lonc e may" ("When the days are long in May"):

Lanquan li jorn son lonc e may	When days are long in May,
M'es belhs dous chans d'auzelhs de lonh,	I delight in songs of birds from far away
E quan mi suy partitz de lay,	and when I have gone away from there,
Remembra'm d'un' amor de lonh.	I remember a love from far away.
Vau de talan embroncx e clis	I go around with my head bent—sullen,
Si que chans ni flors d'albespis	so that singing and the hawthorn's flowers
No-m valon plus que l'yverns gelatz.	are of no more account to me than the icy winter.

(Chiarini 1985: IV, my translation)

Medieval biographies of Rudel identified his "amor de lonh" as Hodierna of Jerusalem, countess of the crusader state of Tripoli and daughter of King Baldwin II of Jerusalem (r. 1118–31). According to one *vida* ("biography"), Rudel fell hopelessly in love with Hodierna merely by overhearing what pilgrims returning from Antioch said about her. The *vida* adds that the love-struck Jaufré voyaged to Tripoli to see his lady with his own eyes, only to contract an illness (*malauita*) aboard ship. While convalescing in Tripoli, news of his plight reached the countess, who visited the unfortunate pilgrim on his sickbed. Moved to compassion, the countess embraced Jaufré, who—overwhelmed—died of bliss in her arms. The countess arranged to have the man who died for love of her buried honorably in the church of the Templars and then took monastic vows, living out the remainder of her life as a nun (Paden 1998: 16–17).

Notwithstanding its fanciful nature, the romanticized biography of Jaufré Rudel reveals an important historical truth: that medieval audiences of troubadour lyric understood the ideal of *amor de lonh* in terms of the material realities that made formerly distant Mediterranean destinations far closer than they had ever seemed before. Indeed, several poems in the troubadour corpus focus on the longing of women left behind in Europe while their lovers are on crusade in the Holy Land (Routledge 1995). And, indeed, one of the first great troubadours wrote his poems under the name Cercamon—literally, "he who wanders—and/or investigates—the world."

Literature, in general, played a vital role in redefining noble and aristocratic identities in relation to emergent modes of mobility. As Sharon Kinoshita has demonstrated, the commercial and crusading interests that made the Mediterranean loom ever larger in the consciousness of Latin Christians left their mark on the most enduringly influential genre of medieval courtly narrative: chivalric romance (Kinoshita 2006). The earliest romances—the *romans d'antiquité*—were French versifications of classical works, such as Virgil's *Aeneid* and Statius's *Thebaid*. In addition to the prestige granted them by virtue of their antiquity, these two Roman epics unfolded in Mediterranean settings in which Francophone audiences were increasingly interested (in both the intellectual and politico-economic senses of that term). Although only one of Chrétien de Troyes's twelfth-century Arthurian romances has a Mediterranean setting (*Cligès*), collectively, his works consolidated the archetype of the knight errant in this age of widening geographical horizons. It was not inevitable that the quintessential hero of romance should be a traveler who elected to leave the comfort and safety of home to win renown; like the courtly lover, the knight errant sprang from the soil of a culture that was actively thinking and living through the implications of its intensified connections to once-remote corners of the world.

The first decade of the thirteenth century witnessed a radical new conception of clerical identity, as well, with the foundation of the Franciscan and Dominican orders. The mendicant orders were, at their core, a repudiation of monastic life, which had been founded on the principle of retirement from the temporal world. Rather that immuring themselves within a religious community, the Dominicans and Franciscans thrust themselves into a world that was being transformed by urbanization and by the related expansion of commerce, banking, and bureaucracy. Over the course of the thirteenth century, the Franciscans and Dominicans fanned out across Latin Christian Europe, northern Africa, the eastern Mediterranean, and—as mentioned earlier—even into east Asia. Their peripatetic ethos made members of both orders supremely useful to some of the most urgent ecclesiastic initiatives of the later Middle Ages, including the education and correction of the laity, the war on heresy, and the crusades. Dominican missionary, travel writer, and polemicist Riccoldo of Montecroce construed the emergence of the fraternal orders as a vital counterweight to the military threat posed by the Mongol empire and the Egyptian sultan:

> All Christian people and all western people should gratefully remember that at the same time the Lord sent the Tartars to the Eastern countries in order to kill and destroy, he also sent his most faithful servants blessed Dominic and blessed Francis to the Western countries in order to illuminate, instruct, and edify. And as much as the latter have accomplished in their building up, the former increased in their destroying (George-Tvrtković 2012: 93).

Franciscans and Dominicans alike found inspiration in Francis of Assisi, who legendarily paid a dangerous and polemical visit to Ayyubid Sultan al-Kamil of Egypt (r. 1218–38). Francis challenged the Muslim clerics at the sultan's court to undergo a trial by fire to determine whose religion was the authentic one. Following Francis's lead, Franciscans such as John of Plano Carpini, Benedict the Pole, William of Rubruck, and Odoric of Pordenone voyaged into the Mongol empire as diplomats and missionaries, leaving behind detailed accounts of their travels. Dominicans Andrew of Longjumeau and Ascelin of Lombardy also voyaged into the Mongol empire, while many others—including Riccoldo of Montecroce and Jordanus of Sévérac—went to Persia and/or India. Jordanus and Odoric both reported the public execution of nine Franciscan friars in Thana (Thane, India) in 1321. Their grisly fate is the subject of the monumental fresco by Ambrogio Lorenzetti, which adorns the chapterhouse of Siena's Franciscan friary, one of numerous indications of the importance of travel and martyrdom to their communal self-image.

The advent of the mendicant orders coincided with the emergence of another self-conscious and increasingly self-assertive social group, whose collective identity was likewise linked to long-distance travel: merchants. A fourteenth-century Catalan manual written for aspiring traders praises the mercantile profession in decidedly chivalric terms, as "the best and most profitable (*la millor e pus profitossa*) of the masculine arts," in part because it requires young men "to withstand great travails and perils"(*sostenir los grans traballs e perills*) associated with long-distance travel.[2] Friars, missionaries, and diplomats bound for Africa and Asia followed trails blazed by Genoese and Venetian navigators and businessmen (Heers 1983: 165–85; Epstein 2006: 113–23). For this reason, merchants and shipmen enjoyed rather remarkable status as geo-ethnographic authorities and were called upon to supplement—and sometimes correct—the deficiencies of clerical learning. Pietro d'Abano's *Conciliator differentiarum philosophorum* (1310) leaned heavily on the testimony of Marco Polo for the cosmographical portions of the work (Polo 1928: cxciv). Francesco Pipino, a Dominican who undertook a widely read translation of Polo's account into Latin, also cited the Venetian merchant as an authoritative source in his universal chronicle (Dutschke 1993: 160–205). In his fourteenth-century translation of *The Book of John Mandeville*, Otto von Diemeringen, a canon of Metz Cathedral, shored up the credibility of the work he was rendering into German by appealing to the authority of "merchants from twenty-eight different countries, who come [regularly] to Bruges, and happily hear this book read."[3] In the fifteenth century, merchant Benedetto Cotrugli extolled the members of his profession for their unrivaled knowledge "of the monarchies of this world"—adding that this knowledge is the reason why "very frequently great scholars come to visit merchants in their homes" (Lopez and Raymond 2001: 418).

As vernacular literature spread and diversified, it offered a number of pliable models and paradigms for understanding mobility as a technique of elite self-fashioning—one whose methods were open to debate and improvisation. Cyriac of Ancona (1391–1453) was born into a wealthy merchant family that fell into economic hardship during his childhood, following the death of his father. Written shortly after Cyriac's death, *The Life of Cyriac of Ancona* by Franceso Scalamonti used its subject's travel diaries and letters to document the resourceful way that the relatively impecunious Cyriac parlayed his bureaucratic expertise into opportunities to explore the ecological and archaeological wonders of the Mediterranean world. Thanks in part to Scalamonti, Cyriac is today recognized as an antiquarian pioneer, famed for devoting his life to the tireless preservation of ancient inscriptions and the documentation of archaeological discoveries.[4] Steeped in humanist discourses, Scalamonti celebrates Cyriac as "the only man in thirteen hundred years, since the time of the great Alexandrian geographer Claudius Ptolemy in the age of Hadrian, whose expansive nature and highborn temper gave him the courage to travel all over the world" (Cyriac of Ancona 2015: 2–3).

The plot conventions of chivalric romance and the precedents of Marco Polo and John Mandeville encouraged other fifteenth-century travelers—including Bertrandón de la Broquière, Pero Tafur, and Arnold von Harff—to document their own, supposedly real-life, feats of knight-errantry. Ramón de Perellòs (traveled 1396–8) deliberately shunned the descriptions of international courts and earthbound wonders that were normally the focus of knightly travel narratives and instead narrated his daring, Dantesque descent into Saint Patrick's Purgatory (Lough Derg, Ireland), on the grounds that "all men of this world desire to know strange and marvelous things" (1914: 3). A study in contrast, courtier Antoine de La Sale's travel account of 1437, *Le Paradis de la Reine Sibylle* (1930), echoes the interests of moral treatises and works of natural philosophy. According to its author, the *Paradis* was written for no other reason than to debunk the supernatural yarns of pilgrims who, in the spirit of Ramón, descended into the subterranean caverns of Mount Vettore and claimed to experience other-worldly visions there.[5] Each of these adventurous knights approached travel—and travel writing—in a different way, and understood their approach to both as an expression of a unique sensibility. To date, scholarship has focused overwhelmingly on the slightly earlier accounts of Latin Christian travel to east Asia, and there is still no book-length overview of the rich, varied corpus of travel writing on Europe and the Mediterranean that emerged in the wake of the Black Death. Urgently needed, such a study would inevitably uncover a surprising range of attitudes toward mobility—and, in particular, the role that particular approaches to travel should play in the ideal journey and in life well-lived.

AMBIVALENCE

In the age of the package tour, the homogenized global airport, and the fortified beach resort, travel is widely portrayed as a release from—and even as remedy for—work-related fatigue. Medieval travel was, by contrast, understood as a dangerous *intensification* of the pains and taxations of everyday labor, rather than a restorative interval away from them. The journey's potential to transform the individual for the better or to produce knowledge about the world depended on the traveler's willingness to endure psychic and somatic shock—and quite possibly death. Fourteenth-century poet Eustache Deschamps succinctly captures the era's ambivalence toward travel:

Ceuls qui ne partent de l'ostel	Those who never leave home
Sanz aler en divers pais	And don't wander through various countries
Ne scevent la dolour mortel	Know nothing of the agony
Dont gens qui vont sont envahis,	Of those who travel:
Les maulx, les doubtes, les perilz	The pains, fears, and perils
Des mers, des fleuves et des pas,	Of sea, river, and land
Les langaiges qu'om n'entent pas,	Nor the languages one cannot understand
La paine et le traveil des corps.	Nor afflictions and labors of the body
Mais combien qu'om soit de ce las:	But as much as man might tire of these:
Il ne scet rien qui ne va hors."	He knows nothing who has not voyaged abroad.

(Deschamps 2003: 185–6; my translation)

The development of penitential pilgrimage offered would-be risk-takers a legitimate, widely recognized, and supremely adaptable set of propositions, which they could use to justify novel, or otherwise circumspect, modes of mobility.[6] The obligatory pilgrimage of Christian penance apparently originated in sixth-century Ireland. By the thirteenth century, it had been appropriated by political authorities across Europe to punish violations of secular law.[7] Perhaps more significant, penitential journeys were increasingly undertaken on a voluntary basis. This development explains, for example, why Margery Kempe says that she suffered "gret thrist [thirst] and gret penawns" during her late-life pilgrimage across continental Europe, even though she (controversially) undertook the journey without the prior knowledge of her confessor (1996: 222). Crusading, meanwhile, was originally conceived as a kind of pilgrimage (*peregrinatio*). The crusader accrued spiritual blessings because he voluntarily subjected himself to the perils of both warfare *and* long-distance travel (Riley-Smith 1997: 1–11, 24–39, 80–97). The quest of Arthurian romance incorporated elements of both pilgrimage and crusade.

The time, expense, and danger involved in even relatively short journeys demanded a careful reckoning of the potential consequences of a prolonged—or possibly permanent—absence from one's home. It was for this reason that pilgrims and crusaders settled their debts, appointed powers-of-attorney, and wrote wills before departing for the Holy Land (Sumption 1975: 168–71; Webb 1999: 133–47). Even when travelers managed to survive their journeys, their homecomings could be marred by tragic news of what had transpired in their absence. Having dwelled in India and China for twenty years, Ibn Battuta returned to Damascus to discover that the son he had left there was dead, as was his own father back in Morocco (Ibn Battuta 2010: IV.916). Shortly after, Ibn Battuta arrived in his native Tangiers, only to learn that his mother, too, had perished during his absence (Ibn Battuta 2010: IV.925). Away on pilgrimage less than a year, Nicola de Martoni painfully discovered that his wife Constanza had succumbed to illness as he was struggling to survive an exceptionally perilous journey back to her. Nicola concludes the account of his travels with a moving Boethian reflection on her death, to which he appended a transcription of the verse epitaph that he composed in her honor (Martoni 1895: 667–9). It is within the context of such misfortunes that one might understand why the tension between the knight's domestic obligations and the allure of adventure abroad became a defining theme of chivalric romance, from Chrétien de Troyes's *Erec and Enide* through Miguel de Cervantes's *Don Quixote*.

Fears about the breakdown of social order fueled an entirely different set of concerns about mobility. The movements of pilgrims, in particular, were routinely singled out for scrutiny. In the early Middle Ages, monastic orders were the most vociferous opponents of pilgrimage, on the grounds that devotional travel exposed monks and nuns to the worldly enticements that they had renounced in taking their vows (Constable 1976; Webb 1999: 246–53). During the high-to-late Middle Ages, it was widely feared that malefactors were adopting the pious guise of the pilgrim in order to engage in various forms of turpitude. Inquisitors accused Cathar preachers of disguising themselves as pilgrims in order to disseminate their heterodox doctrines and evade detection (Bruschi 2009: 69–72). Moralists decried the devotional journeys of women as pretexts for indulging in adultery, fornication, and/or heretical activity (Morrison 2000; Craig 2009). After the Black Death, England witnessed a crackdown on "false pilgrims," which was part of broader efforts to curb heresy, sedition, and the bargaining power of agricultural laborers (Robertson 2006; Legassie 2007). Valentin Groebner (2007) has documented comparable developments in the German-speaking regions of Europe, which invented two novel techniques for regulating "false" pilgrims and other undesirable transients: the passport and the wanted poster.

At their most categorical, medieval critics of mobility drew on classical and biblical precedent to portray trade and travel as the lamentable price one paid for inhabiting a fallen world. The Chorus of Seneca's *Medea* voices a version of the Golden Age myth that proved particularly influential among late-medieval intellectuals:

> Glorious were the ages our forefathers saw
> when deception was far distant.
> Each person lived an unambitious life, at home,
> then growing old on ancestral farmland,
> rich with a little, they knew no wealth
> except what their native soil brought forth.
> The world was once divided into strict partitions,
> but those were broken by the pinewood ship,
> which ordered the ocean to suffer a beating
> and the sea, once inviolate, to turn into
> one of our reasons to fear (Seneca 2010: 82).

Even more influential was Genesis, which forged an enduring link between mobility and the myth of Paradise lost. The banishment of Adam and Eve condemned humanity not only to labor and death, but also to a state of perpetual displacement and wandering. The God of Genesis would scatter humankind twice more for its impiety, in the wake of the destruction of the Tower of Babel and then again with Noah's Flood. The captivity and wanderings of the Israelites—chronicled in the subsequent books of the Pentateuch—reinforced the Christian link between peripatetic existence and divine punishment.

The repercussions of these ancient texts are detected in an astonishing range of medieval contexts. The belief that Paradise was a physical location from which humans were exiled by divine dictate informed historical and fictional treatments of geographical exploration. Walter of Châtillon's *Alexandreis* paints Alexander the Great as a study in overweening geographical ambition; for this reason, demons and pagan gods alike plot Alexander's doom, on the grounds that he "traces out the secrets of the East, and madly strikes against Ocean itself. And if the Fates should lend his sails kind winds, he plans to seek the Nile's source, and lay siege to Paradise" (Walter of Châtillon 1996: 172). In a similar vein, Canto 26 of Dante's *Inferno*, where Ulysses convinces his men to disregard the risks involved in the "mad" scheme to sail through the Straits of Gibraltar, a voyage that—unbeknownst to the pagan explorer—would expose him to Mount Purgatory against the wishes of the Christian God.[8]

Medieval travelers—informed by both classical and Christian accounts of the former age—assessed foreign cultures in terms of their attitudes toward mobility. In their initial fourteenth-century encounters with the indigenous Guanches of the Canary Islands, mainland Europeans romanticized the islanders' apparent ignorance of navigation, drawing explicitly on Seneca's nostalgic rhetoric to do so (Coleman 2013). At the opposite extreme, nomadism was viewed as a symptom of primitivism or underdevelopment. As John Critchley (1992) has observed, Marco Polo and Rusticello da Pisa used the Italian adjective "domestiche" as a synonym for "civilized," particularly when discussing the putatively uncivilized customs of the nomadic peoples of Asia. Several pilgrims to the Holy Land spoke in phobic terms about the Bedouin, arguing that their mobile lifestyle was the symptom of a primordial curse against their kind (Chareyron 2005: 121–6).

Scriptural depictions of exile were also fundamental to medieval Jewish identity—and to medieval anti-Semitism. The twelfth-century travel account of Rabbi Benjamin of Tudela gathered information about the living conditions of Jewish communities in virtually every known region of the world. Benjamin suggests that his book is a kind of prefiguration of the eventual reunification of the Jewish people, a shared future that unites Jews throughout the world:

> When the Lord will remember us in our exile, and raise the horn of his anointed, then everyone will say, "I will lead the Jews and I will gather them." As for the towns which have been mentioned, they contain scholars and communities that love their brethren, and speak peace to those that are near and afar, and when a wayfarer comes they rejoice, and make feasts for him, and say, "Rejoice, brethren, for the help of the Lord comes in the twinkling of an eye" (Benjamin 2004: 138–9).

In the hands of the author of *The Book of John Mandeville*, such sentiments take on a darker, conspiratorial cast. As many have noted, Mandeville draws on discourses that portrayed the diasporic condition of the Jewish people as a divine punishment for killing Christ and suggests that, in the time of antichrist, they will use their common language to unite with the cursed tribes of Gog and Magog in a second outrage against Christendom:

> Know that the Jews do not have their own land [anywhere] in the whole world ... Therefore all the Jews that dwell throughout all lands always learn to speak Hebrew, in the hope that ... [the peoples of Gog and Magog]

know how to speak to them and lead them into Christendom to destroy Christians (Mandeville 2011: 158–9).

It was these precise prejudices that helped foment the pogroms and expulsions that denied Jewish communities throughout medieval Europe the security of a stable home.

The historical experience of Jewish communities underscores the importance of historicizing one's own assumptions about "mobility." In modern English, it is virtually impossible to use this term in a *neutral*—let alone in a negative—way. *Mobility* inevitably evokes the liberal values of prosperity, open dialogue, and self-determination. When left unexamined, such assumptions might cause one to overlook medieval manifestations of "mobility" in which movement through the world was the result of necessity or force. It might even be the case that, by foregrounding relations of political domination and resistance, the student of the Middle Ages stands to gain a critical appreciation of the ideological blind spots that structure the often unqualified celebrations of "mobility" that otherwise seem so commonsensical as to be universal. The particularity of social and politico-economic structures invests each historical manifestation of mobility with its unique texture and hue. This is certainly the case when it comes to the cultural logic of medieval exoticism, which cannot be entirely understood outside the context of political, economic, and technological history.

POWER, PRESTIGE, AND EXOTICISM

In 1255, an unlikely visitor—a native of Africa—alighted on the banks of the River Thames. The London newcomer had first voyaged from Africa to Palestine, where he then boarded a ship destined for France, as part of the retinue that accompanied Louis IX homeward in the wake of the failed crusade of 1248–50. The French monarch subsequently dispatched the foreigner to the court of his estranged cousin, King Henry III of England, as a kind of goodwill ambassador. For the next four years, this native African resided in the Tower of London, enjoying spacious living quarters, a personal attendant, and a strange diet, rich in beef and red wine. The sudden death of the visitor in 1259 was hastened (if not caused) by the cold north Atlantic climate and the idiosyncrasies of English cuisine. Monk, chronicler, and cartographer Matthew Paris said this about the ill-fated wayfarer:

> Around this time an elephant was sent to England, given as a great gift from the Lord King of France to the Lord King of England. We believe that this was the only elephant ever seen in England, and even on this side of the Alps, and because of this, people flocked to behold this strange sight (Paris 1872–83: V.489).[9]

Like most royal luxuries of the Middle Ages, the elephant of Henry III possesses several rare traits that make it desirable to others, including its size, beauty, intelligence, and scarcity. As Matthew Paris observes, this last quality is a function of the infrequency with which elephants were successfully conveyed from their accustomed habitats to the shores of England. The king's elephant can, therefore, be distinguished from the general field of luxury goods as "exotic," since a significant part of its value derives from the difficulty and expense involved in transporting it to its current surroundings. Another way to say this is that, in the Middle Ages, the exotic commodity is distinguished by a mystique that derives from its capacity to embody an awe-inspiring triumph over geographical distance.

The luckless pachyderm was, in fact, among the first inmates of the Tower Menagerie, which—during the reign of Henry III—also boasted lions and camels donated by the Holy Roman emperor and a polar bear sent from the king of Norway and routinely set loose to fish in the Thames (Sands 1912). The traffic in exotic animals formed part of what I have elsewhere called the *prestige economy of long-distance knowledge*—a constellation of material practices, symbolic conventions, and structures of feeling that enabled medieval people to win prestige, influence, and/or profit through participating in the exchange, circulation, and display of "exotic" commodities (see Legassie 2017: 21–58). Anthropologist Mary W. Helms (1988) observes that, in nearly all preindustrial societies, the field of inquiry that we call *geography* overlaps with *cosmology*. For this reason, geographical distance is charged with the powers of the sacred. Knowledge of far-away lands, therefore, assumes a mystical quality, often sustaining cults of royal and priestly charisma. In some cultural settings, monarchs and high priests bolster their authority by voyaging to distant climes in person, returning as what Helms calls "long-distance specialists." In others, elite persons enjoy the mystique of the exotic without ever having to leave home, usually by claiming special or exclusive rights in foreign visitors and exotic commodities. Among medieval rulers, this second approach tended to be the more prevalent (which is perhaps one factor that contributed to the Middle Ages' ambivalent attitudes toward Ulysses and Alexander the Great). As a consequence, in many medieval cultural settings, the circulation of exotic commodities was self-consciously a traffic in—and a symbolic appropriation of—the pains and labors of long-distance travelers.

This explains why courtly exoticism was a common feature of what Anthony Cutler has called "the tributary economies" of the premodern world, which converted the exchange of precious—often exotic—gifts into a gesture of political submission (Cutler 2001). The tributary economies of the Middle Ages drew on the symbolic conventions that originated in the earlier Hellenistic, Roman, and Persian empires. For example, the hand-held sphere that symbolized the Roman emperor's dominion over the world gave rise in the Middle Ages to the nearly ubiquitous image of Christ (or the Pope, or the Holy Roman emperor) holding the *globus cruciger*, an orb topped by a cross (Schramm 1924). The iconography of Christ's nativity is rich in anthropomorphic dramatizations of this ecclesiastical will to *imperium*; consider, for instance, Giotto's depiction of the exotic tributes of the Magi—and in particular the magus-king who not only bows before the newborn god but also, in offering up his far-fetched gift, suffers his bare, uncrowned head to be touched, in a gesture of submission to a greater sovereign (Figure 5.2).

FIGURE 5.2: Adoration of the Magi, by Giotto, detail from the cycle of frescoes Life and Passion of Christ, 1303–5, after the restoration in 2002. Padua, Italy, Scrovegni Chapel. Credit: DeAgostini/Getty Images.

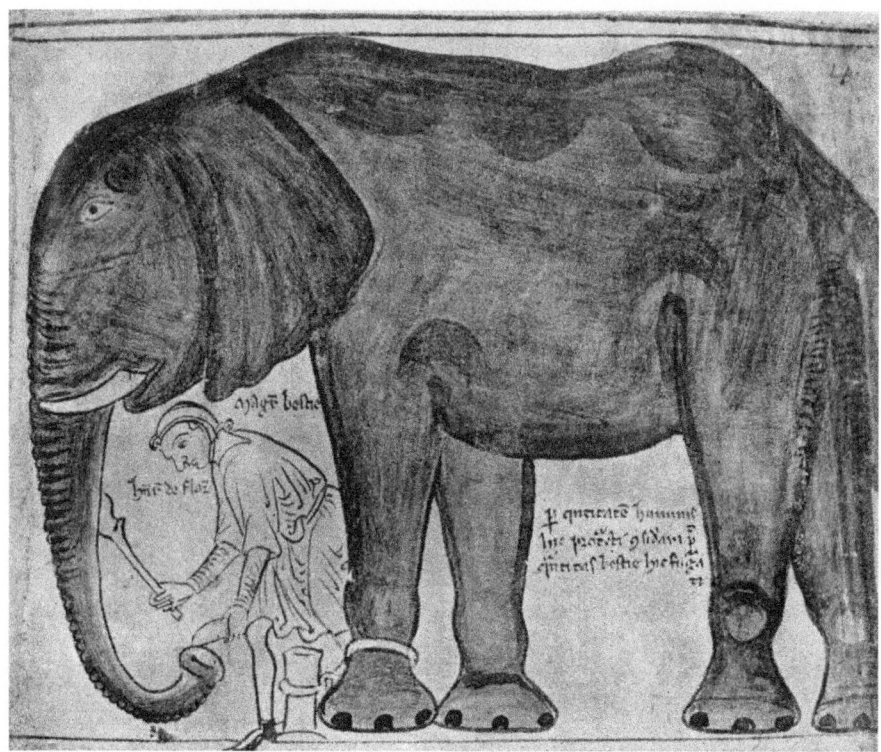

FIGURE 5.3: Matthew Paris, illumination from his "Chronica Major" depicting the elephant sent by St. Louis to Henry III in 1255, *c.* 1200–59. Cambridge, Corpus Christi MS 16. Credit: Culture Club/Getty Images.

The political underpinnings of the prestige economy of long-distance knowledge are vital interpretive context for any instance of medieval exoticism. Matthew Paris' *Chronica majora* (1255), for example, not only documents the arrival of the king's elephant to London, but also features a painting of the pachyderm "drawn from life" (Figure 5.3). Matthew's composition has been praised for its naturalism, especially for the anatomically correct depiction of the animal's knees, located just above its feet, a detail that flew in the face of the widely held claim that elephants did not have leg joints.[10] However, there is reason to doubt that Matthew viewed naturalism or drawing from life as ends in themselves. As painted in the *Chronica*, the king's elephant appears in profile, its jointed leg positioned toward the front of the picture plane. By foregrounding this detail, Matthew calls attention to the shackle that confines the animal. Thus, the very flourish that supposedly exemplifies the illuminator's "naturalism" also situates the elephant within the network of political and social relations that gave rise to its captivity—and to its representation in painting. The same can be said of the depiction of the elephant's caretaker, identified by an authorial gloss as one "Henricus de Flor, Magister Bestiae." In the same caption, Matthew explains that he has included the drawing of Henry "the Beast Master" in order to establish a sense of scale for readers who have never seen an elephant in person. Yet, nothing compelled Matthew Paris to depict the scale-measuring Henry at work; as a result of this homely—almost banal—rendering of the elephant's grooming regime, the viewer infers that Matthew has enjoyed intimate, and perhaps privileged, access to the king's pet. In this illumination, the gaze of the painter is as much an object of representation as the elephant and his caretaker; this gaze makes itself visible by situating itself and the objects that it observes in a triangulated relationship to sovereign power. In crafting this image, Matthew Paris basks in the reflected glory of the monarchs of France and England, whose might is embodied in the captive animal that changes hands between them. Exotic commodities mystify—and are mystified by—the status of those who exchange them. The same can be said of the various medieval middlemen who, like Matthew, insert themselves into the prestige economy of long-distance knowledge by participating in the display and exposition of exotica.

Such appropriations are possible because narratives concerning the origins and chain of custody of exotic commodities—a subcategory of what Igor Kopytoff (1986) called "the cultural biography of things"—played an essential role in the generation and redistribution of prestige within the prestige economy of long-distance knowledge. In the case of luxury imports such as spices, silks, and precious stones, the geographical distance that separated producers and consumers gave rise to inaccurate—and often deliberately fabricated—descriptions of the distant lands where those commodities originated. Paul Freedman has argued that the high price commanded for medieval spices (a category that included not only culinary flavorings but also silks, medicines, and precious stones) was, in part, a function of the mystifying legends that surrounded their origins. The strategies used to harvest black pepper were a particularly fruitful topic for mythographers, while the high price commanded for cinnamon and aromatic aloe wood was partially based on the alleged danger involved in harvesting and transporting them—or on the myth that they were fished out of the Nile, having dropped into it from the inaccessible heights of Terrestrial Paradise (Freedman 2008: 130–45).

The unprecedented popularity of travel writing and cartography during the Middle Ages is, in part, a consequence of the fact that both succeeded in making themselves indispensable conduits in the transmission of (mis)information about the exotic luxuries prized in royal courts, ecclesiastical curiae, and wealthy urban households. The *Catalan Atlas* offers a prime illustration of this point. Dating from around 1375 and attributed to the Mallorcan workshop of Jewish cartographers Abraham and Jehuda Cresques, the *Atlas* was first inventoried in the library of French king Charles V in 1380, and may have been part of a series of reciprocal gift exchanges between the crowns of France and Aragon.[11] The *Atlas* crystalizes (and makes available for appropriation) the travail and long-distance knowledge of a dazzling cross-section of medieval society. The work draws on scholarly, devotional, chivalric, and mercantile approaches to mapping the world. The *Atlas* reproduces the rhumb lines and detailed coastal contours of the portolan chart, a cartographic form based on the observations of merchants and mariners and kept aboard ships as a tool for navigating the Mediterranean as early as the twelfth century (Campbell 1987: I.371–463; Dalché 1995). As Jerry Brotton has observed, the *Atlas* not only depicts merchants traveling along the routes that brought exotic luxuries into the orbit of the French king, but also represents the efforts involved in extracting and transporting the raw materials out of which the Cresques brothers fashioned the masterpiece itself—including the gold and precious stones used to make its costly pigments (1998: 31). Its explanatory glosses, exotic images, and Jerusalem-centered conception of the world harken back to the older traditions of clerical cartography that produced the famous thirteenth-century monumental map produced for Hereford Cathedral. Scholars have also noted the *Atlas*'s reliance on the relatively recent chivalric travel accounts of laymen Marco Polo and John Mandeville.[12] In sum, as the owner of this jewel-like object, Charles held in his hands the labor, pain, and knowledge of countless travelers.

The royal interest in exotica furnished more humble social actors with opportunities to work the prestige economy of long-distance knowledge to their own advantage. Baldassare Ubriachi—a Florentine merchant who traded in diamonds and ivory—wrote to a partner stationed in Mallorca in 1399, asking him to commission *Atlas*-style maps from the Cresques workshop. Baldassare planned to present the maps as gifts to the rulers of the kingdoms where he sold his wares, in the hope that his gesture of liberality would secure him a tax exemption or two (Skelton 1968: 107–13).[13] The earliest surviving manuscript of *The Book of John Mandeville*, produced in 1371, was commissioned as a gift for Charles V by his royal physician, Gervais Chrétien.[14] The year before this manuscript was commissioned, Charles founded a medical college at the University of Paris, which would eventually bear Gervais's name.

Intriguingly, the courtly and scientific vogue for the *Book* contributed to the rumor that Mandeville was not only a knight but also a physician. This claim emboldened one compiler to attribute the authorship of an otherwise anonymous lapidary treatise to Mandeville (De Poerck 1961), suggesting the striking extent to which knowledge of the natural history and medicinal properties of gems was associated with long-distance travel. The frontispiece of this pseudo-Mandevillean lapidary suggests that not only university-educated physicians, but even artisans, could derive social capital from their association with precious stones and the exotic lore that surrounded them. The illumination depicts a quotidian scene in the shop of a prosperous goldsmith (Figure 5.4).

FIGURE 5.4: A goldsmith's shop. Miniature from "The Lapidary" attributed John Mandeville, fifteenth century. BnF, Ms. fr.9136, f.3445, Paris, France. Credit: Leemage/Corbis via Getty Images.

The fashionable couple that owns the shop plies its well-heeled clientele with the shimmering gemstones, which—one presumes—will eventually find homes in custom-made gold or silver settings, like the finished pieces that line the lower shelf behind them. If the artisan family's lap dogs and apparel attest to their prosperity and proximity to their courtly customers, other details situate this generalized tableau of affluence *vis-à-vis* the prestige economy of long-distance knowledge—most obviously, the exotic pet ape that strikes an unpredictable pose in the foreground of the scene. What appears to be a coral rosary dangles from the bottom of the third shelf, while to the right of this object looms a replica of a merchant galley, perhaps destined to serve as a votive offering to a saint who ensured the safe return of one of the goldsmith's well-traveled customers. (It is also possible that the object is a *nef*, a ship-shaped drinking vessel.) More curious still, the doorway on the right opens up onto a miner excavating the raw materials of the jeweler's trade, a vision that seems out of place in the urban setting suggested by the shop's interior. Could it be that the illuminator—less interested in spatiotemporal realism than conceptual consistency—has included this detail as yet another reminder of the goldsmith and his trade are embedded within the broader geographical and economic circuits that allow his social superiors to augment their status and authority through appropriating the knowledge and labor embodied in exotic commodities? Similarly, the far-fetched corals, pearls, and gems in the background right of Petrus Christus's "A Goldsmith in His Shop" (1449) are laid out like a miniature cabinet of curiosities (Figure 5.5), suggesting that the craftsman at the center of the painting shares the intellectual interests of scholars and courtiers—and is, therefore, something more than a "mere" artisan.

The sensation novels and detective fiction of Victorian England preserve, in residual form, this older way of thinking about precious stones and those who traffic in them. In works like Wilkie Collins's *The Moonstone* (1868) and Arthur Conan Doyle's "The Blue Carbuncle" (1892), the long-distance knowledge embodied in the eponymous gem of each narrative gets recoded in menacing

FIGURE 5.5: A goldsmith in his shop, possibly Saint Eligius, by Petrus Christus, Germany, fifteenth century. New York, The Metropolitan Museum of Art. Credit: De Agostini Picture Library/Getty Images.

terms, as a *curse*. Even though these fictional stones are envied for their physical singularity, their allure ultimately derives from the lurid accounts of murder, perfidy, and colonial atrocity that galvanized their journeys to England from an Indian temple (in the case of the Moonstone) and a mythical Chinese riverbed (in the case of the Blue Carbuncle). To compare any of these medieval or Victorian examples to contemporary attitudes toward gemstones is to comprehend the force of Oscar Wilde's witticism regarding the cynic who "knows the price of everything and the value of nothing." It also suggests that a profound gulf separates us—the denizens of a world shrunken by the automobile and the aircraft—from the way that medieval (and even late-nineteenth-century) people perceived geographical distance and the objects that once inspired feelings of wonder by bearing mute witness to the pain and peril involved in surmounting it.

CHAPTER SIX

Sexuality

PATRICIA E. SKINNER

Medieval sexuality has been the focus of substantial recent commentary from a number of perspectives. Ruth Mazo Karras (2005: 5) usefully defines sexuality as "[the] whole realm of human erotic experience—the meanings that people place on sex acts, not the acts themselves—not the history of sex." These meanings have been explored by medievalists from different directions (Bullough and Brundage 1996; Harper and Proctor 2008; Evans 2011). In older scholarship, the range and repetition of ecclesiastical regulation, commentaries, and penitentials dealing with sexual behavior attracted the attention of James Brundage (1985, 1987). These are revealing of changing ideas not only of what constituted a valid marriage, but also of changing attitudes to the sexuality of priests, for whom chastity was increasingly emphasized (and required) from the eleventh century onwards. Brundage also briefly explored the regulation of sexual activity on the First Crusade, to which we shall return. The possibilities of (mainly male) same-sex relationships in the medieval past were the focus of early work by Michael Goodich (1979) and John Boswell (1980, 1994), and then of their critics, who highlighted the relative absence of women in the formulations set up (Murray 1996; Sautman and Sheingorn 2001; Lochrie 2005). Feminist interventions highlighted women's relationships, but the limitations of the gender binary also led to further reflections on male–male relationships and the transgender possibilities open to medieval people (Herdt 1996; Puff 2013).

Medievalists have drawn heavily on—and critiqued—Michel Foucault's (1990) formulation of individual and collective sexual history evolving from a sexual act to a sexual identity (a debate that became particularly focused around same-sex relationships, but had broader implications for what constituted the "norm" and when such an idea emerged). This frame still forms the starting point for more recent work that nuances the arguments still further (Karras 2005: 8–9; Lochrie 2011: 37–40). The title of *Sex Before Sexuality: A Premodern History* (Phillips and Reay 2011) appears to accept the modern invention of the concept, but by structuring its essays along recognizably "modern" lines (examining sex "between men," "between women," and so on), it opens itself up to criticism that reaching the medieval and early modern actuality of sexual behaviors and attitudes is an impossible project. Historians of gender relations have also examined sexuality through the lens of masculinity and feminist theory: how sexual activity "made" a man (in the right places and with the right partners) but might ruin a woman (e.g. Karras 2003: 75–83). There is also an inherent tension in medieval commentaries between the idea of women as passive partners in sexual intercourse, and the fear of their power to entice and entrap men into inappropriate fornication. Finally, the surge of work on medieval affect and the use of emotional or erotic language has also incorporated discussion of how those passions might or might not have resulted in physical relations. Erotic language did not necessarily imply genital contact though, and sexual activity and mutual pleasure did not occupy the same level of importance that it has gained in modern discourse. Complicating things even further, care must be taken here to acknowledge the Islamic medical tradition that saw in *female* sexual pleasure the key to the successful generation of children (Park 2013: 88–92).

What does become clear through these different approaches is how variable "sexuality" is as a category of analysis when applied to the premodern era. Most importantly, the modern binary between hetero- and homosexual, and its associated category "heteronormativity," has been comprehensively rejected in recent interventions related to the medieval situation, not least by Karma Lochrie (2011), whose own studies arguably kicked off its somewhat misplaced popularity among medievalists in the first place (Lochrie 2005). The debate around sexual identity has also spawned a trend for thinking about sexualities (plural) to which Karras (2005: 6) has given short shrift, but which has a powerful hold on historians and literary scholars alike (Fradenburg and Freccero 1996). One of the major drawbacks of essay collections that explore challenges to "prevailing conceptions of gender and sexual identity" is that they set up such cases as exceptions reinforcing a norm, yet the norm itself is rarely articulated (L'Estrange and More 2011).

Somewhat absent from this plethora of work, despite notable studies relating to sexuality within non-Christian communities and cultures (Rosenthal 1979; Roth 1996a, 1996b; Kolten-Fromm 2000; Baskin 2010; Goldin 2011: 121–68; Park 2013; Schüller 2016), has been any consideration of how it mapped onto the ebb-and-flow of medieval empires, in particular the expansion of western European Christian polities (but the Umayyad kingdom of Al-Andalus in Spain, while not an empire, was also an offshoot of one [Ruggles 2004: 66]), and the establishment of the commercial empires across the later medieval Mediterranean and beyond. Such an omission is surprising, given the focus in modern postcolonial studies on the processes of othering and subjection of subaltern peoples through casting their cultures as "backward," inferior, sensual, emotions-driven, and therefore irrational (for postmedieval case studies, see Parker *et al.* 1992). Twenty years ago, Steven J. Kruger (1997: 158–9) highlighted the ways in which a focus on certain categories, such as gender, or religion, both key elements of considerations of medieval sexuality, had in fact elided other categories of consideration, so that race and class, for example, barely registered in surveys of medieval society that "mean[t] a European, Christian society." Since he wrote, there have been isolated responses to his call for a more intersectional approach. A scholar who demonstrates the potential for such work is Kim Phillips, who has explored late medieval travelogues through a gendered and postcolonial lens (K. Phillips 2009, 2011, 2014). Here, it seems, the plurality of "sexualities" can provide a useful analytical tool, as it is clear that medieval writers identified (or fantasized about) the sexual practices of different cultures as a means of othering.

What questions can we draw from modern scholarly explorations of empire and colonialism to interrogate the medieval world's view of sexuality? The penetration of European culture into Africa, Asia, and the Americas in the early modern era was accompanied by both a loosening of sexual restrictions compared with those of the homeland (on male colonists at least) and the sexual exploitation of both women and men in the subject communities (Bryder 1998; Voss and Casella 2012; Meiu 2015). It also saw the export from Europe, with Christian missionaries, of normative ideas of sexuality which condemned—as medieval clerics did—any local or native practices that were "unnatural" and/or did not fit with the norms of "civilized" society (for this process in Polynesia, see, for example, Johnston 2003). The prurient fascination with what lay behind the veil or in the harem fueled an image of the east as mysterious and inaccessible, an image that persisted into modern academic work (Said 1979; critiqued by Hastings 1992; Yegenoglu 1998: 25–7). The tension between colonizers looking to "save" local populations, and the communities within which they worked, is not just a past issue: Leticia Sabsay (2016) highlights the ways in which modern global campaigns for sexual equality still "indicate a process of othering [in which] coloniality and orientalist mentalities have influenced the shaping of the emergent 'sexual rights-bearing subject,' not only at the level of political rhetoric but also in terms of the kind of politics that is generated in the name of this subject."

The possibilities for exploring sexuality against a background of cultural exchange and clash between expanding and contracting medieval empires are therefore rich. This chapter, rather than re-rehearsing the generalities of medieval sexuality, uses it as a way to interrogate "empire," asking whether the dynamics of othering visible in modern colonial enterprises can provide insights into how first medieval empires (and I include here the expansion of Christendom, the ultimate "empire") utilized sexual mores and activities to justify their rule over subject peoples, and often colonized the (mainly) female bodies of those they had conquered as a route to assimilation and control. It works thematically rather than tracing specific empires: although there were moments in the histories of medieval polities where sex came to the fore as a politically charged topic (high-level divorce controversies in the Carolingian empire and the tortuous diplomacy of western marriages with Byzantine princesses serve as examples), these rarely served as "tools of empire," expanding dominance over a subject people, nor did they substantially shift prevailing ideas of sexuality *per se*. Whether the Byzantine emperors, for instance, saw the "export" of princesses to western husbands as a means of expanding the potential boundaries of their empire through the export of cultural practices, rather than simply preserving the *status quo*, has to my knowledge not formed a major topic of enquiry. Obviously, there is much more to say on this topic.

USING POSTCOLONIAL THEORY

Karras' formulation of medieval sex as a "transitive act" (2005: 23) is useful here: if sex was indeed something "done unto others," then its potential as a tool of medieval imperialism (understood here as a coercive force that might or might not have resulted in a recognizable "empire") is worth investigation. There are, however, some important caveats to the discussion. Modern postcolonial theory, as Jerold C. Frakes points out, also makes room for—and is able to access—the voice of the Other not only as object of Euro-Christian hegemony, but as a subject that "writes back." This is a position "that did not or could not exist in the thirteenth century" (Frakes 2011: xiii), and thus in his view potentially compromises the work of medievalists such as Sharon Kinoshita (2006), who make extensive use of postcolonial theory to de-center their analysis of texts that are produced in Europe (in Kinoshita's case, France) but set in more distant lands. Frakes' position is, to my mind, too sweeping: "writing back" can take many forms and is not, for instance, necessarily tied to the writer's own status as an immigrant in the country that has formerly colonized her/his people and appropriated (or suppressed) her/his culture. As will be noted here, there is clear evidence that elite voices among the subjected people in the crusader states were highly skeptical of their new rulers' morals, and not at all afraid to comment upon them. It is, however, true that the present study of necessity mainly positions the western European merchants, crusaders, and other travelers as the dominant voices, subjecting and exploiting the peoples they met. Modern postcolonial studies are only now beginning to compare colonial territories *without* referring back to voices of rule from the "center" (Philips 2006: 21). There is much work yet to be done. A comparative study of the subject Muslim experience in Spain, Sicily, and the Holy Land, for instance, is still a *desideratum*, a project that the late Olivia Remie Constable (2013) signaled but was unable to complete.

Yet there are other areas in which a direct comparison between the medieval and modern are more difficult: the apparent centrality of licensed prostitution as a tonic for the colonizing troops in parts of the British empire, and its opponents among social reformers and missionaries on the ground, does not have an easy equivalent in medieval society, for all that later medieval urban councils often sought to license and regulate the sex trade in their districts (Otis 1985; Karras 1996). Yet Philips (2006: 1–5) uses contemporary accounts condemning the practice of allowing the men access to the sex trade to map the modern licensed areas for prostitution near or in colonial barracks, and there is possibly potential to explore the location of medieval brothels to see whether they, too, were deliberately placed. The striking conversion of the name of Prague's brothel from "Venice" to "Jerusalem," and its housing of repentant prostitutes, hints at the international aspect to the trade and its potential to cater for, and include, foreign bodies in imaginary if not physical locations (Mengel 2014).

One area of enquiry that does resist easy comparison is that of a culture of sexualizing of children. Modern colonial endeavors frequently targeted and reported on the immorality of subject peoples who married off their children at what were deemed shockingly early ages (e.g. Philips 2006: 57–82, on India). Yet while both medieval canon law and several secular law codes in medieval Europe prescribed ages ranging from twelve upwards for valid marriages (meaning those that could be consummated), medieval travelers rarely comment on such issues among the people they encountered. Even quite explicit reports on the availability of sex to the traveler, such as Marco Polo's discussed later, do not include children in their survey.

Work on medieval colonial enterprises, interested more in legal and economic questions, has rather overlooked the day-to-day bodily engagement of colonizer and local. The otherwise excellent volume *Coloniser au Moyen Âge* (Balard and Ducellier 1995) seems not to have considered the appropriation and control of sexuality as a "technique of domination." Yet medieval writers, particularly those describing unfamiliar people or situations, often resorted to both positive and negative descriptions of bodily form (skin, hair, shape, color), and clothing, as ways to mark the "otherness" embedded in their cultural encounters. Such descriptions were rarely straightforwardly negative: there was a fascination, an attraction residing in the strangeness, that often comes through in the descriptions. It should be noted at the outset that the object of the (usually male) writer's gaze was more often than not female, and the issue of gender bias is one that lurks throughout the chapter.

The discussion that follows uses the three categories of "mission", "conquest," and "miscegenation" to explore how medieval sexuality can help to explore the cultural idea of empire. These are not hard and fast divisions, since the first two headings arguably were two sides of the same coin in religiously motivated campaigns, and the third was perhaps their inevitable result. The final section considers the ways in which western, Christian views of "natural" sexual relations were challenged by the de- and re-gendered bodies encountered during the expansion of European horizons.

MISSION: CONVERTING FOREIGN BODIES

The activities of medieval missionaries offer a substantial body of evidence to interrogate, since the expansion of Latin and Byzantine Christianity were both, arguably, colonial projects. The expansion of "Christendom" and its interactions with non-European peoples and polities, so eloquently evoked by scholars such as Richard Southern (1962), who early on explored western views of Islam, and Robert Bartlett (1993), whose portrayal of Norman/French expansion has examined ethnicity as a way of understanding the Frankish domination in the south and east, has mainly been seen in terms of political and cultural clash and accommodation. Southern noted the Christian view of Islam, particularly during the crusading era, that denigrated Muhammad for "his plan of general sexual license as an instrument for the destruction of Christendom" (1962: 30) but focused his attention mainly on intellectual and religious, rather than sociocultural, exchanges. Bartlett, despite dealing with "colonial towns and colonial traders" in his survey, touches only lightly on the issue of "mixed" cultures, exploring law and language rather than sexual encounters.

The "conversion era," so often associated only with Europe in Late Antiquity, in fact extends well into our period when viewed from the perspective of empire. Both south-eastern Europe and the Baltic region were the subject of missions and crusades from the ninth to the thirteenth centuries. To what extent did reports and sermons of missionaries and converts focus on the sexual *mores* of the communities to whom they were preaching? The evidence from papal letters to the newly converted and to the missionaries/crusaders is that while the sexual practices of the new Christians were considered, there seems to have been a considerable degree of leeway and discretion exercised. That is, the popes preferred the greater gain of extending the Christian community, rather than risking apostasy through enforcing canonical law too strictly. Two examples serve to illustrate this pragmatism in practice.

The first is an early case of dealing sensitively with local converts. The Bulgarian khan, Boris, appears to have converted to Christianity around 865

CE. The following year, Pope Nicholas I (858–67) sent a lengthy letter responding to the khan's queries about the proper behavior of a Christian ruler and his people. It includes guidance on degrees of consanguinity in marriage, and the length of time a husband should wait after childbirth before resuming marital relations with his wife, both culture-specific concerns. It is clear from other responses that Nicholas was keen to allow the khan to use his own judgment on some matters (chs. 39 and 64, Perels 1925: 582, 590; English translation in North 1998). More explicit were the letters of Pope Innocent III (1198–1215) to Bishop Albert of Livonia, against the wider background of the Baltic crusades from the later twelfth to mid-thirteenth century. The new converts, he says, might have rather different ideas about marriage, particularly regarding consanguinity, and thus the missionaries should be sensitive in imposing penance for sexual sin such as adultery and fornication, being merciful and lenient rather than overly zealous (Fonnesberg-Schmidt 2007: 117–18).

This conciliatory tone extended to the texts of other Christians traveling outside Europe and reporting back on the communities they visited and observed. Their reports include comments on the morality of those whom they visited, particularly where this diverged from their own "norms." For instance, western travelers to the Mongol empire (whether as missionaries or diplomats) in the thirteenth century include commentaries on the marital and sexual practices of the cultures they encountered, as noted, for example, by Scott Westrem (1990). Such cases have tended to be treated in isolation rather than being seen as a continuation of a discourse that, arguably, is as old as written records themselves, and very rarely has the exploitative gaze of the western writer been understood as such. William D. Phillips (1997), for example, does not mention the possibilities of sexual contact at all. John of Plano Carpini, traveling as an envoy of the pope to the Mongols, noted polygamy among the "Tartars," but later in his report commented that: "Their women are chaste, nor does one hear any mention among them of any shameful behavior on their part; some of them, however, in jest make use of vile and disgusting language" (Dawson 1966/1980: 7 and 15).

While John and the Franciscan missionary William of Rubruck, quite properly given their clerical status, were circumspect in their comments about the sexuality of the peoples they visited on their journeys east, and William gives a description of Mongol women that emphasizes their monstrosity in his eyes, near contemporary lay accounts provided rather more frank details. The merchant traveler Marco Polo, for instance, had no qualms about observing, reporting on, and almost certainly enjoying various sexual relations on his travels. He reports several times, with varying degrees of disapproval, of local customs whereby the inhabitants of a particular region allow a sexual freedom to their womenfolk, or practice polygamy (I.34, I.41, I.47, II.4, II.37–9, III.25,

Colbert 1997: 52, 62, 69, 96, 146–51, 240). He mentions the latter frequently but only rarely compares it with Christian monogamy (II.20, Colbert 1997: 126). Striking is his description of the district of Kamul (I.38, Colbert 1997: 58–9), where the inhabitants "give positive orders to their wives, daughters, sisters, and other female relations, to indulge their guests in every wish . . . and the stranger lives in the house with the females as if they were his own wives," simply paying for this full-scale hospitality when he leaves. Had Marco himself sampled this hospitable culture, to leave what is an extended description of the women who were "in truth very handsome, very sensual and fully disposed to conform in this respect to the injunction of their husbands"? Similarly, had he first-hand knowledge of the prostitutes he reports on in the suburbs of Kanbalu and Tai-du and in Kinsai (II.7, II.17, II.68.iii, Colbert 1997: 102–3, 121, 185)? He also reports on the beauty, or otherwise, of local women: those of northern Persia, in his opinion, are "the most beautiful in the world," while those in Zanzibar are "the most ill-favoured women in the world" (I.21, III.37, Colbert 1997: 38, 250). The extensive harems of eastern rulers also feature in his descriptions (II.31, II.38.ix, III.6, III.20.ii, III.24, Colbert 1997: 140, 148, 213, 227, 238). Simon Gaunt (2013: 138) nevertheless takes issue with scholars convinced that Marco "was preoccupied with sexual mores, alternatively [sic] representing the East as a kind of sexual paradise or betraying his own interests as a sexual tourist." Marco's remarks can perhaps be better understood as those of a young man from a city whose engagement with the cultures of the wider world was already well established, and who would have witnessed first-hand the traffic in female slaves that came through the Italian ports, including those who served in Italian households and were in practice sexually available to their masters. The rigid honor codes of urban Venice, like other Italian cities, precluded young men's sexual dalliances with women from the same social class. Read through a colonial lens, Marco's text represents either the *real* sexual freedoms he experienced away from home, or perhaps an exaggerated fantasy of the sexual availability of foreign wives and daughters, safely distanced from his homeland and thus unverifiable by his readers.

Beside the campaign to extend the geographical boundaries of European Christendom, there was also increasing pressure from the eleventh century onwards on Jewish subjects *within* European kingdoms to convert. Kruger (1997: 166) uses the theme of conversion to explore the connections between the ideas of religion and race in late medieval Europe, and cites the didactic tale of Hermann of Cologne, a convert to Christianity who nevertheless lapses back into the "carnality" of his former Jewish state by contracting a marriage inspired by the devil. Only through the prayers of two religious women is he brought back to the chastity of a Christian life. And this is an important marker between Christianity and both Judaism and Islam, for both the latter religions were characterized by hostile (and sometimes grudgingly fascinated) commentators highlighting their "deviant" marriage practices (Jews marrying bigamously or within degrees of consanguinity not permitted by canon law, Muslim men permitted polygamy, etc.) as a sign of their immorality more generally. There were also degrees of difference within, as well as between, religious groups in sexual practices: Joseph Shatzmiller (2009: 581) points out that the condemnation, by northern European, Ashkenaz rabbis of the southern, Sephardi practice of bigamy fell on deaf ears among the Jewish communities of the Mediterranean world. Here, in fact, the only voices raised against bigamous marriages were from Christian, not Jewish or Muslim, authors.

Did later conversion narratives, in the same way as earlier ones, utilize sexuality in the *topos* of the pious wife/queen converting her husband/king and thus an entire people? It is hard to find direct evidence of this: indeed, the susceptibility of *women* to conversion seems to have been far more common in the central and later medieval texts, and the story of Muslim princesses falling for Christian lords and converting on their marriage became a stock feature of twelfth- and thirteenth-century literary culture (Barton 2011: 18). Elsewhere, the subjection of pagan peoples, such as the Cumans in Hungary, included marriage to and conversion of their high-born women, as in the case of the daughter of a Cuman chieftain married to the future István V (r. 1270–2) and baptized with the name Elizabeth. The Hungarian situation, as Nora Berend has pointed out, was somewhat unusual in that the Hungarian kings were not *colonizing* Cuman territory but instead trying to incorporate a pagan people that had settled voluntarily within their borders. The difficulties inherent in this project found expression in a common *topos*, that of dangerous, pagan men raping Christian women, as a report to the pope by István's father, Béla IV, reveals (Berend 2001a: 220). Elizabeth's son, László IV, acquired the epithet "the Cuman," and trod a precarious path between trying to convert the still-pagan Cumans settled in his kingdom and pacifying the increasing demands of the papacy to either achieve this goal or expel them altogether (Berend 2001b). Yet the later anxieties around the Cumans, most clearly expressed in the "Cuman law" of 1279 outlined by the papal legate, focused mainly on their migratory culture, living in tents, and their worship of pagan religious symbols, rather than their sexual threat to Christians.

CONQUEST: APPROPRIATION OF BODILY SERVICES

The eleventh and twelfth centuries were the age of expansive European aggression. Conquest narratives frequently portray the slaughter of men and the capture and enslavement of women and children (Gillingham 2015). Marriage, rape, and abduction were fluid categories in western warfare, and "strategic intermarriage" a frequent necessity (Finke and Shichtman 1998: 61–3). Western crusade propaganda included regular accusations that Saracen men

(Turks and others) raped young girls and women, and even nuns, and captured women and boys to put in their brothels, although the evidence that this actually happened is scanty (Brundage 1985: 61 cites a few examples). Was their economic value, as slaves, outweighed by the cultural value of their visible subjection? What happened to these women next? James Brundage has highlighted the violence of the *language* used by crusade historians to depict their Muslim enemies as "addicted to lurid forms of sexual debauchery" (Brundage 1985: 60, citing Peter Tudebode), particularly toward virtuous Christian women. He suggests that Muslim females, prostitutes or not, were also "bartered back and forth among themselves" (ibid.).

Modern warfare has included rape as a tool to terrorize people into submission, so did the same hold true in the medieval setting? Rape had a broad spectrum of meanings in medieval culture: the violent seizure and penetration of women (and men) was only one element (Dunn 2013 conveys something of the diversity of interpretations). Racial and ethnic difference was frequently expressed in terms of sexual "crimes," which could include not only perceived promiscuity, but also adultery, rape, incest, and sodomy. In the religiously confused environment of Norman-era southern Italy, the distaste of some Christian authors at the use of Muslim soldiers in King Roger II's (r. 1130–54) army to put down rebellions in the Christian cities of Puglia resulted in reports of atrocities as the Saracens ran amok, raping wives in front of husbands and killing infants in front of their mothers—in fact just the kind of behavior that crusade authors had highlighted (Hysell 2012: 151).

Finke and Schichtman highlight that the age of the crusades gave rise to two genres of writing, vernacular history and romance, that their depictions of the strangeness of others "manage[d] the anxieties—of both conqueror and conquered, the powerful and the exploited—about the chaos that lies beyond what is known" (Finke and Shichtman 1998: 59). In their study of the vernacular histories of King Arthur and the Mont St. Michel giant, it is the latter who is the rapist—a monstrous, foreign being who kills Arthur's niece in his attempt to rape her, and then violates the girl's nurse, who in Wace is presented giving an extended account of her ordeal. The point is to present the giant not only as a monster, corrupting the purity of the young virgin to the point of death (the nurse is rather more matter-of-fact—she is an experienced older woman of a different class, thus her rape does not "count" in quite the same way), but as a *foreign* monster—living in Brittany, not Britain.

The anxieties provoked by warfare may have pushed a Muslim father in Sicily to send his young daughter away from the island with a pilgrim companion of the writer Ibn Jubayr, perhaps to prevent any possibility of harm to her in the face of the Norman conquest. Although the story is told in the context of reports of forced conversions by the Christians, the girl's destiny—to marry the pilgrim or to be found a suitable husband by him—speaks to the dangers inherent in being a female subject (Amari 1880: 179–80; a translation of this story, though with an error on the page reference, is in Skinner and van Houts 2011: 74–5). More explicit is a case, again featuring a Muslim man, reported by the Norman author Geoffrey Malaterra:

> Among them was a young nobleman, a citizen of Messina, who had a very beautiful sister, and as he fled he strove to have her come with him; the girl, who was small and virginal, weak in nature, and a stranger to work, began to lag out of fear and being unused to running. Her brother urged her to flee with the sweetest words, but these did no good, and seeing that she had exhausted her strength, he drew his sword and killed her, so that she should not remain to be corrupted by any of the Normans. And however much he was flooded with tears on account of the sweetness of his sister—for she was his only one—he preferred to be the killer of his sister and to mourn her death, than that she become a traitor to her faith and be unwillingly defiled [*stupraretur*] by another law (book II, ch. 11, Malaterra 1927–8: 33).

This particular episode has received some attention from scholars wishing to show that Geoffrey's intention was to appeal to the courtly culture of his audience and/or express a picture of the Muslims that was not wholly negative (Wolf 1995: 160; Hysell 2012: 147). Yet the Latin *stupraretur* for "defiled" has a twin meaning of "defilement" as well as of "rape or ravishment." The ambiguity of meaning highlights a common problem in the sources: it is not difficult, in various genres, to find reports of a *fear* of rape by members of a foreign group (St. Margaret of Hungary, daughter of King Béla IV, famously asked for permission to deface herself as a protection against rape by the approaching Mongols [Skinner 2015]), but it is actually quite hard to find concrete examples of that fear being realized. The scene in the *Roman de Godefroi de Bouillon*, set against the First Crusade and showing a woman and child being sent up a ladder to escape a besieged city might speak to their ransom value (she is with the king) rather than sexual fears (Figure 6.1). The fears of these commentators in different parts of western Europe simply reflected another reality of medieval life: that situations of conflict regularly led to the capture, enslavement, and/or enforced conversion of women and children from different cultures, who could be transported and sold far from their native lands (for a Catalan contract sending a female slave to Sicily in 1238, see Constable 1996: 235).

Before leaving the subject of warfare and its fallout, it is as well to note that the many female slaves trafficked around Europe from their homelands further east faced the colonization of their bodies not just for sex, but other services. Rebecca Winer (2008) has highlighted the use of enslaved wet nurses in late medieval Spain. Papal Councils in 1179 and again in 1215 threatened excommunication to Christian women who served in Jewish homes, either as

FIGURE 6.1: Miniature taken from the Roman de Godefroi de Bouillon, fifteenth century. Credit: De Agostini Picture Library/Getty Images.

servants or wet nurses, suggesting, in Kruger's words, a "certain visceral repugnance at the bodies that they sought to rope off from Christendom" (1997: 168–9). The reality of life for the colonized Jewish subject in Crete is highlighted by the entangled marital and business history of the female convert to Christianity studied by Lauer (2014). Further east, Genoese merchant records from the Crimea testify to numerous sales of women, with and without children, and there is no doubt that their potential as sexual partners contributed to their value as a commodity (Stuard 1995; Skinner and van Houts 2011: 63–9). The Florentine merchant Gregorio Dati cheerfully acknowledged the son he had fathered with a slave in Barcelona, and sent for that son to be educated into the family business (and by extension acculturated to Italian ways). As one may see, such children could be recognized and supported, if not placed on an equal footing with their step-siblings born of marriage.

We should not forget that it was not only women who could be trafficked as slaves and used for sexual purposes. As early as the ninth century, Muslim raids emanating from North Africa on the Christian central Mediterranean targeted boys who could be enslaved, castrated, and sold for use as eunuchs, although the Byzantine hagiography that reports such raids (and their capture of future saints) does not refer explicitly to the practice (Conant 2015). The account of the Venetian traveler Marco Polo (II.45, Colbert 1997: 163) offers a further angle on the spoils of war and sexuality when he reports that all the [male] prisoners taken in war in the province of Bangala are presently emasculated and used as eunuchs to guard women's quarters, thus fetching high prices as slaves (Figure 6.2).

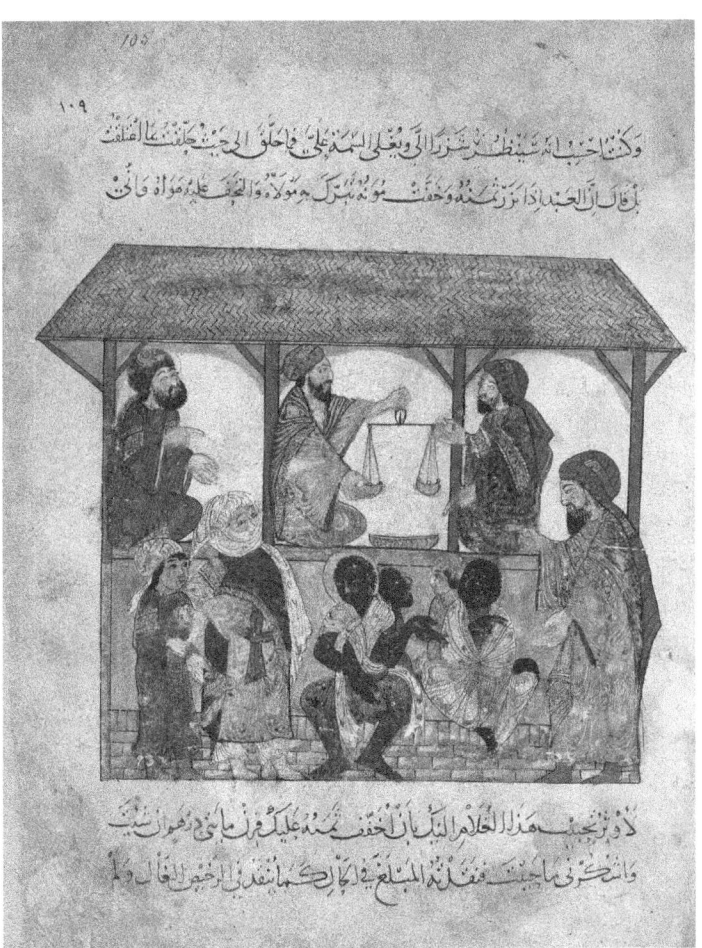

FIGURE 6.2: Slave traders. Arabic miniature, twelfth century. Credit: De Agostini Picture Library/Getty Images.

MISCEGENATION: EMBRACING FOREIGN BODIES

In the aftermath of war, peace could bring with it either a relaxation of cultural boundaries or their strict enforcement. John Gillingham (2015), using western narratives of the First Crusade, has pointed out that the likely use of Muslim women as enslaved sexual partners in the Near East is near invisible except in specific passages such as Fulcher of Chartres' "idyllic picture of a prospering multi-cultural society united by a single faith." Yet Fulcher's famous portrayal contrasts with the continuing anxiety demonstrated by the prohibitions of the Council of Nablus in 1120 of interfaith sexual relations. The drastic punishment threatened in the latter against Christian men who had sex with Muslim women was castration, with the willing woman subjected to having her nose cut off. The reverse situation, a Muslim man taking a Christian woman with her consent, was punished as adultery, that is, with the death penalty (Kedar 1999). Nevertheless, the potential for men to make new lives with different sexual partners in the east might explain the celebratory effigy of Hugh I of Vaudemont being greeted by his wife back in France (Figure 6.3).

The term "miscegenation" is more frequently associated with racialized mixing, and "race" has itself been a contested category within medieval studies (Eliav-Feldon 2005; Heng 2011a, 2011b; Mittman 2015). More frequently, the texts we have display a fear of inter-*religious* rather than interracial sexual relations, but even this distinction is bogus, according to Sara Ahmed (2015). As Karras notes (2005: 107), all three major religions seem to have been reasonably tolerant of men having intercultural sexual relations outside the faith, particularly if they resulted in the female partner's conversion, but were less keen to see "their" women appropriated in this way: even having sex with a prostitute outside the faith caused debate among the authorities. The Fourth Lateran Council's injunction in 1215, that Muslims and Jews should wear distinguishing dress or insignia, derived precisely from the anxieties surrounding "mistaken (*per errorem*)" intercourse by Christian men with Jewish or Muslim women, or Jewish or Muslim men with Christian women. Notably the canons do not attribute a greater weight to the latter, although it was at the heart of the matter that Christian women should not become pregnant by Jews or Muslims (Kruger 1997: 167–8). The anxiety that this caused gave rise to almost fantasy-like portrayals of such mixed-faith relationships, as when the thirteenth-century Provençal rabbi Isaac ben Yedediah expounded at length on the undesirability of uncircumcised men sleeping with Jewish women and bringing them to orgasm first (and thus making them desirous of more intercourse), in contrast with the swift ejaculation that for the rabbi marked sex between Jewish men and their wives, and left the latter "ashamed and confounded" by their unsatisfied desire (quoted at length in Karras 2005: 78).

Such imaginings also permeated more sober legal documents, as in the fifteenth-century Aragonese court cases studied by Martine Charageat. Here,

FIGURE 6.3: Limestone group depicting Hugh I of Vaudemont greeted by his wife Anna of Lorraine, upon returning from the Crusades to the Holy Land, twelfth century. From the Priory of Belval (Vosges), Church of Cordeliers, Nancy, Meurthe et Moselle, Lorraine, France. Credit: De Agostini Picture Library/Getty Images.

the question was pollution of Christian women by Jewish men, a penetration of the "frontière sexuelle," to use her evocative term. Yet as she notes, the cases focus not on the Jewish penetrator, but functioned as a means of interrogating the morals of the Christian woman who would even think to submit to him. These cases were a discourse built by Christians, for Christians (Charageat 2009: 590–1). The colonial subject here was not even invited to the proceedings.

Part—perhaps most—of the anxiety stemmed from the understanding of sex as an act that led not only to cultural mixing but to physical reproduction: medieval Christian theorists (and their counterparts in the other religions) categorized non-reproductive acts as "unnatural." This understanding of the sin of Onan has profound implications for our understanding of sexuality and empire, since it rendered the penetration of women against their will an entirely "natural" act, unless it contravened the rights of another man who had prior claim to the woman in question (thus, in that sense, adultery was "unnatural"). The offspring of such unions occupied an ambivalent cultural space that was explored with fascination by writers of medieval literary works. Lynne Ramey examines how diverse medical models of conception were reflected in twelfth- and thirteenth-century tales of interfaith relationships (Ramey 2011). In the *King of Tars*, for example, the Muslim "sultan of Dammas" marries the daughter of the Christian king whom he is fighting, and she ostensibly converts to Islam and becomes pregnant. Her child, however, is born a formless blob of flesh, which her husband blames on her lack of sincere belief. Yet when a priest baptizes the child a Christian, it miraculously changes form, acquiring limbs, face, and normal functions, and when the sultan follows suit, his black flesh is changed to white.

While tales such as these reflect a worldview of Christian superiority overcoming the challenge of a mixed marriage, Muslims, too, were keen to avoid interfaith relationships. The fear of sexual contact was particularly prevalent in regions where different religious communities lived side by side, such as medieval Sicily and Iberia (Ruggles 2004; Barton 2011). Frakes (2011: xiii) has noted that these regions (and central Europe, already explored) were sites of "Bhabha-esque ... creative interstices," that is, places where the distinctions between Christian rulers and non-Christian subjects were regularly blurred, accidentally or deliberately, by everyday cultural interactions. In multicultural communities such as medieval Sicily, the iconographic depiction of ostensibly Christian courtly culture, on the ceiling of the Norman Palace Chapel in Palermo, includes a dancing girl clad in a full-body costume that emphasizes her curves and speaks to Islamic tropes of a paradise filled with *houris* just like her (Grube and Johns 2005; Kapitaikin 2013), and the Muslim writer Ibn Jubayr speaks of the women of Palermo going about their lives with veiled faces (cited in White 2005: 84). The dynamics of interpenetration in Iberia changed over time, for the conquering elite in early medieval Spain was Muslim, not Christian. Barton (2011: 6) notes that Muslim elite men in early medieval Spain were not only permitted to marry outside the faith, but in many cases strategically did so for economic and political reasons. This aggressive marriage strategy only went into terminal decline when faced with the combination of the concerted opposition of Christian clergy and arrival of Christian warriors after 1050.

The sexual purity of women remained a central facet of religious identity. Although not explicit about the question, the Muslim scholar Ibn Hazm was nevertheless highly critical of the late-eleventh-century rulers of the *taifas*, the Muslim successor states to the caliphate of Cordoba, whose appeasement of aggressive Christian rulers included allowing the latter to take Muslim men, women, and children away to Christian regions as captives (Finke and Shichtman 1998: 69). Following the Christian reconquest of much of the Iberian peninsula, the critical voices continued. David Nirenberg (2001: 71–3) has explored Muslim subjects who did not convert to Christianity, who were permitted to live circumscribed lives as Mudejars, subject to Christian lords. This set up a real tension, particularly in the eyes of external Muslim observers, particularly in North Africa, who wrote of the degradation of the Mudejars as Muslims. How, it was asked, could a Mudejar defend the sexual propriety of his wife when he was not permitted to exact Koranic punishments and was subject to the will of a Christian lord? How might Muslims defend their women from the risk of violation and conversion? Nirenberg illustrates that this was no mere theoretical question, since Mudejar communities in Spain identified numerous women who had transgressed in precisely this way, purchasing privileges from the Christians (and thus ensuring a record survives of each case) to allow them to put such women to death.

No less extreme was the reaction of Christians to interfaith sexual contact: King Alfonso III of Portugal was censured by the pope in 1268 for having permitted Christian men within his kingdom to marry women of Muslim and Jewish origin, regardless of whether these brides had converted to Christianity. The suspicion of converts remained a formidable barrier to their assimilation into Christian society: as Kruger (1997: 166) comments, "religious conversions [were] likely to be accompanied not by an embracing of normative heterosexuality, but rather by a movement from uncontrolled 'luxury' into a more chaste and 'ordered' state."

It was not just male–female interfaith relations that were viewed as suspect: in her study of bathing in Muslim texts, Alexandra Cuffel (2009: 178–80) highlights the suspicion of Muslim and Christian women mixing freely at the bath, or *hammam*, expressed by Islamic writers in Al-Andalus and, later, Syria, who feared same-sex relationships might result from such close proximity and intimacy, or that "community boundaries would completely disintegrate." Cuffel might have included in her survey the requirement on Jewish women to bathe too, particularly after menstruation, although the potential for mixing with women of other faiths was perhaps obstructed by the fact that baths were built specifically for Jewish ritual practices. Ruth Karras (2005: 77) highlights the custom for Jewish women to resume sexual relations with their husbands after such baths, and notes therefore that on seeing a woman emerge from the *mikveh*, "everyone knew that she and her husband would be having sex that night" (Figure 6.4).

CONCLUSION

As we saw earlier, war and conquest could mean the enslavement, subjection, and sexual exploitation of boys as well as women. In both Christian and Muslim cultures, boyhood was celebrated as a time of extreme beauty by male writers,

FIGURE 6.4: Moorish baths of Ronda, c. thirteenth century. Malaga province, Andalusia, Spain. Credit: Education Images/UIG via Getty Images.

giving rise on both sides to accusations of sexual exploitation. Karras (2005: 133) quotes the fourteenth-century William of Adam on "libidinous, vile and abominable men . . . corrupters of human nature"—an attack directed primarily at Muslims— but he is equally scathing of the Christian merchants who buy and sell young slaves for this purpose. Classifying this, in modern terms, as verging on pederasty is not helpful: to reiterate, erotic language did not necessarily lead to full sexual contact (Uebel 2003). Boys "occupied an ambiguous gendered space" in Muslim society

(Clarke 2016: 77). Moreover, the *mukhannathūn* of the medieval Islamic world, men who dressed as women without seeking to *pass* as women, and the existence in the same culture of *ghumaliya* or slavegirls with boyish looks who might be dressed as boys (Ruggles 2004: 73), complicates the supposedly clear gender binary still further. Their very existence may have given rise to further ways in which the Christianizing colonial powers of the twelfth century marked their subjects in predominantly Muslim lands as "other." As we have already seen, the complex and ambivalent relationship between conqueror and conquered was often worked out in cultural outputs such as creative, literary texts. For instance, Kruger (1997: 161) highlights the queerness of foreign bodies as described in Christian texts, in particular Chaucer's "mannish" pagan and Islamic women.

The centrality of dress to the de- and re-gendering of young men and women is worth further consideration, for observers also remarked on costume as a marker of otherness. An early record of clothing differences as gender markers comes in the ninth-century papal letter of Nicholas I to the Bulgarian khan, Boris, introduced earlier. Perhaps in response to an enquiry about appropriate dress for new Christians, the pope's letter refers to the wearing of pants or trousers (*femoralia*—the Latin suggests a cut-off, short garment). While he is dismissive of the problem—"we do not wish the exterior style of your clothing to be changed, but rather the behaviour of the inner man within you"—Nicholas is nevertheless rather uneasy about the fact that a garment that he considers male is being worn by both men *and* women in Boris's realm. "But really, do what you please," he reiterates. The garb of the Bulgarian women might be strange, even slightly transgressive, but of little import in the wider scheme of Nicholas's mission (ch. 59, Perels 1925: 588).

This does, however, highlight an issue that Karras and others have noted—there is a focus, in descriptions of bodies and clothing, on the face and the lower body. The nakedness, or form of covering, of these areas signaled much about the perceived morality of unfamiliar people. Marco Polo, for example, as well as commenting on female bodies, also provides a quite detailed description of trousers worn by the women "of the superior class" of Balashan:

> ... who wear below their waists, in the manner of drawers. A kind of garment, in the making of which they employ, according to their means, an hundred, eighty or sixty ells of fine cotton cloth; which they also gather or plait, in order to increase the apparent size of their hips; those being accounted the most handsome who are the most bulky in that part (I.26, Colbert 1997: 46).

Marco's comment reinforces a clear point about the intersection of sexuality with imperial or colonizing observations in medieval texts: the vast majority of sources focus on women. In Marco's text, for example, femininity (and perceived fertility) was reinforced by the wearing of padded trousers. This is a masculine culture that transcended religious lines: the overwhelming majority of texts were constructed by men for men, and targeted their denigrations at men: the apparent visibility and implied sexual availability of subaltern women, or their seizure by force, was an action that dishonored and emasculated subaltern men.

As such, it would be all-too-easy to focus on the penetrating gaze of western travelers and position those they described as powerless to respond. But some subaltern voices—albeit privileged ones—are audible as well. The Muslim scholar and diplomat Ibn Munqidh's mild bemusement at Frankish sexual mores is expressed in his autobiographical writing:

> One day this Frank went home and found a man with his wife in the same bed. He asked him, "What could have made you enter into my wife's room?" The man replied, "I was tired, so I went in to rest." "But how," asked he, "didst thou get into my bed?" The other replied, "I found a bed that was spread, so I slept in it." "But," said he, "my wife was sleeping together with you!" The other replied, "Well, the bed is hers. How could I therefore have prevented her from using her own bed?" "By the truth of my religion," said the husband, "if thou shouldst do it again, thou and I would have a quarrel." Such was for the Frank the entire expression of his disapproval and the limit of his jealousy . . . (Hitti 1929: 165).

Now the purpose of such a tale is open to question, and amusing his reader with the "strangeness" of the foreigners might be Ibn Munqidh's main aim, but there is perhaps an implicit understanding that had it been a Muslim in the bed, the Frank would not have been so forgiving, and Munqidh's own viewpoint is also clear: this would *never* happen in a good Muslim household.

Other subjects, however, exploited good relations with their colonial rulers to police cultural and sexual boundaries *within* their communities. Precious testimonies from the subject Jewish community in Venetian Crete supported the Christian ban on interfaith relations, including the use of Christian wet nurses and other servants, on the basis of maintaining a peaceful coexistence and preserving proper religious customs, including sexual transgressions. The case study of newcomer Shalom the Sicilian, accused of corrupting good Jewish women and polluting himself in brothels, shows the community acting rapidly, and in collaboration with the Venetian authorities, to expel him (Borysek 2014: 257–8).

A focus on sexuality and empire reveals some of the contradictions and fault lines in medieval Christian Europe's engagement with strange cultures within and outside its borders. As Finke and Shichtman (1998: 71) observe, "As boundaries are extended, those at the margins must be assimilated, pushed to more distant margins, or destroyed." In fact, all three strategies are visible in the examples discussed earlier, and ideas of sexuality, particularly that of females, were central: Jews and Muslims (and pagans) were assimilated through marriage or non-consensual sexual penetration, or they were segregated by laws (including their own) that sought to avoid such relations, or they found themselves displaced, expelled, or converted. And as the physical frontiers of Europe expanded, so the tolerances of sexual behaviors between conqueror and subject, the "sexual frontiers," shifted and adapted too.

CHAPTER SEVEN

Resistance

BRETT E. WHALEN

Historically speaking, resistance to empire can come in many forms, including organized revolts, popular uprisings, conspiracies, and other forms of dissent. From the ninth through the fourteenth centuries, in reality and in symbolic terms, the popes of Rome paradoxically formed the primary enablers and main source of resistance to western empire.[1] At the heart of papal resistance to imperial claims lay a question of political culture, namely that of the "two powers," the temporal might of worldly monarchs versus the spiritual authority of priests. Emperors and popes embodied the two powers before all others. According to medieval thinkers, both the secular and the spiritual powers formed a necessary part of God's plan for history until the end of time. Popes needed emperors as defenders of the church, wielders of the "material sword" against heretics, pagans, and enemies of the faith. Emperors needed popes, who anointed them, bestowed their crowns, and prayed for the stability of their reigns. Working together, the two powers preserved the order of the Christian world (Watt 1988).

And yet, the Roman papacy equally tried to place restraints on medieval empire, limiting its reach over ecclesiastical properties and persons, designating appropriate roles for emperors, and insisting upon the final superiority of the priesthood to the imperial dignity. As the successors to Saint Peter and "Vicars of Christ," enjoying the "fullness of power" over the church, the bishops of Rome claimed not just sweeping spiritual powers, but also the right to intervene in matters of earthly governance. This became the case above all starting in the eleventh century with the emergence of the so-called "papal monarchy," the strong and assertive Roman papacy of the High Middle Ages (Morris 1989). When they believed that the situation called for it, popes turned the "spiritual sword" of excommunication and anathema against obdurate emperors. In certain states of emergency, they offered material support to secular allies battling against imperial rulers, fielded armies against emperors, and even declared crusades against them (Rist 2009). Emperors responded in kind to such acts of resistance, asserting their own supreme authority in matters of temporal governance, defending their traditional rights over church offices and properties, and rejecting the idea that popes could exercise worldly judgment over them. Such battles between the two powers, generated to a great extent by papal resistance to empire, served to define the political culture of the Middle Ages.

As the medieval era drew to a close, however, the dynamics of papal resistance to empire began to change. Suffering from their own internal problems and new external pressures, facing a newly configured political landscape around Europe, the bishops of Rome found themselves increasingly unable or unwilling to resist imperial claims with the same far-reaching impact as during previous centuries. Ironically, by the fourteenth century, emperors and popes began to share a common fate, both yielding ground to the ascendant royal power of kings, while the scope of their own authority diminished. By the end of the Middle Ages, the "Holy Roman Empire" did not provoke much in the way of resistance from anyone, more or less confined to the territories of Germany, surviving as a symbol rather than a genuine source of sovereignty. The clashes of papacy and empire receded into memory, although, according to some, they left behind a crucial legacy of distinction between secular and spiritual forms of sovereignty, between what we now label "religion" and "politics," if not "church" and "state."

THE TWO POWERS IN THE EARLY MIDDLE AGES

The political culture of the two powers dates back to the Christian Roman empire of late antiquity, as summed up by the so-called "Gelasian dictum," a statement attributed to Pope Gelasius I (492–6) about the governance of the world. Addressing the Eastern Roman Emperor Anastasius (r. 491–518), Gelasius drew a clear division between "the sacred authority of priests" and "the royal power," adding "of these that of the priests is weightier, since they have to render an account even for the kings of men in the divine judgment" (Rahner 2006). Just what Anastasius thought about Gelasius's delineation of their respective "spheres" of governance remains unclear. Like most emperors of the time ruling from Constantinople, he probably did not care much one way or another about the bishops of Rome, as long as they obeyed imperial commands. Early medieval popes, who claimed universal jurisdiction over the "spiritual empire" of the church, typically did not possess the sort of political clout or institutional reach that enabled them to contest imperial authority, even if they wanted to do so (Wessel 2008).

Under the Carolingians, the question of the two powers began to assume a higher profile in the politics of western Europe. Indeed, the relationship between popes and emperors stood front and center from the beginning of medieval empire, as seen on Christmas day 800 in St. Peter's basilica at Rome, where Pope Leo III (795–816) crowned Charlemagne (r. 768–814) emperor of the Romans (Ganz 2008: 38). As a symbolic act of cooperation between the pope and the Frankish monarch, the imperial coronation marked the "rebirth" of empire in the west. By this time, Charles and his father Pepin had cultivated a relationship with the bishops of Rome for decades, presenting themselves as the pious defenders of the Roman church. Although Charlemagne did not need Leo's approval to exercise power over his kingdoms, in terms of his legitimacy to rule over the empire, he clearly benefitted from his relationship with the pope. Recently driven from Rome by his enemies, Leo had turned to Charles for aid in recovering his position. For ideological and practical reasons, this "Franco-papal alliance," as it is sometimes called, befitted both sides of this relationship (Noble 1984: 260).

This convergence of papal and Carolingian interests, however, knew its limits. During the decades leading up to the imperial coronation, in large part as a response to the growing Carolingian presence on the Italian peninsula, someone in papal circles crafted *The Donation of Constantine* (Figure 7.1), one of the most famous forgeries in European history (Dutton 2004a). This invented

FIGURE 7.1: Donation of Constantine, Basilica of Santi Quattro Coronati, Rome. Credit: Fine Art Images/Heritage Images/Getty Images.

tradition describes how the first Christian emperor, Constantine, surrendered his imperial power to Pope Sylvester, handing over his tiara and other regalia, bestowing the territorial possessions of the western Roman empire on the Roman church before acting as the pope's groom. Not coincidently, Pepin had made a similar "donation" to Pope Stephen II (752–7), formally recognizing the papacy's lordship over a considerable part of central Italy, the beginnings of the so-called Papal States (Partner 1972). If one believed *The Donation of Constantine*, Pepin merely gave back what rightly belonged to the bishops of Rome. During a meeting with Stephen at Ponthion outside of Paris, according to the *Lives of the Popes*, not long after the pope anointed Pepin as ruler of the Franks, the king even acted as the pope's groom, humbly leading Stephen's horse with pious devotion (Scholz 1970: 39).

A mosaic in the Lateran church commissioned by Pope Leo a few years before he crowned Charlemagne suggests a similar relationship between popes and worldly monarchs (Figure 7.2). It features Saint Peter in the center, handing over the *pallium*—the symbol of a bishop's office—to Pope Leo on his right and a banner—denoting military might—to Charles on his left. The words below read: "Blessed Peter give life to Pope Leo and give victory to King Charles." On one hand, the fresco displays the idea of cooperation between the two powers, both carrying out their divinely assigned roles. But the centrality of Saint Peter, with Leo occupying the privileged spot on his right, suggested a subtle hierarchy or a prioritizing of the pope over the Frankish ruler. Christ left his "power of the keys" on earth to Peter, and Peter assigned the two powers their respective duties. In case someone missed this message, an accompanying fresco features a corollary image with Christ at its center, Pope Sylvester on his right, and Constantine on his left (Noble 1984: 323–4).

If *The Donation of Constantine* and the mosaic in the Lateran church suggested papal resistance to Carolingian authority, in reality, the newly minted emperors of the ninth century clearly held the upper hand in the relationship between the two powers. Needless to say, Charlemagne did not share the papal view of his subordinate relationship with the bishop of Rome. His power as Christian ruler came directly from God, even if the bishops of Rome played a role in consecrating his reign. When Charles wrote to Leo III in 796, asserting his duty "to defend the holy Church of Christ from the attacks of pagans and infidels from without, and within to enforce the acceptance of the catholic faith," he made the pope's role in this relationship clear: "It is your part, most holy father, to aid us in the good fight by raising your hands to God as Moses did, so that by your intercession the Christian people under the leadership of God may always and everywhere have victory over the enemies of His holy name, and the name of our lord Jesus Christ may be glorified throughout the entire world" (Loyn and Percival 1976: 120–1). From this perspective, Charles stood center-stage; Leo played a supporting role. During his stay at Rome in

FIGURE 7.2: Lateran Church mosaic: Saint Peter, Leo III, and Charlemagne, ninth century, lithograph 1880.

800, when he intervened on Leo's behalf to protect him from enemies who had driven him from the city, Charles did so by standing in judgment of the pope and his accusers, a clear indicator of who really held the upper hand. After leaving Rome following his coronation, Charles never returned. The emperor, not the pope, crowned his son Louis (r. 813–40) as co-emperor in 813, although Louis did make his own journey to the holy city to be crowned and anointed by Pope Stephen IV (816–17) three years later (Ganz 2008: 39).[2] Louis's son Lothar (r. 817–55) likewise received his imperial crown at Rome. Such visits came at a price for the Roman popes, allowing Louis and his son to intervene directly in the affairs of the city and its church, receiving oaths of fealty from successive popes as their loyal subjects (Whalen 2014: 74–6).

With the decline of the Carolingian empire in the mid-to-late ninth century, the Roman church experienced new challenges, disruptions, and scaled-down horizons. When imperial power resurfaced in Saxony starting with Otto I (r. 936–73), a new series of emperors emerged that more or less kept the bishops of Rome under their thumbs, even as they looked for the pope to anoint them and place the imperial crown upon their heads. As pious rulers, the Ottonians confirmed earlier imperial donations of properties to the Roman church and swore to respect ecclesiastical liberties, but they also left no doubt who dictated the terms of their relationship with the Roman popes. After Otto's imperial coronation by Pope John XII (955–64) in 962, the contemporary author Liudprand of Cremona tells us, when John turned against him, the emperor called for a church council that deposed John from office and elected a friendlier pope, Leo VIII (963–5) (Squatriti 2007: 219–37). During the reign of Otto III (r. 996–1002), the newly elected pope Gerbert of Aurillac took the suggestive name of Sylvester II (999–1003), but he showed no signs of contesting Otto's rights over Rome as emperor. Indeed, he supported his former pupil's ambitious—albeit short-lived—vision of a renewed Roman empire, recovering the idiom of its ancient glories (Lattin 1961: 294–9). The ensuing Salian imperial dynasty began with a similar "proprietary" sense of their rights over the Apostolic See. When Emperor Henry III (r. 1046–56) faced a three-way schism in the papal office, he did what emperors were expected to do—he intervened, calling for a council at Sutri to toss out the three rivals and assure the election of his preferred candidate, Clement II (1046–7). He did so, in part, so that a proper pope could crown him as emperor of the Romans, which Clement did shortly thereafter. Judging by this episode, the comfortable sense of imperial oversight over the papacy must have seemed as secure as ever (Miller 2005: 63–9).

CHURCH REFORM AND THE INVESTITURE CONTEST

Such business as usual for emperors and popes, however, was about to change in ways that no one could have imagined. During the second half of the eleventh century, papal resistance to empire entered a new phase with the coming of the "church reform movement." After the deaths of Clement II and his briefly lived successor, Henry III arranged for the election of Bruno of Toul, who took the name Leo IX (1049–54). Following his elevation at the emperor's behest, the new pontiff did something unusual: he entered Rome like a penitent pilgrim, asking the clergy and people of the city to affirm his position as their bishop. According to the *Life of Leo* IX, they did so enthusiastically (Robinson 2007: 131–3). This public display of humility signaled Leo's commitment to a new "reformist" sense of what it meant to be a member of the church hierarchy, committed to purifying the clergy from the corrupting outside influences of the world. Such corruption came in many forms: married clergy, stained by carnal relations with their wives; priests who wielded weapons, shedding blood;

bishops and others who paid for their sacred offices, committing the sin of simony. Pope Leo and other supportive "reformers" viewed the supreme authority of the pope as the key to combat these and other sources of pollution (Cushing 2005).

Leo and Henry III remained on good terms, but over time the advocates of this reformist program began to resist the long-held rights of emperors to exercise direct influence over the Roman church. In 1059, while Henry III's underage heir Henry IV (r. 1056–1105) was still in his minority, Pope Nicholas II (1059–61) and the cardinal clergy agreed to new rules for the election of a pope (Robinson 1990: 33–120). The cardinal bishops would choose the pope, with input from the cardinal priests and only then from the wider Roman clergy and laity. The decree still qualified that such an election should happen "without violating what is owed to the honor and reverence of our beloved son Henry, who is at present king and, God willing, in the future hopefully emperor." By formalizing papal elections as an internal affair managed by the cardinal bishops, however, the decree implicitly challenged the young Henry's right to intervene in the selection of any new pope. In later years, alternative versions of the election decree circulated, emphasizing the need for the cardinals to consult the German ruler, a sign that not everyone was eager to see the monarch's traditional prerogatives eroded (Miller 2005: 71–3).

When the hardliner deacon Hildebrand became Pope Gregory VII (1073–84), he transformed this reformist movement—sometimes called the "Gregorian" reform after his name—into a platform for confrontation with the empire. Gregory initially stood on good terms with Henry IV as his spiritual son, even calling upon the king and future emperor to join him on a proposed expedition to rescue the Christians of the east from the "pagans," as the pope called Muslims (Emerton 1990: 56–8; Cowdrey 1998). Gregory's strong view of the papal office and its powers, however, set him on a collision course with the young ruler. As Gregory declared in his *Dictatus papae*, a bullet list of sorts laying out his office's prerogatives, the pope could "depose or restore bishops," could "depose emperors," could "be judged by no one," and could "absolve subjects from fealty to unjust men" (Miller 2005: 81–3). Tensions between Gregory and Henry began to simmer when the young ruler refused to break off ties with several of his counselors whom the pope excommunicated. Eventually, they came to clash openly over the issue of investiture, the question of whether secular princes like Henry could bestow a bishop's ring and staff, the symbols of his sacred office (Blumenthal 1992). In January 1076, Henry called for a synod to meet at Worms, where the assembled bishops denounced the "false monk Hildebrand" and declared his election as pope illegitimate. During a synod at Rome a few weeks later, Gregory excommunicated Henry, depriving him of "the governance of the entire kingdom of Germany and Italy," releasing his subjects from any and all oaths of fealty owed to him (Emerton 1990: 90–1).

Facing local forms of resistance to his rule, Henry was in a vulnerable position. At the beginning of his reign, he had already faced an uprising by a large number of East Saxon nobles. Emboldened by the pope's sentence against the Salian ruler, the Saxons revolted again. In the meanwhile, Henry continued to lose support from a great number of important churchmen in Germany and Lombardy, who refused to obey the excommunicate ruler (Leyser 1983: 409–43). On January 25, 1077, under pressure, Henry appeared at the gates of Canossa castle, seeking an audience with Pope Gregory, who was staying with his supporter Countess Mathilda of Tuscany during his northward journey to meet with the Saxon rebels. The German king waited three days in snowy conditions, wearing humble, penitential garb, before finally meeting with the pope (Figure 7.3). After Henry made numerous promises and concessions, Gregory provisionally reconciled him with the church, although explicitly not settling the matter of his contested kingship in Germany (Emerton 1990: 111–13; Miller 2005: 90–100). This distinction did not matter in the long term. With the sentence of excommunication lifted, Henry turned his attention to crushing the rebellion against him. In March, the Saxons elected their own "anti-king," Rudolf of Swabia, still hoping for the pope's support. Indeed, according to Paul of Bernried in his *Life of Pope Gregory VII*, Gregory's decision to excommunicate Henry for the first time enabled Rudolf's opposition to the illegitimate ruler. "No one could justly accuse King Rudolf and his princes of perjury," Paul observed, since they had been "absolved from that oath by the pope, because the king had been deposed and excommunicated" (Robinson 2007: 338).

Pope Gregory's attempts to broker a peace between the warring factions went nowhere. Confident in his victory over the rebels, Henry began to contravene the commitments he had made to the pope at Canossa. In March 1080, Gregory excommunicated him for a second time, while Henry presided over a synod at Mainz that declared Gregory deposed from the papal office. In a letter to Hermann, archbishop of Mainz, Gregory once again spelled out his reasons for excommunicating Henry as well as the legality of his decision, pointing to the examples of past popes who judged and excommunicated emperors and others. "Does anyone doubt," he asked, "that the priests of Christ are to be considered as fathers and masters of kings and princes and all believers?" (Emerton 1990: 169). In terms of placing political pressure on the Salian ruler, however, the second ban did not work nearly as effectively as the first one. In June 1080, a number of bishops supporting Henry appointed Guibert of Ravenna as the new bishop of Rome, the "anti-pope" Clement III (1080–1100). Rudolf of Swabia died in battle later that fall, strengthening Henry's hand. In March 1084, after Henry marched into Rome, Clement crowned him as "emperor of the Romans" in St. Peter's basilica, a sign that anyone aspiring to the imperial dignity needed the formal sanction of the

FIGURE 7.3: Gregory VII, Henry IV, and Mathilda of Tuscany, after a miniature from the parchment manuscript "Life of Matilda" (1114 completed) by the monk Donizo of Canossa in the Vatican Library in Rome, published in 1880.

pope—as long as it was the right pope for the job. As for Gregory VII, fleeing from Rome to take refuge with his Norman allies, he died in exile at Salerno on May 25, 1085, supposedly saying "I loved justice and I hated iniquity, therefore I die in exile" (Robinson 1990: 398–413; Miller 2005: 114–15).

At that moment, the apparent challenge posed by the "Gregorian papacy" to the empire must have seemed like an aberration more than anything else. But in fact, as the decades passed, a series of reformist popes following in the tradition of Gregory VII continued to pursue his reformist ambitions and resist imperial claims over the church. Pope Urban II (1088–99), who would eventually issue the call for what became known as the First Crusade, showed particular persistence and skill in turning the cities and communes of northern Italy against Henry IV (Cowdrey 1995: 721–42). In 1095, Henry's alienated son, Conrad II, rebelled against his father with Urban's support. During their meeting at Cremona in April of that year, Conrad publically acted as the pope's groom, invoking the memory of the humble Constantine, before swearing an oath of fealty to the pontiff. Urban received him as a "son of the holy Roman church" and promised to aid him in obtaining his "kingdom" and acquiring the "crown of empire."[3] Conrad's rebellion failed, but similar troubles hounded Henry for the rest of his life, including another revolt by his son and heir, Henry V (r. 1099–1125). This time around, Pope Paschal II (1099–1118) threw his support behind Henry IV's rebellious son, hoping that he would prove more amenable than his father to settling the investiture controversy on favorable terms.

After Henry V assumed sole rulership over Germany and northern Italy, his warm relations with Paschal did not last. By this time, the pope and supportive churchmen had worked out a compromise with the kings of France and England over investiture. The monarchs would renounce the right to bestow the signs of the bishop's spiritual dignity (*spiritualia*), guaranteeing the free election of bishops by their peers without royal interference. Newly elected bishops, however, would swear oaths of fealty to their rulers for the properties and other material benefits attached to their positions (the *regalia* or *temporalia*). Kings retained the right to intervene in disputed clerical elections. Negotiations continued for the German ruler to renounce the rights of investiture on similar terms until 1111, when he met with Paschal at Rome, planning for his imperial coronation. A fight broke out between the Germans and Romans: when Henry left the city, he brought the pope and a number of the cardinals with him as virtual prisoners. Under pressure, Paschal conceded the right of investiture to Henry, and promised never to excommunicate him. He also performed the imperial coronation. Henry left Italy with everything he had come for, or so it seemed (Chodorow 1989: 3–25). Paschal, however, quickly renounced the agreement. Facing further uprisings in Germany, Henry and his representatives finally reached a compromise after negotiations with Popes Gelasius II (1118–19) and Callixtus II (1119–24), formally agreeing to the Concordat of Worms in 1122. Henry surrendered "all investiture by ring and staff," assuring free and canonical elections for bishops, restoring any of the Roman church's property seized during their past conflicts and granting "true peace" to the pope. Callixtus conceded that the election of bishops in Germany would take place in Henry's presence, allowing him to intervene in disputed elections, while bishops from that kingdom and the other parts of his empire would receive the *regalia* from him (Miller 2005: 120–1).

While they did not get everything they hoped for, papal resistance to empire had worked to a certain extent. The investiture contest ended in a compromise that both sides could regard as a victory of sorts, leaving the German ruler with considerable influence over ecclesiastical elections, but forcing him to renounce the time-honored rights of investiture. The days when emperors could openly appoint bishops with ring and staff, however, confidently making sure that their preferred candidate occupied the Apostolic See of Rome, had become a thing of the past.

THE AGE OF PAPAL MONARCHY

After the settlement at Worms, both popes and emperors enjoyed the benefits of their "truce" over investiture. Much like other ruling institutions around Europe, the papacy entered into a period of sustained growth in its administrative reach and governing capabilities. In terms of political culture, the pope's primacy as the heir to Saint Peter and "Vicar of Christ" assumed an unprecedented profile in European politics, as the bishops of Rome actualized their claims to spiritual leadership over Christendom like never before.[4] Beneath the surface of apparent concord between the two powers, however, the fundamental dynamics of their complicated relationship had not changed. Simply put, emperors and popes still needed each other's mutual—if sometimes grudging—support, although both sides loudly protested when they felt that the other had overstepped its bounds. In moments of crisis, such papal protests turned into acts of direct resistance to imperial claims, sometimes breaking into a state of open war between "church" and "empire" (Whalen 2014: 111–32).

One can see these dynamics at play in the relationship between Lothar III of Supplinburg (r. 1125–37) and Innocent II (1130–43) (Robinson 2016). Elected king of the Romans after the death of Henry V, Lothar faced persistent opposition in Germany from his Staufer rivals Frederick II and Conrad I. After a disputed election that split the cardinals, Innocent confronted a rival pope, Anacletus II, whose supporters forced him from Rome. Both Lothar and Innocent, therefore, stood to gain from public signals of cooperation. When Lothar met with Innocent at Liège in 1131, he humbly performed the scene reminiscent of Constantine's submission to Sylvester. In the square before the cathedral church in Liège, as the French abbot Suger of Saint Denis described the scene, "the emperor humbly offered himself as a squire," hurrying over to the pope in the middle of his procession. "In one hand he held the scepter to defend the supreme pontiff," Suger continued, "and in the other the reins of his white horse, and he led him about as if he were his lord" (Cusimano and Moorhead 1992: 147). In 1132, Lothar marched into Italy with a small force, not large enough to drive Anacletus from St. Peter's basilica where he had taken refuge, but sufficient to install Innocent in the Lateran church, where the pope crowned Lothar emperor in June 1133. Lothar then returned to Germany, leaving Innocent in a somewhat precarious position until the emperor returned in 1137, reinforcing the pope's position and attacking the Normans—at that point, threatening the Papal States—at the pope's behest.

After the reign of Conrad III (r. 1138–52), never crowned as emperor of the Romans, the assertive Staufer ruler Frederick I (r. 1152–90) made a far more aggressive bid to restore the "Holy Roman Empire" to its former glories in Germany and Lombardy. His efforts set the stage for a renewed round of conflict between the papacy and his imperial rule. In 1154, like many of his predecessors, Frederick marched into Italy to enforce his will and receive his crown. Meeting with Hadrian IV (1154–9) at Sutri in June 1155, Frederick repeated Lothar's ceremonial performance as the pope's groom, but with far more reluctance. According to a later account, the pope objected when Frederick held his left stirrup instead of the right one, as was customary, when he dismounted. Frederick complained about Hadrian's reaction, asking whether the pope expected him to perform this service as a token of his respect or as a legal obligation. In either case, Hadrian should be satisfied. When Frederick's supporters in his camp worried that this dust-up might endanger his planned imperial coronation, they convinced him to repeat the ceremony, this time correctly. Proceeding to Rome, Hadrian crowned Frederick emperor of the Romans in St. Peter's basilica, although the rebellious Romans soon forced both of them from the city (Freed 2016: 140–50).

Over the following years, Frederick and Hadrian's relationship continued to expose deep-seated tensions between their respective offices. The question at the heart of the matter remained an old one: which of the two powers ultimately answered to the other? During an assembly at Besançon in October 1157, imperial and papal representatives began to argue vociferously over Hadrian's description of the empire as a "benefit" from the pope, perhaps indicating his belief that the emperor ruled as a papal vassal. Frederick's followers rejected that idea entirely. They also disputed over the meaning of a mural at the Lateran church that portrayed Lothar's meeting with Innocent II years earlier, when the German ruler acted as his groom. The words under the image ran "Coming before our gates, the king vows to safeguard the city; then, a liegeman of the pope, by him he is granted the crown." Frederick's envoys likewise repudiated this visual suggestion that the emperor served as a subordinate to the pope. The situation grew tense and nearly came to blows when the count of Bavaria threatened one of the papal legates with his sword. In a letter sent to the pope about the incident, Frederick likewise denounced Hadrian's suggestions that the emperor received the "material sword"—symbolizing his worldly jurisdiction—from the pope rather than receiving it from God directly. Writing back to Frederick, Hadrian later tried to smooth things over, insisting that "benefit" only meant "a good deed," namely placing the crown on the emperor's head, not a fief (Mierow 1953: 180–6).[5]

This crisis passed but when the next papal election resulted in schism between Pope Alexander III (1158–81) and the "anti-pope" Victor IV, Frederick backed Victor, chosen by cardinals with more sympathy for his imperial rights. Seeing a chance to intervene, the emperor called for a council to meet at Pavia and settle the division in the papal office. At this point, according to Alexander's biographer Boso, the clergy backing the pope worried greatly: "For some the greatest fear was the persecution at the hands of so powerful a prince that loomed over them, for others, the violations and utter destruction of the church's liberty" (Ellis 1973: 48). When the assembled clergy chose Victor, Alexander denounced Frederick as an "oppressor" of the church and fled to the kingdom of France, seeking refuge there. This situation worsened when some of the cities in Lombardy began to openly resist Frederick, forming the so-called "Lombard League" in 1167 (Raccagni 2010). Italy erupted into war. Seeking to counter Frederick, Alexander threw his support behind the protesting Lombards. The two powers more or less stood in a state of civil war, with kingdoms, communes, and communities around Christian Europe picking sides until the Lombards dealt Frederick a significant defeat at the battle of Legnano in 1176. The following year, the warring parties agreed to the Treaty of Venice, ending their conflict on terms favorable to the Lombards. Frederick denounced the current anti-pope Paschal III and once again acted as groom for Alexander, whose allies had brought the emperor to heel (Ellis 1973: 107–9).

Through their by no means seamless alliance of interests and combined acts of resistance, the Lombard League and the pope had exposed the hard limits of the emperor's abilities to exercise his rule over northern Italy. Frederick's son Henry VI (r. 1190–97), however, continued to press the Staufer dynasty's claims over the Italian peninsula, potentially expanding them through his marriage to Queen Constance of Sicily in 1189. Her nephew William, the Norman king of the Regno (i.e,. Sicily, Apulia, and Calabria), had died childless, leaving Henry as the leading contender for the crown. When the relatively deferential Pope Celestine III (1191–8) crowned Henry emperor of the Romans in 1191, the papacy faced a new and possibly threatening configuration: an emperor who ruled over Germany, Lombardy, and the Regno, boxing in the Papal States on both sides. The Roman church received an unexpected reprieve of sorts, however, when Henry unexpectedly died in 1198, leaving his son and heir Frederick II as still just a child. In Germany, a veritable civil war broke out between Henry's brother, Philip of Swabia, and Otto IV of Brunswick, rivals for the title "king of the Romans" and the imperial office (Whalen 2014: 130–7).

While the state of the empire remained in flux, the papacy benefited from the vigorous and exceptional leadership of Innocent III (1198–1216) (Sayers 1994; Moore 2003). More than any other medieval pope, Innocent III exemplified the "papal monarchy" at the height of its prestige and influence, known for his commitment to the linked goals of church reform, wiping out heresy, and liberating Jerusalem once and for all from the "infidels." The fact that Innocent enjoyed such successes during a period that lacked a strong imperial presence was not a coincidence. Facing a competition between possible emperors, he pressed the claims of the papacy to arbitrate over empire in forceful terms. In a secret address to the cardinals in 1200, the young pope insisted that the provision of the Roman empire belonged "principally and finally" to the Apostolic See: principally, because the pope had transferred the imperial dignity from Greece to the west in the days of Charlemagne; and finally, because the pope rendered the final blessing upon the emperor, crowning him and investing him with his *imperium* (Kempf 1947: 74–91).

Innocent did not just express such views about the limits of imperial power in secret. In a letter to Otto of Brunswick in March 1201, he compared the "two great dignities" of church and empire to the sun and the moon: both placed by God in the heavens, the former shining with spiritual might during the day, the latter shining in the darkness, wielding material power against the church's enemies. The moon reflected the light of the sun, indicating the superiority of the spiritual dignity. Drawing out this analogy, Innocent identified the current gap in the imperial office as something like an eclipse of the moon, a dangerous time allowing heretics to flourish and pagans to rise up against the Christian faith (Kempf 1947: 97–110).[6] During the following years, Innocent backed Otto's claim as king and emperor, and then seemed willing to support Philip until his murder in 1208, before resuming his support for Otto. In October 1209, the pope crowned Otto as emperor of the Romans in St. Peter's basilica. By this time, Innocent had extracted numerous concessions and promises from the would-be imperial ruler, most of which limited his right to interfere with ecclesiastical properties and persons, along with guarantees to recognize and respect the borders of the Papal States. Professing his obedience, reverence, and honor for the Roman church, Otto submitted to most of Innocent's demands. He also swore not to invade Sicily. Within a few months of his coronation, however, he effectively reneged on these agreements with the pope, leading to his excommunication in November 1210. Over the following years, Otto lost his support among the German nobility, who turned instead to the young Frederick II, by then old enough to press his dynastic claims. Innocent likewise threw his support behind the Staufer ruler, a former ward of the Roman church. Civil war again broke out in Germany. After suffering a severe military setback with his English allies at the battle of Bouvines on July 27, 1214, defeated by Frederick's French ally, King Philip II, Otto withdrew to his holdings at Brunswick and abandoned his claims to the throne in 1215. Pope Innocent had outlasted his antagonist (Moore 2003: 63–70, 181–8, 215–19).

FREDERICK II AND THE BATTLE FOR CHRISTENDOM

The way was clear for the rise of Frederick II (r. 1212–50). Most historians seem to agree that Frederick, sometimes called the "Wonder of the World," represented the most dynamic imperial ruler of the High Middle Ages, and certainly the most colorful.[7] Through his various inheritances and marriages, he came to hold an impressive number of titles: king of the Romans, king of Arles, king of Lombardy, king of Sicily, and, after his coronation in 1220 by Pope Honorius III (1216–27), emperor of the Romans. A few years after that, through his marriage to Isabelle of Brienne, he became king of crusader Jerusalem. Although Frederick started his reign on relatively good terms with the papacy, the deeper question of medieval political culture remained unresolved: which of the two powers, the spiritual and the temporal, ultimately answered to the other? As the years passed, the Staufer emperor's ambitions and assertive style of governance provoked the last sustained acts of papal resistance to empire, fighting for control of the Italian peninsula, but also waging a battle of ideas over the relationship between the "Vicars of Christ" and the current occupant of the imperial throne.

The first round of trouble started not long after Gregory IX (1227–41) became pope (Lomax 1992).[8] After years of postponements, Frederick was supposed to depart on crusade to Syria by August 1227, fulfilling his previous vow. When he took ill and failed to set sail, Gregory excommunicated him. Frederick left for Syria in 1228, still excommunicated, and managed to recover Jerusalem by signing a treaty with the Egyptian sultan (Tyerman 2006: 739–55). Back in Italy, accusing the Staufer ruler and his agents of violating ecclesiastical persons and properties in southern Italy and Sicily, Gregory assembled an army to march against Frederick's forces, calling upon the Lombards among others to contribute troops. During the ensuing "War of the Keys," named for the banner featuring the papal symbol associated with Saint Peter, the pope's allies and supporters gained the upper-hand until Frederick returned from Syria, quickly recovering his lost territories in the Regno (Loud 2011). By that point, both sides stood to lose from prolonging their conflict, leading the pope and emperor to make peace in 1230.

Over the following years, Gregory and Frederick remained at peace and found genuine opportunities to cooperate, above all with regard to their plans for the next crusade to the holy places (Weiler 2000). Frederick's prosecution of a war against the re-formed Lombard League, however, and his persistent violation of the church's liberties in the Regno—according to Gregory's complaints—slowly eroded their relationship. In March 1239, accusing the emperor of various sins, crimes, and assaults on the church, Gregory excommunicated him for a second time. The ensuing conflict again turned violent. Frederick besieged Rome in the late winter of 1240, threatening the city until Gregory arranged a show-stopping procession featuring the relics of Saints Peter and Paul, rallying the wavering citizens to his side. He personally marked some of them with the sign of the cross, sanctioning them to fight against the emperor. Over a year later, in May 1241, Frederick's son Enzio and his Pisan allies destroyed a fleet of Genoese ships bound for Rome, bringing a number of highly placed cardinals, bishops, and abbots to a council summoned by the pope. Judging by contemporary chronicles, such dramatic moments of confrontation between the "church" and "empire" shocked and scandalized Europeans, who viewed this in-fighting as a danger to Christendom, threatened from within by heretics and from without by pagans, infidels, and the "Tartars," that is, the Mongols who were menacing Europe's eastern regions at the time (Abulafia 1988).

The pope and emperor continued their confrontation until Gregory died in 1241. After a long vacancy in the papal office, the election of Innocent IV (1243–54) opened a brief window for possible reconciliation between the papacy and Frederick (Melloni 1990). When the negotiations for peace fell through, Innocent fled from Italy entirely, installing himself and the papal curia at Lyons, close to the borders of the sympathetic French kingdom. In June and July 1245, the pope staged a general council at Lyons, summoning clerics and lay representatives from around Europe and beyond to hear his case against Frederick along with other church business. Testimony was given and documents produced as evidence of the Hohenstaufen ruler's abuse of clergy, plundering of ecclesiastical properties, alliances with "infidels," violations of the peace, and other misdeeds. Frederick's envoys, including the imperial judge Thaddues of Suessa, offered a spirited defense of the emperor, accusing the pope and his allies of lying about Frederick's crimes. On July 17, 1245, after consulting with the assembled bishops, Innocent pronounced his judgment, stripping Frederick of all his "every honor, his empire, and his other kingdoms" (Figure 7.4). The pope made sure that the written sentence deposing Frederick circulated around Europe, likewise dissolving all oaths of fealty owed to the former king and emperor by his followers.[9]

In immediate terms, Innocent's deposition of Frederick, perhaps the most controversial act of papal resistance to empire in the Middle Ages, did not settle anything but served to intensify their confrontation. In terms of the wider legal culture, the pope possessed an impressive array of arguments to justify his actions, based on his status as the Vicar of Christ with the "fullness of power" over the church. Frederick, however, who never denied the pope's rights to pass spiritual judgments in matters of sin, denounced the pope's sentence as an illegitimate form of interference in worldly affairs of governance. To enforce his adverse judgment, Innocent continued some of the previous measures taken by the papacy to constrain Frederick: publicizing his state of excommunication, collecting and channeling revenues from ecclesiastical properties to fund his military opponents, sending out letters that denounced Frederick as a wicked tyrant and persecutor of the church. The pope also took new steps to defeat his Staufer opponent, supporting the election of "anti-kings" in Germany and the preaching of crusades against Frederick and his son Conrad as enemies of the church. According to some rumors, he even backed plots to murder Frederick.

FIGURE 7.4: Pope Innocent IV deposes Emperor Frederick II, France, fifteenth century. Credit: De Agostini Picture Library/Getty Images.

Church and empire, as one scholar puts it, had entered into a state of "total war" (Morris 1989: 566).

For some Christians, those struggles between empire and church indicated nothing less than the end of days. Drawing upon a host of prophecies and apocalyptic schemes, some associated with the famous scriptural commentator Joachim of Fiore, others with the British magician Merlin, still others with the ancient pagan sibyls, some Christians came to view Frederick as antichrist, or at least one of his "members" acting in history. This link between the emperor and antichrist features in a "Joachite" image of an apocalyptic dragon (Revelations 12), with a series of seven heads representing various wicked emperors, including Frederick I, Henry VI, and—the sixth head—Frederick II. That left one more head remaining, *the* final antichrist (Figure 7.5). Others, by contrast, declared that Innocent IV was antichrist, presenting the papacy's

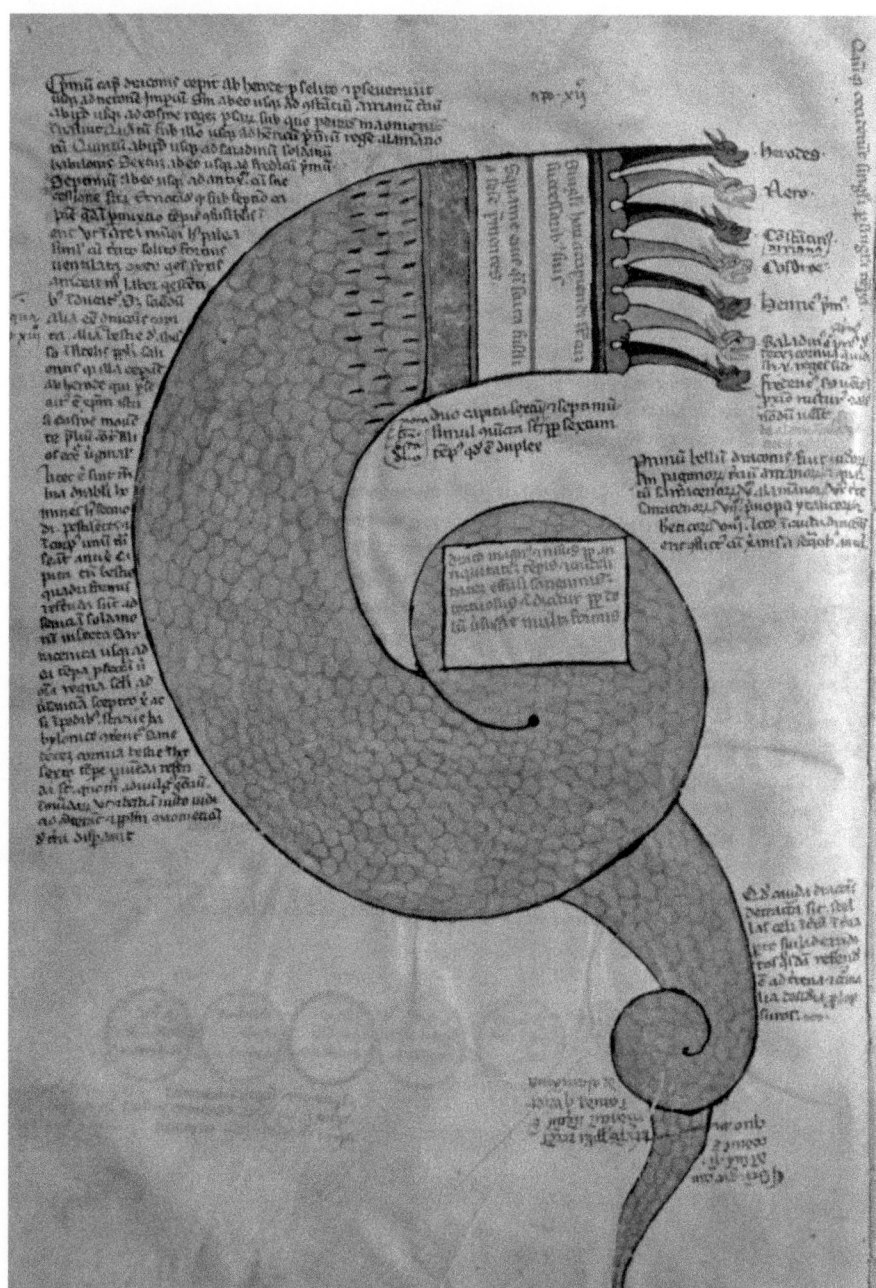

FIGURE 7.5: Joachim of Fiore, Apocalyptic Seven-Headed Dragon, Liber Figurarum, 1132–1202, by Joachim of Fiore, St. Peter's basilica, Perugia, Umbria, Italy. Credit: De Agostini/Archivio J. Lange.

wasteful battles with the emperor as indicative of the church's overall pastoral and moral failings as the apocalypse approached. In these terms, the clash between the "two powers" portended the end of history, or perhaps the opening of a new and marvelous historical age when such violence would give way to peace, prosperity, and spiritual fulfillment (Lerner 1988: 359–84; Patschovsky 1998: 291–322).

EMPIRE AND CHURCH IN THE LATER MIDDLE AGES

In December 1250, after a period of illness, Frederick II died, not reconciled with the Roman pope. Innocent returned to Italy the following year, where he kept up his struggles against Frederick's short-lived or ineffective heirs, Conrad and Manfred. The stakes in such conflicts, however, had changed, focusing more and more on the direct political control of southern Italy rather than any wider sense of struggle between church and empire. After Innocent died in 1254, his successors Alexander IV (1254–61) and Urban IV (1261–4) faced a growing "quagmire" in the unsettled region that lacked a strong Staufer presence to maintain order. To deal with this situation, Pope Urban invited the French prince Charles d'Anjou to assume rulership over the kingdom of Sicily, a gambit that more or less worked until the Sicilians revolted against Charles in 1282, inviting Peter III of Aragon to rule over the kingdom. The papacy rejected Peter's claims and even declared a crusade against him. For years to come, the papacy would pour its energies and considerable sums of money into the region, trying to stabilize the situation on the southern border of the Papal States (Runciman 1958).

In other ways, Frederick II's passing marked a turning point in the history of medieval empire and its sometimes contentious relationship with the papacy. Decades passed before a strong enough candidate emerged to claim the imperial crown, Rudolf of Habsburg (r. 1273–91), whose election ended the "Great Interregnum" in the kingdom of Germany and the Holy Roman Empire. Rudolf, who never came close to wielding the sort of authority enjoyed by Frederick II, made numerous concessions to win the support of Pope Gregory X (1271–6), renouncing his imperial rights over the city of Rome, promising to never claim rulership over Sicily, and committing to lead a new crusade to the Holy Land—one which never actually happened (Fried 2015: 513–20). During the years after Rudolf's death, the German electors responsible for choosing the "king of the Romans" vied for influence over the imperial office, different families and factions seeking the ideal candidate that would favor and protect their own interests. The next two German kings never managed to claim the imperial dignity. Other monarchs around Europe, above all the increasingly assertive French king Philip IV, showed less and less deference to the emperor as the ultimate ruler of Christendom, even in theory.

The next imperial ruler, Henry VII of Luxembourg (r. 1308–13), represented a compromise candidate between the various electors and other interested parties, nervous that Philip might secure the imperial title for his own brother Charles of Valois. Even Henry, however, was a vassal of the French king for some of his holdings. During his royal coronation at Aachen in 1309, he swore "subservience and loyalty" to the pope, a ceremonial gesture meant to spell out the limitations of his position rather than signaling any real strength of the papacy. In 1310, seeking to flex his imperial muscle, Henry marched into Italy to assert his rights over Lombardy. The Italian poet Dante, who believed that only a strong imperial presence could settle the tumultuous political scene in the region, greeted his arrival with great fanfare. Others, however, protested and resisted Henry's attempts to extend his rights over the cities and communes of northern Italy. Robert of Naples, the Angevin ruler of southern Italy, likewise opposed Henry. The aspirational emperor could barely force his way into Rome to be crowned emperor in June 1312 by the cardinal bishop of Ostia, sent to the city for that purpose by Pope Clement V (1305–14) who was residing at Avignon as his successors would do for decades to come. Henry died at Pisa just over a year later, still mired down in his attempt to subdue Italy (Bowsky 1960; Fried 2015: 393–8).[10]

This trajectory of waning imperial clout continued over the following years. After Henry's death, the electors reached a split decision in 1314, some supporting the Wittelsbach candidate Louis the Bavarian (r. 1314–47) and others the Habsburg one, Frederick of Austria (1313–30). A drawn-out fight for the crown followed, ending in 1322 when Louis secured his position as king of the Romans and the next emperor. By this time, however, he faced a divisive confrontation with Pope John XXII (1316–34), who had refused to recognize Louis and excommunicated him in 1324. John also complained about Louis's support for the so-called Spiritual Franciscans, a community of dissident friars banned by the pope for their radical views on apostolic poverty. In January 1328, Louis arrived at Rome for his imperial coronation, a sign of how an emperor's coronation at the city still mattered. His crowning, however, also displayed how much things had changed in the last few generations. He received his crown not from the pope, still residing in Avignon and bitterly opposed to Louis's coronation, or even a cardinal, but rather from the Roman senator Sciarra Colonna. During his months-long stay in the city, Louis formally accused John XXII of heresy for his suspect theological views and set up a Franciscan anti-pope Nicholas V, who repeated the emperor's coronation ceremony before they both left the city (Ullmann 2003: 284–6).

Louis the Bavarian's opposition to John XXII revealed other fissures in the traditional relationship between church and empire, as the emperor turned his court at Munich into a refuge for Franciscan critics of not just the current pope, but the very premise of papal authority in the temporal realm. This shift in political philosophy had developed over decades, emerging in part due to a new intellectual awareness of Aristotelian thought about the "natural" origins of kingship as a form of human governance. Some traditionalists defended the supreme right of the pope to judge emperors and other secular rulers, but more stressed the need for clear delineation between the temporal and spiritual realms, confining the power of the priesthood to the latter. Thinkers like William of Ockham, a dissident friar who fled Avignon in 1328, seeking Louis's protection, pushed such insights in far-reaching directions. According to Ockham, the pope had no more claim over the Roman empire, either by "divine" or "human" law, than he did over any other kingdom—that is to say, none at all. The Roman empire had clearly existed even before there were any bishops of Rome: those who claimed that Christ had somehow transferred its dominion to Saint Peter and his papal heirs misread scripture. As for *The Donation of Constantine*, even if Constantine had surrendered his empire to Sylvester, and Ockham seriously doubted that he did, the emperor would not have actually had the legal right to dispossess his own successors in such a manner. By interfering in the lawful governance of the empire, Ockham concluded, the pope represented a tyrant, overstepping the bounds of his spiritual office.[11]

Over the following decades, these theoretical critiques of papal authority found real-world equivalents, as the German electors began to deny the pope any role in their choice of a ruler, including the right to crown the emperor—any bishop, they proclaimed, could do that. After his coronation ceremony at Rome in 1355, Emperor Charles IV (r. 1346–78) spent barely a few days in the city before returning north of the Alps. Despite his relatively amicable relations with Popes Clement VI (1342–52) and Innocent VI (1352–62), a year later when he approved the "Golden Bull of 1356," clarifying the rules for electing the king and emperor of the Romans, Charles made no mention of the pope's role in that process. That silence spoke volumes. Over five centuries after Leo III had crowned Charlemagne in St. Peter's basilica, the bishops of Rome had been removed from the equation of empire, no longer in a position to legitimate or meaningfully resist Roman emperors and their *imperium*.

* * * * *

By the close of the Middle Ages, therefore, one might say that emperors and popes had become shadows of their former selves, giving way to the nascent power of Europe's late medieval states.[12] The history of their past clashes, however, would continue to shape how people remembered the Middle Ages as a distinct phase in the development of European, if not western, civilization. From this perspective, battles between emperors and popes, assuring that neither side could exercise complete dominion over the other, helped to make room for the eventual separation of church and state, a hallmark of the modern world (Tierney 1982; Oakley 2012). This view of the medieval past, highlighting the cooperative and conflictive relationship between the "two powers" as a key factor in the distinctive shape of European political culture has much to recommend it. But it also seems to rest upon the assumption of a one-way trajectory from the conditions of the medieval world to those of the modern one, viewing history as a "secularizing" process rendering human governance and public life less overtly religious, confining religion to the private realm. In the twenty-first century, when the supposedly clear lines between religion and politics have become somewhat harder to discern, those past struggles between worldly and spiritual powers ironically seem less distant than they might have a few generations ago. As for whether the political culture of the Middle Ages have any lessons to teach about resistance to empire, that remains an open question.[13]

CHAPTER EIGHT

Race

CORD J. WHITAKER

Race has been widely recognized as a major component in the history and development of empire in the west. But its history is far older than that of the early modern and modern empires with which it is usually associated. Race has been traced back as far as the ancient Greek comportment toward other cultures, who were considered barbarians based on the sounds of their languages and other foreign attributes (Snowden 1970: 170; Euben 2008: 60–1). Race has hinged upon the contrast between darkness and lightness of complexions and persists in modernity largely as the distinction between blackness and whiteness of skin. Indeed, historians have noted the widespread use of black and white in ancient Greek art to which interest in their contrast may be traced (Gage 1993: 11–12). Race has been of seminal importance in the development of modern thought in fields as diverse as sociology, philosophy, anthropology, and literature. Race, especially in the development of the "racial sciences" of the eighteenth and nineteenth centuries, has helped spark entirely new fields such as genetics (Morgan *et al.* [1915] 1922: vii; Kant [1775] 1997: 43–4). While race is largely thought of as a modern construct, traced by even some of the twentieth-century's most progressive scholars only as far back as the seventeenth century, race-thinking—the notion that differences in physical appearance and genealogical lineage dictate the characters and abilities of groups as well as individuals—had significant influence on the cultures and conflicts of the Middle Ages (Kelsey 1965: 21–2). The religious conflicts of the Crusades, in particular, established European worldviews that made possible the Age of Exploration, from the fifteenth century forward, and instituted race-thinking as one of the central tools of European empires globally, and in the New World of the Americas especially. This chapter traces the development and utilization of race by considering its characteristics in the Middle Ages and in modernity; examining its central epistemological elements in the Middle Ages with a focus on climate theory; and discussing its reliance on previous and contemporary imperial efforts including the Roman, Mongol, and Holy Roman empires. While medieval and modern western cultures—the social power structures that give shape to polities and periods—are both characterized by conflict, this chapter explores the role of race in the transition from a medieval west defined by race-thinking in the service of crusading to a modernity whose cultures are defined by New World empire and the racial ideology that is its legacy.

DEFINING MEDIEVAL RACE IN MODERNITY

The question of whether or not the term race should be applied to dynamics among human groups in premodernity has been fraught. It prompted historian of the Middle Ages William Chester Jordan to assert, in the postscript to Thomas Hahn's groundbreaking special issue of *The Journal of Medieval and Early Modern Studies*, that his doubts about "the utility of 'race' (an allegedly fixed category) as an analytic concept in the modern world . . . are compounded when 'race' is applied to the Middle Ages." Jordan goes on to speculate that readers will not "sufficiently shed their modern notions of race simply because scholars redefine the concept against the modern grain, so that medieval race can encompass change and independent nonbiological markers" (2001: 169). In a similar move several years earlier, Ivan Hannaford in his ambitious *Race: The History of an Idea in the West* notes the lack of "the dispositions and presuppositions of race and ethnicity" in the Middle Ages. These, he argues, "were introduced—some would say 'invented' or 'fabricated'—in modern times and were the excrescence of recent thought on descent, generation, and inheritance" (1996: 6). Critical consensus has taken race to be the product of the "definitions and presuppositions of race propounded with such certainty in the eighteenth and nineteenth centuries" (Hannaford 1996: 7). Indeed, to locate the rise of race in the seventeenth century, as theologian George Kelsey did in the mid-twentieth century, was in its time a more radical position—and one that has been since corroborated by a number of scholars working in early modern studies (Britton 2014: 5–8).

The definition of race, subject to the historical period in which a scholar contextualizes it, has varied. Though a basic definition of race might involve only a person's skin color and what it implies about her lineage, race is rarely so simply treated. Among even scholars whose concerns are limited to modernity, race is not simple to define. Geneticists R.A. Kittles and J. Benn-Torres write that: "Race is an enigma, exhibiting no clear biological definition yet strong cultural and social meanings, particularly in the United States."

Kittles and Benn-Torres immediately turn to history: "Historically, racial groups have been classified by various physical attributes, such as skull volume and size, skin color, facial features, and other physical attributes" (2009: 82). Sociologist Jason Eastman defines race by the symbolic meanings that attend racial categories: "whiteness becomes a usually unstated, symbolic indicator of a hardworking person with high ethical standards" while "a nonwhite race is a readily visible symbolic indicator of people's unseen, and often supposedly inferior characteristics, character, inner identity, abilities, and morality" (2015: 231–2). Anthropologist Nina Jablonski writes that while "[s]kin color has been the primary characteristic used to assign people to different 'races,'" the category has "always been ill-defined" and "varied tremendously from one place to another." Jablonski continues: "Races have been defined as collectives of physical traits, behavioral tendencies, and cultural attributes. They have been considered real and immutable, so that a person having a particular physical characteristic had, by definition, all of the other attributes of the racial category" (2012: 4). While these definitions vary in their disciplinary perspectives, they share a focus on race's effects in the modern world and they indicate that race's major utilities have been in classification, character judgment, and the crystallization of a racial group into a totalizing and immutable category.

Despite the location of race's beginning in the seventeenth and eighteenth centuries by scholars such as Kelsey or, more recently, in the sixteenth by Valentin Groebner, a growing number of scholars have noted the presence of race-thinking in the Middle Ages (roughly 500–1500 CE) (Kelsey 1965: 21–3; Groebner 2003: 1–18). Investigations into medieval race have produced definitions that take into account the greater breadth of evidence used in race-thinking before the eighteenth and nineteenth centuries' Enlightenment. In his encyclopedia entry, Jeffrey Jerome Cohen states that race in the Middle Ages

> involves differences imagined as innate (such as national character), differences in biology (such as humoral imbalance), differences in bodily features (such as dark skin or a hooked nose), differences in descent or origin still evident in contemporary identity, and especially differences that are visible only as they are performed by bodies in motion (ritual, custom, legal or hospitality codes not in their abstract existence but in their concrete expression) (Cohen 2013: 115).

Cohen's definition presents its elements (national character, humoral imbalance, dark skin) in a way that does not respect the primacy usually accorded to visible, phenotypic traits in modernity. In modernity, theoretically, phenotypic traits such as a hooked nose are observed first and then judgments are made about national character. Cohen's definition, by first mentioning "differences imagined as innate (such as national character)," registers that in medieval race-thinking the

FIGURE 8.1: Medieval knight figurine.

acceptable signs of race are more plentiful than in modernity (Figure 8.1). He also demonstrates that medieval race places abundant value on culture and customs, so that rituals, for instance, can serve as the observed stimuli that indicate racial difference. The breadth of evidence employed in medieval race-thinking made it a useful tool in premodern imperial projects and their modern aftermath.

In addition to offering a view of race that destabilizes the primacy of biology in favor of culture and other indicators, medieval race-thinking makes clearer the spiritual nature of racial character judgments. Geraldine Heng writes that "cultural practices across a range of registers also disclose historical thinking that pronounces decisively on the ethical, ontological, and moral value of black and white" (2011a: 259). She surveys writing that suggests white skin is a sign of courage while dark skin is a sign of cowardice and dishonesty. She considers medieval architectural sculpture that links the execution of a holy figure, John the Baptist, with Africans and that links Africans with lasciviousness, too. Heng concludes that medieval race hinges on a binarism in which:

> Black is damned, white is saved. Black, of course, is the color of devils and demons, a color that sometimes extends to bodies demonically possessed ... In literature, black devilish Saracen enemies—sometimes of gigantic size—abound, especially in the *chanson de geste* and romance, genres that tap directly into the political imaginary ... Elite humans beings of the 14th century have a hue, and it is white (2011a: 259–61).

Heng's work demonstrates that medieval race-thinking goes well beyond character judgments in order to define moral hierarchies whose subject is the very essence of the soul. Beyond mere "national character," medieval racial judgments are concerned with the essence of a people's collective soul. Character as expressed in actions and comportments is no more than a secondary indicator, after appearance, of what is really at stake: essential moral goodness or depravity at the collective and individual levels. Considering medieval physiognomic science—the (pseudo-)scientific judgment of character based on appearance—historian Joseph Ziegler makes a strong case that medieval physiognomy was a "universal practice geared to decipher the personality of individuals" (Ziegler 2009: 199). Though Ziegler argues that medieval learned physiognomy cannot be taken as evidence of race's deployment in the Middle Ages because physiognomy, in his estimation, does not judge groups, it is precisely the confluence of physiognomy's presentation of physical traits that *are* easily visible in groups with the spiritual dichotomy of blackness and whiteness that gives medieval race-thinking its power. In the Middle Ages, individuals and groups are subject to judgments, based on appearance and actions, about their collective *and* individual souls.

To recognize the medieval deployment of race is to use one modern theory to disrupt another: medieval critical race theory unravels the periodizing notion that the Middle Ages and modernity are discrete and incommensurate categories. Heng summarizes critical race theory's near-consensus that "'race' [is] a portable, protean term, empty of stable referent, and without fixed dispositions in referencing ... that the only reference of the term 'race' [is], in fact, its *function*, or *instrumentality* in a historical period" (2003: 13, emphasis original). While this ought to mean that the term is transferrable to any historical period in which similar functions can be discerned, Heng notes that it has led to the opposite effect:

> a history of commitment to countering Enlightenment racisms posited on biology, anatomy, and color binarisms nonetheless raised biology to a position of central importance in deciding what constituted racisms and racial enactments (2003: 13).

It is for this reason, among others, that the Middle Ages have been held apart as "a kind of pre-political infancy, innocent of racial thinking or race-making." Interactions that in other periods would be considered racial are, in the Middle Ages, deemed to "not properly point to authentic, mature racial practices or race logic" (2003: 13). Nonetheless, the implication of the position that race is "portable," "protean," and "empty of stable referent," is that the Middle Ages should not be spared its influence. As Kathleen Davis has noted, periodizing divisions between the Middle Ages and the early modern period have "mask[ed] the existence of 'modern' characteristics in the Middle Ages and 'medieval' characteristics in modernity" to the end of "occlud[ing] minority histories such as those of women and the racially or religiously oppressed" (2008: 4). In fact, Davis shows just how complicated is the relation between medieval and modern race when she notes that the sixteenth-century legal theorist Jean Bodin connected the feudal with slavery, while the colonial slave trade boomed, in order to position feudalism and slavery together as "characteristic of Europe's past and of a non-European present" (Davis 2008: 8). In sum, the culturally hegemonic notion that modernity is the sphere of a progressive Europe is premised upon the identification of racial and temporal others against whom modernity is defined. Recognizing and examining race in the Middle Ages makes apparent the intimacy of the relationship, the interdependence, and in some respects inseparability, of the medieval period and the development of modern cultures, including those imbricated with imperial power in the west.

MEDIEVAL RACE AND THE WIDER WORLD

Western empire has been variably imagined as a political constellation that experiences and relates history as having a "linear teleology," as "a coherent, end-directed story told by [the imperial victor's] own power," and as "an extension of the sovereignty of the European nation-states beyond their own boundaries" (Quint 1993: 9; Hardt and Negri 2000: xii). While these definitions register the cultural mechanisms of power consolidation, empire has also been defined in more material modes as the extension of "the idea of kingship—the protection of the people in return for their absolute allegiance—across the globe" and as "the biggest asset stripping exercise in history" (Lee 2005: 1). Each of these descriptions is from a study of either early (Quint, Lee) or late modernity (Hardt and Negri). It is no coincidence that the Middle Ages are not generally associated with European empire.

In the modern conceptualization, the vast expansion of European power to the east and the west is only fully realized with an increase in European exploration and the creation of colonial settlements by groups of settlers and the early modern European trading companies. Even the suggestion of the Middle Ages' involvement in New World empire has been so unorthodox that

Mary Campbell, in her magisterial treatment of early European travel writing, has to state declaratively that the anonymous fourteenth-century writer of *Mandeville's Travels* "was a good writer, and he became an *auctoritas*" whom Christopher Columbus used and believed in his voyages of discovery (Campbell 1988: 10). Columbus's was a literal reading of the *Travels* that "helped inspire his search for a 'real' terrestrial paradise" (Campbell 1988: 183). It is necessary to note that, far from being a proto-modern text that evidenced a vast departure from its medieval predecessors, the *Travels* was quite indebted to, and of a kind with, medieval encyclopedic writings that sought to identify and categorize the flora and fauna (including humans) of the world.

In order to subject the globe to European sovereignty and obtain access to and power over global assets, it was necessary that political actors had a working understanding of the world that they aimed to control. It aided the execution of Europe's exploratory voyages and the production of early modern texts of discovery that an encyclopedic approach to the world was not at all new with Mandeville. Attempts to categorize the world's people stretch at least as far back as the fifth century BCE in which the so-called "Father of Anthropology" Herodotus reveals in his *Histories* "something of how fifth-century Greeks understood non-Greeks, their own history, and the interrelationship between them" (Evans *et al.* 1908: 125; Euben 2008: 55). In another example, such attempts characterize the first-century CE *Historia Naturalis* in which Roman military man, rhetor, and all-around scholar Pliny produces an "encyclopedic account of the state of science, art, and technology" that includes significant sections on the lands, plants, animals, and peoples of the world. Pliny outright refers to some of Africa's inhabitants—the "Atlas people" who would have lived in the mountains that flank the African continent's north-west corner—as "primitive and subhuman" ([1991] 2004: xv, 57). Medieval Europe's understanding of the world owed much to classical sources, and it drew from them one element in particular that may have had more influence on modern race and western imperial cultures than all the rest: climate theory.

Climate theory, or "the effects of climate in determining the humoral makeup of individuals and the anatomical, physiological, and even behavioral predispositions of nations," was widely disseminated among learned readers in the Middle Ages, and it had its roots in classical and pseudo-classical materials (Akbari 2012: 141). In the "twelfth-century renaissance" and through the thirteenth century, the European intellectual scene was flooded with Aristotelian and other (pseudo-)classical works that were (re-)discovered in Middle Eastern libraries, translated into Latin, and made available in Europe (Abulafia 1994: 23–33). Around 1100, only two of Aristotle's logical works were known in Latin and these works, along with Porphyry's *Isagoge*, became known as the "old logic" (*logica vetus*). From this point forward the recovery, translation, and European circulation of Aristotelian and related texts took place at breakneck pace: by 1300, some fifty Aristotelian works and commentaries were in circulation along with more than twenty other pseudo-Aristotelian and related works (Dod 1982: 45–79). Medieval Aristotelianism proved fertile ground for the race-thinking's rise as a major influencer of social and political cultures.

Among the classical works flooding the Latin west were those that treated blackness as a part of physiognomy, such as Rhazes' *Liber ad regem Almansorem*, the physiognomy book of which had been translated from Arabic into Latin by Gerard of Cremona and circulated independently in the Latin west beginning in the early thirteenth century. Rhazes writes, in a chapter titled "Significationes colorum" [The meanings of colors]:

> Red color or redness of blood and heat refers to a multitude (of conditions). In truth, color midway between red and white signifies a temperate complexion, if the skin were also without hair. He, however, whose color is like a flame of fire is irascible and a maniac. He whose color appears to be red and bright, he is modest. Also, he whose color appears green or black is irascible (1994: 163–4).[1]

Rhazes's work reflects the standard medieval physiognomic ideal: a temperate complexion signifies a temperate person, and a temperate person is the best person to have in one's employ. A man's character can be discerned through his skin color, and temperate skin color is that immediately in between red and white. Too much red, and any greenness or blackness, means that a man has an extreme personality and tends toward anger. Medieval classicism is thus directly implicated in the association of skin color with character judgments.

In climate theory inhere elements that facilitate race-thinking's role as a driver of culture as well as those that trouble race-thinking and its assumptions. Take, for example, William de Mirica's mid-fourteenth-century commentary on pseudo-Aristotle's *Phisonomia*. In it, William writes that:

> Blackness in Ethiopians and Mauritanians is indeed by the heat of the sun. For Mauritania is that region in Ethiopia that is hottest. In which, on account of the unrelenting heat and fire of the sun, the subcutaneous blood is burned and thus having been burned it is made black. In him whose blood has been blackened by diffusion between the skin and the flesh all members are generally blackened (Ziegler 2005: 533, n. 81).

While later medieval, and more compressed, physiognomies sidestep the causes of color in favor of its effects on character, William's work reflects the fact that the learned physiognomer would generally have understood that color was the effect of climate. Furthermore, William's work demonstrates learned physiognomies' interest in tracing the etiology of appearance from climate's effects through physical changes that are not readily visible and finally through their exterior and visible effects. As physiognomies circulated more widely, they became increasingly compressed and began to favor visible effects and their meanings for character while eliding etiologies. Etiologies often provided the interpretive spaces through which negative character judgments could be de-emphasized in favor of positive attributes (Whitaker 2009). In the increasing absence of etiologies, negative judgments were given more room to thrive. The compression of physiognomies laden with climate theory has facilitated the strategic use of race-thinking in imperial projects and the development of post-imperial cultures in which racial judgments are made quickly, appear to be based solely on phenotype, and masquerade as facts rather than interpretations.

By 1444, when Portugal's Prince Henry the Navigator initiated Europe's economic dependence on the African slave trade by receiving a cargo of 235 African men, women, and children at Lagos, Portugal, climate theory was already an established part of the European view of the world, and it was increasing in power. The fourteenth-century travel narrative *The Book of Knowledge of All Kingdoms* was one of Henry's "indispensable guides as he envisions further conquest of Africa." In it, the people are "black as pitch" but also Christian. They "burn themselves with fire on their foreheads with the sign of the Cross in recognition of their baptism." The text intimates that their blackness was considered at odds with their faith and reason: "*although* these people are black, they are men of good understanding and good mind" (Marino 1999: 61; Jennings 2010: 23). Their blackness is attributed to the heat of their land that, as William points out, burns their blood. Climate is a complicated thing, however; *The Book of Knowledge* notes that Indians are also black because they live in a hot land, but their towns are adjacent to the sea and the moist air changes the quality of the heat such that "they derived beautiful bodies and elegant forms and fine hair, and the heat does nothing else to them except make them brown in color" (Marino 1999: 83–4). Proximity to the sea is a caveat that racial climate theory maintains until at least the late eighteenth century when Johann Gottfried von Herder writes that "where the heat is diminished, or cooled by the sea breeze, the black [skin] is softened into yellow. The cool heights are inhabited by white, or whitish people . . ." (Herder 1997: 75). Neither the recognition of "good minds" nor "beautiful bodies" spared Africans and Indians the horrors of colonial oppression. Skin color was the primary indicator for deciding who should rule and who should be ruled. Climate theory had direct implications for the rise in the economic expediency of the trade in enslaved African people, other imperial projects such as colonization in India, and the development of the character judgments that reinforced them.

Lest it seem that climate theory was mostly a southern European matter, occasioned by the Iberian peninsula's Mediterranean location, it is important to note that climate theory intimates the development of a culture of race-thinking in more northerly medieval texts, too. Take, for instance, the Latin *De proprietatibus rerum* by the thirteenth-century English encyclopedist known as Bartholomeus Anglicus, and John Trevisa's Middle English translation *On the Properties of Things*. The text states that, on one hand, men in Africa have humors burnt and wasted by the sun that lead ultimately to their being black and "cowardes of herte." On the other hand, men of the north due to coldness are white, their humors are retained because they are not evaporated by sun and heat, and they are, as a result, "bolde and hardy" (Bartholomeus Anglicus [1601] 1964: 648, 752–3; Akbari 2012: 144–5). Climate theory, with the influence of Aristotelian texts throughout western Europe in the later Middle Ages, pervaded northern as well as southern European thought about the world and its people.

In fact, climate theory's role in the development of western imperial race-thinking culture is evident in its influence on early iterations of English colonization. In 1580, some 240 years after the Portuguese landing in the Canary Islands and thirty-seven years before the establishment of the British settlement at Jamestown, Virginia, Edmund Spenser moved to Ireland to serve under Arthur Grey, 14th Baron Grey de Wilton, the newly appointed Lord Deputy of the Kingdom of Ireland. Sixteen years later, Spenser published *A Vewe of the Present State of Ireland* (Figure 8.2). The text's aim is to argue for colonial reform by

FIGURE 8.2: Edmund Spenser is portrayed in this engraving produced in 1834.

pointing out the failures of English rule in that the Irish are "nowe accompted/ the most barbarous nation in Cristendome" (Spenser 1596: 53). Spenser expends no small amount of effort presenting theses for Irish ancestry, and his text supports its claim that the Irish are depraved with a number of assumptions based in climate theory. Relying on a number of classical sources, including Herodotus, *A Vewe* suggests different origins for the people who populate different parts of Ireland. Two interlocutors, Irenius and Eudoxus, discuss Ireland's situation at length. Irenius offers an account of Irish heritage from traditional Irish chronicles:

> . . . an other nation
> Cominge oute of Spaine arryved in the weste
> partes of Ireland & findinge it waste or
> weaklie inhabited possessed it, whoe whither
> they were native *Spanierdes* or *Gaules* or
> *Affricanes* or *Gothis* . . . it is vnpossible to affirme . . . (Spenser 1596: 47).

The notion that the Irish may be of African descent appears again and again in different guises, and the treatment reaches its climax in the assertion that Spain's history has seen so much mixing of various peoples that Spanish ancestry is unknowable:

> Northerne nacions findinge the Compleccion
> of that soyle and vehement heat theare farre
> diffringe from their natures, tooke noe felicitye
> in the Countrye but from thence passed over &
> ded spreed them selues into all Countries in Christendome
> of all which theare is none but hathe some mixture
> and sprincklinge, yf not throughe peoplinge of
> them, And yet after all these the Mores and
> Barbarians breakinge over out of *Affrica* ded
> finallie possesse all *spayne* or the moste parte therof
> and treade downe vnder the faule heathnishe foote
> whate ever litle they founde theare yet standinge
> the which thoughe afterwardes they were beaten out
> by *Ferdinando* of *Arygon* and Elizabeth his wief yet
> they were not soe Clensed but that thorowe the
> marriages which they hadd made and mixture with
> the people of the land duringe their longe contynuance
> theare they hadd lefte noe pure drop of *Spannishe*
> bloud noe nor of Romane nor of *Scythian*, so that of
> all nations under heavene I suppose the *Spanierd* is the
> moste mingled moste vncerteine & moste bastardlie (Spenser 1596: 54).

Spenser's use of "compleccion" to describe Spain's soil and climate reflects the pre- and early modern etymology of complexion, in which it means the condition resulting from the blending of four qualities, or in the case of persons the four humors. Indeed, the modern use of complexion, meaning skin tone, is the effect of compression in the word's lexical range. That compression in turn reflects the development of modern race theory, in which the signs considered meaningful in judging character gradually become restricted to skin tone. "*Compleccion*," for Spenser, however, necessarily involves the climate of the lands in question.

Hanging on the suggestion that the Irish may be of African stock is the notion that they are intemperate in their passions. Irenius and Eudoxus discuss Irish "cryes," from war cries to mourning lamentations,

> which savor greatlye of the *Scythian* barbariscme as their
> lamentacions att their burialls with dispaierfull out-
> cries, and imorderate waylinges . . . .
> the same is not proper spannishe but alltogither
> heathnishe brought in first thither either by the
> *Scythians* or by the Mores which were *Affricanes*
> but longe possessed that Country for it is the maner
> of the *Pagans & Infidells* to be intemperate in their
> waylinges of their dead for that they hadd noe
> faithe nor hope of saluacion . . . (Spenser 1596: 68–69).

In this passage, the source of inordinate mourning is the lack of Christian faith, but another passage links immoderate lamentation directly to climate:

> those Northerne Nations havinge bene vsed to
> be annoyed with muche Coulde & darknes are
> wont therfore to haue the fier & the sonne
> in greate veneracion like as Contrarywise the
> mores and *Ægyptians* which are muche offended
> and greived with muche extreame heate of
> the sunne doe everie morninge when the sunne
> Riseth fall to Cursinge and blaminge of him
> as their plague and Cheif scourge (Spenser 1596: 72).

Irenius, in expounding on the "manner of [Irish] Armes & arraye in Battell with other Customes," registers, like William de Mirica and Bartholomeus Anglicus before him, the profound effect of the sun on the characters of people. The sun, in addition to producing cowardice, also produces intemperance; people in sunny climates begin each day by cursing and blaming the sun. Unlike some more compressed climate theories, Spenser's work registers the etiology of intemperance: the character of people from sunny geographies has its origin and definition in their reactions to the sun itself. The Irish, despite their northern location, are intemperate and immoderate; they are held up as an example of the negative effects of southerly origins on national and individual character.

Long after Spenser and well into modernity, climate theory continued to have an outsized effect on the idea of race and its deployment in imperial efforts. It features in the racial "sciences" of the Enlightenment naturalists and philosophers including Georges Louis Leclerc, Comte de Buffon (1707–88); Immanuel Kant (1724–1804); Kant's student Johann Gottfried von Herder (1744–1803); and Georg Wilhelm Friedrich Hegel (1770–1831). Each thinker offers a theory in which, in one way or another, light-skinned Europeans reside at the top of a hierarchical scale of intellectual ability, rational capacity, and social advancement. The primacy of binaristic race-thinking, in which a person's or people's character is judged according to their blackness or whiteness, in modern imperial and post-imperial western cultures is largely the effect of climate theory's persistence from classical antiquity through the Middle Ages and into modernity.

IN THE SHADOW OF ANCIENT AND CONTEMPORARY EMPIRES

From Julius Caesar's first-century-BCE conquests in England to Pope Gregory's (540–604) famous pun about Briton slave boys in the Roman market—*Angli* ("Angles") recalls *Angeli* ("Angels") and he thought their white skin and blond hair made the name fitting—to the belief that London was founded by a Trojan who originally named it *Troia Nova* ("New Troy") and subsequent efforts to "restore" the name *Troynovant* from the 1380s until Spenser's *Faerie Queene* (1590–6), England wrestled with its former identity as a Roman colonial backwater. England was far away from Rome; in Rome-centered maps it appeared at the edge of the world (Lavezzo 2006: 2). In addition to the Roman imperial past, English and, more broadly, European Christian identity was shaped by conflict with contemporary imperial power to the east, especially that of Genghis Khan and his descendants. At the same time, western European Christendom had already fashioned itself into a multi-kingdom political constellation that shifted Christendom's power center north and west into Germany and away from Rome. England and Europe's Roman heritage along with late medieval religious, economic, and military competition helped consolidate, as an integral part of the European imperial project, ideas of difference into the concept of race.

The Roman empire cast the longest shadow on late medieval England's increasingly imperial aspirations. Indeed, the influential myth of *Troynovant* is a major element in Geoffrey of Monmouth's *History of the Kings of Britain*, a text that also posits the English sovereign, in the person of Arthur, as the rightful heir to the Roman imperial throne. Here, Roman general Lucius Tiberius writes a scathing letter to King Arthur, rebuking him for refusing to pay tribute to Rome and demanding he appear before the Roman senate to "make satisfaction to [his] masters" (Geoffrey 1848: 9.xv). Arthur calls together his council and responds by laying out his own claim to tribute *from* Rome:

> For if Rome has decreed that tribute ought to be paid to it from Britain, on account of its having been formerly under the yoke of Julius Caesar, and other Roman emperors; I for the same reason now decree, that Rome ought to pay tribute to me, because my predecessors formerly held the government of it. For Belinus, that glorious king of the Britons, with the assistance of his brother Brennus, duke of the Allobroges, after they had hanged up twenty noble Romans in the middle of the market-place, took their city, and kept possession of it a long time. Likewise, Constantine, the son of Helena, and Maximian [Maximus], who were both my kinsmen, and both wore the crown of Britain, gained the imperial throne of Rome. Do not you, therefore, think that we ought to demand tribute of the Romans? (Geoffrey 1848: 9.xv).

Arthur claims that his ancestors ruled Rome and that he therefore ought to as well. He reverses Rome's claim and begins a myth that extends through the development of the English literary canon; it appears in various guises in such texts as Chaucer's *Man of Law's Tale* in the fourteenth century, Thomas Malory's *Le Morte d'Arthur* in the fifteenth, and Spenser's *Faerie Queene* in the sixteenth. During the late Middle Ages and as Britain begins to lay the groundwork for the early modern empire that will follow, London is positioned as the new Rome and Britain as the inheritor of Roman imperial power.

Europe did not have to look only to its Roman past for imperial inspiration. During the thirteenth and fourteenth centuries, the Mongol empire came to power under Genghis Khan in central Asia. In 1206, Genghis Khan proclaimed the formation of the Great Mongolian State (Figure 8.3). Within three generations, it became the largest land empire in world history, stretching from Asia's eastern coast westward to the Levant and the edge of eastern Europe (Allsen 2004: 17) (Figure 8.4). Christian Europe's comportment toward the Mongol empire ranged from excitement about possible collaboration and emulation to fear and loathing. The Mongol empire served several purposes in Europe's program toward a Christian empire in the Middle East. Among these was the idea that the Mongol emperor was a friend to Christianity. Indeed, for many in Europe Genghis Khan became conflated with the myth of Prester John, a perfectly Christian king in the east (Kaplan 1985: 58–9). If western

FIGURE 8.3: Portrait of Genghis Khan. Ink and watercolor on silk. Bridgeman Art Library. Credit: ullstein bild via Getty Images.

Christendom could reach him, the story went, he would join forces with Europe and together they would surround and defeat the Muslims (Bisgaard 2005: 127). The Mongol empire's obvious and storied power, coupled with the hopeful possibility of its alliance with Latin Christendom, loomed large in late medieval Europe's cultural and political imaginations.

The political reality of the Mongol empire's independence from Christendom started to become apparent as early as the 1240s. Only several decades into the empire's rapid growth, it began attacking the fringes of eastern Europe. Nevertheless, the imagined alliance of Europe with the Mongol empire under the banner of Latin Christianity spawned cultural products that long postdated the possibility of its realization. Take, for example, the late thirteenth- or early fourteenth-century text *King of Tars*. In it, the beautiful daughter of the Christian king of Tars attracts the attentions of a "heathen high lord of Damascus the sultan" (Perryman 1980: 5–6). He promises to wage war on Tars unless he can marry the princess. The princess goes to him, and in the story that ensues she bears him a child who is born a lifeless lump of flesh. When prayer to the Christian God transforms the "lump-child" into a beautiful little baby, the

FIGURE 8.4: A forty-meter-tall statue of Genghis Khan stands atop the Genghis Khan Statue Complex and Museum at Tsonjin Boldog, Tov Province, Mongolia. Credit: Nick Ledger.

sultan converts to Christianity and wages war on his former fellow Saracen kings (Calkin 2009: 114). The story's sources—the Anglo-Latin *Flores historiarum*, Villani's Italian *Istorie Fiorentine*, Rishanger's Anglo-Latin *Chronica*, a Hispano-Latin letter to Jayme II of Aragon, the Germano-Latin *Annales Sancti Rudberti Salisburgenses*, and Ottokar's German *Österreichische Reimchronik*, all datable to the late thirteenth or early fourteenth century— identify the princess as the daughter of the Christian king of Armenia and her to-be-converted husband as a pagan king of Tartars who attacks Saracens (Perryman 1980: 46; Calkin 2009: 105). The Tartars (or Tatars), formerly rivals to Genghis Khan's people, were already consolidated under his power by the time the Great Mongolian State was formed in 1206 (Allsen 2004: 17, 51, 63). Thus, the romance's characterization of the king of Tars as a Christian king reflects the continued hope in the late 1200s and early 1300s that Genghis Khan and his descendants were Christians, soon-to-be Christians, or at very least friends to Christendom, who would aid it against Islam.

In the *King of Tars*, race-thinking is part and parcel of Christendom's imperial aspirations. By the late thirteenth century, it was common to imagine Christendom's religious competitors, including pagans and Muslims, Africans and non-Africans alike, as black. Nonetheless, the *King of Tars* is notable for the spectacular nature of its race-thinking. When the sultan converts to Christianity, "His hide, þat blac & loþely was,/ Al white bicom, þurth Godes gras/ & clere wiþouten blame" (928–30). White skin very clearly indicates the Christianity of its bearer while dark or black skin indicates the religious alterity of its bearer. When the sultan changes religious allegiances, his skin shows it. The sultan's transformation, however, is not the uncomplicated religious conversion it at first appears to be (Whitaker 2013: 169–93). It does, however, intimate the political effects of race when his skin-color transformation *causes* the sultan to believe in Christ (931–2). The resulting change in identity drives home its political point when the sultan wages war on five Saracen kings, his former coreligionists and political allies. After his transformation, he is allied instead with his white, Christian, and—in some later iterations of the narrative, including Geoffrey Chaucer's—*imperial* father-in-law. Race, in the literature and culture of medieval Christendom, delineates political loyalties and indicates access to European imperial power.

Though the Roman and Mongol empires were certainly models, Europe did not have to look to the past or to the east for examples of empire. Hopes of Mongol imperial Christianity and military aid were deeply imbricated with the political designs of Europe's own Holy Roman Empire. From 800, when Charlemagne, king of the Franks, was crowned Roman emperor by Pope Leo III, the lands around the Rhine became one of the most important spaces in Christendom, rivaled only by Rome (Bryce 1899: 2–4) (Figure 8.5). Other than momentary gaps in real power along the way, the empire continued for nearly a millennium until its dissolution in 1806 (Bryce 1899: 3).

The integral role of race in the late medieval Holy Roman Empire's dominance is demonstrated by Carmelite friar John of Hildesheim's Latin *Historia trium regum*, or the *History of the Three Kings*. It was written in Germany, likely around 1364 in celebration of the two-hundredth anniversary of the translation to Cologne Cathedral of the bodies of the three kings, or *magi*, who famously venerated the infant Christ (Kaplan 1985; Schaer 2000: 17). The *Historia* had appeared in English as *The Three Kings of Cologne* by 1400. Its subject matter, registering the Holy Roman Empire's influence, is the direct result of Frederick I Barbarossa's political machinations (Figure 8.6). Frederick I (r. 1152–90) took advantage of the 1159 papal schism when "pro-imperial" cardinals elected Victor IV while "anti-imperial" cardinals elected Alexander III. The emperor supported Victor IV, and when Victor died in 1164 Frederick's chancellor Rainald of Dassel oversaw another election. These pro-imperial cardinals elected Paschal III. After the election, Rainald traveled to Milan, which had submitted to Frederick, and "impounded certain relics," including three bodies held outside Milan at the church of St. Eustorgius and supposed to be those of the three kings. The bodies, according to lore, had been found in the east by Saint Helena, Emperor Constantine's mother (who was

FIGURE 8.5: The Coronation of Emperor Charlemagne by Pope Leo III. Credit: French School/Getty Images.

known for collecting Christian relics) and brought to Constantinople. They had subsequently been translated to Milan (Hamilton 1985: 187). They were translated to the Cathedral at Cologne in 1164, the same year that Victor IV died. This action was meant to valorize kingship and exalt the power of the Holy Roman emperor above even that of the pope (Hamilton 1985: 182–3). Indeed, the long shift to describing the three holy men as kings rather than magi may have, in part, been the result of Rainald and Frederick's efforts (Hamilton 1985: 182–90; Bisgaard 2005: 122).

In the magi inheres the intersection of the empire's aspirations toward global domination and the medieval development of race-thinking. The magi, from as early as the eleventh century, represented the world's three known continents: Europe, Asia, and Africa. Saint Bruno, founder of the Carthusian order, wrote of them: "three men, of the three parts of the globe, Asia, Europe, and Africa" (Kaplan 1985: 34; Saint Bruno 1844–45, *Commentarium in*

FIGURE 8.6: The Emperor Frederick I Barbarossa with his sons Henry VI and Frederick, Duke of Swabia, from the Welfenchronik chronicle produced at the Abbey of Weingarten, Germany, in the twelfth century. Credit: De Agostini Picture Library/Getty Images.

Matthaeum, in *PL*, 168, col. 1338) (Figure 8.7). Examining the related myth that each continent's people are the progeny of one of the biblical figure Noah's three sons, historian Benjamin Braude has shown that "the racial identities [of Noah's three sons] have been remarkably unstable. Shem, Ham, and Japhet have been ever-changing projections of the likes and dislikes, hatreds and loves, prejudices and fears, needs and rationales through which society continually constructs and reconstructs its selves and its opposites" (1997: 119, 142). In other words, the continents with which Shem, Ham, and Japhet were identified—usually Asia, Africa, and Europe respectively— also became reflections of the observing society's predilections and how that society used these to construct its view of itself. In addition, the magi myth's coalescence of the three kings with the three continents testified to Roman

FIGURE 8.7: Adoration of the Magi by Gerard David. Fifteenth-century work demonstrating the conventional depiction of the three wise men representing Asia, Africa, and Europe. The depiction of the African magus is particularly noticeable. Credit: Superstock.

Christendom's world domination. The entire world had come to worship the Christ child.

Despite the potentially unifying effect of Roman Christendom's intercontinental reach, the *Historia* and the *Three Kings* demonstrate the simultaneous presence of the conflicts more commonly associated with race. Catalogs, referred to by scholars as "lists of nations" and common in classical and medieval encyclopedic works, dominate the text (Akbari 2012: 118). These encyclopedic descriptions detail the differences in customs and practices among various Christian sects, largely in the east. These sects are introduced in the latter half of the Latin *Historia*:

> Also it has been noted in what and how much honor and reverence these three blessed kings are held by all heretics and schismatics in all provinces and parts of the East who continue and remain to this day, and it has been understood that in the East and in all parts overseas the Christian faith is divided into diverse parts and sects of men, following these men whose

names follow: Nubiani, Soldini, Nestorini, Latini, Indi, Armeni, Greci, Siriani, Georgiani, Nycolaite, Jacobite, Copti, Ysini, Marronini and Mandopolos, and from these all Christians in that place are over all previously named men and heretics other than in these heretics' own lands and realms, in which they have always held rule (Horstmann 1886: 277).

The existence of far-flung Christians such as the Soldini, Siriani, and Nestorini support the Holy Roman Empire's aspirations to world domination at the same time that their practices challenge the empire's claim to singular control of the Christian religion. The text takes pains to assert Roman Christendom's dominion when it notes that "all Christians in that place are over all previously named men and heretics." "All Christians in that place" refers to all orthodox Roman Christians and the "previously named men and heretics" are the Soldini, Siriani, etc. Nonetheless, the text continues to register that the Roman Church's power is somewhat insecure with the admission that the "heretics" continue to rule in their own lands. Anxiety about the implementation and maintenance of power is central to the imperial enterprise, and the *Historia*'s list of nations exhibits such anxiety.

As the list of nations makes its way from the Latin *Historia* into abbreviated vernacular texts, such as the *Three Kings*, the race-thinking impulses behind the list of nations becomes more apparent. While the *Historia* follows its list by elucidating the differences between various sects with such details as whose priests marry and whose remain celibate, the *Three Kings* lumps together heretics in an indistinct mass and juxtaposes them to orthodox Christians:

there are also diverse sects and parties of Christian men, and each one holds his opinion and his belief by himself, and does certain devotions and reverence to these three kings and to the feast of the Epiphany; for all these Christian men, although they are heretics and of misbelief, they do great reverence to these three worthy kings, as you will hear afterward. For all these Christian men and heretics, no matter of what degree, they fast on Christmas day until nighttime . . . (London, British Library: fol. 67b; Horstmann 1886: 141).

Though the sects are named at this point in the *Historia* and in the corresponding passages of other English versions, they are not named at this point in this abbreviated version of the *Three Kings*. This version, appearing in what would become the English royal household's manuscripts as well as those of the important sixteenth- and seventeenth-century collector Robert Cotton, distills difference down to "Cristenmen and heretikes" (Whitaker 2009: 1–4). The *Three Kings*' othering of non-western Christians evokes the us-and-them, or in-group/out-group, dynamic that has been central to the history of race-thinking and is integral to modern racial ideology.

In addition to racial binarism, the Latin *Historia* and the English *Three Kings* also demonstrate the empire's increasing reliance on the most salient element of modern race: black-and-white color ideology. The *Historia* attributes blackness to Jaspar, the king who represents Africa, and his people the Nestorians. Jaspar is holy and righteous while his people are depraved and heretical. Blackness persists in both, however, because it is not seen as a marker of exclusivity or essential difference. Late medieval Europeans considered black skin a "vulgar and superficial corporeal conceptualization of ancestry and relationships" (Braude 1997: 126–7). This does not remain Europe's estimation of skin color for long, however. The *Three Kings* omits the *Historia*'s powerful assertions of the Nestorians' blackness while retaining and emphasizing Jaspar's blackness. While the English text does not bind blackness with evil, it does register the impulse, growing in the late Middle Ages, to bind blackness with either evil or good. Blackness and whiteness increasingly become, in the later Middle Ages, the binary and racial conditions on which the Roman Church's, and with it the Holy Roman Empire's, power relies. Medieval Europe's Roman imperial past, its contemporary competition with the Mongol empire, and its Holy Roman imperial present all imbued it with a culture of delineation and demarcation in which race-thinking helped to facilitate and consolidate social and political power. Race-thinking, nascent in its medieval form, has thrived beyond the Middle Ages in order to become the better established and more firmly binaristic racial ideology that buoys up western imperial and post-imperial cultures.

MANDEVILLE AND "REASONABLE" RACES

As the purported dawn of the early modern period broke upon the Middle Ages, the imperial aspirations that would define the Age of Exploration perhaps reached their zenith in one of Europe's most popular travel narratives: the *Book* (or *Travels*) *of John Mandeville* from the mid-fourteenth century. By the fifteenth century, it would be found, in addition to English, translated into Latin, French, German, Irish, Italian, Czech, and Danish, and it survives in nearly 300 manuscripts. For comparison, Chaucer's *Canterbury Tales* survive in whole or in part in merely eighty-two (Hanna 1987: 1118; Kohanski and Benson 2007). C.W.R.D. Moseley asserts that "few literate men in the fourteenth and fifteenth centuries could have avoided coming across the *Travels* at some time" (1975: 126). The *Travels*' importance to the project of empire extends beyond its linguistic reach. Its material attendance upon the imperial project was so pronounced that it was an important resource for European explorers in the Americas, including Walter Raleigh, Martin Frobisher, and Christopher Columbus, who "all read it earnestly." Frobisher even brought it with him to Baffin's Bay off of Greenland in 1576 (Campbell 1988: 126). In addition to its transmission, popularity, and material use in empire-building, the *Travels* reveals the rhetorical structure upon which racial ideology helps European empires to flourish. The *Travels* puts into perspective the long history of race and empire—classical and medieval encyclopedism, climate theory, colonization within and outside Europe, and the influence of empires past and present—with its presentation of the world's so-called "monstrous races." The text's establishment of a binaristic relationship between the "monstrous" and the normal intimates the ever-stronger presence of race-thinking in medieval western culture and the resultant centrality of racial ideology to modern western imperial cultures.

The *Travels* posits a norm in the character of the English knight Sir John Mandeville and then depicts a great number of creatures that differ significantly from the norm. Creatures of classical and medieval myth, encyclopedias, and travel writing, such as Cyclopes with one eye in the middle of their foreheads; Epiphagi with no heads, their ears in their shoulders, and their mouths in the middle of their chests; and Blemmyes with no heads and their eyes and mouths behind their shoulders, have been referred to as "monstrous races." The term has often been untroubled, used "without sufficient thought," and is central to such magisterial works as John Block Friedman's *The Monstrous Races in Medieval Art and Thought* (Mittman 2015: 37–8). It has occasioned scholars, such as William Chester Jordan and Asa Mittman, to question its use with regard to the Middle Ages—though Jordan and Mittman do so in remarkably different ways (Jordan 2001: 165–74; Mittman 2015: 36–51). Jordan and Mittman alike conclude that the dangers of using the word "race" outweigh its benefits. Nevertheless, the rhetorical strategy by which the *Travels* depicts its human or quasi-human subjects means that no other term does as good a job as race when it comes to how the text manufactures and propagates judgments about character and spiritual worth or depravity.

The *Travels* continues in the tradition of compression that pervades physiognomy and climate theory: its judgments rely on pronouncements that give little if any attention to evidence. Take, for example, the case of the people who live by the smell of apples:

> And another ile is ther which they calle Pytan. Men of this ile tylyeth no corn lond, for they ete noght. And they ben smale men, but noght so smale as ben pigmans. These men lyven with the smel and savour of wild apples. And when they goth fer out of contré they berith apples with hem, for also sone as they leveth the savour of the apples they deye. And they ben noght ful resonable, but as bestes (Kohanski and Benson 2007: 2638–42).

These people who do not eat certainly count as "monstrous" in that they are significantly different from the text's assumed norm: they do not eat, and they live only by the fragrance of apples. When they are out of the fragrance's range, they die. This is evidence of difference indeed, but the text's claim that they are not "reasonable, but as beasts" is not borne out by their description at all. Instead, the evidence logically leads to the opposite conclusion. That they make certain to take apples with them when they travel, so that they will survive, is very prudent and suggests that the apple-smelling people in fact have a great deal of reason. The judgment that they are "noght ful resonable" stands in for their difference and has little to do with their actual rational capacity.

In another example of the late Middle Ages' race-thinking rhetoric, the *Travels* assumes the irrationality of the people of Tracota. While this passage does not exactly ignore clear evidence of reason, as the section on the apple-people does, it colors its information from the outset:

> Than is ther another ile that is y-called Tracota, wher men beth as beestes and noght resenable, for they eten eddres and they speke noght but make soch noyse as eddres don. And they make noon fors of no rychesse, but of oon stone that hath 40 colouris that is y-called traconyghte. And they knowe noght the vertu of that stone, but they coveyte hym for the gret fayrenesse of hym (Kohanski and Benson 2007: 1848–53).

There is little room for interpretation after the text introduces the Tracotans as "beestes and noght resenable." The evidence introduced with "for they . . ." is an afterthought to the initial pronouncement; it is as if the evidence is merely rehearsing the obvious. Furthermore, the Tracotans' economic system appears reasonable indeed: they assign monetary value to a stone they consider quite "fayre," or beautiful. Instead, the text calls their system into question, claiming that they do not know the "vertu" of the stone and linking their estimation of it to the Judeo-Christian sin of covetousness. The primacy of value judgments, efforts to make evidence fit with those judgments, and the presumption that beliefs or practices that do not accord with a European Roman Christian norm are abhorrent and irrational are part and parcel of the race-thinking that deems some people more and some less human. Race-thinking is the process of interpretation upon which imperial projects in the west have their foundations.

CONCLUSION: RACE AND "PERPETUAL SLAVERY"

Race's integral role in the development of western European imperial culture is also demonstrated by the Church's attempts to regulate slavery. The Portuguese landing in the Canary Islands off the west coast of Africa in 1341 touched off a debate between Portugal and Spain for control of the archipelago that lasted for over a century. The Castilian and Portuguese crowns each claimed the islands for their own. While a number of papal bulls were issued in favor of each power, the dispute was not settled until 1479 when Portugal ceded control to Castile (Davenport 1917: 9–10). From the fourteenth through the seventeenth centuries, popes were of multiple minds about the justifications for and conditions of slavery. In his October 3, 1434 bull, Pope Eugenius IV (1431–47) warns against slaving in the Canaries, writing:

> But some from [the Canary Islands] already converted to the faith were by some sea pirates, Christians in name, taken captive; set them free in order that for all faithful Christians and especially such recent converts we be shepherds and guardians and care to provide that the same already converted persons, owed security, may rejoice, and others may not draw back from conversion for fear of captivity (Campos 1901: 207–8).

In 1434, the Pope's main concern was that Christians should not be enslaved by other Christians. Religious identity is the most important component in the justification of enslavement. Furthermore, in order for the Church, and western Europe's imperial aspirations, to continue to grow, potential Christians must not be scared away by the possibility of enslavement. The regulation of enslavement was necessary to Latin Christian evangelism.

A pair of papal bulls from 1452 and 1455, known as *Dum Diversas* and *Romanus Pontifex* respectively, shows how quickly and significantly the Church's official position on identity and slavery shifted. Pope Nicholas V, Eugenius's successor, writes in *Dum Diversas*:

> and your Royal Majesty, deserving of reward, by way of this most holy decree, we have cared for you to invade, conquer, assault, and subjugate the Saracens, and pagans, and other infidels, and whichever enemies of Christ, and wherever are constituted kingdoms, dukedoms, retinues, principalities and other dominions, lands, places, villages, fortresses, and whichever other possessions, both movable and immovable and consisting in whatever things, and held in whatever name, by the same Saracens, pagans, infidels, and enemies of Christ detained and possessed, and also whichever dukedoms, camps, principalities, or other dominions, lands, places, villages there were, whether ruled by king, or prince, or kings, or princes, dukes, fortresses, possessions, and goods, and their persons to *reduce to perpetual servitude* (Davenport 1917: 17, n. 37, my emphasis).

Unlike Eugenius's bull, Pope Nicholas's support for "perpetual servitude" does not make any exceptions for recently or potentially converted Christians. In *Romanus Pontifex*, Nicholas refers back to *Dum Diversas*.

> We [therefore] weighing all and singular the premises with due meditation, and noting that since we had formerly by other letters of ours granted among other things free and ample faculty to the aforesaid King Alfonso—to invade,

search out, capture, vanquish, and subdue all Saracens and pagans whatsoever, and other enemies of Christ wheresoever placed, and the kingdoms, dukedoms, principalities, dominions, possessions, and all movable and immovable goods whatsoever held and possessed by them and to *reduce their persons to perpetual slavery,* and to apply and appropriate to himself and his successors the kingdoms, dukedoms, counties, principalities, dominions, possessions, and goods, and to convert them to his and their use and profit (Davenport 1917: 16–17, 23, my emphasis; Davenport's translation).

In 1455, Nicholas reasserts the position that those whom the Portuguese conquer are to be reduced to "perpetual slavery." This is in stark contrast to Eugenius IV's concerns.

For Nicolas V, Christian conversion is no barrier to perpetual slavery. While Eugenius invokes the fear of slavery as an evil that obstructs potential conversions, Nicholas explicitly discusses conversion as a benefit of conquest.

Thence also many Guineamen and other negroes, taken by force, and some by barter of unprohibited articles, or by other lawful contract of purchase, have been sent to the said kingdoms. A large number of these have been converted to the Catholic faith, and it is hoped, by the help of divine mercy, that if such progress be continued with them, either those peoples will be converted to the faith or at least the souls of many of them will be gained for Christ (Davenport 1917: 16, 22; Davenport's translation).

Converting "Guineamen and other negroes" to the catholic faith and saving their souls is certainly part of Nicholas's program for Portuguese dominion. He hopes that the imperial work is girded with "divine mercy" and that "continued progress" will produce more Christian converts. For Nicholas, however, nowhere does this imperial project require that converts be freed from slavery. On the contrary, it is slavery itself—the sending of Africans to Portugal—that promises to produce ever more converts. Furthermore, Nicholas appends to Eugenius's overwhelming concern with faith identity the geographical and phenotypic identity of enslaved converts. He is concerned in a general sense with "Saracens, and pagans, and other infidels, and whichever enemies of Christ," but more specifically he is concerned with "negroes." In Nicholas's fifteenth-century hands, imperial race-thinking has already begun to take on the tenor of modern racial ideology in that phenotype has become a category's primary definitional focus.

The early modern and modern empires of Britain, France, Spain, Portugal, and other European nations modeled themselves on and against the Roman empire, the Mongol empire, and the Holy Roman Empire in addition to related projects such as the Crusades. English and European literary examples—the Arthurian tradition in France and England and its assertion of English Romanness, English romances using eastern European stories and engaging trans-European concerns about Mongolian power, and German and English imaginings of the Holy Roman Empire's and the Roman Church's world domination—convey the multifaceted and hegemonic nature of the imperial impulse in the west through the Middle Ages and into modernity. European kingdoms, at the late medieval and early modern dawn of the nation-state, were in need of mechanisms to produce political cultures in which access to power could be easily discerned and maintenance of power readily facilitated. Race develops alongside and as a preeminent tool of imperial projects. The development and growth of its influence is apparent in classical and medieval encyclopedic texts as well as in the importance of climate theory from classical antiquity through the work of naturalists such as Carl von Linnaeus, Immanuel Kant, and Charles Darwin in the eighteenth and nineteenth centuries. Imperial race has been just as important in intra-European colonial projects, such as the construction of English domination in Ireland, as it has been in extra-European colonial projects, such as those in Asia, Africa, and the Americas. In the history of its engagement with empire, race supersedes even as it foregrounds our modern notion that race is about skin color.

NOTES

Introduction

1. My thanks to Brett Edward Whalen and Mauro J. Caraccioli, who assisted with various aspects of this essay. All errors and omissions, of course, remain my own.
2. Translation here my own, based on McGinn's original.
3. See also the (expanding) bibliography curated by medievalists at http://bit.ly/2rXsroO.

Chapter 2

1. In the late nineteenth century, the Cairo Geniza collection was uncovered in a sealed room of a synagogue in Old Cairo. The collection preserves materials, including thousands of medieval letters and other papers written in Arabic using Hebrew characters. They document the world of Jewish merchants trading in and out of Egypt during the eleventh and twelfth centuries.
2. A new emphasis on the Mediterranean and Mediterranean Studies will in some sense lead to this. Although less work has centered strictly on economic networks.

Chapter 3

1. The Medieval Warm Period has been dangerously politicized in arguments "that 'natural' fluctuations alone could explain current conditions, since greenhouse gases were only ~280 ppmv during Medieval time (versus 400 ppmv today)" (Bradley *et al.* 2016: 990).
2. Riché (1993: 136) notes the placement of royal lands in "the valleys of the Aisne and the Oise (at Quierzy, Attigny, Verberie, and Compienge), the Meuse and the Mosel (at Herstal and Thionville), along the Rhine (at Ingelheim, Frankfurt, Worms, and frutehr north, at Nijmegen), and finally in Saxony (at Paderborn). There remained,

however, literally hundreds of other royal stopovers and villae that are known to us only from textual references.".
3. Hoffmann (2014: 81) notes that while Carolingians used *villa* instead of *mansus*, the landed estates (*mansus indominicatus*) of the Carolingians included "organized land of all types—arable, pasture, woodland, farmsteads."

Chapter 5

1. For vital context on this long-lived cartographic conundrum, see Scafi (2006).
2. My translation (Gual Camarena 1981: 57).
3. My translation (Ridder 1991: 227): "Vnd do etteliche stücke lihte vngelöplich sint do han ich frömeder meistere von naturen zů zůgnůsse zů latine geschriben die man wol mag lesen der sú hören wil die die meistere pfaffen von naturen wol verston süllent."
4. Cf. Legassie (2017: 152–9), where it is argued that similar interests animate the accounts of late-medieval pilgrims to the Holy Land.
5. For modern edition, see Antoine de la Sale (1930).
6. On the plasticity of the concept of pilgrimage, see Dyas (2001) and Holloway (1998). The term *pilgrimage* was already flexible in late antiquity, as shown by Dietz (2005).
7. On the origins and development of penitential pilgrimage, see Vogel (1964).
8. Dante Alighieri (2004a), *Inferno*, 26.79–142; cf. Dante Alighieri (2004b), *Paradiso*, 27.67–96.
9. "Tempore quoque sub eodem, missus est in Angliam quidam elephas, quem dominus rex Franciae pro magno munere dedit domino regi Anglorum. Nec credimus quod unquam aliquis elephas visus est in Anglia, immo nec etiam in partibus cisalpinis, praeter illum; unde confluebant populi ad tantae spectaculum novitatis" (my translation).
10. Druce (1919: 3–4). On the naturalism of Matthew's renderings, see Lewis (1987: 212–16). As the argument of this essay suggests, I do not agree with Lewis' contention (at 215–16) that Matthew Paris' interest in the elephant "had nothing to do with politics" and that he was simply exploiting its "sensational value." Sensation, spectacle, and the exotic are in no way antithetical to medieval politics. For other accounts of Matthew Paris as long-distance specialist to the king, see Birkholz (2004) and Connolly (2009).
11. For a more detailed treatment, see Legassie (2017: 51–3).
12. On form and sources, see Grosjean (1978) and Massing (1991).
13. Skelton (1968: 107–13).
14. For details on the production, presentation, and use of this manuscript, see Röhl (2006: 282) and Kupfer (2008).

Chapter 7

1. Cf. Matthew 16:18–19. On the origins of the Roman church and papacy, including papal claims to primacy over the universal church, see Demacopoulos (2013) and Whalen (2014: 7–33).

2. In October 816, during a meeting with Louis at Reims, Pope Stephen IV (816–17) crowned and anointed him as emperor of the Romans, as described by the so-called Astronomer in his *Life of Emperor Louis*; see Noble (2009: 252–3).
3. Described by the chronicler of Berthold of Reichenau; vol. 5, *Monumenta Germaniae Historica* (1844: 463).
4. In addition to Morris (1989), on the "papal monarchy," see also the influential work of Walter Ullmann (1949, 1965), with cautions about Ullmann's tendency to read his sources selectively and create an overly seamless picture of papal ideology (Watt 1964: 179–317).
5. On the theology and politics of the "two swords," see Chodorow (1972).
6. On Innocent's attitude toward secular powers, see Pennington (1984).
7. There are numerous biographies of Frederick II, some openly biased against the papacy for opposing him. See, among others, Kantorowicz (1957), van Cleve (1972), and Abulafia (1988).
8. On Gregory IX's papacy generally speaking, see the recent volume of essays edited by Egger and Smith (forthcoming).
9. For an anonymous, most likely eye-witness account of the proceedings, vol. 2, *Monumenta Germaniae Historica: Constitutiones* (1896: 513–16); for the text of Innocent's sentence, vol. 2, *Monumenta Germaniae Historica: Epistolae XIII* (1887: 88–94). See also Kempf (1968).
10. On Dante's attitude toward empire, captured in his 1318 tract *On Monarchy*, see also Cassell (2004).
11. Among other works, see William of Ockham's *A Short Discourse on the Tyrannical Government over Things Divine and Human, but Especially over the Empire and Those Subject to the Empire, Usurped by Some Who are Called Highest Pontiffs* (McGrade 1992) and *On the Power of Emperors and Popes* (Brett 1998).
12. As observed by Ullmann (2003: 290), "The idea of universalism had been dropped by both the papacy and the empire."
13. For a penetrating critique of such views on the progressive relationship between medieval and the modern era, see Davis (2008).

Chapter 8

1. All translations are mine unless otherwise noted.

FURTHER READING

Abels, Richard P. (1998), *Alfred the Great: War, Kingship and Culture in Anglo-Saxon England*, Harlow: Pearson.
Aberth, John (2013), *An Environmental History of the Middle Ages: The Crucible of Nature*, New York: Routledge.
Abulafia, Anna Sapir (1994), *Christians and Jews in the Twelfth-Century Renaissance*, London: Routledge.
Abulafia, David (1988), *Frederick II: A Medieval Emperor*, London: The Penguin Press.
Abulafia, David (1994), *A Mediterranean Emporium: The Catalan Kingdom of Majorca*, Cambridge: Cambridge University Press.
Abulafia, David (1995), "Trade and Crusade, 1050–1250," in *Cross Cultural Convergences in the Crusader Period: Essays Presented to Aryeh Grabois on His Sixty-Fifth Birthday*, ed. Michael Goodich, Sophia Menache, and Sylvia Schein, 1–20, New York: Peter Lang.
Abu-Lughod, Janet L. (1989), *Before European Hegemony: The World System A.D. 1250–1350*, Oxford: Oxford University Press.
Adams, G.B. and Stephens, H.M., eds (1901), "Assize of the Forest or of Woodstock, Henry II," in *Select Documents of English Constitutional History*, New York: Macmillan.
Adso of Montier-en-Der (1979), "De antichristo," in *Apocalyptic Spirituality*, trans. Bernard McGinn, 89–96, New York: Paulist Press.
Ælfric (1993), "Colloquy," in *Anglo-Saxon Prose*, ed. Michael Swanton, 169–77, New York: J.M. Dent.
Ahmed, Sara (2015), "Race as Sedimented History," *Postmedieval, Supplement: Making Race Matter in the Middle Ages*, 6 (1): 94–7.
Ainsworth, Peter F. (1990), *Jean Froissart and the Fabric of History: Truth, Myth, and Fiction in the Chroniques*, Oxford: Clarendon Press.
Akbari, Suzanne Conklin (2012), *Idols in the East: Representations of Islam and the Orient, 1100–1450*, Ithaca, NY: Cornell University Press.
Alighieri, Dante (2004a), *Inferno*, trans. Allen Mandelbaum, New York: Bantam.
Alighieri, Dante (2004b), *Paradiso*, trans. Allen Mandelbaum, New York: Bantam.

Allsen, Thomas T. (2004), *Culture and Conquest in Mongol Eurasia*, Cambridge: Cambridge University Press.
Allsen, Thomas T. (2006), *The Royal Hunt in Eurasian History*, Philadelphia, PA: University of Pennsylvania Press.
Amari, M. (1880), *Biblioteca Arabo-Sicula*, Vol. I, Rome/Turin: Loescher.
Archer, Janice (1995), "Working Women in Thirteenth-Century Paris," PhD dissertation, University of Arizona.
Arnold, Benjamin (1997), *Medieval Germany, 500–1300: A Political Interpretation*, Basingstoke: Macmillan.
Arnold, Ellen (2013), *Negotiating the Landscape: Environment and Monastic Identity in the Medieval Ardennes*, Philadelphia, PA: University of Pennsylvania Press.
Arnold, John H. (2008), *What is Medieval History?*, London: Polity.
Baker, Keith Michael (1990), *Inventing the French Revolution: Essays on the Political Culture of the Eighteenth Century*, Cambridge: Cambridge University Press.
Balard, Michel and Alain Ducellier, eds (1995), *Coloniser au Moyen Âge: méthodes d'expansion et techniques de domination en Méditerranée du 11ᵉ au 16ᵉ siècle*, Paris: Armand Colin.
Baldwin, John (2010), *Paris 1200*, Stanford: Stanford University Press.
Ballantyne, Tony and Antoinette Burton, eds (2009), *Moving Subjects: Gender, Mobility, and Intimacy in an Age of Global Empire*, Urbana, IL: University of Illinois Press.
Bang, Peter Fibiger (2007), "Trade and Empire—In Search of Organizing Concepts for the Romany Economy," *Past and Present*, 195: 3–54.
Barber, Malcolm C. (1994), *The New Knighthood: A History of the Order of the Temple*, Cambridge: Cambridge University Press.
Barlow, Frank (2002), *The Godwins: The Rise and Fall of a Noble Dynasty*, London: Pearson.
Bartholomew Anglicus ([1601] 1964), *De proprietatibus rerum*, trans. John Trevisa, Frankfurt: Minerva.
Bartlett, Robert (1986), *Trial by Fire and Water: The Medieval Judicial Ordeal*, Oxford: Clarendon Press.
Bartlett, Robert (1993), *The Making of Europe: Conquest, Colonization and Cultural Change*, London: Allen Lane.
Bartlett, Robert (2008), *The Natural and the Supernatural in the Middle Ages*, New York: Cambridge University Press.
Barton, Simon (2011), "Marriage across Frontiers: Sexual Mixing, Power and Identity in Medieval Iberia," *Journal of Medieval Iberian Studies*, 3 (1): 1–25.
Baskin, Judith (2010), "Jewish Private Life: Gender, Marriage and the Lives of Women," in *The Cambridge Guide to Jewish History, Religion and Culture*, ed. Judith Baskin and Kenneth Seeskin, 358–80, Cambridge: Cambridge University Press.
Bates, David (2016), *William the Conqueror*, New Haven, CT: Yale University Press.
Bautier, Robert-Henri (1991), *Sur l'histoire économique de la France médiévale: la route, le fleuve, la foire*, Aldershot: Variorum.
Benjamin of Tudela (2004), *The Itinerary of Benjamin of Tudela: Travels in the Middle Ages*, trans. Marcus Nathan Adler, New York: Nightingale Press.
Bennett, Judith M. (1986), "The Village Ale-Wife: Women and Brewing in Fourteenth-Century England," in *Women and Work in Preindustrial Europe*, ed. Barbara A. Hanawalt, 20–36, Bloomington, IN: Indiana University Press.
Bennett, Judith M. (1999), *Ale, Beer, and Brewsters in England: Women's Work in a Changing World, 1300–1600*, New York: Oxford University Press.

Berend, Nora (2001a), *At the Gates of Christendom: Jews, Muslims and "Pagans" in Medieval Hungary, c. 1000–c. 1300*, Cambridge: Cambridge University Press.
Berend, Nora (2001b), "How Many Medieval Europes? The 'Pagans' of Hungary and Regional Diversity in Christendom," in *The Medieval World*, ed. Peter Linehan and Janet L. Nelson, 77–92, Abingdon: Routledge.
Berkhofer, Robert (2004), *Day of Reckoning: Power and Accountability in Medieval France*, Philadelphia, PA: University of Pennsylvania Press.
Beullens, Pieter (2007), "Like a Book Written by God's Finger: Animals Showing the Path Towards God," in *A Cultural History of Animals in the Medieval Age*, ed. Brigitte Resl, 17–151, New York: Berg.
Birkholz, Daniel (2004), *The King's Two Maps: Cartography and Culture in Thirteenth-Century England*, New York: Routledge.
Bisgaard, Lars (2005), "A Black Mystery: The Hagiography of the Three Magi," in *Medieval History Writing and Crusading Ideology*, ed. Tuomas M.S. Lehtonen and Kurt Villads Jensen, 120–38, Helsinki: Finnish Literature Society.
Bisson, Thomas (2010), *The Crisis of the Twelfth Century*, Princeton, NJ: Princeton University Press.
Black, Antony (1984), *Guilds and Civil Society in European Political Thought from the Twelfth Century to the Present*, Ithaca, NY: Cornell University Press.
Bloch, Marc (1962), *Feudal Society*, trans. L.A. Manyon, 2nd edn, London: Routledge & Kegan Paul.
Blumenthal, Debra (2009), *Enemies and Familiars: Slavery and Mastery in Fifteenth-Century Valencia*, Ithaca, NY: Cornell University Press.
Blumenthal, U.-R. ([1988] 1992), *The Investiture Controversy: Church and Monarchy from the Ninth to the Twelfth Century*, 2nd edn, Philadelphia, PA: University of Pennsylvania Press.
Borysek, Martin (2014), "The Jews of Venetian Candia: The Challenges of External Influences and Internal Diversity as Reflected in *Takkanot Kandiyah*," *Al-Masāq: Journal of the Medieval Mediterranean*, 26 (3): 241–66.
Boswell, John (1980), *Christianity, Social Tolerance and Homosexuality: Gay People in Western Europe from the Beginning of the Christian Era to the Fourteenth Century*, Chicago, IL: University of Chicago Press.
Boswell, John (1994), *Same-Sex Unions in pre-Modern Europe*, New York: Random House.
Bowsky, William M. (1960), *Henry VII in Italy: The Conflict of Empire and City-State, 1310–1313*, Lincoln, NB: University of Nebraska Press.
Boyle, John Andrew (1977), "The Alexander Romance in the East and West," *Bulletin of the John Rylands University Library of Manchester*, 60: 13–27.
Bracciolini, Poggio (1857), *The Travels of Nicolo Conti in the East, in the Early Part of the Fifteenth Century* (translated from the original of Poggio Bracciolini), trans. J.W. Jones, London.
Bradley, Raymond, Heinz Wanner, and Henry Diaz (2016), "The Medieval Quiet Period," *The Holocene*, 26: 990–3.
Brady, Lisa (2015), "Has Environmental History Lost Its Way," *Process: a blog for American history*, http://www.processhistory.org/has-environmental-history-lost-its-way/, accessed June 2016.
Braude, Benjamin (1997), "The Sons of Noah and the Construction of Ethnic and Geographical Identities in the Medieval and Early Modern Periods," *The William and Mary Quarterly*, 54 (1): 103–42.

Braudel, Ferdnand (1966), *Méditerranée et le monde méditerranéen à l'époque de Philippe II*, 2 vols, 2nd edn, Paris: Armand Colin.
Braudel, Ferdnand (1972), *The Mediterranean and the Mediterranean World in the Age of Philip II*, 2 vols, trans. Siân Reynolds, New York: HarperCollins, reprinted (1995), Berkeley, CA: University of California Press.
Bressler, Richard (2010), *Frederick II: Wonder of the World*, Yardley, PA: Westholme Publishing.
Brett, Annabel S., ed. and trans. (1998), *On the Power of Emperors and Popes*, Bristol: Thoemmes Press.
Britton, Dennis A. (2014), *Becoming Christian: Race, Reformation, and Early Modern English Romance*, New York: Fordham University Press.
Brotton, Jerry (1998), *Trading Territories: Mapping the Early Modern World*, Ithaca, NY: Cornell University Press.
Brown, Warren C. (2011), *Violence in Medieval Europe*, Harlow: Pearson.
Brubaker, Leslie (2004), "The Elephant and the Ark: Cultural and Material Interchange Across the Mediterranean in the Eighth and Ninth Centuries," *Dumbarton Oaks Papers*, 58: 175–95.
Bruce, Scott (2015), *Cluny and the Muslims of La Garde-Freinet: Hagiography and the Problem of Islam in Medieval Europe*, Ithaca, NY: Cornell University Press.
Brundage, James A. (1960), "An Errant Crusader: Stephen of Blois," *Traditio*, 16: 380–95.
Brundage, James A. (1985), "Prostitution, Miscegenation and Sexual Purity in the First Crusade," in *Crusade and Settlement: Papers read at the First Conference of the Society for the Study of the Crusades and the Latin East*, ed. Peter W. Edbury, 57–65, Cardiff: University College Cardiff Press.
Brundage, James A. (1987), *Law, Sex and Christian Society in Medieval Europe*, Chicago, IL: University of Chicago Press.
Bruno, Saint (1844–5), *Commentarium in Matthaeum*, in *Patrologiae Cursus Completus: Series Latina*, ed. J.P. Migne, 168, Paris.
Bruschi, Caterina (2009), *The Wandering Heretics of Languedoc*, Cambridge: Cambridge University Press.
Bryant, Lawrence (1986), *The King and the City in the Parisian Royal Entry Ceremony: Politics, Ritual and Art in the Renaissance*, Geneva: Droz.
Bryce, James (1899), *The Holy Roman Empire*, London: Macmillan.
Bryder, Linda (1998), "Sex, Race and Colonialism: An Historiographical Review," *The International History Review*, 20: 806–22.
Bull, Marcus (1993), *Knightly Piety and the Lay Response to the First Crusade: The Limousin and Gascony, c. 970–1130*, Oxford: Clarendon Press.
Bull, Marcus (2005), *Thinking Medieval: An Introduction to the Study of the Middle Ages*, London: Palgrave Macmillan.
Bullough, Vern L. and James A. Brundage, eds (1996), *The Handbook of Medieval Sexuality*, New York: Garland.
Büntgen, Ulf and Len Hellmann (2014), "The Little Ice Age in Scientific Perspective: Cold Spells and Caveats," *Journal of Interdisciplinary History*, 44: 353–68.
Büntgen, Ulf, Willy Tegel, Kurt Nicolussi, Michael McCormick, David Frank, Valerie Trouet, Jed O. Kaplan, Franz Herzig, Karl-Uwe Heussner, Heinz Wanner, Jürg Luterbacher, and Jan Esper (2011), "2500 Years of European Climate Variability and Human Susceptibility," *Science*, 331 (6017): 578–82.
Büntgen, Ulf, Vladimir S. Myglan, Fredrik Charpentier Ljungqvist, Michael McCormick, Nicola Di Cosmo, Michael Sigl, Johann Jungclaus, Sebastian Wagner, Paul J. Krusic, Jan Esper, Jed O. Kaplan, Michiel A.C. de Vaan, Jürg Luterbacher,

Lukas Wacker, Willy Tegel, and Alexander V. Kirdyanov (2016), "Cooling and Societal Change During the Late Antique Little Ice Age from 536 to Around 660 AD," *Nature Geoscience*, 9: 231–6.

Burbank, Jane and Frederick Cooper (2010), *Empires in World History: Power and the Politics of Difference*, Princeton, NJ: Princeton University Press.

Burckhardt, Jacob (1904), *The Civilization of the Renaissance in Italy: An Essay*, trans. S.G.C. Middlemore, London: Macmillan.

Burgess, Glynn, trans. (1990), *The Song of Roland*, New York: Penguin Classics.

Burton, Antoinette (2015), *The Trouble with Empire: Challenges to Modern British Imperialism*, Oxford: Oxford University Press.

Calkin, Siobhan Bly (2009), *Saracens and the Making of English Identity: The Auchinleck Manuscript*, New York: Routledge.

Camille, Michael (1995), "'When Adam Delved': Laboring on the Land in English Medieval Art," in *Agriculture in the Middle Ages*, ed. Del Sweeney, 247–76, Philadelphia, PA: University of Pennsylvania Press.

Campbell, Darryl (2010), "The Capitulare de Villis, the Brevium exempla, and the Carolingian Court at Aachen," *Early Medieval Europe*, 18 (3): 243–64.

Campbell, Mary B. (1988), *The Witness and the Other World: Exotic European Travel Writing, 400–1600*, Ithaca, NY: Cornell University Press.

Campbell, Tony (1987), "Portolan Charts from the Late Thirteenth Century to 1500," in *The History of Cartography*, Vol. 1, ed. J.B. Harley and David Woodward, 371–463, Chicago, IL: University of Chicago Press.

Camporeale, Salvatore I. (1996), "Lorenzo Valla's *Oratio* on the Pseudo-Donation of Constantine: Dissent and Innovation in Early Renaissance Humanism," *Journal of History of Ideas*, 57: 9–26.

Campos, Don Rafael Torres (1901), *Carácter de la conquista y colonización de las Islas Canarias: Discursos leídos ante la Real Academia de la Historia*, Madrid: Imprenta y litografía del depósito de la guerra.

"Capitulare de Villis" (2008), In *Carolingian Polyptyques*, University of Leicester, https://www.le.ac.uk/hi/polyptyques/capitulare/trans.html, accessed December 2016.

Cary, George (1956), *The Medieval Alexander*, Cambridge: Cambridge University Press.

Cassell, Anthony K. (2004), *The* Monarchia *Controversy: An Historical Study with Accompanying Translations of Dante Alighieri's* Monarchia, *Guido Vernani's Refutation of the "Monarchia" Composed by Dante, and Pope John XXII's Bull* Si fratrum, Washington, DC: Catholic University Press of America.

Catlos, Brian (2014), *Muslims of Medieval Latin Christendom, c. 1050–1614*, Cambridge: Cambridge University Press.

Charageat, Martine (2009), "Les juifs et la sexualité interdite dans la rhétorique judiciaire chrétienne (Aragon, XV siècle)," in *Cristianos y judíos en contacto en la Edad Media*, ed. Flocel Sabaté Curell and Claude Denjean, 589–604, Lleida: Editorial Milenio.

Chareyron, Nicole (2005), *Pilgrims to Jerusalem in the Middle Ages*, trans. W. Donald Wilson, New York: Columbia University Press.

Cheyette, Fredric (2008), "The Disappearance of the Ancient Landscape and the Climatic Anomaly of the Early Middle Ages: A Question to be Pursued," *Early Medieval Europe*, 16: 127–65.

Chodorow, Stanley (1972), *Christian Political Theory and Church Politics in the Mid-Twelfth Century: The Ecclesiology of Gratian's Decretum*, Berkeley, CA: University of California Press.

Chodorow, Stanley (1989), "Paschal II, Henry V, and the Origins of the Crisis of 1111," in *Popes, Teachers, and Canon Law in the Middle Ages*, ed. James Ross Sweeney and Stanley Chodorow, 3–25, Ithaca, NY: Cornell University Press.

Clanchy, Michael (2013), *From Memory to Written Record, England 1066–1307*, 2nd edn, Chichester: Wiley-Blackwell.

Clarke, Nicola (2016), "Heirs and Spares: Elite Fathers and Their Sons in the Literary Sources of Umayyad Iberia," *Al-Masāq: Journal of the Medieval Mediterranean*, 28 (1): 67–83.

Cobb, Paul M., trans. (2008), *The Book of Contemplation: Islam and the Crusades*, New York, Penguin.

Cobb, Paul M. (2014), *The Race for Paradise: An Islamic History of the Crusades*, Oxford: Oxford University Press.

Cohen, Jeffrey Jerome (2013), "Race," in *A Handbook of Middle English Studies*, ed. Marion Turner, 109–22, Chichester: Wiley-Blackwell.

Cohen, Meredith (2015), *The Sainte-Chapelle and the Construction of Sacral Monarchy: Royal Architecture in Thirteenth-Century Paris*, Cambridge: Cambridge University Press.

Colás, Alejandro (2007), *Empire*, London: Polity.

Colbert, Benjamin (1997), *The Travels of Marco Polo*, Ware: Wordsworth Editions.

Coleman, James K. (2013), "Boccaccio's Humanistic Ethnography," in *Boccaccio: A Critical Guide to the Complete Works*, ed. Victoria Kirkham, Michael Sherberg, and Janet L. Smarr, 265–75, Chicago, IL: University of Chicago Press.

Conant, Jonathan P. (2015), "Anxieties of Violence: Christians and Muslims in Conflict in Aghlabid North Africa and the Central Mediterranean," *Al-Masāq: Journal of the Medieval Mediterranean*, 27 (1): 7–23.

Connolly, Daniel (2009), *The Maps of Matthew Paris: Medieval Journeys through Space, Time and Liturgy*, Woodbridge: Boydell Press.

Constable, Giles (1976), "Opposition to Pilgrimage in the Middle Ages," *Studia Gratiana*, 19: 125–46.

Constable, Giles (1995), "The Orders of Society," in *Three Studies in Medieval Religion and Social Thought*, 249–360, Cambridge: Cambridge University Press.

Constable, Olivia Remie (1994), *Trade and Traders in Muslim Spain: The Commercial Realignment of the Iberian Peninsula, 900–1500*, Cambridge: Cambridge University Press.

Constable, Olivia Remie (1996), *Trade and Traders in Muslim Spain*, Cambridge: Cambridge University Press.

Constable, Olivia Remie (2013), "Islamic Practice and Christian Power: Sustaining Muslim Faith Under Christian Rule in Medieval Spain, Sicily and the Crusader States," in *Co-Existence and Co-Operation in the Middle Ages*, IV European Congress of Medieval Studies, Palermo, 23–27 June 2009, ed. A. Musco and G. Musotto, 25–36, Palermo: F.I.D.E.M.

Constable, Olivia Remie (2014), "From Hygiene to Heresy: Changing Perceptions of Women and Bathing in Medieval and Early Modern Iberia," in *La cohabitation religieuse dans les villes européennes, X–XVe siècles*, ed. S. Boissellier and J. Tolan, 185–206, Turnhout: Brepols.

Contamine, Philippe (1984), *War in the Middle Ages*, trans. Michael Jones, Oxford: Basil Blackwell.

Contamine, Philippe, Marc Bompaire, Stéphane Lebecq, and Jean-Luc Sarrazin (2003), *L'économie médiévale*, 3rd edn, Paris: Armand Colin.

Coulson, Charles L.H. (2003), *Castles in Medieval Society: Fortresses in England, France, and Ireland in the Central Middle Ages*, Oxford: Oxford University Press.

Cowdrey, H.E.J. (1969), "Bishop Ermenfrid of Sion and the Penitential Ordinance following the Battle of Hastings," *Journal of Ecclesiastical History*, 20 (2): 225–42.

Cowdrey, H.E.J. (1995), "Pope Urban II and the Idea of Crusade," *Studi Medievali*, 36: 721–42.

Cowdrey, H.E.J. (1998), *Gregory VII, 1073–1085*, Oxford: Clarendon Press.

Craig, Leigh Ann (2009), *Wandering Women and Holy Matrons: Women as Pilgrims in the Later Middle Ages*, Leiden: Brill.

Creighton, Oliver H. (2012), *Early European Castles: Aristocracy and Authority. AD 800–1200*, London: Bristol Classical Press.

Critchley, John (1992) *Marco Polo's Book*, Aldershot: Variorum.

Crouch, David (1992), *The Image of the Aristocracy in Britain, 1000–1300*, London: Routledge.

Cuffel, Alexandra (2009), "Polemicising Women's Bathing among Medieval and Early Modern Christians and Muslims," in *The Nature and Function of Water, Baths, Bathing and Hygiene from Antiquity through the Renaissance*, ed. Cynthia Kosso and Anne Scott, 171–88, Leiden: Brill.

Cushing, Kathleen (2005), *Reform and the Papacy in the Eleventh Century: Spirituality and Social Reform*, Manchester: Manchester University Press.

Cusimano, Richard and John Moorhead, trans. (1992), *Deeds of Louis the Fat*, Washington, DC: Catholic University Press of America.

Cutler, Anthony (2001), "Gifts and Gift Exchange as Aspects of the Byzantine, Arab, and Related Economies," *Dumbarton Oaks Papers*, 55: 247–78.

Cutler, Anthony (2004), "Realities, *Realia*, and Realism: An Introduction to the Symposium," *Dumbarton Oaks Papers*, 58: 155–74.

Cyriac of Ancona (2015), *Life and Early Travels*, ed. and trans. Charles Mitchell, Edward W. Bodnar, and Clive Foss, Cambridge, MA: I. Tatti Renaissance Library, Harvard University Press.

Dalché, Patrick Gautier (1995), *Carte marine et portulan au XIIe siècle: le Liber de existencia riveriarum et forma maris nostri Mediterranei (Pise, circa 1200)*, Rome: École française de Rome.

Dalton, Paul (2009), "The Outlaw Hereward 'the Wake': His Companions and Enemies," in *Outlaws in Medieval and Early Modern England: Crime, Government and Society, c. 1066–c. 1600*, ed. John C. Appleby and Paul Dalton, 7–36, Farnham: Ashgate.

Davenport, Frances Gardiner, ed. and trans. (1917), *European Treaties Bearing on the History of the United States and its Dependencies*, Washington, DC: Carnegie Institution.

Davis, Jennifer R. (2015), *Charlemagne's Practice of Empire*, Cambridge: Cambridge University Press.

Davis, Kathleen (2008), *Periodization and Sovereignty: How Ideas of Feudalism and Secularization Govern the Politics of Time*, Philadelphia, PA: University of Pennsylvania Press.

Davis-Secord, Sarah (2017), *Where Three Worlds Met: Sicily in the Early Medieval Mediterranean*, Ithaca, NY: Cornell University Press.

Dawson, Christopher, ed. (1966), *The Mongol Mission: Narratives and Letters of the Franciscan Missionaries in Mongolia and China in the Thirteenth and Fourteenth Centuries*, New York: Harper, reprinted (1980) as *Mission to Asia*, Toronto: University of Toronto Press.

Demacopoulos, George E. (2013), *The Invention of Peter: Apostolic Discourse and Papal Authority in Late Antiquity*, Philadelphia, PA: University of Pennsylvania Press.

De Poerck, Guy (1961), "Le corpus mandevillien du ms Chantilly 699," in *Fin de Moyen Age et Renaissance: Mélanges de philologie offerts à Robert Guiette*, ed. Guy De Poerck, 31–48, Antwerp: De Nederlansche Boekhandel.

Devroey, Jean-Pierre (1993), *Études sur le grand domaine carolingian*, Aldershot: Ashgate.

Devroey, Jean-Pierre (2017), "Ordering, Measuring, and Counting: Carolingian Rule, Cultural Capital and the Economic Performance in Western Europe, 750–900," http://www.academia.edu/1867212/Ordering_measuring_and_counting_Carolingian_rule_cultural_capital_and_the_economic_performance_in_Western_Europe_750-900_, accessed November 10, 2017.

Dietz, Maribel (2005), *Wandering Monks, Virgins, and Pilgrims: Ascetic Travel in the Mediterranean World, A.D. 300–800*, University Park, PA: Pennsylvania State University Press.

Dillard, Heath (1984), *Daughters of the Reconquest: Women in Castilian Town Society, 1100–1300*, Cambridge: Cambridge University Press.

Ditchfield, Simon, Charlotte Methuen, and Andrew Spicer, eds (2017), *Translating Christianity*, Studies in Church History 53, Cambridge: Cambridge University Press.

Dod, Bernard (1982), "Aristoteles latinus," in *The Cambridge History of Later Medieval Philosophy*, ed. Norman Kretzmann, Anthony Kenny, Jan Pinborg, and Eleonore. Stump, Cambridge: Cambridge University Press.

Douglas, David C. and George W. Greenaway, eds (1981), *English Historical Documents II: 1042–1189*, 2nd edn, London: Eyre Methuen.

Doyle, Michael W. (1986), *Empires*, Ithaca, NY: Cornell University Press.

Druce, George C. (1919), "The Elephant in Medieval Legend and Art," *Journal of the Royal Archaeological Institute*, 76: 1–73.

Duby, Georges (1978), *The Three Orders: Feudal Society Imagined*, trans. Arthur Goldhammer, Chicago, IL: University of Chicago Press.

Dunn, Caroline S. (2013), *Stolen Women in Medieval England: Rape, Abduction and Adultery, 1100–1500*, Cambridge: Cambridge University Press.

Dutschke, Consuelo Wager (1993), "Francesco Pipino and the Manuscripts of Marco Polo's Travels," PhD dissertation, University of California, Los Angeles.

Dutton, Paul Edward (1994), *The Politics of Dreaming in the Carolingian Empire*. Lincoln, NE: University of Nebraska Press.

Dutton, Paul Edward (2004a), *Carolingian Civilization*, 2nd edn, Toronto: University of Toronto Press.

Dutton, Paul Edward (2004b), *Charlemagne's Mustache and other Cultural Clusters of a Dark Age*, New York: Palgrave Macmillan.

Dutton, Paul Edward (2009), *Charlemagne's Courtier: The Complete Einhard*, Toronto: University of Toronto Press.

Dyas, Dee (2001), *Pilgrimage in Medieval English Literature, 700–1500*, Woodbridge: D.S. Brewer.

Eastman, Jason T. (2015), "The Wild (White) Ones: Comparing Frames of White and Black Deviance," *Contemporary Justice Review: Issues in Criminal, Social, and Restorative Justice*, 18 (2): 231–47.

Echard, Siân (1998), *Arthurian Narrative in the Latin Tradition*, Cambridge: Cambridge University Press.

Edbury, Peter and John Gordon Rowe (1988), *William of Tyre: Historian of the Latin East*, Cambridge: Cambridge University Press.
Effros, Bonnie (2017), "The Enduring Attraction of the Pirenne Thesis," *Speculum*, 92: 184–208.
Egerton, Frank (2012), *Roots of Ecology; Antiquity to Haeckel*, Berkeley, CA: University of California Press.
Egger, C. and D. Smith, eds (forthcoming), *Pope Gregory IX (1227–41)*, New York: Routledge.
Einhard and Notker the Stammerer (1969), *Two Lives of Charlemagne*, ed. and trans. Lewis G.M. Thorpe, London: Penguin Books
Eliav-Feldon, Miryam (2005), *The Origins of Racism in the West*, Cambridge: Cambridge University Press.
Ellenblum, Ronnie (2002), "Were there Borders and Borderlines in the Middle Ages? The Example of the Latin Kingdom of Jerusalem," in *Medieval Frontiers: Concepts and Practices*, ed. David Abulafia and Nora Berend, 105–19, Burlington, VT: Ashgate.
Ellis, G.M., trans. (1973), *Boso's Life of Alexander III*, Totowa, NJ: Rowan & Littlefield.
Emerton, Ephraim, trans. ([1932] 1990), *The Correspondence of Pope Gregory VII: Select Letters from the Registrum*, New York: Columbia University Press.
Emmerson, Richard K. and P.J.P. Goldberg (2000), "'The Lord Geoffrey had me made:' Lordship and Labour in the Luttrell Psalter," in *The Problem of Labour in Fourteenth-Century England*, ed. James Bothwell, P.J.P. Goldberg, and W.M. Ormrod, 43–63, Rochester, NY: Boydell & Brewer.
Epstein, Steven (1991), *Wage Labor and Guilds in Medieval Europe*, Chapel Hill, NC: University of North Carolina Press.
Epstein, Steven (2001a), *Speaking of Slavery: Color, Ethnicity and Human Bondage in Italy*, Ithaca, NY: Cornell University Press.
Epstein, Steven (2001b), *Genoa & the Genoese, 958–1528*, Chapel Hill, NC: University of North Carolina Press.
Epstein, Steven (2006), *Purity Lost: Mixing Relationships in the Eastern Mediterranean*, Baltimore, MD: Johns Hopkins University Press.
Epstein, Steven (2012), *The Medieval Discovery of Nature*, New York: Cambridge University Press.
Euben, Roxanne (2008), *Journeys to the Other Shore: Muslim and Western Travelers in Search of Knowledge*, Princeton, NJ: Princeton University Press.
Evans, Arthur J., Andrew Lang, Gilbert Murray, P.B. Jevons, J.L. Myres, and W. Warde Fowler (1908), *Anthropology and the Classics*, ed. R.R. Marrett, Oxford: Clarendon Press.
Evans, Ruth, ed. (2011), *A Cultural History of Sexuality in the Middle Ages*, New York: Bloomsbury Press.
Evergates, Theodore (2016), *Henry the Liberal: Count of Champagne, 1127–1181*, Philadelphia, PA: University of Philadelphia Press.
Fagan, Brian (2000), *The Little Ice Age: How Climate Made History, 1300–1850*, New York: Basic Books.
Fagan, Brian (2008), *The Great Warming: Climate Change and the Rise and Fall of Civilizations*, New York: Bloomsbury Press.
Farmer, Sharon (2002), *Surviving Poverty in Medieval Paris: Gender, Ideology, and the Daily Lives of the Poor*, Ithaca, NY: Cornell University Press.
Farmer, Sharon (2017), *The Silk Industries of Medieval Paris: Artisanal Migration, Technological Innovation, and Gendered Experience*, Philadelphia, PA: University of Pennsylvania Press.

Ferguson, Wallace (1948), *The Renaissance in Historical Thought: Five Centuries of Interpretation*, New York: Houghton Mifflin.

Fernández-Armesto, Felipe (1987), *Before Columbus: Exploration and Colonisation from the Mediterranean to the Atlantic, 1229–1492*, Philadelphia, PA: University of Pennsylvania Press.

Finke, Laurie A. and Martin B. Shichtman (1998), "The Mont St Michel Giant: Sexual Violence and Imperialism in the Chronicles of Wace and Layamon," in *Violence Against Women in Medieval Texts*, ed. Anna Roberts, 56–74, Gainesville, FL: University of Florida Press.

Flecker, Michael (2001), "A Ninth-Century AD Arab or Indian Shipwreck: First Evidence of Direct Trade with China," *World Archaeology*, 32: 335–54.

Fletcher, Richard A. (2003), *Bloodfeud: Murder and Revenge in Anglo-Saxon England*, Oxford: Oxford University Press.

Flury-Lemberg, Mechthild (1988), *Textile Conservation and Research: A Documentation of the Textile Department on the Occasion of the Twentieth Anniversary of the Abegg Foundation*, Bern: Schriften der Abegg-Stiftung.

Fonnesberg-Schmidt, Iben (2007), *The Popes and the Baltic Crusades, 1147–1254*, Leiden: Brill.

Forey, Alan J. (1986), "Recruitment to the Military Orders (Twelfth to Mid-Fourteenth Centuries)," *Viator*, 17: 139–71.

Forey, Alan J. (1992), *The Military Orders from the Twelfth to the Early Fourteenth Centuries*, Basingstoke: Macmillan.

Foucault, Michel (1990), *History of Sexuality, Vol. 1: An Introduction*, trans. Robert Hurley, New York: Vintage.

Fradenburg, Louise O. and Carla Freccero, eds (1996), *Premodern Sexualities*, New York: Routledge.

Frakes, Jerold C., ed. (2011), *Contextualising the Muslim Other in Medieval Christian Discourse*, Basingstoke: Palgrave.

Frederick II of Hohenstaufen (1943), *The Art of Falconry, being the De Arte Venandi cum Avibus*, ed. and trans. Casey A. Wood and F. Marjorie Fyfe, London: Oxford University Press.

Freed, John B. (2016), *Frederick Barbarossa: The Prince and the Myth*, New Haven, CT: Yale University Press.

Freedman, Paul (1999), *Images of the Medieval Peasant*, Stanford, CA: Stanford University Press.

Freedman, Paul (2008), *Out of the East: Spices in the Medieval Imagination*, New Haven, CT: Yale University Press.

Freedman, Paul (2012), "Peasants, the Seigneurial Regime, and Serfdom in the Eleventh to Thirteenth Centuries," in *European Transformations: The Long Twelfth Century*, ed. Thomas F.X. Noble and John Van Engen, 259–78, Notre Dame, IN: Notre Dame University Press.

Fried, Johannes (2015), *The Middle Ages*, trans. Peter Lewis, Cambridge, MA: The Belknap Press of Harvard University Press.

Fried, Johannes (2016), *Charlemagne*, trans. Peter Lewis, Cambridge, MA: Harvard University Press.

Froissart, Jean (1978), *Chronicles*, trans. Geoffrey Brereton, Harmondsworth: Penguin.

Fry, Timothy, ed. (1981), *RB 1980: The Rule of St. Benedict in English*, Collegeville, MN: Liturgical Press.

Gabriele, Matthew (2008), "The Provenance of the *Descriptio qualiter Karolus Magnus*: Remembering the Carolingians at the Court of King Philip I (1060–1108) before the First Crusade," *Viator*, 39: 93–117.

Gabriele, Matthew (2011), *An Empire of Memory: The Legend of Charlemagne, the Franks, and Jerusalem before the First Crusade*, Oxford: Oxford University Press.

Gabriele, Matthew (2016), "Frankish Kingship and the Ghost of Charlemagne in the Exegetical Diplomas of King Philip I of Francia," in *The Charlemagne Legend in Medieval Latin Texts*, ed. William J. Purkis and Matthew Gabriele, 9–32, Woodbridge: Boydell & Brewer.

Gage, John (1993), *Color and Culture: Practice and Meaning from Antiquity to Abstraction*, Berkeley, CA: University of California Press.

Ganz, David, trans. (2008), *Two Lives of Charlemagne*, London: Penguin.

Garipzanov, Ildar H. (2008), *The Symbolic Language of Authority in the Carolingian World (c. 751–877)*, Leiden: Brill.

Garmonsway, G.N., ed. and trans. (1990), *Anglo-Saxon*, London: J.M. Dent.

Garver, Valerie L. (2009), *Women and Aristocratic Culture in the Carolingian World*, Ithaca, NY: Cornell University Press.

Gaunt, Simon (2013), *Marco Polo's* Le Divisement du Monde: *Narrative Voice, Language and Diversity*, Cambridge: D.S. Brewer.

Geoffrey of Monmouth (1848), *History of the Kings of Britain*, in *Six Old English Chronicles, of Which Two are Now First Translated from the Monkish Latin Originals*, ed. and trans. J.A. Giles, London: Henry G. Bohn, http://d.lib.rochester.edu/camelot/text/geoffrey-of-monmouth-arthurian-passages-from-the-history-of-the-kings-of-britain, accessed March 11, 2017.

Geoffrey of Monmouth (2007), *The History of the Kings of Britain*, ed. Michael D. Reeve, trans. Neil Wright, Woodbridge: Boydell Press.

George-Tvrtković, Rita (2012), *A Christian Pilgrim in Medieval Iraq*, Turnhout: Brepols.

Georgopoulou, Maria (2001), *Venice's Mediterranean Colonies: Architecture and Urbanism*, Cambridge: Cambridge University Press.

Gillingham, John (2015), "Crusading Warfare, Chivalry and the Enslavement of Women and Children," in *The Medieval Way of War: Studies in Medieval Military History in Honor of Bernard S. Bachrach*, ed. Gregory Halfond, 133–52, Aldershot: Ashgate.

Gillis, Matthew Bryan (2017), *Heresy and Dissent in the Carolingian Empire: The Case of Gottschalk of Orbais*, Oxford: Oxford University Press.

Goitein, S.D. (1967–93), *A Mediterranean Society: The Jewish Communities of the World as Portrayed in the Documents of the Cairo Geniza*, 6 vols, Berkeley, CA: University of California Press.

Goldberg, Eric (2013), "Louis the Pious and the Hunt," *Speculum*, 88: 613–43.

Goldberg, Jessica (2012), *Trade and Institutions in the Medieval Mediterranean: The Geniza Merchants and Their Business World*, Cambridge: Cambridge University Press.

Goldin, Simha (2011), *Jewish Women in Europe in the Middle Ages*, Manchester: Manchester University Press.

Goodich, Michael (1979), *The Unmentionable Vice: Homosexuality in the Later Medieval Period*, Santa Barbara, CA: ABC-CLIO.

Goodson, Caroline, Anne Lester, and Carol Symes, eds (2010), *Cities, Texts, and Social Networks, 400–1500: Experiences and Perceptions of Medieval Urban Space*, Aldershot: Ashgate.

Goswami, Manu (2004), *Producing India: From Colonial Economy to National Space*, Chicago, IL: University of Chicago Press.

Grafton, Anthony with April Shelford and Nancy Siraisi (1992), *New Worlds, Ancient Texts: The Power of Tradition and the Shock of Discovery*, Cambridge, MA: The Belknap Press of Harvard University Press.

Green, Caitlin (2016, May 23), "A Note on the Evidence for African Migrants in Britain from the Bronze Age to the Medieval Period" [Blog], http://www.caitlingreen.org/2016/05/a-note-on-evidence-for-african-migrants.html, accessed August 17, 2017.

Green, Monica, ed. (2014), *Pandemic Disease in the Medieval World: Rethinking the Black Death*, Special Issue of *The Medieval Globe*, Kalamazoo: Arc Medieval Press.

Groebner, Valentin (2003), "Haben Hautfarben eine Geschichte? Personenbeschreibungen und ihre Kategorien zwischen dem 13. und dem 16. Jahrhundert," *Zeitschrift für Historische Forschung*, 30: 1–18.

Groebner, Valentin (2007), *Who Are You? Identification, Deception, and Surveillance in Early Modern Europe*, trans. Mark Kyburz and John Peck, New York: Zone Books.

Grosjean, Georges (1978), *Mapamundi. The Catalan Atlas of the Year 1375*, Zurich: Urs Graf Verlag.

Grube, Ernest J. and Jeremy Johns (2005), *The Painted Ceilings of the Cappella Palatina*, Genoa/New York: Bruschettini Foundation for Islamic Art/East-West Foundation.

Gual Camarena, Miguel, ed. (1981), *El primer manual hispánico de mercadería (siglo XIV)*, Barcelona: Consejo Superior de Investigaciones Científicas, Instituto de Geografía, Etnología e Historia.

Guizot, François (1838), *General History of Civilization in Europe*, trans. William Hazlitt, Oxford: D.A. Talboys.

Hahn, Cynthia J. (2012), *Strange Beauty: Issues in the Making and Meaning of Reliquaries, 400–1204*, University Park, PA: Pennsylvania State University Press.

Hahn, Cynthia J. and Holger A. Klein (2015), *Saints and Sacred Matter: The Cult of Relics in Byzantium and Beyond*, Washington, DC: Dumbarton Oaks Research Library and Collection, Harvard University Press.

Haldon, John (1993), *The State and the Tributary Mode of Production*, London: Verso.

Halsall, Guy (2003), *Warfare and Society in the Barbarian West, 450–900*, Abingdon: Routledge.

Hamilton, Bernard (1985), "Prester John and the *Three Kings of Cologne*," in *Studies in Medieval History Presented to R.H.C. Davis*, ed. Henry Mayr-Harting and R.I. Moore, London: The Hambledon Press.

Hammer, Carl I. (1997), *Charlemagne's Months and their Bavarian Labors: The Politics of the Seasons in the Carolingian Empire*, Oxford: Archaeopress.

Hanawalt, Barbara A. (1986), "Peasant Women's Contribution to the Home Economy in Late Medieval England," in *Women and Work in Preindustrial Europe*, ed. Barbara A. Hanawalt, 3–19, Bloomington, IN: Indiana University Press.

Hanawalt, Barbara and Lisa J. Kiser (2008), "Introduction," in *Engaging with Nature: Essays on the Natural World in Medieval and Early Modern Europe*, ed. Barbara Hanawalt and Lisa J. Kiser, 1–10, Notre Dame, IN: University of Notre Dame Press.

Hanna, Ralph, III (1987), "The Canterbury Tales," in *The Wadsworth Chaucer*, ed. Larry D. Benson, 1118–35, Boston, MA: Wadsworth, Cengage Learning.

Hannaford, Ivan (1996), *Race: The History of an Idea in the West*, Baltimore, MD: Johns Hopkins University Press/Woodrow Wilson Center Press.

Hardt, Michael and Antonio Negri (2000), *Empire*, Cambridge, MA: Harvard University Press.
Harper, April and Caroline Proctor, eds (2008), *Medieval Sexuality: A Casebook*, New York: Routledge.
Harris, Jonathan (2015), *The Lost World of Byzantium*, New Haven, CT: Yale University Press.
Haskins, Charles Homer (1921), "The 'De Art Venandi cum Avibus' of the Emperor Frederick II," *English Historical Review*, 36 (143): 334–55.
Haskins, Charles Homer (1924), *Studies in the History of Mediaeval Science*, Cambridge, MA: Harvard University Press.
Hastings, Tom (1992), "Said's Orientalism and the Discourse of (Hetero)sexuality," *Canadian Review of American Studies*, 23: 127–48.
Hayward, John (1988), "Hereward the Outlaw," *Journal of Medieval History*, 14 (4): 293–304.
Heers, Jacques (1983), *Marco Polo*, Paris: Fayard.
Helms, Mary W. (1988), *Ulysses' Sail: An Ethnographic Odyssey of Power, Knowledge, and Geographical Distance*, Princeton, NJ: Princeton University Press.
Heng, Geraldine (2003), *Empire of Magic: Medieval Romance and the Politics of Cultural Fantasy*, New York: Columbia University Press.
Heng, Geraldine (2011a), "The Invention of Race in the European Middle Ages I: Race Studies, Modernity, and the Middle Ages," *Literature Compass*, 8 (5): 315–31.
Heng, Geraldine (2011b), "The Invention of Race in the European Middle Ages II: Locations of Medieval Race," *Literature Compass*, 8 (5): 332–50.
Heng, Geraldine (2014), "An African Saint in Medieval Europe: The Black Saint Maurice and the Enigma of Racial Sanctity," in *Sainthood and Race: Marked Flesh, Holy Flesh*, ed. Molly H. Bassett and Vincent W. Lloyd, 18–44, New York: Routledge.
Henning, Joachim (2008), "Strong Rulers—Weak Economy? Rome, The Carolingian and the Archeology of Slavery in the First Millennium AD," in *The Long Morning of Medieval Europe: New Directions in Early Medieval* Studies, ed. Jennifer R. Davis and Michael McCormick, 33–54, London: Ashgate.
Herder, Johann Gottfried von ([1784–91] 1997), *Ideas on the Philosophy of the History of Mankind*, in *Race and the Enlightenment: A Reader*, ed. Emmanel Chukwudi Eze, 70–8, Malden, MA: Blackwell.
Herdt, Gilbert (1996), *Third Sex, Third Gender: Beyond Sexual Dimorphism in Culture and History*, Cambridge, MA: Zone Books.
Heywood, Andrew (2015), *Political Theory: An Introduction*, 4th edn, London: Palgrave Macmillan.
Hill, David H. (1969), "The Burghal Hidage: The Establishment of a Text," *Medieval Archaeology*, 13: 84–92.
Hill, David H. (1981), *An Atlas of Anglo-Saxon England*, Oxford: Basil Blackwell.
Hill, Rosalind M.T., ed. and trans. (1962), *Gesta Francorum et aliorum Hierosolimitanorum*, London: Nelson.
Hitti, Philip K., trans. (1929), *An Arab-Syrian Gentleman and Warrior in the Period of the Crusades: Memoirs of Usamah ibn Munqidh*, New York: Columbia University Press.
Hoffmann, Richard (2008), "Homo et Natura, Homo in Natura: Ecological Perspectives on the European Middle Ages," in *Engaging with Nature: Essays on the Natural World in Medieval and Early Modern Europe*, ed. Barbara Hanawalt and Lisa J. Kiser, 11–38, Notre Dame, IN: University of Notre Dame Press.

Hoffmann, Richard (2014), *An Environmental History of Medieval Europe*, New York: Cambridge University Press.
Holloway, Julia Bolton (1998), *Essays on Pilgrimage and Literature*, New York: AMS Press.
Hoofnagle, Wendy Marie (2013), "Taming the Wilderness: The Exploration of Anglo-Norman Kingship in the Vie de Saint Gilles," *Haskins Society Journal*, 25: 165–86.
Hoofnagle, Wendy Marie (2016), *The Continuity of the Conquest: Charlemagne and Anglo-Norman Imperialism*, University Park, PA: Pennsylvania State University Press.
Horden, Peregrine and Nicholas Purcell (2000), *The Corrupting Sea: A Study of Mediterranean History*, Oxford: Blackwell.
Horstmann, C., ed. (1886), *The Three Kings of Cologne: An Early English Translation of the "Historia Trium Regum"*, London: Early English Text Society.
Howe, Stephen (2002), *Empire: A Very Short Introduction*, Oxford: Oxford University Press.
Howell, Martha (1986), *Women, Production, and Patriarchy in Late Medieval Cities*, Chicago: University of Chicago Press.
Howell, Martha (2010), *Commerce Before Capitalism in Europe, 1300–1600*, Cambridge: Cambridge University Press.
Husain, Adnan (2011), "From Mission to Crusade: Friar William of Rubruck's Journey to the Mongols," in *The Middle Ages in Texts and Texture: Reflections on Medieval Sources*, ed. Jason Glenn, 245–58, Toronto: University of Toronto Press.
Hysell, Jesse (2012), "*Pacem portantes advenerint*: Ambivalent Images of Muslims in the Chronicles of Norman Italy," *Al-Masāq: Islam and the Medieval Mediterranean*, 24 (2): 139–56.
Ibn Battuta (2010), *The Travels of Ibn Battuta, AD 1325–1354*, 4 vols, trans. H.A.R. Gibb, Farnham: Ashgate.
Jablonski, Nina G. (2012), *Living Color: The Biological and Social Meaning of Skin Color*, Berkeley, CA: University of California Press.
Jackson, Peter (2017), *The Mongols and the Islamic World: From Conquest to Conversion*, New Haven, CT: Yale University Press.
Jankulak, Karen (2010), *Geoffrey of Monmouth*, Cardiff: University of Wales Press.
Jennings, Willie James (2010), *The Christian Imagination: Theology and the Origins of Race*, New Haven, CT: Yale University Press.
Jocelin of Brakelond (1989), *Chronicle of the Abbey of Bury St Edmunds*, trans. Diana E. Greenaway and Jane E. Sayers, Oxford: Oxford University Press.
John of Salisbury ([n.d.] 1909), *Policraticus*, ed. C.C.W. Webb, Oxford: Clarendon Press.
Johnston, Anna (2003), *Missionary Writing and Empire, 1800–1860*, Cambridge: Cambridge University Press.
Jones, Chris (2007), *Eclipse of Empire? Perceptions of the Western Empire and its Rulers in Late-Medieval France*, Turnhout: Brepols.
Jones, Gwyn (1968), *A History of the Vikings*, Oxford: Oxford University Press.
Jordan, William Chester (1979), *Louis IX and the Challenge of Crusade*, Princeton, NJ: Princeton University Press.
Jordan, William Chester (2001), "Why 'Race'?," *Journal of Medieval & Early Modern Studies*, 31 (1): 165–74.
Justice, Steven (1994), *Writing and Rebellion: England in 1381*, Berkeley, CA: University of California Press.

Kaeuper, Richard W. and Elspeth Kennedy, trans. (1996), *The Book of Chivalry of Geoffroi de Charny: Text, Context, and Translation*, Philadelphia, PA: University of Pennsylvania Press.
Kant, Immanuel ([1775] 1997), *On the Different Races of Man*, in *Race and the Enlightenment: A Reader*, ed. Emmanel Chukwudi Eze, 38–48, Malden, MA: Blackwell.
Kantorowicz, Ernst ([1931] 1957), *Frederick the Second, 1194–1250*, trans. E.O. Lorimer, New York: Richard R. Smith.
Kapitaikin, Lev (2013), "'The Daughter of al-Andalus': Interrelations between Norman Sicily and the Muslim West," *Al-Masāq: Islam and the Medieval Mediterranean*, 25 (1): 113–34.
Kapelle, William E. (1979), *The Norman Conquest of the North: The Region and its Transformation, 1000–1135*, Chapel Hill, NC: University of North Carolina Press.
Kaplan, Paul H.D. (1985), *The Rise of the Black Magus*, Ann Arbor, MI: UMI Research Press.
Karras, Ruth Mazo (1988), *Slavery and Society in Medieval Scandinavia*, New Haven, CT: Yale University Press.
Karras, Ruth Mazo (1996), *Common Women: Prostitution and Sexuality in Medieval England*, Oxford: Oxford University Press.
Karras, Ruth Mazo (2003), *From Boys to Men: Formations of Masculinity in Late Medieval Europe*, Philadelphia, PA: University of Pennsylvania Press.
Karras, Ruth Mazo (2005), *Sexuality in Medieval Europe: Doing Unto Others*, New York: Routledge.
Kedar, Benjamin Z. (1999), "On the Origins of the Earliest Laws of Frankish Jerusalem: The Canons of the Council of Nablus 1120," *Speculum*, 74: 310–35.
Keen, Maurice H. (1984), *Chivalry*, New Haven, CT: Yale University Press.
Keen, Maurice H., ed. (1999), *Medieval Warfare: A History*, Oxford: Oxford University Press.
Kelly, Morgan and Cormac Ó Gráda (2014), "Debating the Little Ice Age," *Journal of Interdisciplinary History*, 45: 57–68.
Kelly, Samantha (2003), *The New Solomon: Robert of Naples (1309–1343) and Fourteenth-Century Kingship*, Leiden: Brill.
Kelsey, George (1965), *Racism and the Christian Understanding of Man*, New York: Charles Scribner's Sons.
Kempe, Margery (1996), *The Book of Margery Kempe*, ed. Lynn Staley, Kalamazoo, MI: Medieval Institute Publications.
Kempf, Friedrich, ed. (1947), *Regestum Innocentii III papae super negotio Romani imperii*, Miscellanea Historia Pontificae, Vol. 12, Rome: Pontificia Università Gregoriana.
Kempf, Friedrich (1968), "La deposizione di Federico II alla luce della dottrina canonistica," *Archivio della Società Romana di Storia Patria*, 21: 1–16.
Keynes, Simon D. (1997), "The Vikings in England, *c.* 790–1016," in *The Oxford Illustrated History of the Vikings*, ed. Peter H. Sawyer, 48–82, Oxford: Oxford University Press.
Keynes, Simon D. and Michael Lapidge, trans. (1983), *Alfred the Great: Asser's Life of King Alfred and Other Contemporary Sources*, Harmondsworth: Penguin.
Khanmohamadi, Shirin A. (2014), *In Light of Another's Word: European Ethnography in the Middle Ages*, Philadelphia, PA: University of Pennsylvania Press.
King, Edmund (2010), *King Stephen*, New Haven, CT: Yale University Press.
Kingsley, Charles ([1866] 1889), *Hereward the Wake: Last of the English*, London: Macmillan.

Kinoshita, Sharon (2006), *Medieval Boundaries: Rethinking Difference in Old French Literature*, Philadelphia, PA: University of Pennsylvania Press.

Kinoshita, Sharon (2008), "Chrétien de Troyes's 'Cligés' in the Medieval Mediterranean," *Arthuriana*, 18, 48–61.

Kiser, Lisa (2007), "Animals in Medieval Sports, Entertainment, and Menageries," in *A Cultural History of Animals in the Medieval Age*, ed. Brigitte Resl, 103–26, New York: Berg.

Kittles, R.A. and J. Benn-Torres (2009), "Race and Genetics," in *Contemporary Cardiology: Cardiovascular Disease in Racial and Ethnic Minorities*, ed. K.C. Ferdinand and A. Armani, 81–91, New York: Humana Press.

Kohanski, Tamarah and C. David Benson, eds (2007), *The Book of John Mandeville*, Kalamazoo, MI: Medieval Institute Publications, http://d.lib.rochester.edu/teams/text/kohanski-and-benson-the-book-of-john-mandeville-introduction, accessed March 23, 2017.

Kolten-Fromm, Naomi (2000), "Sexuality and Holiness: Semitic Christian and Jewish Conceptualizations of Sexual Behavior," *Vigiliae Christianae*, 54: 375–95.

Kopytoff, Igor (1986), "The Cultural Biography of Things: Commoditization as Process," in *The Social Life of Things: Commodities in Cultural Context*, ed. Arjun Appadurai, 64–91, Cambridge: Cambridge University Press.

Kowaleski, Maryanne, ed. (2006), *Medieval Towns: A Reader*, Toronto: Broadview.

Krauze, Friedrich, ed. (1895), *Annales Regni Francorum, MGH SRG 6*, Hannover: Monumenta Germaniae Historica.

Kruger, Steven J. (1997), "Conversion and Medieval Sexual, Religious and Racial Categories," in *Constructing Medieval Sexuality*, ed. Karma Lochrie, Peggy McCracken, and James A. Schultz, 158–79, Minneapolis, MN: University of Minnesota Press.

Kupfer, Marcia (2008), ". . . lectres . . . plus vrayes": Hebrew Script and Jewish Witness in the Mandeville Manuscript of Charles V," *Speculum*, 83 (1): 58–111.

Laiou, Angeliki, ed. (2005), *Urbs Capta: The Fourth Crusade and its Consequences: La IVe Croisade et ses conséquences*, Paris: Lethielleux.

Lamb, H.H. (1965), "The Early Medieval Warm Epoch and its equel," *Palaeogeography, Palaeoclimatology, Palaeoecology*, 1: 13–37.

Lamb, H.H. (1982), *Climate, History and the Modern World*, London: Methuen.

Latowsky, Anne A. (2013), *Emperor of the World: Charlemagne and the Construction of Imperial Authority, 800–1229*, Ithaca, NY: Cornell University Press.

Lattin, Harriet Pratt, trans. (1961), *The Letters of Gerbert with his Papal Privileges as Sylvester II*, New York: Columbia University Press.

Lauer, Rena (2014), "Jewish Women in Venetian Candia: Negotiating Intercommunal Contact in a Premodern Colonial City, 1300–1500," in *La cohabitation religieuse dans les villes européennes, X-XVe siècles*, ed. S. Boissellier and J. Tolan, 293–310, Turnhout: Brepols.

Lavelle, Ryan (2010), *Alfred's Wars: Sources and Interpretations of Anglo-Saxon Warfare in the Viking Age*, Woodbridge: Boydell Press.

Lavezzo, Kathy (2006), *Angels on the Edge of the World*, Ithaca, NY: Cornell University Press.

Lecaque, Thomas (2018), *Raymond of Saint-Gilles: Occitanian Culture and Piety at the Time of the First Crusade*, New York: Routledge.

Lee, Christopher (2005), *This Sceptred Isle: Empire*, London: BBC Books.

Legassie, Shayne Aaron (2007), "Chaucer's Pardoner and Host—On the Road, in the Alehouse," *Studies in the Age of Chaucer*, 29: 183–223.

Legassie, Shayne Aaron (2017), *The Medieval Invention of Travel*, Chicago, IL: University of Chicago Press.
Le Goff, Jacques (1980), *Time, Work, and Culture in the Middle Ages*, trans. Arthur Goldhammer, Chicago, IL: University of Chicago Press.
Lerner, Robert (1988), "Frederick II, Alive, Aloft and Allayed, in Franciscan-Joachite Eschatology," in *The Uses and Abuses of Eschatology in the Middle Ages*, ed. Werner Verveke, Daniel Verhelst, and Andries Welkenhuysen, 359–84, Leuven: Leuven University Press.
Lester, Anne E. (2011), *Creating Cistercian Nuns: The Woman's Religious Movement and its Reform in Thirteenth-Century Champagne*, Ithaca, NY: Cornell University Press.
Lester, Anne E. (2014), "What Remains: Women, Relics and Remembrance in the Aftermath of the Fourth Crusade," *Journal of Medieval History*, 40: 311–28.
Lester, Anne E. (2017), "Translation and Appropriation: Greek Relics in the Latin West in the Aftermath of the Fourth Crusade," in *Translating Christianity*, Studies in Church History 53, ed. Simon Ditchfield, Charlotte Methuen, and Andrew Spicer, 88–117, Cambridge: Cambridge University Press.
L'Estrange, Elizabeth and Alison More, eds (2011), *Representing Medieval Genders and Sexualities in Europe: Construction, Transformation and Subversion*, Aldershot: Ashgate.
Lewis, Suzanne (1987), *The Art of Matthew Paris in the Chronica Majora*, Berkeley, CA: University of California Press.
Leyser, Henrietta (1984), *Hermits and the New Monasticism: A Study of Religious Communities in Western Europe*, New York: St. Martin's Press.
Leyser, Karl J. (1965), "The Battle at the Lech, 955," *History*, 50: 1–25.
Leyser, Karl J. (1968), "Henry I and the Beginnings of the Saxon Empire," *English Historical Review*, 83: 1–32.
Leyser, Karl J. (1983), "The Crisis of Medieval Germany," *Proceedings of the British Academy*, 69: 409–43.
Lipton, Sara (2014), *Dark Mirror: The Medieval Origins of Anti-Jewish Iconography*, New York: Metropolitan Books.
Little, Lester K. (1971), "Pride Goes before Avarice: Social Change and the Vices in Latin Christendom," *American Historical Review*, 76 (1): 16–49.
Lochrie, Karma (2005), *Heterosyncrasies: Female Sexuality when Normal Wasn't*, Minneapolis, MN: Minnesota University Press.
Lochrie, Karma (2011), "Heterosexuality," in *A Cultural History of Sexuality in the Middle Ages*, ed. Ruth Evans, 37–40, Oxford: Bloomsbury Press.
Lomax, Derek W. (1978), *The Reconquest of Spain*, London: Longman.
Lomax, John Phillip (1992), "A Canonistic Reconsideration of the Crusade of Frederick II," in *Proceedings of the Eighth International Congress of Medieval Canon Law*, ed. Stanley Chodorow, 207–26, Vatican City: Biblioteca Apostolica Vaticana.
London, British Library, MS Cotton Vespasian E.16.
Lopez, Robert S. (1956), "Back to Gold, 1252," *Economic History Review*, 9: 219–40.
Lopez, Robert S. (1976), *The Commercial Revolution of the Middle Ages, 950–1350*, New York: Cambridge University Press.
Lopez, Robert S. (1987), "The Trade of Medieval Europe: The South," in *The Cambridge Economic History of Europe, Vol. 2: Trade and Industry in the Middle Ages*, ed. Edward Miller, Cynthia Postan, and M.M. Postan, 306–401, Cambridge: Cambridge University Press.

Lopez, Robert S. and Irving W. Raymond, trans. (2001), *Medieval Trade in the Mediterranean World: Historical Documents*, New York: Columbia University Press.

Loud, G.A. (2011), "The Papal 'Crusade' against Frederick II in 1228–1230," in *La papauté et les croisades: actes du VIIe congrès de la Society for the Study of the Crusades and the Latin East*, ed. Michel Balard, 91–103, Farnham: Ashgate.

Loyn, H.R. and John Percival, trans. (1976), *The Reign of Charlemagne: Documents on Carolingian Government and Administration*, New York: St. Martin's Press.

MacCormack, Sabine (2002), "The Virtue of Work: An Augustinian Transformation," *Antiquité Tardive/Late Antiquity*, 9: 219–37.

MacKay, Angus (1977), *Spain in the Middle Ages: From Frontier to Empire, 1000–1500*, London: Macmillan.

MacKay, Angus with David Ditchburn, eds (1997), *Atlas of Medieval Europe*, London: Routledge.

Malterra, Geoffrey (1927–8), *De Rebus Gestis Rogerii Calabriae et Siciliae Comitis et Roberti Guiscardi Ducis Fratris Eius*, ed. E. Pontieri, Bologna: Zanichelli.

Mandeville, John (2011), *"The Book of John Mandeville" with Related Texts*, ed. and trans. Iain Macleod Higgins, Indianapolis, IN: Hackett.

Mann, Michael E., Zhihua Zhang, Scott Rutherford, Raymond Bradley, Malcolm K. Hughes, Drew Shindell, Caspar Ammann, Greg Faluvegi, and Fenbiao Ni (2009), "Global Signatures and Dynamical Origins of the Little Ice Age and Medieval Climate Anomaly," *Science*, 326 (5957): 1256–60.

Margariti, Roxani (2014), *Aden and the Indian Ocean Trade: 150 Years in the Life of a Medieval Arabian Port*, Chapel Hill, NC: University of North Carolina Press.

Marino, Nancy F., ed. (1999), *El Libro del Conoscimiento de Todos los Reinos*, Tempe, AZ: Arizona Center for Medieval and Renaissance Studies.

Markovits, Claude, Jaques Pouchepadass, and Sanjay Subrahmanyam, eds (2003), *Society and Circulation: Mobile People and Itinerant Cultures in South Asia, 1750–1950*, London: Anthem.

Martin, Therese, ed. (2012), *Reassessing the Roles of Women as "Makers" of Art and Architecture*, 2 vols, Leiden: Brill.

Martin, Therese (2016), "The Margin to Act: A Framework of Investigation for Women's (and Men's) Medieval Art-Making," *Journal of Medieval History*, 42: 1–25.

Martoni, Nicolas (Nicola) de (1895), Liber peregrinationis ad Loca Sancta, in "Relation du pèlerinage à Jérusalem de Nicolas de Martoni, notaire italien (1394–1395)," in *Revue de l'Orient latin*, 3.

Marvin, Garry (2012), *Wolf*, London: Reaktion Books.

Massing, Jean Michel (1991), "Observations and Beliefs: The World of the Catalan Atlas," in *Circa 1492: Art in the Age of Exploration*, ed. Jay A. Levenson, 27–33, New Haven, CT: Yale University Press.

McCormick, Michael (2001), *Origins of the European Economy: Communications and Commerce, AS 300–900*, Cambridge: Cambridge University Press.

McCormick, Michael (2002), "New Light on the 'Dark Ages:' How the Slave Trade Fuelled the Carolingian Economy," *Past and Present*, 77: 17–54.

McCormick, Michael (2011), *Charlemagne's Survey of the Holy Land: Wealth, Personnel, and Buildings of a Mediterranean Church between Antiquity and the Middle Ages*, Washington, DC: Dumbarton Oaks Medieval Research Library and Collection, Harvard University Press.

McCormick, Michael, Paul Edward Dutton, and Paul A. Mayewski (2007), "Volcanoes and the Climate Forcing of Carolingian Europe, AD 750–950," *Speculum*, 82: 865–95.

McCormick, Michael, Ulf Büntgen, Mark A. Cane, Edward R. Cook, Kyle Harper, Peter Huybers, Thomas Litt, Sturt W. Manning, Paul Andrew Mayewski, Alexander F.M. More, Kurt Nicolussi, and Willy Tegel (2012), "Climate Change During and After the Roman Empire: Reconstructing the Past from Scientific and Historical Evidence," *Journal of Interdisciplinary History*, 43 (2): 169–220.

McGrade, Arthur S., ed. and John Kilcullen, trans. (1992), *A Short Discourse on the Tyrannical Government over Things Divine and Human, but Especially over the Empire and Those Subject to the Empire, Usurped by Some Who are Called Highest Pontiffs*, Cambridge: Cambridge University Press.

McKitterick, Rosamond (2008), *Charlemagne: The Formation of a European Identity*, Cambridge: Cambridge University Press.

Meiu, George Paul (2015), "Colonialism and Sexuality," in *The International Encyclopaedia of Human Sexuality*, ed. Patricia Whelehan and Anne Bolin, 197–200, London: Wiley.

Melloni, Alberto (1990), *Innocenzo IV: La concezione e l'esperienza della cristianità come regimen unius personae*, Genoa: Marietti.

Mengel, David C. (2014), "From Venice to Jerusalem and Beyond: Milíč of Kroměříž and the Topography of Prostitution in Fourteenth-century Prague," *Speculum*, 79: 407–42.

Menocal, María Rosa (1987), *The Arabic Role in Medieval Literary History: A Forgotten Heritage*, Philadelphia, PA: University of Pennsylvania Press.

Metcalfe, Alex (2009), *The Muslims of Medieval Italy*, Edinburgh: Edinburgh University Press.

Mierow, C.C., trans. (1953), *The Deeds of Frederick Barbarossa*, New York: Columbia University Press.

Miller, Maureen C., ed. (2005), *Power and the Holy in the Age of the Investiture Conflict: A Brief History with Documents*, Boston, MA: Bedford St. Martin.

Miller, Peter, ed. (2013), *The Sea: Thalassography and Historiography*, Ann Arbor, MI: University of Michigan Press.

Mittman, Asa (2015), "Are the 'Monstrous Races' Races?," *Postmedieval, Supplement: Making Race Matter in the Middle Ages*, 6 (1): 36–51.

Moore, John C. (2003), *Pope Innocent III (1160/61–1216): To Root up and to Plant*, Leiden: Brill.

Morgan, T.H., A.H. Sturtevant, H.J. Muller, and C.B. Bridges ([1915] 1922), *The Mechanism of Mendelian Heredity*, revised edn, New York: Henry Holt.

Morris, Colin (1989), *The Papal Monarchy: The Western Church from 1050–1250*, Oxford: Clarendon Press.

Morris, Ian and Walter Scheidel, eds (2009), *The Dynamics of Ancient Empires: State Power from Assyria to Byzantium*, Oxford: Oxford University Press.

Morrissey, Robert (2003), *Charlemagne and France: A Thousand Years of Mythology*, trans. Catherine Tihanyi, Notre Dame, IN: University of Notre Dame Press.

Morrison, Susan Signe (2000), *Women Pilgrims in Late Medieval England*, London: Routledge.

Moseley, C.W.R.D. (1975), "Availability of *Mandeville's Travels* in England," *The Library*, s5-XXX (2): 125–33.

Mummey, Kevin and Kathryn Reyerson (2011), "Whose City is This? Hucksters, Domestic Servants, Wet-Nurses, Prostitutes, and Slaves in Late Medieval Western Mediterranean Urban Society," *History Compass*, 92: 910–22.

Murray, Jacqueline (1996), "Twice Marginal and Twice Invisible: Lesbians in the Middle Ages," in *The Handbook of Medieval Sexuality*, ed. Vern L. Bullough and James A. Brundage, 191–222, New York: Garland.

Murry, James (2005), *Bruges, Cradle of Capitalism, 1280–1390*, Cambridge: Cambridge University Press.

Muthesius, Anna (1997), *Byzantine Silk Weaving, AD 400 to AD 1200*, ed. Ewald Kislinger and Johannes Koder, Vienna: Verlag Fassbaender.

Muthu, Shankar, ed. (2012), *Empire and Modern Political Thought*, Cambridge: Cambridge University Press.

Nelson, Janet (2002), "The Church and a Revaluation of Work in the Ninth Century?," in *The Use and Abuse of Time in Christian History*, Studies in Church History 37, ed. R.N. Swanson, 35–43, Woodbridge: Boydell & Brewer.

Newfield, Timothy P. (2013), "The Contours, Frequency and Causation of Subsistence Crises in Carolingian Europe (750–950 CE)," in *Crisis Alimentarias en la Edad Media: Modelos, Explicaciones Y Preprestaciones*, ed. Pere Benito I Monclús, 117–72, Lleida: Editorial Milenio.

Newfield, Timothy and Inga Labuhn (2016), "Towards a Messy History of Crisis and Climate in Carolingian Europe," *Historical Climatology Blog*, http://www.historicalclimatology.com/blog/towards-a-messy-history-of-dearth-and-climate-in-carolingian-europe, accessed December 2016.

Newman, Martha G. (1996), *The Boundaries of Charity: Cistercian Culture and Ecclesiastical Reform*, Stanford, CA: Stanford University Press.

Newman, Martha G. (2012), "Labor: Insights from a Medieval Monastery," in *Why the Middle Ages Matter: Medieval Light on Modern Injustice*, ed. Celia Chazelle, Simon Doubleday, Felice Lifshitz, and Amy Remensnyder, 106–20, Abingdon: Routledge.

Nicholas, David (1997), *The Later Medieval City, 1300–1500*, London: Longman.

Niermeyer, Jan F., ed. (1997), *Mediae Latinitatis Lexicon Minus*, Leiden: Brill.

Nirenberg, David (2001), "Muslims in Christian Iberia, 1000–1526: Varieties of Mudejar Experience," in *The Medieval World*, ed. Peter Linehan and Janet L. Nelson, 60–76, Abingdon: Routledge.

Noble, Thomas F.X. (1984), *The Republic of Saint Peter: The Birth of the Papal State, 680–825*, Philadelphia, PA: University of Pennsylvania Press.

Noble, Thomas F.X., trans. (2009), *Charlemagne and Louis the Pious: The Lives by Einhard, Notker, Ermoldus, Thegan, and the Astronomer*, University Park, PA: Pennsylvania State University Press.

North, W.L., trans. (1998), "The Responses of Pope Nicholas I to the Questions of the Bulgars AD 866 (Letter 99)," http://sourcebooks.fordham.edu/basis/866nicholas-bulgar.asp.

Oakley, Francis (2012), *The Mortgage of the Past: Reshaping the Ancient Political Inheritance, The Emergence of Western Political Thought in the Latin Middle Ages*, New Haven, CT: Yale University Press.

Ohlgren, Thomas, ed. (2005), *Medieval Outlaws: Twelve Tales in Modern English Translation*, revised edn, West Lafayette, IN: Parlor Press.

Orderic Vitalis (1968), *The Ecclesiastical Histor*, Vol. II, ed. and trans. Marjorie M.M. Chibnall, Oxford: Clarendon Press.

Orme, Nicholas (1984), *From Childhood to Chivalry: The Education of the English Kings and Aristocracy, 1066–1530*, London: Methuen.

Otis, Leah Lydia (1985), *Prostitution in Medieval Society: The History of an Urban Institution in Languedoc*, Chicago, IL: University of Chicago Press.

Ottewill-Soulsby, Samuel (2017), "Carolingian Diplomacy with the Islamic World, 751–888," PhD dissertation, University of Cambridge.
Ovitt, George, Jr. (1987), *The Restoration of Perfection: Labor and Technology in Medieval Culture*, New Brunswick, NJ: Rutgers University Press.
Paden, William D. (1998), *An Introduction to Old Occitan*, New York: Modern Language Society Press.
Pagden, Anthony (2003), *Peoples and Empires: A Short History of European Migration, Exploration, and Conquest from Greece to the Present*, New York: Random House.
Pálsson, Hermann and Paul Edwards, trans. (1976), *Egil's Saga*, New York: Penguin Classics.
Pamuk, Sevket (2007), "The Black Death and the Origins of the 'Great Divergence' Across Europe, 1300–1600," *European Review of Economic History*, 11: 289–317.
Paris, Matthew (1872–83), *Chronica Majora*, 7 vols, ed. H.R. Luard, London: Longman.
Park, Katherine (2013), "Medicine and Natural Philosophy: Naturalistic Traditions," in *The Oxford Handbook of Women and Gender in Medieval Europe*, ed. Judith Bennett and Ruth Mazo Karras, Oxford: Oxford University Press.
Parker, Andrew, Mary Russo, Doris Sommer, and Patricia Yaeger, eds (1992), *Nationalisms and Sexualities*, London: Routledge.
Parsons, Timothy (2010), *The Rule of Empires: Those Who Built Them, Those Who Endured Them, and Why They Always Fall*, New York: Oxford University Press.
Partner, Peter (1972), *The Lands of St. Peter: The Papal State in the Middle Ages and the Early Renaissance*, Berkeley, CA: University of California Press.
Pastoureau, Michel (2007), *The Bear; History of a Fallen King*, trans. George Holoch, Cambridge, MA: The Belknap Press of Harvard University Press.
Patschovsky, Alexander (1998), "The Holy Emperor Henry 'the First' as One of the Dragon's Heads of Apocalypse: On the Image of the Holy Roman Empire Under German Rule in the Tradition of Joachim of Fiore," *Viator*, 29: 291–322.
Paul, Nicholas L. (2012), *To Follow in Their Footsteps: The Crusades and Family Memory in the High Middle Ages*, Ithaca, NY: Cornell University Press.
Pennington, Kenneth (1984), "Pope Innocent III's Views on Church and State: A Gloss to *Per Venerabilem*," in *Law, Church, and Society: Essays in Honor of Stephan Kuttner*, ed. Kenneth Pennington and Robert Somerville, 1–25, Philadelphia, PA: University of Pennsylvania Press.
Perels, E., ed. (1925), *Nicolae I Papae Epistolae*, in MGH Epp. Karol. Aevi, IV, 568–600, Berlin: Weidmann.
Perryman, Judith, ed. (1980), *The King of Tars, ed. from the Auchinleck MS, Advocates 19.2.1*, Heidelberg: Universitätsverlag Carl Winter.
Petrarch (2005), *Letters of Old Age (Rerum senilium libri)*, 2 vols, trans. Aldo S. Bernardo, Saul Levin, and Reta A. Bernardo, New York: Italica Press.
Philips, Richard (2006), *Sex, Politics and Empire: A Postcolonial Geography*, Manchester: Manchester University Press.
Phillips, J.R.S. (1988), *The Medieval Expansion of Europe*, Oxford: Oxford University Press.
Phillips, Kim (2009), "Oriental Sexualities in European Representation," in *Old Worlds, New Worlds: European Cultural Encounters, c. 1000–c. 1750*, ed. Laura Bailey, Lindsay Diggelmann, and Kim Phillips, 53–74, Turnhout: Brepols.
Phillips, Kim (2011), "Warriors, Amazons and Isles of Women: Medieval Travel Writing and Constructions of Asian Femininities," in *Intersections of Gender,*

Religion and Ethnicity in the Middle Ages, ed. Cordelia Beattie and Kim Phillips, 183–207, Basingstoke: Palgrave Macmillan.

Phillips, Kim (2014), *Before Orientalism: Asian Peoples and Cultures in European Travel-Writing, 1245–1510*, Philadelphia, PA: University of Pennsylvania Press.

Phillips, Kim M. and Barry Reay, eds (2011), *Sex Before Sexuality: A Premodern History*, Cambridge: Polity.

Phillips, William D., Jr. (1997), "Voluntary Strangers: European Merchants and Missionaries in Asia During the Late Middle Ages," in *The Stranger in Medieval Society*, ed. F.R.P. Akehurst and Stephanie P. Cain van D'Elden, 14–26, Minneapolis, MN: Minnesota University Press.

Phillips, William D., Jr. (2013), *Slavery in Medieval and Early Modern Iberia*, Philadelphia, PA: University of Pennsylvania Press.

Pliny the Elder ([1991] 2004), *Natural History: A Selection*, trans. John F. Healy, London: Penguin.

Pluskowski, Aleksander (2006), *Wolves and the Wilderness in the Middle Ages*, New York: Boydell Press.

Polo, Marco (1928), *Il milione: Prima edizione integrale*, ed. Luigi Foscolo Benedetto, Florence: Olschki.

Polo, Marco (2016), *The Description of the World*, ed. and trans. Sharon Kinoshita, London: Hackett.

Poole, Kevin R., trans. (2014), *Chronicle of Pseudo-Turpin*, New York: Italica Press.

Postan, Michael (1987), "The Trade of Medieval Europe: The North," in *The Cambridge Economic History of Europe, Vol. 2: Trade and Industry in the Middle Ages*, ed. Edward Miller, Cynthia Postan, and M.M. Postan, 168–304, Cambridge: Cambridge University Press.

Potter, Kenneth R., ed. and trans. (1976), *Gesta Stephani*, Oxford: Clarendon Press.

Powers, James F. (1971), "Townsmen and Soldiers: The Interaction of Urban and Military Organization in the Militias of Mediaeval Castile," *Speculum*, 46 (4): 641–55.

Powers, James F. (1988), *A Society Organized for War: The Iberian Municipal Militias in the Central Middle Ages, 1000–1284*, Berkeley, CA: University of California Press.

Pryor, John H (2006), *Logistics of Warfare in the Age of the Crusades*, Proceedings of a Workshop held at the Center for Medieval Studies, University of Sydney, September 30 to October 4, 2002, London: Routledge.

Puff, Helmut (2013), "Same-Sex Possibilities," in *The Oxford Handbook of Women and Gender in Medieval Europe*, ed. Judith Bennett and Ruth Mazo Karras, 379–95, Oxford: Oxford University Press.

Purkis, William J. (2008), *Crusading Spirituality in the Holy Land and Iberia, c. 1095–c. 1187*, Rochester, NY: Boydell & Brewer.

Quint, David (1993), *Epic and Empire: Politics and Generic Form from Virgil to Milton*, Princeton, NJ: Princeton University Press.

Raccagni, Gianluca (2010), *The Lombard League, 1167–1225*, Oxford: Oxford University Press.

Rahner, Hugo ([1961] 2006), *Church and State in Early Christianity*, San Francisco, CA: Ignatius Press.

Raich, Susan (2015), "Wreck of the Sea in Law and Practice in Eleventh- and Twelfth-Century England," *Anglo-Norman Studies: Proceedings of the Battle Conference*, 38: 141–54.

Ramey, Lynn (2011), "Medieval Miscegenation: Hybridity and the Anxiety of Inheritance," in *Contextualising the Muslim Other in Medieval Christian Discourse*, ed. Jerold C. Frakes, 1–20, Basingstoke: Palgrave.

Ramey, Lynn T. (2014), *Black Legacies: Race and the European Middle Ages*, Gainesville, FL: University Press of Florida.

Ramón de Perellòs (1914), *Viatge al Purgatori de Sant Patrici*, ed. R. Miquel y Planas, Barcelona.

Ranft, Patricia (2006), *The Theology of Work: Peter Damain and the Medieval Religious Renewal Movement*, New York: Palgrave.

Refling, Mary (2005), "Frederick's Menagerie," Paper read at the *Second Annual Robert Dombrowski Italian Conference*, Storrs, CT, http://faculty.fordham.edu/refling/Frederick's%20Menagerie.pdf, accessed September 2016.

Remensnyder, Amy (1995), *Remembering Kings Past: Monastic Foundation Legends in Medieval Southern France*, Ithaca, NY: Cornell University Press.

Remensnyder, Amy (1996), "Legendary Treasure at Conques: Reliquaries and Imaginative Memory," *Speculum*, 71: 884–906.

Reuter, Timothy (1985), "Plunder and Tribute in the Carolingian Empire," *Transactions of the Royal Historical Society*, s5-35: 75–94.

Reuter, Timothy (1991), *Germany in the Early Middle Ages c. 800–1056*, London: Longman.

Reyerson, Kathryn L. (1999), "Commerce and Communication," in *The New Cambridge Medieval History, Vol. 5: c. 1198–1300*, ed. David Abulafia, 50–70, Cambridge: Cambridge University Press.

Reyerson, Kathryn L. (2016), *Women's Networks in Medieval France: Gender and Community in Medieval Montpellier, 1300–1350*, New York, Palgrave.

Rhazes (1994), *Liber ad regem Almansorem*, in *Scriptores Physiognomonici Graeci et Latini*, Vol. 2, ed. Richard Foerster, Stuttgart: B.G. Teubner.

Riché, Pierre (1993), *The Carolingians: A Family Who Forged Europe*, trans. Michael Allen, Philadelphia, PA: University of Pennsylvania Press.

Ridder, Klaus (1991), *Jean De Mandevilles "reisen": Studien Zur Überlieferungsgeschichte Der Deutschen Übersetzung Des Otto Von Diemeringen*, Munich: Artemis Verlag.

Riley-Smith, Jonathan (1987), *The Crusades: A Short History*, New Haven, CT: Yale University Press.

Riley-Smith, Jonathan (1997), *The First Crusaders, 1095–1131*, Cambridge: Cambridge University Press.

Rist, Rebecca (2009), *The Papacy and Crusading in Europe, 1198–1245*, London: Continuum.

Robertson, Kellie (2006), *The Laborer's Two Bodies: Literary and Legal Productions in Britain, 1350–1500*, New York: Palgrave.

Robinson, I.S. (1990), *The Papacy 1073–1198: Continuity and Innovation*, Cambridge: Cambridge University Press.

Robinson, I.S., trans. (2007), *The Papal Reform of the Eleventh Century: Lives of Leo IX and Gregory VII*, Manchester: Manchester University Press.

Robinson, I.S. (2016), "Innocent II and the Empire," in *Pope Innocent II (1130–43): The World vs the City*, ed. John Doran and Damian J. Smith, 27–68, London: Routledge.

Rogers, Daniel, Bhavani Raman, and Helmut Reimitz (2014), *Cultures in Motion*, Princeton, NJ: Princeton University Press.

Röhl, Suzanne (2006), "Le livre de Mandeville à Paris autour de 1400," in *Patrons, Authors and Workshops: Books and Book Production in Paris around 1400*, ed. Godfried Croenen and Peter Ainsworth, 281–95, Leuven: Peeters.

Rosenthal, Franz (1979), "Fiction and Reality: Sources for the Role of Sex in Medieval Muslim Society," in *Society and the Sexes in Medieval Islam*, ed. A. Lutfi al-Sayyid Marsot, 3–22, Malibu, CA: Undena Publications.

Roth, Norman (1996a), "A Note on Research into Jewish Sexuality in the Medieval Period," in *The Handbook of Medieval Sexuality*, ed. Vern L. Bullough and James A. Brundage, 309–17, New York: Garland.

Roth, Norman (1996b), "A Research Note on Sexuality and Muslim Civilization," in *The Handbook of Medieval Sexuality*, ed. Vern L. Bullough and James A. Brundage, 319–27, New York: Garland.

Rothman, E. Natalie (2012), *Brokering Empire: Trans-Imperial Subjects between Venice and Istanbul*, Ithaca, NY: Cornell University Press.

Rothwell, Harry, ed. (1975), "Magna Carta," in *English Historical Documents 1189–1327*, Vol. III, London: Eyre & Spottiswoode.

Routledge, Michael (1995), "Songs," in *The Oxford Illustrated History of the Crusades*, ed. Jonathan Riley-Smith, 91–111, Oxford: Oxford University Press.

Ruggles, E. Fairchild (2004), "Mothers of a Hybrid Dynasty: Race, Genealogy and Acculturation in al-Andalus," *Journal of Medieval and Early Modern Studies*, 34 (1): 69–73.

Ruiz, Teofilo F. (2012), *A King Travels: Festive Traditions in Medieval and Early Modern Spain*, Princeton, NJ: Princeton University Press.

Runciman, Steven (1958), *The Sicilian Vespers: A History of the Mediterranean World in the Later Thirteenth Century*, Cambridge: Cambridge University Press.

Russell, P.E. (2000), *Prince Henry "the Navigator": A Life*, New Haven, CT: Yale University Press.

Rustow, Marina et al. (2017–), *The Geniza Lab initiative*, Princeton University, https://www.princeton.edu/~geniza/about.html.

Sabsay, L. (2016), "From being Sexual to having Sexual Rights," *Dark Matter*, 14, http://www.darkmatter101.org/site/2016/05/16/from-being-sexual-to-having-sexual-rights/, accessed December 8, 2016.

Sahlins, Peter (1991), *Boundaries: The Making of France and Spain in the Pyrenees*, Berkeley, CA: University of California Press.

Said, Edward (1979), *Orientalism: Western Conceptions of the Orient*, New York: Vintage.

Sale, Antoine de la (1930), *Le Paradis de la Reine Sibylle*, ed. Fernand Desonay, Paris: E. Droz.

Sands, Harold (1912), "Extracts from the Documentary History of the Tower of London," *Archaeological Journal*, 69 (1): 161–72.

Sautman, Francesca Canadé and Pamela Sheingorn, eds (2001), *Same-Sex Love and Desire among Medieval Women*, New York: Palgrave.

Sayers, Jane (1994), *Innocent III: Leader of Europe 1198–1216*, London: Longman.

Scafi, Alessandro (2006), *Mapping Paradise: A History of Heaven on Earth*, Chicago, IL: University of Chicago Press.

Schaer, Frank, ed. (2000), *The Three Kings of Cologne, Edited from London, Lambeth Palace MS 491*, Heidelberg: Universitätsverlag Carl Winter.

Schoenfeld, Edward J. (1995), "Anglo-Saxon *Burhs* and Continental *Burgen*: Early Medieval Fortifications in Constitutional Perspective," *Haskins Society Journal*, 6: 49–66.

Scholz, Bernhard Walter with Barbara Rogers, trans. (1970), *Carolingian Chronicles: Royal Frankish Annals and Nithard's Histories*, Ann Arbor, MI: University of Michigan Press.

Schramm, Percy Ernst (1924), "Das Herrscherbild in der Kunst des frühen Mittelalters," *Vorträge der Bibliothek Warburg*, 2: 145–239.

Schüller, Tonia (2016), "Marriage Policy in Medieval Islam: The Example of Timür," in *Muslim Bodies: Body, Sexuality and Medicine in Muslim Societies/Körper, Sexualität und Medizin in muslimischen Gesellschaften*, ed. Susanne Kurz, Claudia Preckel, and Stefan Reichmuth, 191–212, Berlin: LIT Verlag.

Seaver, Kirsten A. (1996), *The Frozen Echo: Greenland and the Exploration of North America, ca. AD 1000–1500*, Stanford, CA: Stanford University Press.

Sénac, Philippe (2002), *Les carolingiens et al-Andalus (VIIIe-IXe siècles)*, Paris: Maisonneuve et Larose.

Seneca (2010), *Six Tragedies*, trans. Emily Wilson, Oxford: Oxford World's Classics.

Shatzmiller, Joseph (2009), "La bigamie juive dans l'Espagne médiévale," in *Cristianos y judíos en contacto en la Edad Media*, ed. Flocel Sabaté Curell and Claude Denjean, 581–7, Lleida: Editorial Milenio.

Shen, Hsueh-man, ed. (2006), *Gilded Splendor: Treasures of China's Liao Empires (907–1125)*, New York: Asia Society.

Skelton, R.A. (1968), "A Contract for World Maps at Barcelona, 1399–1400," *Imago Mundi*, 22: 107–13.

Skinner, Patricia (2015), "Marking the Face, Curing the Soul? Reading the Disfigurement of Women in the Later Middle Ages," in *Medicine, Religion and Gender in Medieval Culture*, ed. Naoë Kukita Yoshikawa, 287–318, Woodbridge: Boydell, https://www.ncbi.nlm.nih.gov/books/NBK311275/.

Skinner, Patricia and Elisabeth van Houts, eds (2011), *Medieval Writings on Secular Women*, London: Penguin.

Smets, An and Baudouin van den Abeele (2007), "Medieval Hunting," in *A Cultural History of Animals in the Medieval Age*, ed. Brigitte Resl, 59–79. New York: Berg.

Smith, Julia M.H. (2012), "Portable Christianity: Relics in the Medieval West (c. 700–1200)," *Proceedings of the British Academy*, 181: 143–67.

Snowden, Frank M., Jr. (1970), *Blacks in Antiquity: Ethiopians in the Greco-Roman Experience*, Cambridge, MA: The Belknap Press of Harvard University Press.

Southern, R.W. (1962), *Western Views of Islam in the Middle Ages*, Cambridge, MA: Harvard University Press.

Spenser, Edmund (1596), *A Vewe of the Present State of Ireland, from Gonville and Caius College, Cambridge MS 188/221*, 53, ed. Andrew Zurcher, https://www.english.cam.ac.uk/ceres/haphazard/vewe/index.html, accessed March 19, 2017.

Spiegel, Gabrielle M. (1997). *The Past as Text: The Theory and Practice of Medieval Historiography*, Baltimore, MD: Johns Hopkins University Press.

Spufford, Peter (1987), "Coinage and Currency," in *The Cambridge Economic History of Europe, Vol. 2: Trade and Industry in the Middle Ages*, ed. Edward Miller, Cynthia Postan, and M.M. Postan, 788–863, Cambridge: Cambridge University Press.

Spufford, Peter (1988), *Money and its Use in Medieval Europe*, Cambridge: Cambridge University Press.

Squatriti, Paolo, trans. (2007), *The Complete Works of Liudprand of Cremona*, Washington, DC: Catholic University of America Press.

Stine, S. (1994), "Extreme and Persistent Drought in California and Patagonia during Medieval Time," *Nature*, 369 (6481): 546–9.

Strathern, Alan (2016), "Religion and Empire," in *The Encyclopedia of Empire*, ed. Nigel Dalziel and John M. MacKenzie, 1–11, Wiley Online Library, https://doi/10.1002/9781118455074.wbeoe223, accessed February 2017.

Strayer, Joseph R. (1969a), "France, the Holy Land, the Chosen People, and the Most Christian King," in *Action and Conviction in Early Modern Europe*, ed. T.K. Rabb and J.E. Seigel, 3–16, Princeton, NJ: Princeton University Press.

Strayer, Joseph R. (1969b), "Political Crusades of the Thirteenth Century," in *The Crusades: Vol. 2: The Later Crusades, 1189–1311*, ed. Robert Lee Wolff and Harry W. Hazard, 343–76, Madison, WI: University of Wisconsin Press.

Strickland, Matthew (1996), *War and Chivalry: The Conduct and Perception of War in England and Normandy, 1066–1217*, Cambridge: Cambridge University Press.

Strohm, Paul (1992), *Hochon's Arrow: The Social Imagination of Fourteenth-Century Texts*, Princeton, NJ: Princeton University Press.

Stuard, Susan Mosher (1986), "To Town to Serve: Urban Domestic Slavery in Medieval Ragusa," in *Women and Work in Preindustrial Europe*, ed. Barbara A. Hanawalt, 39–55, Bloomington, IN: Indiana University Press.

Stuard, Susan Mosher (1995), "Ancillary Evidence on the Decline of Medieval Slavery," *Past and Present*, 149: 3–32.

Stubbs, William, ed. (1913), *Selected Charters of English Constitutional History*, revised edn, Oxford: Clarendon Press.

Sumption, Jonathan (1975), *Pilgrimage: An Image of Mediaeval Religion*, London: Faber & Faber.

Talbot, Charles H., trans. (2008), *The Life of Christina of Markyate*, ed. Samuel Fanous and Henrietta Leyser, Oxford: Oxford University Press.

Thomas Aquinas ([n.d.] 1948), *Summa theologica*, trans. Fathers of the English Dominican Province, New York: Benzinger Brothers.

Thomas Walsingham, ([n.d.] 1867–9), *Historia Anglicana*, ed. Henry Thomas Riley, London: Rolls Series 28.4.

Thommen, Lukas (2012), *An Environmental History of Ancient Greece and Rome*, trans. Philip Hill, New York: Cambridge University Press.

Tierney, Brian (1982), *Religion, Law, and the Growth of Constitutional Thought 1150–1650*, Cambridge: Cambridge University Press.

Toch, Michael (2005), "The Jews in Europe 500–1050," in *The New Cambridge Medieval History*, Vol. 1, ed. Paul Fouracre, 547–70, Cambridge: Cambridge University Press.

Toohey, Matthew, Kirstin Krüger, Michael Sigl, Frode Stordal, and Henrik Svensen (2016), "Climatic and Societal Impacts of a Volcanic Double Event at the Dawn of the Middle Ages," *Climatic Change*, 136 (3): 401–12.

Trouet, V., J. Esper, N.E. Graham, A. Baker, J.D. Scourse, and D.C. Frank (2009), "Persistent Positive North Atlantic Oscillation Mode Dominated the Medieval Climate Anomaly," *Science*, 324 (5923): 78–80.

Tyerman, Christopher (2006), *God's War: A New History of the Crusades*, Cambridge, MA: The Belknap Press of Harvard University Press.

Uebel, Michael (2003), "Re-Orienting Desire: Writing on Gender Trouble in Fourteenth-Century Egypt," in *Gender and Difference in the Middle Ages*, ed. Sharon Farmer and Carol Braun Pasternack, 230–57, Minneapolis, MN: University of Minnesota Press.

Ullmann, Walter (1949), *Medieval Papalism: The Political Theories of the Medieval Canonists*, London: Methuen.

Ullmann, Walter ([1955] 1965), *The Growth of Papal Government in the Middle Ages: A Study in the Ideological Relation of Clerical to Lay Power*, 2nd edn, London: Methuen.

Ullmann, Walter ([1972] 2003), *A Short History of the Papacy in the Middle Ages*, London: Routledge.
Unger, Richard (2015), "Commerce, Communication, and Empire: Economy, Technology and Cultural Encounters," *Speculum*, 90: 1–27.
Upton-Ward, Judith M., trans. (1992), *The Rule of the Templars*, Woodbridge: Boydell Press.
Van Cleve, Thomas C. (1972), *The Emperor Frederick II of Hohenstaufen, Immutator Mundi*, Oxford: Clarendon Press.
Van den Hoven, Birgit (1996), *Work in Ancient and Medieval Thought: Ancient Philosophers, Medieval Monks and Theologians and Their Concept of Work, Occupations, and Technology*, Amsterdam: J.C. Gieben.
Van Engen, John H. (1983), *Rupert of Deutz*, Berkeley, CA: University of California Press.
Van Houts, Elisabeth M.C. (1999a), *Memory and Gender in Medieval Europe, 900–1200*, Toronto: University of Toronto Press.
Van Houts, Elisabeth M.C. (1999b), "Hereward and Flanders," *Anglo-Saxon England*, 28: 201–23.
Vauchez, André (1997), *Sainthood in the Later Middle Ages*, trans. J. Birrell, Cambridge: Cambridge University Press.
Verdon, Jean (2003), *Travel in the Middle Ages*, trans. George Holoch, Notre Dame, IN: University of Notre Dame Press.
Verhulst, Adriaan (2002), *The Carolingian Economy*, Cambridge: Cambridge University Press.
Vogel, Cyrille (1964), "Le pèlerinage pénitentiel," *Revue des Sciences Religieuses*, 38 (2): 113–53.
Voss, Barbara L. and Eleanor Conlin Casella, eds (2012), *The Archaeology of Colonialism: Intimate Encounters and Sexual Effects*, New York: Cambridge University Press.
Walter of Châtillon (1996), *The Alexandreis of Walter of Châtillon*, trans. David Townsend, Philadelphia, PA: University of Pennsylvania Press.
Warner, David A., trans. (2001), *Ottonian Germany: The Chronicon of Thietmar of Merseburg*, Manchester: Manchester University Press.
Watson, Sethina (2010), "City as Charter: Charity and the Lordship of English Towns, 1170–1250," in *Cities, Texts, and Social Networks 400–1500: Experiences and Perceptions of Medieval Urban Space*, ed. Caroline Goodson, Anne E. Lester, and Carol Symes, 235–62, Farnham: Ashgate.
Watt, J.A. (1964), "The Theory of Papal Monarchy in the Thirteenth Century," *Traditio*, 20: 179–317.
Watt, J.A. (1988), "Spiritual and Temporal Powers," in *The Cambridge History of Medieval Political Thought c. 350–c. 1450*, ed. J.H. Burns, 367–423, Cambridge: Cambridge University Press.
Webb, Diana (1999), *Pilgrims and Pilgrimage in the Medieval West*, London: I.B. Tauris.
Weiler, Björn (2000), "Gregory IX, Frederick II, and the Liberation of the Holy Land," in *The Holy Land, Holy Lands, and Christian History*, ed. R.N. Swanson, 192–206, Woodbridge: Boydell Press.
Wessel, Susan (2008), *Pope Leo the Great and the Spiritual Rebuilding of Universal Rome*, Leiden: Brill.
Westermann, Edwin J. (1939–41), "Emperor Charles IV and Pope Innocent VI," *University of Colorado Studies*, 1: 301–6.

Westrem, Scott D. (1990), "Medieval Western European Views of Sexuality Reflected in Narratives of Travelers to the Orient," in *Homo Carnalis: The Carnal Aspect of Medieval Human Life*, ed. Helen Rodnite Lemay, 141–56, Binghamton, NY: SUNY Press.

Whalen, Brett Edward (2009), *Dominion of God: Christendom and Apocalypse in the Middle Ages*, Cambridge, MA: Harvard University Press.

Whalen, Brett Edward (2014), *The Medieval Papacy*, London: Palgrave Macmillan.

Whitaker, Cord J. (2009), "Race and Conversion in Late Medieval England," PhD dissertation, Duke University.

Whitaker, Cord J. (2013), "Black Metaphors in the *King of Tars*," *Journal of English and Germanic Philology*, 112 (2): 169–93.

Whitaker, Cord J. (2015), "Race-ing the Dragon: The Middle Ages, Race and Trippin' into the Future," *Postmedieval*, 6: 3–11.

White, Lynn, Jr. (1962), *Medieval Technology and Social Change*, Oxford: Oxford University Press.

White, Lynn, Jr. (1967), "The Historical Roots of our Ecologic Crisis," *Science*, 155 (3767): 1203–7.

White, Pamela, ed. (2005), *Exploration in the World of the Middle Ages, 500–1500*, New York: Facts on File.

Wickham, Christopher (1994), *Land and Power: Studies in Italian and European Social History*, London: British School at Rome.

Wickham, Christopher (2005), *Framing the Early Middle Ages: Europe and the Mediterranean, 400–800*, Oxford: Oxford University Press.

Wickham, Christopher (2008), "Rethinking the Structure of the Early Medieval Economy," in *The Long Morning of Medieval Europe: New Directions in Early Medieval Studies*, ed. Jennifer R. Davis and Michael McCormick, 19–32, London: Ashgate.

Widukind of Corvey (2014), *Deeds of the Saxons*, trans. Bernard S. Bachrach and David S. Bachrach, Washington, DC: Catholic University of America Press.

William of Rubruck (1990), *The Mission of Friar William of Rubruck: His Journey to the Court of the Great Khan Möngke, 1253–1255*, ed. and trans. Peter Jackson and David Morgan, London: Hakluyt Society.

Williams, James (2012), "Working for Reform: *Acedia*, Benedict of Aniane and the Transformation of Working Culture in Carolingian Monasticism," in *Sin in Medieval and Early Modern Culture: The Tradition of the Seven Deadly Sins*, ed. Richard G. Newhauser and Susan Ridyard, 19–42, York: York Medieval Press.

Williams, Raymond (1983), *Keywords: A Vocabulary of Culture and Society*, revised edn, New York: Oxford University Press.

Wilson, David M., ed. (1985), *The Bayeux Tapestry*, London: Thames & Hudson.

Winer, Rebecca (2008), "Conscripting the Breast: Lactation, Slavery and Salvation in the Realms of Aragon and the Kingdom of Majorca, *c.* 1250–1300," *Journal of Medieval History*, 34: 164–84.

Wolf, Kenneth Baxter (1995), *Making History: The Normans and their Historians in Eleventh-Century Italy*, Philadelphia, PA: University of Pennsylvania Press.

Wood, Diana (2002), *Medieval Economic Thought*, Cambridge: Cambridge University Press.

Wyatt, David R. (2009), *Slaves and Warriors in Medieval Britain and Ireland, 800–1200*, Leiden: Brill.

Wyngaert, Anastasius van den, ed. (1929), *Sinica Franciscana: Itinera et relationes Fratrum Minorum Saeculi XIII et XIV*, Vol. 1, Quaracchi-Florence: Collegium S. Bonaventurae.

Xiaodong, Xu (2009), "Multi-Cultural Characteristics of Liao Amber and the Source of Raw Material: Amber from the Tomb of Princess Chen and her Consort," in *Amber in Archaeology: Proceedings of the Fifth International Conference on Amber in Archaeology, Belgrade 2006*, ed. Alexandar Palavestra, Curt W. Beck, and Joan M. Todd, 238–49, Belgrade: National Museum.

Xoplaki, Elena, Dominik Fleitmann, Juerg Luterbacher, Sebastian Watgner, John Haldon, Eduardo Zorita, Ioannis Telelis, Andrea Toreti, and Adam Izdebski (2016), "The Medieval Climate Anomaly and Byzantium: A Review of the Evidence on Climate Fluctuations, Economic Performance and Societal Change," *Quaternary Science Reviews*, 136: 229–52.

Yegenoglu, Meyda (1998), *Colonial Fantasies: Towards a Feminist Reading of Orientalism*, Cambridge: Cambridge University Press.

Young, Nicolás, Avriel D. Schweinsberg, Jason P. Briner, and Joerg M. Schaefer (2015), "Glacier Maxima in Baffin Bay During the Medieval Warm Period Coeval with Norse Settlement," *Science Advances*, 1 (11): e1500806, http://advances.sciencemag.org/content/1/11/e1500806.full.

Yule, Henry, ed. and trans. (1914–16), *Cathay and the Way Thither*, 2nd edn, revised by Henri Cordier, Hakluyt Society, 2nd ser., nos. 38–41, 4 vols, London: Hakluyt Society.

Ziegler, Joseph (2005), "Skin and Character in Medieval and Early Renaissance Physiognomy," *Micrologus: Natura, Scienze e Societa Medievali/Nature, Sciences and Medieval Societies*, 13: 511–35.

Ziegler, Joseph (2009), "Physiognomy, Science, and Proto-racism 1200–1500," in *The Origins of Racism in the West*, ed. Miriam Eliav-Feldon, Benjamin Isaac, and Joseph Ziegler, 181–99, Cambridge: Cambridge University Press.

NOTES ON CONTRIBUTORS

Marcus Bull is Andrew W. Mellon Distinguished Professor of Medieval and Early Modern Studies at the University of North Carolina, Chapel Hill. His research interests include the cultural resources that were available to medieval writers when narrating the experience of warfare.

Matthew Gabriele is Professor of Medieval Studies in the Department of Religion & Culture at Virginia Tech. His first book was *An Empire of Memory: The Legend of Charlemagne, the Franks, and Jerusalem before the First Crusade* (Oxford University, 2011) and he has published widely on the Charlemagne legend, empire, apocalypticism and reform, medievalism, and Jewish–Christian relations.

Shayne Legassie is an Associate Professor of English and Comparative Literature and Adjunct Associate Professor of Romance Studies at the University of North Carolina, Chapel Hill. He is the author of *The Medieval Invention of Travel* (University of Chicago Press, 2017), co-editor of *Cosmopolitanism and the Middle Ages* (Palgrave, 2013), and book reviews editor for *Studies in the Age of Chaucer*.

Anne E. Lester received her PhD from Princeton University (2003) and is Associate Professor and the John W. Baldwin and Jenny Chair in Medieval History at the John Hopkins University. She is the author of *Creating Cistercian Nuns: The Women's Religious Movement and Its Reform in Thirteenth-Century Champagne* (Cornell University Press, 2011) and co-editor of five collections of essays. Her research focuses on religion, gender, memory, materiality, and premodern conceptions of empire and the state during the High Middle Ages. She is completing a book entitled, *Fragments of Devotion: Relics and Remembrance in the Aftermath of the Fourth Crusade*.

Martha Newman is an Associate Professor of History and Religious Studies at the University of Texas at Austin. She is the author of *The Boundaries of Charity: Cistercian Culture and Ecclesiastical Reform* (Stanford University Press, 1996), as well as articles that explore gender and labor in Cistercian exempla and saints' lives. Between 2007 and 2016, she was the founding chair of the Department of Religious Studies at the University of Texas at Austin.

Patricia Skinner holds a personal chair in History at Swansea University. Her work focuses on gender, disability, and minority groups in medieval Europe. She is the author of *Living with Disfigurement in Early Medieval Europe* (2017) and *Studying Gender in Medieval Europe: Historical Approaches* (2018), both published by Palgrave.

Vicki Szabo, author of *Monstrous Fishes and the Mead Dark Sea* (Brill 2008), is an Associate Professor of Ancient, Medieval, and Environmental History at Western Carolina University. Her current research focuses on interdisciplinary reconstruction of medieval Norse exploitation of marine mammals through archaeology, history, and ancient DNA analysis.

Brett Whalen is an Associate Professor of Medieval Religious and Intellectual History at the University of North Carolina, Chapel Hill. His past works include *Dominion of God: Christendom and Apocalypse in the Middle Ages* (2009) and *The Medieval Papacy* (2014). He teaches courses on the medieval church, the crusades, and apocalypticism.

Cord J. Whitaker teaches medieval literature and the history of race at Wellesley College. His research in medieval romance, race, religious conflict, and modern politics has appeared in numerous journals, blogs, and edited collections, including his own *postmedieval* special collection "Making Race Matter in the Middle Ages." He is currently completing a book project on race and rhetoric in late medieval English literature and beginning another on Harlem Renaissance medievalism.

INDEX

Aachen 9, 10, 12, 15, 48, 84, 88, 90, 180
Abano, Pietro d' 123
Abul Abbas 88–9
acculturation, of elite males 34
Adalbero of Laon 103
Adam and Eve 95, 96, 97, *105*, 107, *112*, 120, 127
administrative regimes 50
Adoration of the Magi *131*
Adso 1, 2–3
Aelfric 103
Ælfric, Abbot 75–6
Aeneid 122
Africans, on the British Isles 17
Age of Exploration 117–18, 183, 189, 204
aggression, and conquest 147–51 (*see also* violence)
agricultores 108
agricultural labor 111, 113
agricultural production, destruction of 32
agricultural surpluses 30, 49, 50
Ahmed, Sara 152
al-Kamil of Egypt (r. 1218–38), Sultan 123
Albert of Livonia, Bishop 145
Albertus Magnus (c. 1200–80) 75, 82
Alcuin 99
Alexander III (1158–81), Pope 172–3, 199
Alexander IV (1254–61), Pope 179
Alexander the Great 119, 127
Alexandreis 127

Alexandria 63
Alfonso III of Portugal (1210–79) 155
Alfred of Wessex (r. 871–99) 27–9, 103
Allsen, Thomas 88
Americas, "discovery" of 119
Anacletus II (1130–38), Antipope 171
Anastasius (r. 491–518), Emperor 162
Angevin empire 86
Anglo-Norman empire 86
Anglo-Saxon Chronicle 85, 86
Anglo-Saxons 29, 86
antichrist 1–2, 177
Apostolic See 166, 171, 174
aratores 103
Aristotle 81, 189–90
army(ies)
    of Alfred of Wessex (r. 871–99) 27–9
    destructive power of 32–4
Arthur, King 39–41, 42, 196
Arthurian romance 126
artisans 106, 134–5
Asia 118, 119
assarting 50
Asser 28
assimilation, and trade 63
Atlantic, explorations of the 117–18
Aucassin and Nicolette 100
Augustine of Hippo 5, 97, 107–8
authority, and display 58
autonomy, of the peasantry 49

Bacon, Roger 83
Baghdad 15
Ball, John 93
Baltic crusades 145
barbarian peoples, civilization of 13
Bartholomeus Anglicus 192
Bartlett, Robert 60, 144
Bartolomeo of Santo Concordio 118
basileus 13
Bayeux Tapestry 31
Benedictine Rule 107
Benjamin of Tudela, Rabbi 128
Benn-Torres, J. 184–5
Berend, Nora 147
Berkhofer, Robert 50
Bernard of Clairvaux 109
Bernard of Tiron 109
Bible(s)
    Genesis 95–6, 97, 107, 127
    and human difference 98
    Moutier-Grandval Bible 97
    New Testament 96
    Vulgate Bible 120
bipartite estates 99
bishops of Rome. *See* popes
Black, Antony 106
Black Death 79, 91, 118
Black Sea 118
blackness 17–18, 187, 190, 191, 199, 204
    (*see also* race)
Bloch, Mark 33
"Blue Carbuncle, The" 136, 137
Bodin, Jean 188
Bohemond 30
Book of John Mandeville, The 124, 128, 134, 204–6
Book of Knowledge of All Kingdoms, The 191
Book on the Game of Chess 104
Borgarnes 71–2
Boris I of Bulgaria (r. 852–889) 144–5, 157
Boswell, John 139
bourgeoisie class 66
Bouvines, battle of (1214) 174
Bracciolini, Poggio 119
Braude, Benjamin 201
British empire 196
British Isles (*see also* England)
    Africans on the 17
    Viking invasions of 27–8

Brotton, Jerry 134
Brundage, James 139, 148
Burbank, Jane 94
Burckhardt, Jacob 4–5
Burghal Hidage 28
burghers 66
burhs 27–9
Burton, Antoinette 48
Byzantine empire 13, 15, 117

caballeros 26, 27
Caesarius of Arles 100, 108
Cairo Geniza 51–2, 211n.2:1
Callixtus II (1119–24), Pope 170
Campbell, Mary 189
Canary Islands 206, 207
Capetians, *imperium* of 11–12
capital, growth and accumulation of 46
capitalism, and production 113
Capitulare de Villis 84, 87–8, 90, 102
Carolingian empire 22, 51, 78, 84–5, 98, 99, 102, 163–4
Carthusians 109–10
cartography 133–4
castles, late medieval 23–4
Catalan Atlas 133–4
Catalonia 15, 100
Celestine III (1191–8), Pope 173
character, and race 187
Charageat, Martine 152–3
Charlemagne (r. 768–814 CE)
    and the bishop of Rome 164–5
    canonization of 10–11
    and climate 78
    coronation of 6–9, 15, 21, 163, *200*
    dominion over nature 83–5, 87–92
    environmental crisis 91
    fictional exploits of 12
    imperium of 11–12, 19, 42
    as king and emperor 12
    power of 8–9, 10
    practice of empire of 9
    recognition in the east 48
    relations with other rulers 15
    and serfdom 100
    and social classification 102
    violence of his military campaigns 41
    and warfare 21–2
Charles d'Anjou 179
Charles IV (r. 1346–78), Emperor 181

INDEX 249

Charles Martel (d. 741) 21
Charles V of France 133–4
Chaucer, Geoffrey 196
childbirth 145
children
   sexualizing of 143
   of slave women 150
   slavery of 151, 156
China 118
chivalric romance 122, 126
chivalry 34
Christendom
   the battle for 174–9
   Charlemagne as protector of 9
   Christian territorial gain in Iberia 25, 26
   Frederick II and the battle for 174–9
   and imperial power 47
   imperialism of 198–204
   missionaries converting foreign bodies 144–7
   and the Mongol empire 197–8
   power moving from Rome 195
Christianity
   Christian *imperium* 57, 58–9
   classification of groups within society 111
   conversions to 16, 144, 147, 155
   fear of the antichrist 1
   and interfaith sexual relations 152–4, 158
   and Judaism and Islam 144, 146–7
   and labor 107–12
   Latin 197
   and race 202
   and slavery/serfdom 97, 99–100
   supporting the social order 96
   and white skin 199
Christina of Markyate 23
Christus, Petrus 136
Chronica majora 77, 132
Chronicles 32
Chronicon ex chronicis 104
Church
   and elite males 34
   and empire 171, 176–7, 179–81
   and sins committed by armies 33–4
   and slavery 206–8
Cistercians 109, *110*

Civilization of the Renaissance in Italy, The 4
civilizing barbarian peoples 13
class, burgher and merchant class 66 (see also elites)
Clement II (1046–7), Pope 166
Clement III (1080–1100), Pope 168
Clement V (1305–14), Pope 180
Clement VI (1342–52), Pope 181
Cligés 61
climate (*see also* environment)
   climate change 77–9, 91
   climate theory 189–95
   Little Ice Age (LIA) 78, 79
   Medieval Warm Period (MWP)/ Medieval Climatic Anomaly (MCA) 73, 78–9, 211n.3:1
   modern approaches to medieval 77–80
cloth, trade in 52–3
Cluny 108
Cohen, Jeffrey Jerome 185
coinage
   denarius depicting Charlemagne 6
   regulation of 53
   and trade 54–5
   Viking 116
Collins, Wilkie 136
Colloquy 75–6
colonialism (*see also* empire(s); imperialism)
   Christianity and sexuality 144–7
   of Henry II 13
   and oppression 191
   and sexuality 141–7, 157
   and trade 188
   of the Vikings 116
Coloniser au Moyen Âge 143
Columbus, Christopher 118, 189, 204
commodities, exotic 130
communication, technologies of 56
Conan Doyle, Arthur 136
Conciliator differentiarum philosophorum 123
Concordat of Worms (1122) 170, 171
Conques, abbey of 57–8
conquest, and the appropriation of bodily services 147–51
Conrad I of Germany (c. 881–918) 171
Conrad II (c. 990—1039), Emperor 170
Conrad III (r. 1138–52), Emperor 172

Constance of Sicily, Queen 173
Constantine (r. 306–312 AD), Emperor 57, 164, 181
Constantinople 13, 64
consumption
  and culture 64
  exotic commodities 130
  and imperial power 46
  and trade 53
  and women 65–6
Conti, Nicolò di 119
Cooper, Frederick 94
cooperation, mutual 113
corruption, of the clergy 166–7
cosmology, and geography 130
Cotrugli, Benedetto 124
Cotton, Robert 203
Council of Nablus (1120) 152
craftsmen 136
credit mechanisms 54, 55–6
Cresques, Abraham and Jehuda 133–4
Critchley, John 128
crusade movement
  Baltic crusades 145
  Christian view of Islam 144
  First Crusade (1095–9) 30, 36, 62, 117, 169
  Fourth Crusade (1202–4) 63–4, 117
  as pilgrimage 126
  and race-thinking 183
  Third Crusade (1189–92) 117
  and trade 56, 62–4
Cuffel, Alexandra 155
culture(s)
  and consumption 64
  cross-cultural integration in Eurasia 117
  cultural biography of things 133
  cultural commerce 69
  cultural diaspora 59–64
  cultural dissent 86
  cultural transmission and diffusion 66–7
  and empire 53, 64, 65
  extending across geographic barriers 15
  material 65
  political culture 161, 162, 171, 175, 182
  of production 65
  and race 186
  religious 64
  and sexuality 157–8

Cuman people 147
customs, to fund warfare 30
Cutler, Anthony 130
Cyriac of Ancona (1391–1453) 124

Damascus 63
Dante 128, 180
Dark Ages 115, 116
Dati, Gregorio 150
Davis, Jennifer R. 9
Davis, Kathleen 188
De animalibus 81
De Arte Venandi cum Avibus 81, 82
De opere monachorum 107
De proprietatibus rerum 192
Deeds of Hereward, The 39
Deschamps, Eustache 125
Descriptio qualiter Karolus Magnus 12
desire, erotic 120
Dhuoda 15
diaspora
  cultural and trade 59–64
  elite 60–4, 65, 117
Diemeringen, Otto von 124
difference(s)
  the Bible and human difference 98
  and *imperium* 18
  between marginalized groups 101
  and religious groups 147
disease, plague 69, 79, 91, 118
dissent, cultural 86
Divine punishment 78
Domesday Book 32, 85
domination, and control of sexuality 143
Dominicans 122–3
Donation of Constantine, The 163, 164, 181
Duby, Georges 103, 105
Dum Diversas 207–8
Dutton, Paul Edward 88, 90

East Frankish (German) kingdom 22
Eastman, Jason 185
economic development 113
economic growth, and agricultural surpluses 49, 50
economies
  prestige 133, 135
  tributary economies 130
education 121

Edward, the Black Prince 32–3
Edward the Elder of Wessex (r. 899–924) 28
Egil 71–2
Egil's Saga 71, 73
Egypt, Fatimid 61
Einhard 21, 23, 84, 88
elephants, gifts of 129–30, 132–3
elites
  burghers 66
  diaspora 60–4, 65, 117
  and empires 94
  enculturation and identity reproduction of 85
  fantasy histories of 37–43
  and gift giving 37
  identity of 85, 120
  and local production 50
  military identity of 30, 34, 36–7
  and mobility 120, 124
  religious 107, 108, 109, 112
  and slavery 98
  of subjected people 142
Emperor of France, title of 18
emperors (*see also* names of individual emperors)
  control of the natural world 80
  and kings 12, 21, 94
  and popes 161–3, 181
  power of 161–71, 174–9
  resistance of 162
empire(s) (*see also* colonialism; imperialism; *imperium*; names of individual empires)
  Christian culture of 64
  and Church 171, 176–7, 179–81
  and culture 53, 64, 65
  defined 94
  empire-building and race 204–5
  imperial ideology 96
  and *imperium* 19
  and labor 94
  medieval 13, 15, 19, 113
  and the Middle Ages 6
  and the movement of things 63
  and the natural world 74–5
  power of 46, 47, 67
  resistance to 161
  and sexuality 141–2, 158–9
  subjects and objects of 67
  and trade 46, 65
  and warfare 22
  and wealth 61
England (*see also* British Isles)
  Anglo-Norman empire 86
  Norman Conquest of 31–2, 33
  Norman kings of 13
  Roman heritage of 195–6
Enlightenment 5, 6
environment (*see also* climate)
  environmental history 74, 76
  environmental legacy of Rome 77, 84
  and premodern societies 74
Epstein, Steven 98, 106
Ermenfrid of Sion 33
erotic desire 120
Espistola Generalis 84
estate management 50
Eugenius IV (1431–47), Pope 207, 208
eunuchs 151
Eurasia, cross-cultural integration 117
Europe
  growth of 60
  Roman heritage of 195
exile 128
exoticism, and mobility 129–37
exploitation 96, 100, 103, 109
  sexual 141, 155–6
explorations
  Age of Exploration 183, 204
  of the Atlantic 117–18
  "discovery" of the Americas, 119
  and European sovereignty 189

Faerie Queene 196
falconry 81, 83
famine, following warfare 32
Farmer, Sharon 65, 113
Fatimid Egypt 61
Ferguson, Wallace 4
feudal society 51
feuds 23
Finke, Laurie A. 148, 158–9
fire, as a weapon 30–2
First Crusade (1095–9) 30, 36, 62, 117, 169
forests, control of 85–7
fortifications
  burhs 27–8
  of Henry I of Germany 29

Foucault, Michel 139
Fourth Crusade (1202–4) 63–4, 117
Fourth Lateran Council's injunction (1215) 152
Frakes, Jerold C. 142
France
French Revolution 19, 105
    nation of 11
    and serfdom 100, 101
    taxation 106
Francia 45–6
Francis II (r. 1792–1806), Emperor 18
Francis of Assisi 123
Franciscans 122–3
Franco-papal alliance 163
Franks 1, 2–3, 9, 84
Frederick I Barbarossa (r. 1152–90), Emperor 10, 16, 102, 172–3, 199, 201
Frederick II (1194–1250), Emperor
    and the battle for Christendom 174–9
    coinage of 55
    crusading campaigns of 117
    death of his father 173
    and Lothar III 171
    military expeditions to Jerusalem 16
    and the natural world 80–2, 83
    power of 17
    sacrum imperium of 18
Frederick III (1831–1888), Emperor 99
Frederick of Austria (1313–30) 180
Freedman, Paul 98, 99, 101, 103, 133
French Revolution 19, 105
Friedman, John Block 205
Frobisher, Martin 204
Froissart, Jean 32, 33
frontier life, Spanish 26
fueros 25–6
Fulcher of Chartres 152
fyrd 28

Gaunt, Simon 146
gaze, of western travellers 145, 158
Gelasian dictum 162
Gelasius I (492–6), Pope 162
Gelasius II (1118–19), Pope 170
gender (*see also* women)
    and labor 97, 111–12
    and sexuality 140
General History of Civilization in Europe 6

Genesis 95–6, 97, 107, 127 (*see also* Adam and Eve)
Genghis Khan 196–7, *198*
Genoa, empire of 118
genocide 32
Geoffrey of Monmouth 39–40, 41, 196
Geoffroi de Charny 34
geographical knowledge 118–20, 130–1
geography, and cosmology 130
Gerard I of Alsace, Count 23
Gerard of Cambrai 103
Gerard of Cremona 190
Gerberga, Queen 1
Gerson, Jean 105
gift giving and receiving 37, 48–9, 129–30, 132–3
Gillingham, John 152
Giotto 131
globus cruciger 131
God, and nature 75, 76, 82
Godescalc Evangelistary 89
Godfrey II of Lower Lotharingia, Duke 23
Golden Bull of 1356 181
"Goldsmith in His Shop, A" 136
Goodich, Michael 139
Goswami, Manu 48
Grafton, Anthony 118
Great Council in Dubrovnik 99
Great Famine 91
Great German Pilgrimage 61
Greenland 79
Gregorian reform movement 56, 167
Gregory I (590–604), Pope 98, 195
Gregory VII (1073–84), Pope 56, 167–9
Gregory IX (1227–41), Pope 175
Gregory X (1271–6), Pope 179
Grey, Arthur 192
Groebner, Valentin 185
Guelph Treasure (*Welfenschatz*) 58, 59
guilds 106
Guizot, François 6
Guy of Lusignan 117

Hadrian IV (1154–9), Pope 172
Hahn, Cynthia 57
Hahn, Thomas 184
Haimo of Auxerre 102
Ham, sin of 98, 99, 100
Hammer, Carl 102
Hanawalt, Barbara A. 75

Hannaford, Ivan 184
Harald Fairhair of Norway 71
Harold II of England (c.1022–1066) 31
Harrying of the North 32, 33
Harun al-Rashid (r. 786–809) 7, 9, 15, 48
Hastings, battle of 31
Haymo and Heiric of Auxerre 108
Helena, Saint 57, 199–200
Helms, Mary W. 130
Heng, Geraldine 17, 186–7
Henry I, Count of Champagne 52
Henry I of England (c. 1068–1135) 53, 103, *104*
Henry I of Germany (876–936) 22, 29
Henry II of England (r. 1154–89) 13, *14*, 35, 113
Henry III of England (1207–1272) 129–30
Henry III (r. 1046–56), Emperor 166–7
Henry IV (r. 1056–1105), Emperor 167–70
Henry V (r. 1099–1125), Emperor 170
Henry VI (r. 1190–97), Emperor 173
Henry VII of Luxembourg (r. 1308–13), Emperor 180
Henry of Essex 35
Henry the Navigator, Prince of Portugal 191
Herder, Johann Gottfried von 191
Hereward the Wake 38–9, *40*
Herodotus 189
Hincmar of Reims 109
Historia Naturalis 189
Historia trium regum (*History of the Three Kings*) 199, 202, 203–4
Historia Turpini 41–3
"Historical Roots of our Ecologic Crisis, The" 76
Histories 189
History of the Kings of Britain 39–40, 196
Hodierna of Jerusalem 121
Hoffmann, Richard 76, 80, 84
Holy Land, intervention in 61 (*see also* crusade movement)
holy objects 64 (*see also* relics)
Holy Roman Empire 10, 18, 162, 199, 203, 204
honestiores and *humiliores* 101
Honorius Augustondunensis 100
Honorius III (1216–27), Pope 175
Hoofnagle, Wendy 13

Horden, Peregrine 116
Hospitallers 37, 56
Howell, Martha 66, 106
Hrabanus Maurus 99
Hugh Capet (r. 987–96), King 11
Hugh I of Vaudemont 152, *153*
human trafficking 150–1
humanism 119
Humbert of Romans 111, 112
Hundred Years War (1337–1453) 32, 33
Hungary, and serfdom 100–2
hunting, royal 88–9, 91

Iberia 15, 16–17, 25–6, 154–5
Ibn Battuta 126
Ibn Hazm 154
Ibn Jubayr 154
Ibn Munqidh 158
Iceland 71, 73–4
identity(ies)
    clerical 122–3
    of elites 85, 120
    Englishness 101
    European Christian 195
    medieval Jewish 128–9
    of merchants 123–4
    military 30, 34, 36
    and mobility 61, 120–5
    religious 154, 207
    sexual 140
    and travel 122–3
imperialism (*see also* colonialism; empire(s))
    of Christendom 198–204
    imperial claims of the Church 107
    and race 209
    and sexuality 141–3, 157
imperium (*see also* empire(s))
    of the Capetians 11–12
    of Charlemagne 11–12, 19, *42*
    Christian 57, 58–9
    derivations of 19
    and difference 18
    ecclesiastical will to 131
    and empire 19
    encompassing people 15–16
    in the Middle Ages 9
    reframing of 10
    of rulers 16

sacrum imperium 10, 16, 18
   term 22
imports, luxury items 133
India 118
indigenous peoples, encounters with 128
Inferno 128
Innocent II (1130–43), Pope 171
Innocent III (1198–1216), Pope 145, 173–4
Innocent IV (1243–54), Pope 176–7
Innocent VI (1352–62), Pope 181
integration, and trade 63
intellectuals, medieval 119
international orders 56
Investiture Contest 13
Irene (r. 797–802), of Byzantium 7, 15
Isabelle of Brienne 175
Isidore of Seville 98, 120
Islam, and Christianity 144, 146–7 (*see also* Muslims)
Islamic world, gold coinage 55
Italy, merchants from 62–3
iudices 90

Jablonski, Nina 185
Jacques de Vitry 111, 112
Jerusalem 16, 61, 62, 63
Jewish communities 16, 128–9, 146, 150, 155
Joachim of Fiore 177–8
John of England (r. 1199–1216) 86–7
John of Hildesheim 199
John of Montecorvino 118, 119–20
John of Plano Carpini 145
John of Salisbury 103–5
John of Worcester 85, 103
John XII (955–64), Pope 166
John XX II (1316–34), Pope 180
Jordan, William Chester 184, 205
Jordanus of Sévérac 123
Journal of Medieval and Early Modern Studies, The 184

al-Kamil of Egypt (r. 1218–38), Sultan 123
Karras, Ruth Mazo 98, 139, 142, 152, 155–6
Kelsey, George 184, 185
Kempe, Margery 126
"king-emperor" 12
King of Tars 154, 197–8

kings, and emperors 12, 21, 94
kingship 181, 188
Kingsley, Charles 38
Kinoshita, Sharon 122, 142
Kiser, Lisa J. 75
Kittles, R.A. 184–5
knights
   commoner 26
   knight errants 122, 124
   Knights Templar 117 (*see also* Templars)
   Teutonic Knights 37
knowledge
   codification of 81
   geographical 118–20, 130–1
   long-distance 130, 135, 136
Kopytoff, Igor 133
Kruger, Steven J. 141, 146, 150, 155
Kveldulf 71

La Sale, Antoine de 124
labor
   agricultural 111, 113
   artisans 106, 134–5
   and Christianity 107–12
   craftsmen 136
   and empires 94
   and gender 97, 111–12
   medieval 94–5
   mutuality and concord 101–7
   as penance 113
   regulation of 106
   rural 105
   servitude and serfdom 96–101 (*see also* slavery)
   and trade 64–5
   urban citizens 105–6
   of women 65–6, 68, 97, 104, 106, 108, 111–12
   and work 95–6
   work, penance and self-production 107–12
laboratores 103
Langton, Stephen 109, 113
language
   erotic 140, 156
   expansion of French 13, 117
"Lanquan li jorn son lonc e may" 121
Lapidary, The 134–6
"Last Emperor" legend 2, 3

INDEX

Latin Empire of Constantinople (1204–61) 64
Lauer, Rena 150
Le Goff, Jacques 95
legends, creation of 57
Legnano, battle of (1176) 173
Leo III (795–816), Pope 6–9, 163, 164–5
Leo VIII (963–5), Pope 166
Leo IX (1049–54), Pope 166–7
Levant 62, 63
Liber ad regem Almansorem 190
Life of Cyriac of Ancona, The 124
Life of Leo IX 166
Life of Pope Gregory VII 168
Limoges, storming of 32–3
Lincoln, battle of (1141) 36
literacy 49
literature
    Arthurian romance 126
    chivalric romance 122, 126
    classical works 189–90
    and mobility 121–2
    and trade 56
    travel writing 124–5, 133, 189, 191, 204–5
    vernacular 66, 124, 148
    Victorian novels/fiction 136–7
Little Ice Age (LIA) 78, 79
Liudprand of Cremona 166
Lives of the Popes 164
Livre de métiers 106
Lochrie, Karma 140
Lombard kingdom, and Charlemagne 22
Lombard League 173, 175
Lorenzetti, Ambrogio 123
Lothar I (r. 817–55), Emperor 165
Lothar III of Supplinburg (r. 1125–37), Emperor 171
Louis I (the Pious) (r. 813–40), Emperor 21, 87, 91, 165, 213n.7:2
Louis IV of France (r. 936–54) 1
Louis IV (the Bavarian) (r. 1314–47) 180
Louis IX of France (r. 1226–70) 16, 55, 64, 117, 129
love
    from afar 121, 122
    courtly love 120–1
Luttrell Psalter 102
luxury items, trade in 62–3

Magdeburg Cathedral, Saint Maurice at 17–18
magi 199–200
    Adoration of the Magi 202
Magna Carta 86
Magyars 22
Malaterra, Geoffrey 149
Malory, Thomas 196
Man of Law's Tale 196
Mandeville, John 128–9, 134–5, 204–6
Mandeville's Travels 189
Marco Polo 66, 119, 123, 128, 134, 145–6, 151, 157
Marignolli, John 119, 120
maritime trade routes 47, 118
markets
    development and regulation of 52
    international 55
marriage 143, 145, 147, 154–5
Martoni, Nicola de 126
Matilda, empress 36
Maurice, Saint 17–18
McCormick et al. 77
McCormick, Michael 49, 98
medieval age, boundaries of 4
medieval empire 13, 15, 19, 113
medieval Europe, as societies "organized for war" 23–6
Medieval Quiet Period [MQP] 79
Medieval Warm Period (MWP)/Medieval Climatic Anomaly (MCA) 73, 78–9, 211n.3:1
Mediterranean
    Aragonese influence in 117
    and Frankish Europe 116–17
    importance of 122
    the Mediterranean world 15
    and trade 47
menageries 88–90, 129–130, 132–3
mendicant orders 122–3
Menentillus of Spoleto 118
merchants 62, 64–5, 66, 123–4
Middle Ages
    construction of 5–6
    and empire 6
    imperium in the 9
    mobility in the 15–17, 115
Military Orders 36–7
militias, of towns 25–6
mills 50

missionaries
   Dominican 122–3
   and sexuality 144–7
Mittman, Asa 205
mobility
   aristocratic diaspora 60–4, 65, 117
   and the collapse of the Roman empire 115
   and the crusades 117
   and elites 120, 124
   and exploration 117–18
   and identity 61, 120–5
   and literature 121–2
   Medieval 125–9
   medieval critics of 126–7
   of merchants 66
   in the Middle Ages 15–17, 115
   new horizons 118–20
   penitential pilgrimage 125–6
   of people 66
   power, prestige and exoticism 129–37
   social mobility 26
   and trade 116
   of wealthy peasantry 50
   of women 65
modernity, and defining medieval race 184–8
Mongol empire 16, 45, 118, 123, 145, 196–8
Mongol Khan 16
Monstrous Races in Medieval Art and Thought, The 205
Moonstone, The 136, 137
moral hierarchies, and race-thinking 187
morality, and missionaries 145
Morte d'Arthur, Le 196
Moutier-Grandval Bible 97
Mudejars 155
Muslims 16, 61 (*see also* Islam)
mutuality and concord 101–7

Napoleon I Bonaparte (r. 1804–14, 1815) 18–19
nature
   control of 74–5, 76, 80
   and God 75, 76, 82
   god, emperors and dominion over 80–92
   intellectual dominion of 83

medieval climate 77–80 (*see also* climate)
medieval conceptions of 75–7
networks
   merchant 65, 66
   of power 23–4
   trade 50, 52, 53, 54, 56, 62, 64, 66, 68–9
   trade in luxury items 49
Nicholas I (858–67), Pope 145, 157
Nicholas II (1059–61), Pope 167
Nicholas V (1328–1330), Anti-pope 180
Nicholas V (1447–1455), Pope 207–8
Nirenberg, David 155
nomadism 128
Norman conquests, England and southern Italy 31–2, 33, 117, 141
Norman kings of England 13
North Atlantic 79
Norway 71, 73
Notker the Stammerer (d. 912) 83, 84

objects, and trade 58
Odoric of Pordenone 123
"old logic" (logica vetus) 189
On the Antichrist 1, 3
On the Properties of Things 192
oppression 93, 191
Orderic Vitalis 32, 85
orientalism 141
others
   peasants as 100, 101
   and sexuality 141, 143–4, 148, 156–7
   and trade 63
Otto I (r. 936–73), Emperor 22, 166
Otto III (r. 996–1002), Emperor 166
Otto IV of Brunswick (1175–1218), Emperor 173, 174
Ovitt, George, Jr. 95

pagan peoples 147
Pagden, Anthony 5
Papal States 164
Paradis de la Reine Sibylle, Le 124
Paris, Matthew 77, 129–30, 132–3, 212n.6:10
Parsons, Tim 94
Paschal II (1099–1118), Pope 170
Paschal III (1164–1168), Anti-pope 173, 199

Paul of Bernried 168
pax Romana 102
peasantry
  autonomy of the 49
  and Christianity 111
  exploitation of 100, 109
  funding warfare 30
  genocide of 32–3
  mobility of 50
  as others 100, 101
  production of 49–50
Peasants' Revolt (1381) 93, 94
penance, labor as 107–12, 113
peones 26, 27
Pepin 91, 163, 164
Perellòs, Ramón de 124
Peter III of Aragon 179
Petrarch 119
Philip I of Francia (r. 1060–1108) 11
Philip II (Augustus) of France (r. 1180–1223) 11, 12, 105, 174
Philip IV of France (1268–1314) 179
Philip of Swabia (1198–1208) 173
Philippiad 105
Philips, Kim 143
Phillips, Richard 141
Phillips, William D. 145
physiognomic science 187, 190–1, 205
pilgrimage 56, 61, 125–7
pillaging, by armies 30
Pipino, Marco 123
Pippin the Short (d. 768) 21
Pisa, Rusticello da 119, 128
Pius VIII (1829–30), Pope 19
plague 69, 79, 91, 118
Pliny the Elder 189
plundering, by armies 30, 33
Policraticus 103
politics
  medieval 113
  political culture 161, 162, 171, 175, 182
  political hierarchies 93
  political power 94, 96, 113
  and race 199
polygamy 145
poor people, funding warfare 30
popes (*see also* names of individual popes)
  election of 167
  and emperors 161–3, 181

papal monarchy 161–2, 171–4
power of 161–71, 174–9
power to make and unmake 10
resistance to western empire 161–2, 175–6
sanctioning armed campaigns against Muslims 61
ports 62, 63
postcolonial theory, and sexuality 142–4
power
  of Byzantium 13
  of Charlemagne 8–9, 10
  and emperors/popes 161–71, 174–9
  of Frederick I Barbarossa 10
  of guilds 106
  imperial 46, 47, 67
  Latin Christian 117
  and the medieval world 22
  and mobility 129–37
  and the natural world 73
  networks of 23–4
  political 94, 96, 113
  Roman and Christian 3
  of the Roman church 203
  royal 103–4
  and sexual violence 33
  and trade 53, 65
  the two powers 161–6, 171, 172–3, 175, 179, 182
Prester John 16, 196
prestige, and mobility 129–37
pride, as a sin 37
Primitive Rule of the Templars 37, 38 (*see also* Templars)
production
  artistic 58–9
  and capitalism 113
  production and surplus 49–52, 107
  technologies of 65
property rights, of women 26
prostitution 143, 146
protections, of trade 53–4
Pseudo-Turpin Chronicle 100
Purcell, Nicholas 116

race
  and character 187
  and Christianity 202
  climate theory of 189–95

defining medieval race in modernity 184–8
and empire-building 204–5
history of 183
and imperialism 209
Mandeville and "reasonable" races 204–6
medieval race and the wider world 188–95
and perpetual slavery 206–9
and politics 199
race-thinking 183, 185–7, 190, 192, 195, 198–9, 200, 203, 204, 205–6
and religion 146–7
and sexuality 152–4
in the shadow of ancient/contemporary empires 195–204
skin color 17–18, 99, 185, 186–7, 190, 191, 194, 199, 204
term 187
Race: The History of an Idea in the West 184
Rainald of Dassel 199
Ramey, Lynne 154
Ranft, Patricia 95
rape, and warfare 33, 147–9
record-keeping 50
Refling, Mary 81
reform, Roman church 166–7, 169
regulation
of coinage 53
of labor 106
of social order 102–4
of trade 46, 52–6, 65
relics 56–8, 59, 60, 64, 67–8, 199–200
religion
imperial claims of the Church 107
and interfaith sexual relations 152–4, 158
new religiosity 56
in the private realm 182
and race 146–7
relics 56–8, 59, 60, 64, 67–8, 199–200
religious culture 64
religious elites 107, 108, 109, 112
religious identity 154, 207
role of saints 56–7
and trade 61, 62
Renaissance in Historical Thought: Five Centuries of Interpretation, The 4

Renaissance, The 4, 117
repartimiento 25
resistance
the age of papal monarchy 171–4
church reform and the investiture contest 166–71
of emperors 162
to empire 161
empire and church in the later middle ages 179–81
forest 86
Frederick II and the battle for Christendom 174–9
Papal 164
the two powers 162–6, 171, 172–3, 175, 179, 182
resources, natural 72–3
Rex-Imperator ("king-emperor") 12
Rhazes 190
Rhine 16
Riccoldo of Montecroce 122–3
rituals, and race 186
rivers, and trade 47, 52
road construction 13, 115–16
Robert of Naples 180
Roman de Godfrey de Bouillon 149–50
Roman empire
collapse of and mobility 115
environmental legacy of 77, 84
meaning of Rome/Roman 7
Roman *imperium* 1, 2–4
and slavery 96, 98
social classification in 101
Romanus Pontifex 207
royal estates 88–90
Royal Frankish Annals 6, 48
Rubruck, Friar William 66
Rudel, Jaufré 121–2
Rudolf of Habsburg (r. 1273–91), Emperor 179
Rudolf of Swabia 168
Rupert of Deutz 110
rustici 105

Sabsay, Leticia 141
sacrum imperium 10, 16, 18 (*see also imperium*)
Saint-Denis, abbey 11
saints, role of 56–7
Saladin 63

Salian imperial dynasty 166–8
Saxony 166, 168
Scalamonti, Franceso 124
Schichtman, Martin B. 148
seigneurial revolution 99
Seljuk Turks 61
sevitude and serfdom 96–101, 107 (*see also* slavery)
Sex Before Sexuality: A Premodern History 140
sexuality
  and colonialism 141–3, 157
  conquest, and the appropriation of bodily services 147–51, 155
  and culture 157–8
  defined 139
  and dress 157
  and empire 58–9, 141–2
  and gender 140
  and imperialism 141–3, 157
  interfaith sexual relations 152–4, 158
  miscegenation, embracing foreign bodies 152–5
  missionaries converting foreign bodies 144–7
  and others 141, 143–4, 148, 156–7
  same-sex relationships 155
  sex trade 143 (*see also* prostitution)
  sexual exploitation 141, 155–6
  sexual identity 140
  sexual violence 33–4
  sexualizing of children 143
  use of postcolonial theory 142–4
  and women 111, 152, 153, 154, 159
Shatzmiller, Joseph 147
Shichtman, Martin B. 158–9
shipping routes 49 (*see also* trade)
Sicily 154, 179
Silk Road 45, 66
sin, pride as 37
sinfulness, and servitude 97–8, 99
Skalla-Grímr 71–3
slavery (*see also* servitude and serfdom)
  becoming serfdom 98
  of boys 151, 156
  and the church 206–8
  European dependence on 191
  New World slavery 99
  and the Roman empire 96, 98
  sexual abuse of female 146
  slave trade 67, *68*, 98–9, *151*
  and warfare 147–8
  women slaves 146, 147–8, 149–50, 159
social classification, Carolingian empire 102
social hierarchies 113
social mobility 26
social order, regulation of 102–4
Song of Roland 12–13, 15, 61, 88, 91
Southern, Richard 144
sovereignty 94, 189
space, and imperial power 47
Spain (*see also* Catalonia; Iberia)
  Spanish towns 26
  trade in Muslim Spain 51–2
Spenser, Edmund 192–5, 196
Spiegel, Gabrielle 12
Spiritual Franciscans 180
Statius 122
Stavelot Tryptic 58
Stephen II (752–7), Pope 164
Stephen IV (816–17), Pope 165, 213n.7:2
Stephen of Blois 36
Stephen of England (r. 1135–54) 36
Stephen of Muret 110
Sturluson, Snorri 71–2
subjection, and mutuality 107
Suger of Saint Denis 171
Summa theologica 111
superiority, Christian 154
surveillance, royal 106
Sylvester II (999–1003), Pope 164, 166

Tartars (Tatars) 198
taxation
  France 106
  to fund warfare 30
  and trade 53–4
techne 65
technologies
  of communication 56
  of production 65
Templars 37, *38*, 56 (*see also* Knights Templar)
Teutonic Knights 37
Thaddues of Suessa 176
Thebaid 122
Thietmar of Merseburg 23
things, cultural biography of 133
Third Crusade (1189–92) 117

Thomas Aquinas 111
Thomas of Cantimpré (d. 1272) 83
Three Kings of Cologne, The 199, 202, 203–4
tolls 53–4
towns, militias of 25–6
Tracotans 206
trade
　acceleration of 64
　and assimilation 63
　in cloth 52–3
　and colonial settlements 188
　credit mechanisms 54, 55–6
　and the crusade movement 56, 62–4
　and cultural diaspora 59–64
　and empire 46, 65
　extent of 116
　and integration 63
　and interaction 56
　international 60
　and literature 56
　in luxury items 62–3
　maritime trade routes 47, 118
　merchants 62, 64–5, 66, 123–4
　in Muslim Spain 51–2
　networks 50, 52, 53, 54, 56, 62, 64, 66, 68–9
　and objects 58
　people and things 64–7
　and power 53, 65
　production and surplus 49–52, 107
　protections of 53–4
　regulation of 46, 52–6, 65
　and relics 57, 58, 59
　and religion 61, 62
　and rivers 47, 52
　during the Roman period 47
　scale/scope of imperial trade 46–9
　Silk Road 45, 66
　slave trade 67, 68, 98–9, *151*
　spaces of 47–8
　and spread of plague 69
　structure and regulation 52–6
　and taxation 53–4
training, for warfare 34
travel
　and identity 122–3
　medieval 125
　travel writing 124–5, 133, 189, 191, 204–5

treasury collections, aristocratic and ecclesiastical 58
Treaty of Venice (1177) 173
Trevisa, John 192
troubadour *canso* 120, 121, 122
Troyes, Chrétien de 61, 100, 122
Turpin of Reims, Archbishop 42

Ubriachi, Baldassare degli 134
Unger, Richard 65
urban citizens, labor of 105–6
Urban II (1088–99), Pope 169–70
Urban IV (1261–4), Pope 179
urbanization 50, 122

Van den Hoven, Birgit 95
Venice
　empire of 118
　honor codes of 146
Verden, massacre 41
Verhulst, Adrian 98, 99
vernacular, use of 66, 124, 148
Vewe of the Present State of Ireland, A 192–3
Victor IV (1159–1164), Anti-pope 172–3, 199
Vikings
　invasions of Britain 27–8
　mobility of 116
villesneuves (new towns) 50
Vincent of Beauvais (c. 1190–1264) 75
violence
　cultural ennobling of 43
　as a fact of life 23
　legitimate 41
　medieval Europe 18, 33
　sexual 33–4
Virgil 122
Vulgate Bible 120

Walsingham, Thomas 93
Walter of Châtillon 127
War of the Keys 175
warfare
　aristocratic ethos of 40
　and Charlemagne 21–2
　costs of 30
　and empire 22
　fire as a major weapon of 30–2
　holy war 41

INDEX

impact of on people's lives 27–8
medieval 23–4, 29–30
as a norm 41
plight of peasants/poor people 32–3
and rape 33, 147–9
and slavery 147–8
training for 34
and women 147–9
water mills 50
wealth
   imperial 61
   moveable 66
Wessex 27–9
West Frankish kingdom 11
West Saxons 29
White, Lynn 76, 95
whiteness 185, 187, 199, 204 (*see also* race)
Wickham, Christopher 96, 113
Widukind of Corvey 29
William, Duke of Normandy 31
William of Adam 156
William of Ockham 181
William of Rubruck 16, 120, 145
William the Conqueror (c. 1028–1087) 85, 86, 190–1

Williams, Raymond 95
Winchester 28
Winer, Rebecca 149
women
   of the Carolingian world 15
   Cistercian 109
   conversion of 147
   Iberia 26
   labor of 65–6, 68, 97, 104, 106, 108, 111–12
   mobility of 65
   pilgrims 126–7
   property rights of 26
   prostitution 143, 146
   and sexuality 111, 152, 153, 154, 159
   slaves 146, 147–8, 149–50, 152
   and warfare 147–9
work, and labor 95–6 (*see also* labor)
written language (Latin) 51 (*see also* literature)
Wulfstan 103
Wyatt, David 98

Yorkshire 32

Ziegler, Joseph 187